TOKYO

A WORLD FINANCIAL CENTRE

Odakyu
地下鉄
5:14
CITIZEN
シチズン
OLYMPUS
PIONEER
STUDIO ALTA
AKAI
AIWA
東京都宝くじ

TOKYO
A WORLD FINANCIAL CENTRE

By Brian Robins

Published by
Euromoney Publications
in association with

Canadian Imperial Bank of Commerce

Chase Manhattan Securities Japan

Clifford Chance

Cresvale

The Lloyds Bank Group

Morgan Stanley International

The Nikko Securities Co

Nippon Life Insurance Company

Shearson Lehman Brothers

Showa Ota & Co and Ernst & Whinney

Published by
Euromoney Publications PLC
Nestor House, Playhouse Yard
London EC4V 5EX

ISBN 1 870031 36 9

Typeset by PW Graphics
Printed in England by
Balding & Mansell Ltd

Contents

Ginkatuji Temple, Kyoto, a reminder of a less commercial age.

Financial surplus or deficit by sector, 1954–85

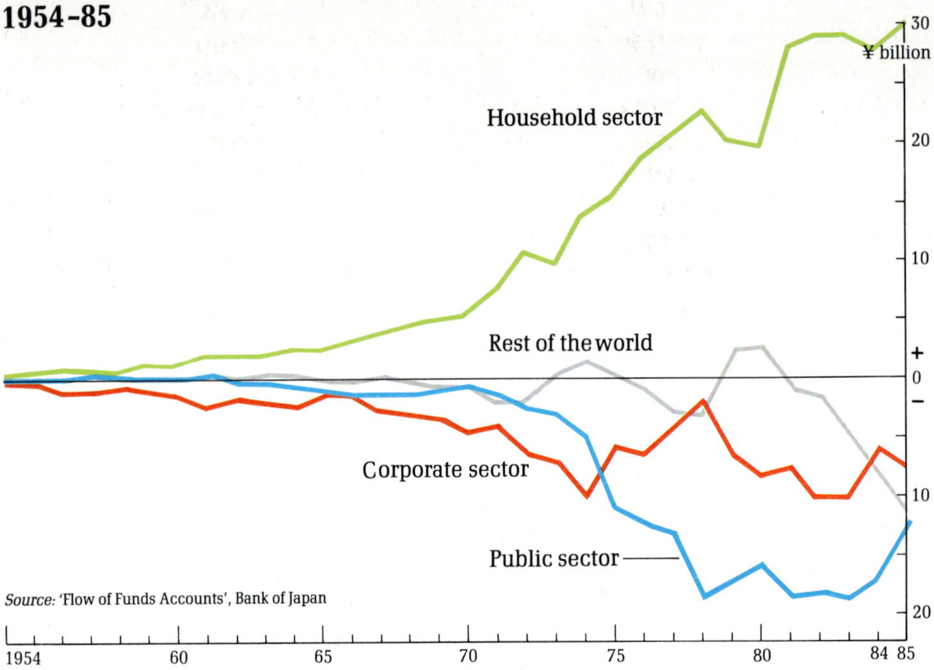

Source: 'Flow of Funds Accounts', Bank of Japan

Financial surplus or deficit of central and local government, 1954–85

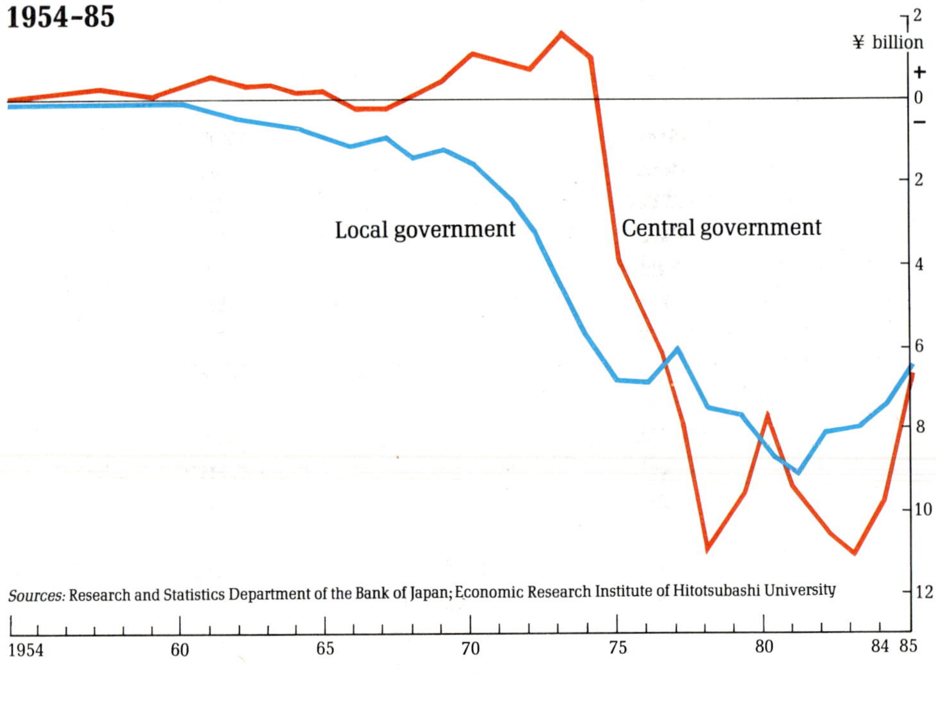

Sources: Research and Statistics Department of the Bank of Japan; Economic Research Institute of Hitotsubashi University

Historical introduction

by Fumimasa Hamada
Professor of Economics
Keio University, Tokyo

The modern Japanese banking system, which had been established by the beginning of this century, has been at the core of the development of Japan's financial system. The divisions within the banking system, laid down by the government, and government controls and regulations have played a crucial role in the development of Japan's financial markets. In 1986, however, changes became apparent with the remarkable shift in portfolio selection, particularly of the private financial institutions, from 'safe' to high-risk, high-return assets such as stocks, industrial bonds and public bonds. Since then, there has been an extraordinary rise in the price of those securities, and the ratio of industrial assets to total assets in Japan has declined. The internationalisation of Japanese financial markets is now in progress.

The development of the banking system

The origins of banking in Japan are said to be exchanges or brokers called 'fudasashi' in Edo (Tokyo) and 'kuramoto' in Osaka, established in the early 1730s and owned by the rice merchants. A type of commercial paper issued by the central or local government, called 'rice stamp', was traded as the speculative financial asset between brokers in Osaka.

In those days, the senior officials of the central or local government introduced laws and regulations for commercial and financial business virtually at their discretion.

Some of these exchanges grew rapidly into trading companies with large capital funds, among them Mitsui, Sumitomo, Kohnoike and Shiroki.

After the Meiji restoration in 1868, the government established the modern financial system to stimulate and promote the industrial development of Japan, with the main aim of modernising and building up the armaments industry. The government proclaimed laws and regulations for the organisation of the banking system, which was composed of various types of special banks whose key function was to supply long-term funds to the basic industries such as iron and steel, textiles, mining and agriculture.

These banks, partly state-owned institutions since the government supported them financially, were called 'national banks'. The laws and regulations for national banks provided for a division of the banking system, with separate regulations for savings banks, banks for foreign trade financing, banks for industrial financing, banks for agricultural financing, etc. In 1882, the Bank of Japan Act came into force, which established the Bank of Japan as the central bank. Most of the national banks have since become private banks, such as savings banks, trust banks, mutual savings banks (which grew out of mutual finance associations) and private commercial banks.

Thus, the financial system, with a segregated banking system at its core, had been established before the end of the 19th century. The Japanese banking system then established was very different from the banking system in Europe, which focused on the commercial banks.

In the 1870s and 1880s, there were few securities. At the beginning of this century, the issuing of government bonds accelerated, and the amount of debentures and stocks increased. Government bond issues, which were about ¥1.8 billion (US$12.8 million) in 1905, rose to ¥132 billion (US$900 million) in

1939. Other securities expanded similarly during this period. This rapid increase in the amount of security issues reflected the increased government expenditure on armaments, as well as the growth of the large corporations engaged in the development of the basic industries.

Personal savings, which were held in the form of long-term deposits, financial trusts and mutual savings deposits, were the major source of funds for the financial institutions in the development of industry. These funds were distributed through the established banking system.

This was the foundation of the indirect financing system, which has been operating as an efficient and reliable system for more than 70 years.

The dual structure of the financial system

The number of banks had been increasing since the national banks became privately owned. But most of the small banks, whose business was regionally confined, have faced problems. During and after the depression which followed World War I, and especially after the financial crisis of 1927, the small and local banks started to merge. The proclamation of the Bank Law in 1927 accelerated this process.

According to a study by Juro Teranishi on the Japanese banking system before World War I, the banking system had a dual structure. The big five banks – Mitsui, Mitsubishi, Sumitomo, Yasuda and Daiichi – had close contact with companies in the modern industrial sectors, such as iron and steel, electricity, rail transportation, chemicals, mining, shipping, and trading companies. Those banks based on the zaibatsu, for example Mitsui, Sumitomo and Yasuda, were very powerful, with massive funds at their disposal, and they supplied funds to industry on a large scale.

The small and regional banks were mostly lending funds to small companies which were engaged in traditional industries such as textiles, silk manufacture and agriculture.

The national loan market, dominated by the large national banks, was completely separate from the small and regional loan markets, leading to a financial system that had a dual structure. Even after World War II, although the small and regional businesses changed and developed, the division of the loan markets remained.

Accumulation of financial assets

In the second half of the 1950s and in the 1960s, the Japanese economy showed high rates of growth. Domestic demand for manufactured goods grew rapidly, reflecting the increase in earnings. Exports also continued to rise, leading to increased investment in plant and equipment. The key policy of the government at this time was to increase Japan's competitiveness in international trade. In order to import the raw materials and oil necessary for a higher output of manufactured goods, Japan had to earn increasing amounts of foreign currencies, especially US dollars. The Ministry of International Trade and Industry (MITI) argued that the allocation of funds to industry must be as efficient as possible. For this purpose, the Council of Industrial Development was established to advise MITI on industrial policy, such as allocation of funds, industrial organisation and improvements in the utilisation of existing capital equipment by industry.

Among the committees of the Council of Industrial Development, the committee for the allocation of funds to industry, on which the long-term credit banks were represented, played a major role in making adjustments to industrial development planning. The decisions made by this committee had a considerable impact on the financial policy of private ordinary banks and long-term credit banks.

Private commercial banks could have raised the necessary funds for companies with good investment opportunities. However, since private commercial banks were not permitted to extend long-term credits to companies directly, these banks accepted financial bonds issued by the long-term credit banks, such as the Industrial Bank of Japan, the Long-Term Credit Bank of Japan and the Nippon Fudosan Bank (now Nippon Credit Bank), and in exchange, the long-term credit banks agreed to the private commercial banks lending money to industry. These indirect financings were a daily routine in those days.

In order to stimulate private investment in industry, the government had set interest rates at a lower level than the market equilibrium rates laid down in the Temporary Interest Rate Adjustment Law, which had been enacted by the occupation authorities in 1947 to regulate the fluctuations of interest rates caused by the post-war inflation. Since interest rates were kept below their equilibrium level, there was excess demand for funds in the financial markets, and private commercial banks were restricted in the amount of funds they could make available to industry.

At the same time, there was excess demand for short-term funds in the money markets, reflecting a shortage of working funds, which, in turn, brought about a rise in the call money rate.

The Bank of Japan controlled the credit policy of the private commercial banks through 'window guidance'. This required the banks to allocate funds to industry according to the government's policy on industrial development.

The economist R. W. Goldsmith, who classified the structure of financial activity into eight types, pointed out that Japan had attained the most advanced financial structure compared to the United States, the United Kingdom and Western Europe. Goldsmith's 'Financial Interrelation Ratio' (FIR) is the ratio of total financial assets to national wealth. In Japan, this ratio was 0.4 in 1913, and had risen to 1.7 in 1963, an increase of about 275 per cent during those 50 years, whereas the average increase of this ratio for the US, the UK, W. Germany, France, Italy and Japan was 47 per cent during the same period. Goldsmith argues that the reasons for this rapid increase in the FIR in Japan were the high rate of economic growth, the dominance of the indirect financing system and the industry's strong dependence on this system.

Personal savings

Personal savings ratios, net of personal debt, rose from 8 per cent to 17 per cent during the period 1953–60, and remained at a level of 18 per cent for the period 1961–68. The Japanese savings ratio has been at a high level since 1955, and is very high compared to that of the United States and European countries. Since the income of unincorporated business owners was declining during the same period, the high personal savings ratio reflects the savings of workers and property owners. The high rate of growth of financial assets was due to the high rate of growth of personal incomes. Savings held in short- and long-term deposits, investment trusts, insurance and securities increased rapidly in the 1950s and 1960s. The total amount of personal savings less personal debt rose from ¥394 billion (US$2.8 billion) in 1953 to ¥6,563 billion (US$46.5 billion) in 1968.

The main purpose of personal savings in Japan is to accumulate funds for house purchase or children's education, and, since savers preferred 'safe' assets, most of the savings were deposited in the Post Office savings system. Recently deposits in the Post Office savings system have exceeded ¥100 trillion (US$710 billion). A comparison with bank time deposits, now about ¥154 trillion (US$1.1 trillion), shows how large the postal savings account is.

Dominance of indirect financing

During the period of high economic growth, indirect financing expanded at a remarkable rate, as is shown by the shift in the composition of personal financial assets since 1953. The ratio of indirect securities to total financial assets held by individuals rose from about 66 per cent in 1953 to about 77 per cent in 1969. The total of indirect financial assets held by individuals was about ¥4,441 billion (US$31 billion) in 1954, and rose to ¥58.52 trillion (US$415 billion) in 1968.

The dominance of indirect financing in the years of rapid economic growth and excess demand for funds had strengthened the position of the commercial and long-term credit banks. Since the banks could ration funds, corporate management needed strong negotiating ability to raise funds from the banks, which were the main source of finance. The proportion of funds supplied by the banks was about 79 per cent for the period 1960–64, and rose to 92 per cent for the period 1965–73.

Investment financing 1953–68

The factors producing the high rate of economic growth in Japan were government investments (sustained for several years by the 'income doubling' plan) and the expectation that, if the government's economic policy was adhered to, the Japanese economy would grow steadily, independent of social or political changes. The lowering of corporate and personal income tax at the same time stimulated demand, and investments increased considerably: by about 40 per cent in nominal and annual terms during the period 1956–60, and by about 25–30 per cent during the period 1961–68.

Despite the rapid increase in investments by companies, the proportion of companies' internal funds used for investment increased during these periods. This proportion was on average 80 per cent in the period 1953–56, and rose to about 90 per cent for the period 1965–68. Therefore, corporate business must have obtained high profits during the expansion of the domestic markets, and most of the profits were reinvested in capital goods, which, in turn, brought about an increase in domestic demand for manufactured goods. Since a considerable proportion of corporate profits was used for new investments, dividends paid to shareholders were low, but stock prices continued to rise, reflecting the market value of companies.

Companies raised funds for investment from four sources: first from their internal funds, secondly from the commercial banks through the long-term credit banks, thirdly from issuing debenture or convertible bonds and fourthly from issuing new stock.

TSE average stock yield and yield of NTT bond, 1952-85

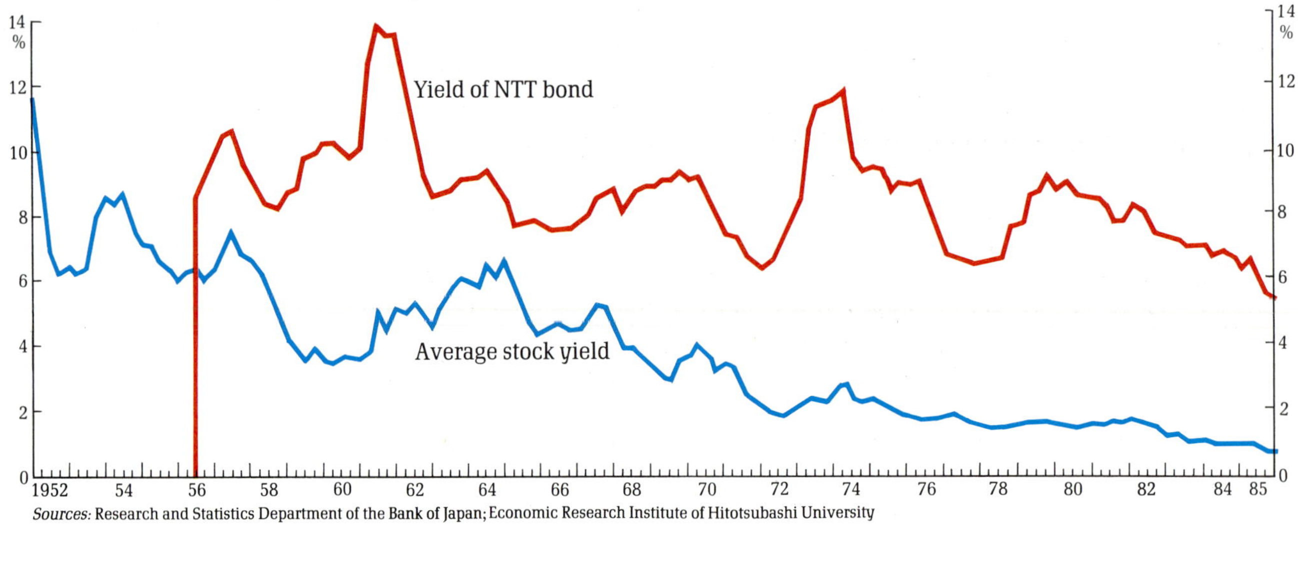

Sources: Research and Statistics Department of the Bank of Japan; Economic Research Institute of Hitotsubashi University

Interest rates

The flow of funds is usually adjusted by changes in interest rates, which balances demand for and supply of funds. In Japan, however, fluctuations of interest rates are very small compared with those in the United States and Western Europe. In Japan, the interest rate on ordinary deposits was 2.19 per cent from April 1952 to May 1957, 2.56 per cent from May 1957 to March 1961, 2.19 per cent from April 1961 to March 1970, and 2.25 per cent from April 1970 to 1981. The yield of the Telegraph and Telephone Public Corporation (now Nippon Telegraph and Telephone) bond is representative of long-term financial investments. Since 1957, this yield has fluctuated between 6.33 and 14.6 per cent.

Interest rates on bank deposits are still regulated at a low level by the Temporary Interest Rate Adjustment Law, and therefore time and savings deposits, as well as ordinary deposits and demand deposits, are basically used only to store assets, rather than to accumulate interest.

Up to now, the authorities have set interest rates at artificial levels. Under the Temporary Interest Rate Adjustment Law, the prime rate on long-term credits is set first, and other rates are then set with some constant differential relative to the prime rate. Although those differentials have been fluctuating, influenced by the changes in market conditions, this rule appears to have held until recently. This rule has also applied to the yields on bonds and the issue terms of public and corporate bonds. The yields on long-term government bonds also appear to have had a strong influence on the determination of the prime rate of long-term credit.

The first oil crisis

As economic growth slowed down, the Japanese financial markets changed in many respects. First, although exports continued to rise, investment in plant and equipment declined. Secondly, with the economic slowdown and relative increase in tertiary or service industries, tax revenues declined, but government expenditure increased. Thirdly, because of a decline in investment by industry, demand for funds contracted, which resulted in excess liquidity in the markets.

Consequently, the corporate sector became cash-rich, whereas the government deficit increased because capital gains were not taxable. Long-term central and local government bonds were bought on a large scale. The price of public bonds fell, and the yield of public bonds rose, at least until 1981.

The securities market

The first Securities and Exchange Law was enacted in 1874, but it was the revised Securities and Exchange Law of 1878 which established the securities markets in Tokyo and in Osaka. The main securities dealt in were government bonds. Only a very small proportion of stocks was traded in the stock market, which showed some highly speculative transactions. The large corporations, the zaibatsu, were not active in the stock market before World War I, and the Japanese stock market therefore played only a minor role in the economic development of Japan.

After World War II, a new Securities and Exchange Law was enacted in 1948, which prohibits banks underwriting securities except public bonds and debentures. Article 65 of this Law prescribes the segregation of the banking system. Banks cannot act as underwriters, but can buy and sell securities on behalf of their customers. They can also buy new issues of government bonds through a syndicate. Trust business is also permitted under this law, and banks can buy and sell securities including stocks on their customers' account.

However, since the proportion of securities held by the banks has constantly been increasing (from 30 per cent in 1953 to 50 per cent in 1986), it appears that the ban on banks' underwriting of securities has not been effective.

The securities market during the recession

Since the Spring of 1983, stock prices have risen, reflecting the large excess liquidity resulting from the sale of foreign bonds at US dollar prices by Japanese and foreign companies. The main reason for the excess liquidity in the Japanese financial markets was the large foreign trade surplus. This gave rise to uncertainty about future developments of Japan's economy. It is generally assumed in Japan that exports will decline in the near future. Also, the yen has appreciated considerably, and this, too, has created an atmosphere of uncertainty.

Investment in industry has declined gradually since 1983, and the corporate sector has become cash-rich. Profits of corporate business, which before had been used for investment in plant and equipment, are now mostly invested in financial assets. Private savings are also invested in financial assets such as saving deposits, trusts, insurance and other securities.

A review of the yields of stocks over the past 30 years shows that the average yield was about 8 per cent for the period 1952–57, fell to about 4 per cent until 1961, but recovered to about 6 per cent in 1964. Then yields again fell, although there was some cyclical recovery, to below 1 per cent. In mid-1986, the average yield was 0.74 per cent. This implies an extraordinarily high price of stocks. In the 1950s and 1960s, the years of rapid growth, high stock prices were not unreasonable for companies which invested heavily to produce goods and/or services, and could expect a high rate of return on their investment. The stock prices then also reflected the increased market value of the companies' intangible assets. Now, however, such increases in the market value of the intangible assets of companies are difficult to justify.

Since the start of the rapid appreciation of the yen in the Spring of 1986, the stock price average on the Tokyo Stock Exchange has risen at an unprecedented rate. To stem the rise of the yen, the Bank of Japan intervened in the foreign exchange markets and bought US dollars. This led to a large increase in the money supply, which added to the excess liquidity.

Internationalisation

In 1951, the Export Import Bank of Japan was established to supply funds for exports. A year later, the bank also became responsible for supplying funds for imports. This was the first step in the internationalisation of the Japanese financial system. As Japan began to develop an industrialised economy, imports and exports increased at a rapid pace, and the foreign exchange business expanded. Many banks in Japan established foreign branches in the United States and Europe to help international trade. In the 1980s, Japanese financial institutions started to operate in many countries. However, true internationalisation of the Japanese financial system means that foreign financial institutions are permitted to take an active part in banking and other financial activities in Japan. At the moment, there still remain many regulations which restrict foreign banks and foreign financial institutions.

Since the second half of the 1980s, stimulated by the boom in the Japanese securities market, and also attracted by the investment opportunities, many foreign banks have opened branches in Japan. Among them are Morgan Trust Bank, Chase Manhattan Trust and Banking Company, Chemical Trust and Banking Company, Lloyds Bank, Union Bank of Switzerland, Canadian Imperial Bank of Commerce and Manufacturers Hanover Trust Bank. Some foreign securities companies are now active on the Tokyo Stock Exchange: Goldman Sachs, Jardine Fleming, Merrill Lynch, Morgan Stanley, Shearson Lehman, S. G. Warburg and Vickers da Costa.

Moreover, foreign banks are now permitted to participate in the syndication of government bonds, although the number of participants is still limited. Furthermore, in 1984, foreign private corporations were permitted to issue Euroyen bonds without restrictions on the number or size of issues.

CHAPTER ONE

Introduction

Fundamental to the changes occurring in the world capital markets is the deregulation of Japan's financial system, which has unleashed a torrent of funds into world markets, as layer after layer of controls has been stripped away.

The recycling of Japan's massive trade surplus immediately brings to mind the flow of petrodollars through the world financial system during the 1970s, and the increased importance of Middle Eastern countries as portfolio investors.

In addition to Japan's staggering trade surplus, there is also significant excess liquidity created by the high savings rate which, combined with low capital spending by industry, is adding to the country's burgeoning cash surplus. With net external assets exceeding US$200 billion, Japan's heightened role as a key player in the international financial system is readily apparent.

Its emergence has coincided with the US becoming one of the most indebted nations in the world, with its large budget deficit requiring a rising volume of imported funds. Since a short-term deterioration of Japan's external prosperity is unlikely, the optimists in Tokyo predict that external assets could top the US$1 trillion mark over the next 15 years.

Whether this happens is not especially important, since Japan's rise to pre-eminence in international capital markets will continue for some time, at least until the US brings its surging budget deficit under control and reduces the trade deficit from the levels registered during 1986 and 1987.

Critical to the rise of Japan in world capital markets is deregulation of the complex web of controls surrounding the various institutions in the financial system. Many of the changes that have been implemented over the past three years have been specifically aimed at boosting Japan's capital outflow, to stem the rise of the yen. More broadly, the deregulation that has occurred to date was specifically intended to be isolated from the domestic financial system. But, as the authorities have found, the increasingly international nature of capital markets has made this aim impossible.

Change within Japan has often followed foreign pressure, or 'gai-atsu', and the same pattern is now evident in the shift now underway in Japan's financial system.

The pressures to liberalise

Foreign pressure on Japan to liberalise its domestic financial system has been common enough in recent years as its domestic institutions have reached a position of unprecedented strength in international financial markets.

The sharp revaluation of the Japanese yen against the US dollar which began in September 1985, following the Group of Five meeting in New York, has only served to heighten the strength of Japan's financial institutions, underscoring a pattern of change in the weighting in the international financial system that was already underway.

Prior to that meeting, Japan's banks and securities houses were already increasingly apparent in the US and Europe, where steady acquisitions had consolidated their position.

A high domestic savings rate, combined with the flexibility and dynamism of the industrial sector, has thrust Japan into the limelight – an unwelcome occurrence for a country that has usually tended towards isolationism.

The pressure on Japan to change, and make its domestic financial system more accessible to non-Japanese financial institutions, has grown with the increasing cohesion of international capital markets, making full and reciprocal access to Japan's financial system important for the continued stability of the international financial environment.

One stumbling block here is the fact that each country's financial system is different; and many of the pressure points between Japan, the US and Europe that emerged during 1986 and 1987 reflect the need to change financial structures to achieve greater uniformity of standards, particularly with capital adequacy ratios, the main point of conflict during much of 1987.

Japan's financial institutions are already concerned about their 'over-presence' in the main international financial centres, but as the capital outflow continues their position can only be strengthened. Not only has the role of Japanese investors become more important in world capital markets, but also many of the barriers within Japan's domestic financial system have become international issues, especially as Japan's banks and securities houses have broadened their scope of international operations.

Deregulation of Japan's domestic financial system has international implications as well. Establishment of a domestic commercial paper market, combined with further steps to revamp the domestic bond market, may result in a reduction in offshore borrowings by Japanese corporations, which will directly affect the level of financial activity in Europe.

Indirect controls by the Japanese government to force its banks and industrial companies to reduce speculation in the US dollar during May and June 1987 immediately removed much of the pressure from the US dollar, bringing stability to foreign exchange markets for the first time in 12 months.

However, for the international banking and financial community, the critical issue remains deregulation of Japan's domestic financial system.

Structure of the financial system

Japan's highly segregated financial system served the country well in harbouring scarce financial resources during much of the post-war period, when Japan's industrial sector was starved of cash. Rapid growth at a time when international credit markets were not as well developed or sophisticated as they are today, meant that Japan's corporate sector had to rely on domestic funds to finance its expansion.

Now, with the industrial sector recycling an increasing amount of cash, the financial system is overdue for change. Looked at in isolation, it is easy to claim that developments have been slow. Since 1984, and especially since 1986, the converse has been true, with the Ministry of Finance (MoF) and the Bank of Japan actively imposing a range of changes of rules and regulations, in recognition of the fundamental shift underway.

Not only is the financial system changing, but the entire industrial system is changing gear in the wake of the large currency revaluation that has taken place since the beginning of 1986. Smokestack industries that played a pivotal role during the 1950s and 1960s are faced with a drastic reduction not only of capacity, but also of their role within the domestic economy over the next decade. Equally, service industries will come to the fore.

The change Japan's economic system is presently undergoing has given rise to growing tensions which are bubbling beneath the surface as Japan is forced to come to grips with the prospects of sizeable unemployment for the first time in its post-war history. Old corporate alliances are coming under renewed pressures as the industrial system changes.

Equally, changes are being fuelled by the liquidity within the domestic economy. Falling interest rates have meant that small savers are aggressively seeking new investment outlets to generate higher returns which is, in turn, forcing a wholesale change in the weightings within Japan's financial system, with the role of the banks declining, and that of the rival savings sectors such as investment trusts and the insurance companies on the rise.

Opposite: 29 April, the Emperor's birthday, depicts two aspects of the national character: discipline and nationalistic fervour.

The pace of deregulation

The pace of deregulation of Japan's financial system over the past five years has been on the one hand startling and on the other disappointing.

A number of developments have been imposed from above by MoF, as it has repeatedly moved ahead of developments sought by domestic financial institutions; and changes adopted since 1984 have served to create pressure from within the financial sector for further liberalisation, although whether it is moving as fast as is demanded by many foreign governments and financial institutions is still open to doubt. With the deregulation now underway, the process mirrors Japan's overall attitude to change – that is, in a tightly controlled manner giving those groups that may suffer the opportunity to prepare fully well ahead of the event.

In this, Japan is very different from either Europe or the US, where a decision is made and quickly imposed, with the stronger institutions consolidating their positions, leaving the smaller institutions scrambling in their wake.

It is easy to argue that many of the changes that have been implemented have been in response to foreign pressure; equally, government officials concede that, even though this pressure has strengthened their hand, change was inevitable and already underway. Japan's financial system was solely oriented towards raising funds to be lent for the massive industrial rebuilding and development process after the end of World War II.

Even as little as 12 years ago, Japan's industrial sector was still cash-short, with industrial borrowers seeking funds literally forming queues outside the big city banks and trust banks. Company officials could regularly be seen trekking across the countryside visiting regional banks in their quest for funds to finance industrial expansion.

However, the first, and particularly the second, oil crisis changed that. From a financial system geared to providing funds for industrial investment, the progressive slowing in demand for new funds by the industrial sector forced a fundamental reappraisal, especially as the high savings rate continued, leading inevitably to an excess of funds for domestic investment. This has been exacerbated since the early 1980s by the build-up of Japan's current account surplus.

The realisation of the need to change the policies and attitudes that had built up Japan's strong industrial machine, and to allow the much freer development of domestic capital markets, has taken time, particularly in a country which goes through an exhaustive process of consensus building on the need for change, and how to achieve it, before making a move.

MoF has taken the initiative with much of the progress that has occurred since 1984, moving ahead of pressure from within the financial system, as it was faced with the growing realisation that, unless some concessions were made, Japan's guaranteed access to international capital markets would come under pressure. The full implications of this have only become apparent since 1985, as Japan's institutional investors have played a crucial role in helping to finance the snowballing budget deficit of the US.

The attitude of Japanese investors is now vital to the smooth development of a number of capital markets worldwide. Against the background of the recent massive growth of Japan's current account surplus – US$92.6 billion in 1986 and likely to remain at around this level until 1990 – it is easy to forget that until the mid-1970s, Japan was cash-short, with a very limited volume of funds left over for consumer lending after feeding the voracious appetite of its industrial machine.

In the early 1960s, for example, a limited number of foreign banks, including Citicorp and Chase Manhattan, made a US$200 million loan to the Bank of Japan – a modest sum by today's standards. At that time, however, it far exceeded the entire foreign exchange reserves of the country and naturally carried with it sizeable risk. In this context, the transformation that has occurred over the past 20 years is startling.

Internationalisation of the markets

The key event which sparked off the present deregulatory developments occurred in December 1980, when new legislation revising foreign exchange controls, the Exchange Control Law, was introduced. The next fundamental step was the yen/dollar accord between the US and Japanese governments which was aimed specifically at internationalising the yen. Under the terms of this agreement, Japan committed itself to deregulating the Euroyen market, beginning to liberalise domestic interest rate controls, establishing a yen-denominated bankers' acceptance market, and permitting the entry of foreign banks into the domestic trust banking sector.

Since then the pace of change has been swift. Activity in the Euroyen market has boomed, with yen-denominated issues the second most popular after US dollar issues in 1986. In the first quarter of 1987 they surpassed temporarily the level of funds raised in US dollar issues.

Also, an offshore banking centre has started up, a limited number of foreign houses have been allowed to join the Tokyo Stock Exchange, a bond futures market has begun operation, an equity futures contract has commenced trading, and a commercial paper market has been established, although under tight controls. Similarly, steps have been taken to put Japan's usually overlooked commodity markets onto a firmer footing, with a gradual expansion in the number and variety of contracts.

Tight controls limiting the offshore investments of many big financial institutions have been eased significantly and, in the process, trading in new instruments such as US Treasuries and UK Gilts has become far more active in Tokyo than was thought possible just a few years ago. Turnover in US Treasuries in Tokyo often exceeds US$5 billion a day – puny when compared with trading levels in New York, or in government bonds in Japan, but nevertheless significant given the fact that this market was virtually non-existent until a few years ago.

Other changes contemplated include further interest rate deregulation, including rates offered for small deposits, changes to the method of government bond issuance, with a gradual shift towards increasing the amount offered for tender, a further expansion of the number of foreign houses with direct access to the floor of the Tokyo Stock Exchange, an expansion of trading in government bond futures, steps to boost the capital adequacy ratios of domestic banks, and possible liberalisation of pension fund management, which is at present limited to trust banks and insurance companies.

In isolation, many of these steps appear modest but, looked at together, they constitute rapid change for a financial system which was all but closed until earlier this decade. Key areas of difficulty remain but, in the light of the more liberal attitudes of senior government officials, some of the key problems will be solved in the not too distant future.

The dramatic shift in Japan's industrial structure over the past decade has fuelled the change. The two Opec-inspired oil crises of the 1970s resulted in a sharp reorientation of new investment, away from capital intensive heavy industry in favour of more skill intensive industries.

The corporate sector, unfamiliar with the concept of distributing its burgeoning cash reserves to shareholders, uses it for a range of investments – both domestic stock and bond markets, and increasingly overseas.

The cash surplus of Japan's most profitable company, Toyota Motor Corporation, for example, easily exceeds US$2 billion, which is by no means unusual among Japanese industrial groups. Matsushita Electric has a cash surplus of over US$10 billion. The cash-rich position of Japanese corporations has contributed to the massive capital outflow from Japan as it recycles its trade surplus and excess savings.

With the dramatic changes underway, Japan's financial institutions have emerged as among the most profitable in the world, even though their overall return on assets falls far below that of many of their international rivals.

The scope for change

Foreign banks are still forced to operate on the periphery of the financial system, unable to obtain financing on an equal footing with domestic banks, and thus unable to compete effectively with the giants of Japan's banking system.

Although Tokyo's short-term capital markets have undergone significant deregulation and hence rapid expansion over the past five years, they are still dominated by direct 'window guidance' by the Bank of Japan whereby it puts pressure on the limited number of short-term market brokers, or 'tanshi gaisha', to retain indirect control over this market.

Consumer banking activities are slow and expensive and there is no automated clearing system for the banking system, with all dealings and transfers being carried out by physical delivery. The exhaustive reporting systems for MoF require the employment of a number of staff whose primary occupation is simply to fill in the forms in the manner required by the ministry. Automation may still be some way off.

The most striking differences emerge in the international market place. Japan's banks and securities houses are now major participants in all major financial centres, particularly London, where they typically offer services from commercial banking through to underwriting and advisory services.

In Japan, however, they are specifically prohibited from doing so, due to the strict operation of Article 65 of the Securities Exchange Law Act, which separates the banking and securities industries along the same lines as the Glass-Steagall Act in the US, upon which it was modelled. Even though there have been significant developments in the US over the past five years, with the lines of distinction between these two sectors becoming increasingly blurred, the Japanese government will not formally permit any significant change unless the US does so. Recently, however, a limited number of European and North American banks have been given approval to move into the securities industry, albeit indirectly. They have been forced to set up convoluted structures to do so while maintaining their banking licences.

Because of the increasingly difficult lending market for foreign banks, some have opted simply to give up their banking licences in favour of entering the securities industry directly.

Eager to move into the domestic securities industry, Japan's long-term credit and trust banks pushed hard behind the scenes for foreign banks to be allowed to enter Japan's securities business, with the clear aim of hoping to be able to do so themselves in the not too distant future.

Japan's long-term credit banks such as the Industrial Bank of Japan and the Long-Term Credit Bank have been keen for some time to return to the domestic securities sector, since it forms a logical extension of their existing activities. Before World War II, the Industrial Bank of Japan, for example, was the dominant force in underwriting in Japan. With the separation of the two businesses during the post-war occupation, it opted to continue with its banking licence. The Industrial Bank of Japan in particular has pressed for change. In early 1987 it took legal advice on its US primary dealer affiliate, Aubrey J. Lanston, opening a representative office in Tokyo. After some hesitation, MoF eventually yielded. This move represents the first crack in the wall separating the securities and banking sectors within Japan's financial system.

The commercial paper market

A further change that will redefine Japan's financial sectors is the decision to establish a commercial paper market. Both the banks and the securities houses have been engaged in a long-running war over this development. The banks opposed the introduction because of the impact it would have on their commercial lending activities, while the securities houses supported starting up this market, preferably without the direct participation of banks. The decision was finally taken to allow a commercial paper market to develop, but with both banks and securities houses participating.

The impact which this market will have on the overall financial system will be comparatively minor at first, since tight controls over who can tap the market, along with onerous stamp duty charges and the like, will continue to make this new market uncompetitive with the more relaxed borrowing procedures in foreign capital markets. Even so, once the structure is in place, the potential for relaxing or removing many of the strictures is real, so that commercial paper may emerge as a competitive financing alternative in the future.

Breaking down the zaibatsu

The securities houses have been lobbying hard for greater freedom and they have steadily worked at arriving at a consensus for change which may go some way towards bringing back onshore some of the offshore borrowing activities of Japan's corporate sector. This has significant implications for rival capital markets not only in the Asian region, but also in Europe and North America.

The changes forced by the dramatic currency revaluation are beginning to affect the relations between the big city and commercial banks and the industrial sector.

At the core of Japan's industrial structure are extensive closely intertwined business groupings, the 'zaibatsu'. Japan's industrial groups are among the most powerful in the world. Typically, each zaibatsu is organised around its own bank – the Mitsui Group and Mitsui Bank, the Mitsubishi Group and Mitsubishi Bank, and the Fuyo Group and Fuji Bank.

Others, such as the Industrial Bank of Japan, have forged their own network of companies, which form in effect its own zaibatsu. The Industrial Bank of Japan's group, for example, includes Nippon Steel Corporation, the largest independent steel company in the world, along with Nissan Motors, Fuji Heavy Industries and a number of others. But with the restructuring underway, many of the old allegiances are breaking down.

All large companies, whether formally members of a clearly defined zaibatsu or not, have their own 'main bank' which has traditionally provided not only banking services, but also corporate and management advice. If a corporation gets into financial difficulties, it is the main bank's responsibility to help.

Thus, when one of Japan's biggest trading houses, Ataka and Co, failed in the late 1970s, it was up to Sumitomo Bank to find suitable merger partners for the various sections of the company. Similarly, when Mazda Motor Corporation (then known as Toyo Kogyo) ran into financial difficulties, it was its main bank, again Sumitomo Bank, which was responsible for the subsequent reorganisation, which resulted in Ford Motor Co of the US being brought in as a major shareholder. With the more recent difficulties surrounding Japan's shipping and shipbuilding industries, the main bank relationships have again come to the fore in the reorganisation and merger options being studied.

But as the corporate sector becomes increasingly independent, these longstanding relationships have weakened. One reason is that the shift from bank to direct financing through capital markets has reduced the hold of the banks over the industrial sector's borrowing needs. So, Sumitomo Bank was sacked as the main bank of Daishowa Paper Co, after the founding family regained control of the company following a financial rescue carried out by Sumitomo Bank.

Also, many of Japan's larger banks find that the balance of power in their relations with corporate customers has shifted dramatically since the mid-1980s. Now that most of Japan's larger companies are cash-rich, they have little need for new bank borrowings. Consequently, in their negotiations with corporate clients, the banks find that they are being pressed hard to cut interest rates to uneconomic levels.

The move ahead

It is in international capital markets where Japanese institutions – both corporate and financial – have made their mark over the past two years.

Capitalising on the enormous interest in equity markets worldwide, they have aggressively raised funds through instruments aimed at tapping the interest of investors in equity-linked issues. As a result, bonds with detachable warrants and convertible bonds issued in Europe have become remarkably popular.

On one day alone in April 1987, new issues topping the US$1.4 billion level were announced. In the first half of 1987, new issues exceeding US$10 billion were brought to market, surpassing the total raised in calendar 1986. Towards the middle of 1987, much of these funds were being raised, after swapping the proceeds into yen, at negative interest rates, making it an especially attractive form of fund raising for Japanese corporations.

Of total offshore fund raisings by Japanese corporations during 1986, equity-linked issues accounted for 40 per cent, totalling US$12.55 billion, triple the amount raised the previous year and rivalling the total for ordinary bond issues of US$15.4 billion.

The aggression of Japanese corporations in raising funds in this manner highlights what is termed 'zaiteku' in Japanese – financing innovation. In this, Japan's corporate finance officers are merely catching up with the active handling of surplus cash holdings which has been the norm in both North America and Europe. While unremarkable to the outsider, it represents a fundamental change of perceptions within Japan because, until recently, this sort of activity has been viewed with considerable moral disapproval.

For many traditional manufacturing concerns, the enormous profits generated from their financial trading activities have become a key factor in survival. Hitachi, for example, generated 40 per cent of pre-tax profits on an unconsolidated basis from zaiteku activities during fiscal 1986. Most of the new fund raising of Japanese corporations is not for new investment in plant or research, since new capital spending forecasts point to a continued decline. Rather, these funds are being reinvested in a variety of instruments on offer.

The enormous power of Japanese corporations was highlighted in the first quarter of 1987, when reported Euroyen capital raisings exceeded Eurodollar raisings – the first time that the US dollar has ever been eclipsed by a rival investment currency. Most of that new fund raising activity was by Japanese corporations raising straight yen funding.

With the large surplus liquidity flowing through Japan's financial system, it is now much easier for new ventures to obtain risk funding, with a variety of specialised venture capital financing vehicles in operation. These companies, primarily spin-offs from the big securities houses, have had a checkered history, particularly during a spate of failures of start-ups in 1985 and 1986. The failures stemmed basically from many of these companies being taken public too early, before either management systems or new products were successfully in place. The lack of borrowing demand by the corporate sector has meant that consumer lending has become an attractive outlet of new lending for all financial institutions, from life insurance companies to the big city banks.

Due to the difficulty of borrowing funds from the banks, consumers had been forced to turn to 'sarakin' (loan sharks) for emergency funds, which often involved interest rates of over 100 per cent per annum. Legislation introduced in 1985 placed a 40 per cent ceiling on the interest charges of these sarakin lenders. With consumer finance now more readily available, the need to tap such fringe financing sources has become less important.

Insulation of the domestic market

One of the key features driving the deregulation of Japan's financial sector has been the desire to insulate the domestic financial system from moves to internationalise the yen, especially through the deregulation of the Euroyen market.

When yen borrowings were first approved, through so-called Samurai bond issues, the authorities limited access to this market to sovereign and supranational borrowers such as the World Bank and the Asian Development Bank.

For a time, after the impact of the two Opec oil crises of the mid-1970s, this market was completely shut down. Even after it reopened, tight strictures remained, which severely limited the amount of new issue activity. Gradually, further liberalisation was effected, with a limited number of top-ranking commercial borrowers allowed to tap the market.

The opening up of the domestic yen market to foreign borrowers was a similar story. This market even today remains highly regulated.

When Euroyen borrowings by foreign corporations were first approved in late 1984, MoF heavily restricted the participation of Japan's institutional investors, ensuring that there was a six-month gap between when an issue was made and when an investment in the paper issued could be made by Japanese investors. The dominant reason was to insulate domestic capital markets from the impact of the rapid expansion of this market.

Nevertheless, the driving force behind most of the dramatic expansion of the Euroyen market was in fact Japanese investors. Few North American or European groups tapping the Euroyen market had any real desire for yen; rather, the funds were quickly swapped into US dollars for the borrower, with the yen funds flowing to Japanese groups.

Specifically, this provided Japanese banks, particularly the city banks and long-term credit banks, with access to long-term paper at significant interest rate advantages over existing borrowings. As a result, Japan's city banks, which have traditionally been limited to raising funds short-term, even though often lending long-term, have been able to build up a portfolio of longer-term liabilities, enabling them to even out their mismatched portfolio.

With all of Japan's big financial institutions enjoying the fruits of liberalisation in the capital centres in Europe and New York, they are now hankering after similar freedom in their home market.

Attempts to limit the fall-out from the development of the Euroyen market on the domestic capital markets have failed, and equally, the raising of funds by Japanese corporations offshore, where the controls over issuers are far less restrictive, is bringing with it change within Japan.

Many of the rules surrounding domestic bond issues for corporate issuers are in the process of being relaxed. This will allow some reinvigoration of this domestic market, which was all but dead. Increasingly, the impediments to further deregulation within Japan's domestic capital markets hinge on the strict divisions within the financial system. However, any concession means overhauling Section 65 of the Securities Exchange Law, something that cannot be countenanced until the US is in a position to move on the Glass-Steagall Act.

Developments in international capital markets may leave the authorities with little choice. The securitisation of world capital markets, for example, has fuelled the desire of Japanese banks to move into the securities field domestically as well as offshore, where they are usually free to do so. Most Japanese financial institutions are active players in underwriting in offshore markets, although they are strictly prohibited to do so domestically.

At the same time, with the pressure on their traditional lending operations, Japan's big commercial banks have been deriving an ever larger portion of their profits from trading, both in Japanese government bonds and in foreign exchange markets, as capital markets worldwide have become more volatile.

Increasingly, the commercial banks have become far less shy about their affiliations with some of the smaller securities companies, on occasion taking overt steps to improve the management of these smaller concerns, as they wait for the inevitable liberalisation of present divisions between securities and banking businesses.

But the changes flowing through Japan's financial system do not start and end with the banks and securities companies. As interest rate liberalisation is pursued, it brings fundamental changes in the fund raising techniques of the corporate sector, with clear consequences for banks and securities houses. Equally, Japan's legion of small investors is being offered increasingly attractive savings alternatives to the low-yielding term deposits with the banks.

The introduction of new products

The general insurance sector, which is subject to strict government controls, making it the most profitable general insurance industry in the world, has achieved strong growth over the past five years by introducing products which tap the strong urge to save on the part of the Japanese. New savings-linked policies have given the general insurance companies a new lease of life.

Life companies have also begun offering a new range of flexible interest rate policies, with returns far in excess of what is available through most other options. The companies selling these policies were subjected to unofficial pressure to reduce the rate of return to policy holders, as the authorities feared a massive shift of funds from other savings instruments.

Investment trusts (or mutual funds, as they are sometimes called) have also experienced a new lease of life, with the funds under management spiralling over the past two years as small investors have scrambled to profit from the strong boom in equity markets in Japan.

The corporate sector has also invested more and more funds in various trust accounts in order to profit from strong equity markets worldwide.

The rapid maturing of Japan's financial system has resulted in non-mainstream financing groups experiencing exceptionally strong growth. Consumer finance companies, for example, have, in broad terms, doubled the size of their operations since the early 1980s. Leasing finance has become far more attractive, with specialised lease financing companies doubling the scale of their operations over the past four years.

The strong growth curve of both sectors has attracted stiff competition from the giants of the financial sector, with the big commercial banks and long-term credit and trust banks pushing hard for business in the same areas.

Interest rate deregulation

Pivotal to the changes underway in Japan's financial system has been the deregulation of interest rates. Similar to the moves that began in the US in the 1970s, when the gradual relaxation of interest rate controls brought in its wake wholesale changes in the financial system, the steady reduction of many of the controls over Japan's interest rates is also bringing with it considerable change. The shift of funds in search of higher interest rates that has occurred in Japan has been exacerbated by the progressive slowdown in new investment spending. The growing volume of funds searching for a higher rate of return at a time of declining interest rates has fuelled the boom in Japan's equity markets and also raised capital outflow.

The sector of Japan's financial system most exposed to the shift underway is the big commercial banks, which have been hit by slowing demand for new funds by industry – historically their main outlet for lending. At the same time, the growing sophistication of the corporate sector, as it taps financial markets directly and also uses techniques such as convertible bonds or issues with warrants, has brought further pressure for change. Japan's commercial banks have progressively been forced to adopt 'spread lending' techniques, as their overall cost of funds has risen as interest rates on large deposits have been deregulated.

The boom in equity markets since early 1985 has made fund raising through various equity-linked instruments a more attractive option for most large corporate borrowers. With the division between the banking and securities industries, the banks have been unable to capitalise on the shift within Japan.

Consumer lending, long overlooked by nearly all of Japan's financing institutions, is one of the few areas remaining which offers significant growth potential. The progressive reduction in the size of deposits that are subject to interest rate controls has seen a large shift of funds out of the banking system into the short-term money market, particularly money market certificates (MMCs) and certificates of deposit (CDs), which offer better rates of return.

The government bond market

The need to expand Japan's short-term money markets has also been demonstrated by the dramatic increase in the size of the bond markets, which have been all but swamped by national bonds, following the big increase in government spending during the 1970s as the authorities sought to offset the recessionary impact of the sharp rise in energy prices.

Many of these issues were of 10-year paper, and they have progressively come due for redemption since the mid-1980s, which has added significantly to the volume of funds needing to be placed. Many of these government bond issues are of over ¥2 trillion (US$12.5 billion) each and, while most are quickly rolled over into new government issues, the interest rate differential between new and old issues is sizeable, fuelling the drive to seek out alternative investments offering a higher rate of interest.

Interest rates on many of these older issues are around the 8 per cent mark, with new issues offering just 4.7 per cent as of mid-1987. With government debt accounting for over 50 per cent of total outstandings in domestic bond markets, there have been fears of a 'crowding out' effect although, given the development of secondary bond markets over the past decade, these fears have by and large proved to be unfounded.

Aiding the distribution process, commercial banks were allowed to distribute government bonds over the counter for the first time in 1984. Overall distribution was also aided by the introduction in 1980 of medium-term government bond funds, 'chuki kokusai', marketed by the securities companies, which have attracted a significant volume of funds, helping the overall deficit financing process.

Banks were also allowed to participate in dealing in government bond markets from mid-1985, and volumes traded soared from around the ¥300 trillion level in 1983 to ¥2,484 trillion in 1986.

Against the backdrop of the pressures on Japan's financial system stemming from the government's substantial borrowing programme, the measures undertaken to liberalise progressively interest rates on large-sized deposits have also had significant ramifications. The developments here followed the US-Japan yen/dollar committee report released in May 1984, when MoF committed itself to a broad policy of freeing interest rate controls on large deposits.

Initially, in October 1985, interest rate controls on deposits of more than ¥1 billion were removed, with the limit lowered to ¥500 million in April 1986, and to ¥300 million in September. Plans to cut controls on rates to ¥100 million are in hand, although there are no plans beyond that level. Even so, the shift of funds has already been dramatic, with a large volume of funds flowing into MMCs, which operate with flexible interest rates. By June 1987, MMCs totalled ¥11.3 trillion.

Along with the approval for issuance of MMCs, the authorities liberalised many of the outstanding controls covering CDs. When first introduced in 1979, the minimum size was ¥500 million, with a three- to six-month time period. Now, the minimum issued amount is ¥100 million, with the time period varying between one and six months. Many of these changes were long overdue and simply serve to bring Japan's markets more into line with those of other major financial centres; but further progress in liberalising interest rates is difficult. Despite repeated assurances that the authorities are negotiating to take the final, and fundamental, step in liberalising Japan's interest rate structure, they are clearly holding back.

At the heart of the difficulties is the nationwide Post Office savings system, the largest savings institution in the world, through which the government finances much of its spending on public works, as well as raising funds for government institutions such as the Export Import Bank of Japan and the Japan Development Bank.

Funds deposited in the Post Office savings system are in turn lodged with the

Trust Fund Bureau of MoF. If used for government spending, they are channelled through the Fiscal Investment and Loan Programme.

Thus, any move to free interest rates on small deposits would in turn affect government financing of public works programmes, as well as the cheap export financing available through the Export Import Bank. The issues at stake for the government in fully liberalising interest rates are clear. Equally, the big banks have been strongly hostile to the fact that the Post Office savings system usually offers depositors slightly higher deposit rates than they can offer. Also, the Post Office does not have to comply with any prudential requirements, nor earn a profit.

Problems of excess liquidity

Along with recycling Japan's staggering trade surplus, the steady rise in the liquidity of the corporate sector has added to the capital outflow, threatening to bring with it new difficulties. The growth of financial assets held by the private sector within Japan is rising faster than the increase in total assets, underscoring both the rapid maturing of the Japanese economy and the increasing emphasis being placed by the corporate sector on managing its financial assets more aggressively. By 1986, the proportion of real assets of the private sector (excluding property holdings) had fallen to 56 per cent of total assets, compared with well over 60 per cent a decade ago.

In addition, the diversification of funding sources of the private sector has also accelerated. In 1981, for example, the corporate sector raised just 8.1 per cent of its funding offshore. By 1985, that had grown to 17.5 per cent, and is now believed to have exceeded 20 per cent, in line with the massive growth of the Euroyen market and the big overseas investment push by Japan's private sector following the appreciation of the yen against the US dollar. Japan's monetary authorities are cautiously watching developments. Since the early 1980s they have adopted an easy money policy, although concerns have risen that heavy speculation in both equity and property markets in Japan threatens an upturn in inflationary pressures.

The corporate sector is increasingly investing in high-risk, high-return investments. The boom in stock prices in Japan during 1986 and the first half of 1987 has fuelled a boom in property prices which increased by an average of 28.8 per cent in fiscal 1986, with further rises since then, especially in the major city areas such as Tokyo. Even with the slowdown in new investment being undertaken by the private sector, there is a steady increase in new fund raising which is partly to retire existing, expensive debt, along with the overriding attraction of raising cheap funds which can in turn be reinvested in other markets.

A notable development seen for the first time during the second quarter of 1987 was negative real interest rates on convertible bond issues, or issues with detachable equity warrants. The coupon for many of these issues during the second quarter of 1987 was a little over 1 per cent which, when swapped from US dollars into yen, resulted in net income being generated for the borrower; this accounted for much of the boom in new issue activity seen during 1987.

Heavy fund raising through these markets resulted in saturation by mid-1987, which was compounded by uncertainty over future movements in equity markets, following their rapid rise over the previous 18 months. Even so, the rise in liquidity in Japan was usually cited as underlying the continued expansion of these markets.

Successive cuts in the official discount rate since early 1986 have fuelled the growth in domestic liquidity, and by mid-1987 the monetary authorities, while voicing increasing concern over the prospects of a build-up of inflationary pressures, were unwilling to move quickly to raise interest rates, following the repeated international commitments given to stimulate domestic economic demand.

The first steps towards liberalisation

The first tangible steps taken by the Japanese government to liberalise controls over its finance sector were implemented in December 1980, when legislation controlling foreign investment and foreign exchange controls was totally revised, following the introduction of new legislation, the Foreign Exchange and Trade Control Law. This legislation made foreign investment and foreign exchange transactions 'free in principle' the norm, rather than 'controlled in principle'.

With this change, the Japanese authorities brought the country up to date with overseas developments in one quick move. The yen had been liberalised earlier but it was not until the passage of this legislation that the changed attitude of the authorities was made clear. The Bank of Japan has intervened in foreign exchange markets at times of rapid market movement when, for example, the yen has moved quickly in one direction. In this instance, the central bank intervenes heavily to stem the flow, although typically with only limited success. Its most noted success, and perhaps its most profitable decision ever, was when it plunged into foreign exchange markets following the Plaza Hotel agreement of the Group of Five in September 1985 – one of the few occasions when any central bank has been able to impose its will on foreign exchange markets.

The next move, and central to the changes now underway both within Japan and externally with the yen, was the agreement of the US-Japan yen/dollar working group on 29 May 1984. Prior to the talks that led to this agreement, there was a considerable body of opinion within the US, and to a lesser extent in Europe, that Japan manipulated the yen so that it was chronically undervalued, giving its industry an unfair advantage in export markets, and in particular in the US. At that time, the US dollar was itself overvalued in the wake of the sharp rise in US government spending in the early years of President Reagan's term of office.

Japan's real interest rates were also kept artificially low, it was argued in the US, which helped depress interest in the yen, as well as giving its industry an additional competitive edge. Low domestic interest rates led to a steady capital outflow from Japan, primarily into US government securities, as investors sought to take full advantage of the interest rate differential between investment alternatives within Japan and those available offshore. This, in turn, kept up pressure on the yen vis-à-vis the US dollar. Central to the yen/dollar committee accord was:

- the liberalisation of barriers within Japan against the outflow and inflow of capital;
- the internationalisation of the yen;
- improved treatment of foreign banks and other foreign financial institutions in the Japanese market; and
- the deregulation of domestic capital markets, including interest rate deregulation.

At the time this agreement was reached, few could have predicted the startling changes that have subsequently occurred. Even though this series of moves followed US pressure for change, the speed with which the Japanese government responded reflected changes in the domestic economy.

The entire structure of Japan's post-war financial system was to channel scarce funds to the industrial sector, primarily from the general savings sector. The two oil crises of the 1970s fundamentally changed the nature of economic growth, away from large-scale, capital intensive heavy industry in favour of more dispersed economic growth, with greater emphasis on communications and the services sector generally. In line with this, the demand for new funds by the corporate sector dwindled rapidly.

At the same time, with the government spending heavily to help the Japanese economy out of the recession of the 1970s, massive fund raising programmes were initiated, which required that the secondary bond market and short-term money market be developed more fully, particularly by the mid-1980s when many of these bonds would be maturing.

These external factors were consolidated by the new Foreign Exchange Law of 1980. After a series of policy reversals, aimed at encouraging either capital inflow or capital outflow, depending on the domestic situation in Japan, the complete liberalisation that occurred with the adoption of new legislation marked a switch from previous policy attitudes.

As a result of the mounting frustration in the US over trade relations with Japan, pressure for basic changes to Japan's financial system was pursued through the yen/dollar committee.

Liberalisation of capital flows

One of the first changes involved liberalising the restrictions covering Samurai bond issues, reducing the waiting period and also boosting the maximum size of issue to be allowed. The impact was immediate, with a sharp growth in the volume of new issues undertaken.

In a similar vein, the quantitative limits imposed on the foreign lending of Japanese banks were largely removed, along with most country limits. Also, the ban on the sale of foreign commercial paper and CDs was lifted in early 1984, along with the designated company system, whereby domestic companies in which foreigners could buy shares were specified. Real estate purchases were liberalised at the same time.

One of the long-term aims of the US government was to increase the use of the yen as an international currency which, it was believed, would add to international demand and also result in further strength of the currency. The yen, however, still only accounts for an estimated 6 per cent of official foreign exchange reserves – half the figure for the Deutschmark.

Little progress has been achieved on this point, although the removal of the 'real demand rule' in early 1984, which previously limited foreign exchange dealings to those covering an underlying transaction, has resulted in foreign exchange trading in Tokyo surging.

The most significant area of change has been the freeing of Euroyen market controls. The yen is now the second most popular issuing currency after the US dollar. Non-Japanese corporations are allowed to tap the market for funds, as are a limited number of domestic groups. The participation of Japanese institutions has resulted in a dramatic increase in the overall level of activity and in the degree of sophistication of instruments on offer in this market.

Treatment of non-Japanese financial institutions

One of the most dramatic changes has been in the treatment of foreign banks and securities houses in the Tokyo market. Foreign banks are now allowed to trade in the secondary market for government bonds and there has been a move to boost the participation of foreign securities houses in the underwriting syndicates for new government debt issues. The government has gradually increased the portion of debt it has put up for tender, as opposed to using the syndication method. Equally, a number of foreign banks have been allowed to enter the trust banking sector, targeting the massive growth in pension funds that is commonly forecast for the next decade.

Similarly, foreign securities houses have been permitted to join the Tokyo Stock Exchange, and are also active in the newly-established securities futures contract in Osaka.

The Japanese view

Even with the changes that have occurred since 1984, and those in the pipeline, getting MoF to move away from its traditional stance of ensuring the protection particularly of investors, even if it stifles overall market development, will take time.

In Japan, the normal maxim of 'let the buyer beware' is still a foreign concept. Even though it clearly applies to any purchases made in Japan's rough and tumble equity markets, it does not apply to debt markets. Change is proceeding, although in some areas at a snail's pace. The advent of 'financial friction' has strengthened the hand of the International Finance Bureau of MoF, but it is still often involved in disputes with other departments of the ministry, most notably the Taxation Bureau and the Securities Bureau, in trying to achieve meaningful change.

Not all of the liberalisation that has occurred within Japan has followed foreign pressure, or 'gai-atsu'. In retrospect, one of the key decisions which subsequently had a profound impact on the liberalisation of Japan's capital markets was the approval for the Asian Development Bank to make a publicly floated yen bond issue in 1970. Approval was finally given after intense lobbying by the then Governor of the Asian Development Bank, Takeshi Watanabe.

Prior to this issue, only two private placements had occured – one by the World Bank, and the second by the Inter-American Development Bank. Watanabe, himself a former MoF official, won the support of senior officials, who were keen to enhance the development of Tokyo as an international financial centre. His argument to senior government ministers was that the proposed issue represented an expression of support for international cooperation, and the Asian Development Bank in particular.

In paving the way for this issue, a number of key difficulties had to be overcome. First, while Japan's banks were at that time allowed to participate freely in private placements, they could not underwrite public issues. Eventually a compromise was reached, whereby a part of the underwriter's fee was returned to the banks after the issue was completed. Secondly, problems over collateral were ultimately circumvented by treating the Asian Development Bank as a sovereign borrower, which exempted it from the established collateral requirements.

More general changes to the domestic bond market were prevented by the requirements of the collateral system, which formed a key part of the activities and earnings of the long-term credit banks. If the domestic bond market were totally liberalised, this would pose a direct loss for the long-term credit banks – the Industrial Bank of Japan, the Long-Term Credit Bank and the Nippon Credit Bank. Their entrenched opposition prevented the development of an unsecured bond market in Japan for some time, and it was not until the late 1970s that a suitable solution was arrived at, whereby a limited number of overseas and domestic corporations were allowed to issue unsecured bonds.

The cautious attitude of the authorities in allowing the development of the yen bond market (Samurai bonds) in Tokyo during the 1970s reflected concerns about isolating the deregulation of the yen from the domestic financial system.

Throughout much of the 1970s, the authorities severely controlled new Samurai bond issues, and it was not until 1984 that this market witnessed a rapid growth in new issue activities, in line with the overall attitude of promoting the internationalisation of the yen. This catchphrase is, in fact, a misnomer since much of the activity in this market has followed the increased aggression of Japanese institutions in foreign capital markets. The rapid growth in new issues in the Euroyen market, for example, gave Japan's banks access to medium-term yen funding for the first time at attractive rates. Similarly, the extraordinary array of instruments that have been offered, from dual currency bonds through to heaven-and-hell swaps were all targeted at the specific needs of Japan's institutional investors.

Even with the progress made in deregulating both the yen and Japan's capital markets, the authorities are still in an enviable position in terms of controlling developments through so-called 'window guidance'.

In the run up to the Venice Summit in June 1987, the Japanese government became increasingly concerned about Japanese investors selling US dollars aggressively, and thus putting pressure on the US dollar vis-à-vis other major currencies. Consequently, MoF put overt pressure on the banks to slow their foreign exchange trading, while the Ministry of International Trade and Industry called in all the major trading companies and manufacturers and put similar pressure on them. Both ministries continue to monitor the foreign exchange trading activities of the banks and the big manufacturing groups closely.

During 1986, the rapid and highly competitive development of new Euroyen instruments, such as heaven-and-hell bonds, caused concern in MoF circles that some of Japan's institutional investors could find themselves in difficulties if they needed to liquidate these investments, for whatever reason, in the future. Accordingly, the ministry forced all institutions developing and purchasing these instruments to reduce their level of activity. As a result, activity in this area has been virtually non-existent since late 1986.

The formal changes in the controls covering the activities of Japan's financial institutions have been mirrored by shifts in the investment alternatives allowed. In a bid to slow the dramatic appreciation of the yen against the US dollar, layer after layer of controls were stripped away, allowing principally the life insurance groups to lift the portion of their total offshore assets from less than 20 per cent to the present level of 40 per cent. Most of this investment was unhedged, so that the life companies have suffered massive foreign exchange losses. With the increased freedom given to overseas investments by the trust banks, however, MoF was more cautious, forcing them to protect their offshore investments against any untoward currency shifts.

Future needs and opportunities

With the changes that have taken place over the past five years, the groundwork has been laid for further deregulation given the conflicting claims that are now arising within the financial sector. But change from here becomes much harder. The power of the Taxation Bureau within MoF has made the anticipated CP market and, similarly, the recently-established Japan offshore market, of little immediate interest.

Nonetheless, Japan's financial markets are in a process of steady transition. Even though the principal structures are still in place, the shift of external conditions, combined with the changing nature of financial markets and capital flows, has meant that although Japan's financial authorities are trying to hold on to a static structure, the roles and lines of demarcation are becoming increasingly blurred. Japan's big commercial banks are increasingly emerging as universal banks in the major financial centres of the world, yet in Japan their hands are bound. At the same time foreign banks have been given approval to enter Japan's securities sector, Japan's banks must abide by increasingly anachronistic lines of demarcation.

The securities houses have, in turn, formed close links with a number of regional banks that give them the potential to develop their medium-term government bond funds quickly into cash management funds; although, following stiff lobbying opposing this development by the larger banks, same-day withdrawal facility has been blocked.

Much of the future deregulation of Japan's financial system will revolve around each sector giving up control over a portion of its traditional ground in return for the freedom to move into other, related areas. Given the entrenched interests involved and the potential impact of many of these changes on the smaller and weaker financial organisations, the more fundamental liberalisation will prove difficult. A smooth transition of Japan's financial system would require mergers of a number of the weaker players, particularly among the smaller regional and mutual banks and the credit associations. There has been minor merger activity among some of the small, regional entities, but this is difficult to effect smoothly among the larger institutions.

Legislative constraints, for example those limiting the role of the mutual ('sogo') banks to being basically savings institutions channelling their deposits to small and medium-sized industrial concerns, are increasingly out of date, particularly as competition among all savings institutions has intensified and the battle to lend to small and medium-sized industrial concerns is fierce. Similarly, a number of the government-sponsored financial institutions, such as the Japan

Development Bank, and some of the many public financial corporations need to have their roles redefined if they are to survive a tougher competitive climate.

Tax reforms

Apart from the deregulation that is flowing from relaxation of controls over specific sections of the financial system, the implication of changes in other areas may also be profound. For much of the latter part of 1986 and 1987, the government sought to revamp the taxation system by shifting the tax burden from direct to indirect taxes. MoF has been keen for some time to overhaul the tax system as a means of bringing the budget deficit under control, since reductions in government spending will not achieve the objective quickly enough. On all previous occasions when the government has attempted to effect changes in this area, it has run into opposition, and this time around was little different. By trying to marry taxation reform with a cut in personal tax levels, the government thought that the proposed package would be politically acceptable, but its ambitions were ultimately frustrated.

One of the most significant aspects of the proposed change was abolishing the 'maruyu' savings system, an issue which generated a great deal of discussion. Under the present tax system, the annual interest income from bank deposits of more than ¥3 million is taxable. To get around this, depositors open several bank accounts with different banks or in different names to avoid incurring this tax liability.

The government wanted to tighten up controls, but the fear of incurring additional tax liabilities resulted in a large shift of small depositors' funds out of the banking system into rival investment alternatives, primarily the share market (through investment trusts) and the flexible policies marketed by the life insurance companies.

For the big banks, this shift of funds removed a source of cheap deposits, which severely affected their balance sheets and added to the prosperity of the securities houses.

Many smaller businesses avoid paying any tax, although the evasion would be jeopardised if a value added tax were introduced, which was the government proposal. Consequently, there was a large groundswell of opposition among the ranks of small business, which forms the backbone of support for the government. As with previous reform attempts, the government was forced to back down, although it is still hoping to achieve smaller, incremental changes.

With the tax proposals pursued during 1987, MoF insisted that they would be revenue neutral, although it was widely expected that once in place, the ministry would slowly move to boost tax revenues to enable a reduction of the government deficit.

Further deregulation of Japan's financial markets will also expose weaknesses among some of its domestic institutions. In late August 1987, Moody's downgraded the long-term debt and deposit ratings of four Japanese banks – the Bank of Tokyo, the Long-Term Credit Bank of Japan, Mitsubishi Trust and Banking Corporation and Sanwa Bank. Its caution stemmed from the rising risks for some of Japan's financial institutions following deregulation, which is bringing with it stiffer competitive pressures.

Subsequently, the Bank of Japan said that it intended closer monitoring of the off-balance sheet assets and liabilities, in particular interest rate and currency swaps, of all banks. The Bank of Japan decision was aimed at ensuring that the city banks, long-term credit banks and trust banks were fully aware of the risks being carried, so as to be fully prepared in the event of any bank running into problems.

CHAPTER TWO

The outlook for deregulation

By 1987, with most of the easier deregulation moves completed, there was a growing perception in Tokyo that the deregulatory process had ground to a halt. Virtually all of the major features of the earlier deregulation packages had been implemented but further steps need to be taken. Deregulation in the future will involve trade-offs within the financial sector, as well as political compromises.

The most fundamental step to be taken is the abolition of Article 65 of the Securities Exchange Law, which would permit banking and broking services to be merged. Any step along these lines will only be contemplated when the US government agrees to a similar step, that is to either abolish or amend the Glass Steagall Act.

Even though this formal barrier remains, Japan's city banks have become much more open about their links with smaller securities houses, indicating an increasingly tolerant attitude being taken by the Ministry of Finance (MoF).

Entrenched interests between the competing sections of the financial sector will slow progress. But with the steps that have been taken to date, the pressure for further liberalisation is intense.

And ironically, for a time at least, foreign institutions have been given a potentially significant advantage over domestic institutions. Foreign banks, for example, have been allowed to open securities branches in Tokyo, while some also have commercial and trust banking arms, and others are seeking membership of the Tokyo Stock Exchange. Citibank, for example, has a commercial banking licence, a trust bank and representation on the Tokyo Stock Exchange through its affiliate Vickers da Costa.

The fact that MoF has given foreign groups access to sections of the market that domestic institutions have not gained was partly to deflect foreign criticism that although Japanese financial institutions are allowed free access to most parts of foreign financial markets, this has not been fully reciprocated by Japan.

The deregulation that has occurred to date has not yet had any impact on the lines of demarcation between the major sectors of the Japanese financial system.

Moving beyond the present deregulation is problematical, given the entrenched interests involved. The long-term credit banks still effectively control the domestic bond market and have been reluctant to respond to pressure for change. Stifling domestic controls have resulted in a progressive shift of corporate sector borrowings offshore over the past four years. Equally, the commercial banks are unwilling to relax their grip on foreign exchange trading, a point of tension with the securities houses, which are seeking direct access. City banks may yield ground here if they can obtain free access to trading in domestic bond markets. At present they are limited to trading on their own account and cannot conduct any trading for clients.

The main concern of MoF is to ensure that deregulation proceeds at a pace which will not harm the existing participants.

Further banking deregulation would erode the position of some of the smaller institutions such as the regional and mutual (sogo) banks, and the credit and labour associations. To avoid this, government officials are quietly encouraging a range of mergers among the smaller groups to put them onto a firmer financial footing.

Further interest rate deregulation will be slow, as will be further moves to lift the present lines of demarcation within the financial system.

And, in the short-term capital markets, for example, there has been a dramatic growth, but further steps are essential if some of the existing anomalies in the market are to be overcome.

The more fundamental changes involve a complex series of trade-offs between the competing sections of the finance system, with MoF or the Bank of Japan acting as the arbitrator.

There may also be some external pressures. The need to ensure pensions are adequate in the future may lead to some relaxation of the present controls, which limit pension fund management to just trust banks and life insurance companies – a highly restricted group given the massive sums involved. There is growing perception that outside fund managers will gain some access to pension fund management in the future.

Also, MoF has indicated that it is prepared to allow life insurance companies to access capital gains in determining returns to policyholders – a change that will have a profound impact on investment strategies once it is implemented.

Most of the controls over foreign exchange trading have been removed. But even with the deregulation that has occurred so far, the powers of 'moral suasion' wielded by MoF and the Bank of Japan still ensure that all dealings are fully reported and closely monitored. If activities in one area are thought to be too speculative, then pressure is usually applied to reduce the level of activity.

Equally, MoF was concerned about many of the complex Euroyen swap instruments that were brought to market during 1986, and pressured for a slowing down of market activity.

Concerned by investment excesses which led to surging property prices in the first half of 1987, the Bank of Japan put strong pressure on the commercial banks to cut the volume of new lending. Similarly, in the wake of the heavy losses incurred on ill-fated investments by Tateho Chemical, announced in early September 1987, the Bank of Japan intervened more actively to slow down what it termed excessive speculative investment.

The need for further liberalisation is recognised by most government officials but many of the attending problems stem, at least in part, from the power of the Taxation Bureau within MoF. With the parlous condition of the government's finances, the Taxation Bureau has been a powerful obstacle to change in a range of areas. With the start-up of the new offshore market, for example, it refused to sanction the various tax exemptions that were sought, which would have made the proposed market a strong rival to other offshore markets. The start-up of the commercial paper market may also be hampered by the levying of additional taxes.

There has been a growing realisation in political circles that one of the main stumbling blocks to further deregulation is the Taxation Bureau. The failure of the attempted reform of Japan's taxation system in 1987 may slow the deregulatory process in the future.

US pressure

Central to much of the deregulation of Japan's financial markets that occurred during the 1980s has been pressure from the US. The broad perception in the US that Japanese industry enjoyed an unfair competitive advantage over its US rivals, due to both controlled interest rates in Japan and manipulation to ensure that the yen remained undervalued, lay behind much of the thrust of the US government in seeking to force the Japanese government to relax many of its controls.

Interest rate deregulation, in particular, was hoped to help put the industries of both countries onto an equal footing in future competition.

In response to the lifting of most interest rate controls on larger deposits, Japanese corporations have actively sought out alternative sources of financing. During 1986 and 1987, this has resulted in a significant boost in the volume of funds raised through issuing convertible bonds domestically, and bonds with detachable warrants in Europe.

Subway commuters: Japan's close-knit financial élite have made it difficult for foreign competitors to gain equal access.

With only a partial deregulation of Japan's interest rate structure completed to date, it is too early to tell whether much of the US argument was correct. Deregulation of interest rates on small deposits will, over time, make some of the cheap financing by the Japan Export-Import Bank and the Japan Development Bank more difficult. Equally, Government spending which is financed through the Fiscal Investment Loans Programme will be more difficult to fund.

As the US pressured the Japanese government to lift many of the controls over its financial sector, Japan's biggest financial institutions have risen to pre-eminence in international capital markets. The role of Japanese investors in absorbing the rising level of US government debt has been an important factor in holding down US interest rates.

Conclusion

Japan's financial institutions will have a clear edge over their international rivals in the coming few years since they are well positioned to aid the recycling of Japan's burgeoning trade surplus. In addition, their close and longstanding links with Japan's institutional investors have helped underwrite their expansion into international capital markets during the 1980s. These links permeate all sections of Japan's financial and industrial élite, making it difficult, but not impossible, for many international competitors in the financial services area to obtain equal access.

The deregulation of Japan's capital markets has helped catapult its banks and securities houses to the fore in world capital markets – a development that was unforeseen when the US government first focused on its strategy of forcing Japan to open its tightly controlled domestic financial sector.

Fundamental to much of the shift that occurred in international capital markets during the mid-1980s is the reweighting of the major currencies, with the decline of the US dollar against both the yen and the Deutschmark. Consequently, Japanese institutions are convinced that both the yen and the Deutschmark will become much more important currencies, not only for trade settlement but also as issuing currencies for borrowers tapping world capital markets. This will result in a further expansion of the power of both Japanese and German financial institutions in world capital markets over the coming decade.

CHAPTER THREE

The Ministry of Finance

In a four-storey building directly opposite the Ministry of International Trade and Industry's new office block in central Tokyo, sits the ministry of Finance (MoF), arguably the most powerful ministry in Japan, ranking alongside the US Federal Reserve and the Bank of England in its influence over international capital market developments.

MoF is central to the functioning of Japan's financial system, establishing financial policy as well as being the primary vehicle for monitoring and controlling the activities of all participants. Regular audits of all banks and securities houses, both foreign and domestic, are carried out, and MoF also exerts considerable unofficial 'guidance' to direct the activities of all participants in Japan's financial system.

It has played the key role in deregulating the financial system and its continued support is vital if this process is to be sustained. Senior MoF officials play the lead role in international negotiations in defining and pursuing the process of deregulation in Japan.

In direct terms, MoF is responsible for setting fiscal and monetary policy, collecting taxes and customs duties, organising and allocating the national budget, and overseeing foreign exchange transactions, foreign borrowings and foreign investment. It also directly manages the Trust Fund Bureau, which effectively forms a bank within MoF.

Its powers extend far beyond the statutes, however, with extensive private-level contact and consultation with all participants in the industry. Little occurs without approval, either implicit or explicit, from MoF. In addition, a large number of senior officials regularly retire from MoF in their early fifties to take up senior positions with banks and securities houses, as either directors or advisors, a practice known as 'amakudari', which consolidates the close network of controls between MoF and the bank and finance sectors. Officials joining MoF are almost exclusively from Japan's top university, the University of Tokyo.

Power rivalries between bureaux of MoF play an important role in determining the outcome of negotiations for deregulation or changes to the financial system. There are, equally, factions across party political lines, which may also have a bearing on the ministry's attitude on issues at hand.

The notorious 'three bureaux' ruling between the Securities Bureau, Banking Bureau and International Finance Bureau has entrenched the position of the securities houses in lead managing offshore financings by Japanese companies, much to the chagrin of the banks, especially the long-term credit banks. This sort of ruling is typical of the agreements reached within MoF to keep the pecking order within the financial system. As a result, the position of power of the various sectors of the financial system can hinge on the power of some divisions within MoF relative to other divisions. Equally, the power of the Taxation Bureau in limiting the tax advantages of using the offshore market was critical in creating this market's present structure and thus its comparative unattractiveness.

Given the varying strengths of each of the bureaux within MoF, it is hardly surprising that deregulation has moved fastest where it has not overtly threatened domestic interests. So, for example, the International Finance Bureau of MoF could support the opening up of the Samurai and Shogun bond markets during the 1970s since it posed no threat to the existing financial structure. On the other hand, deregulation in areas threatening the vested interests of

Japanese financial institutions has been slow. For example, because of the conflict between the long-term credit banks and the securities houses over the expansion of the domestic corporate bond market, the opening up of this market came about only after extensive discussions, with only a small amount of ground conceded each time.

One of the surprising features of Japan's financial system is that the central bank, the Bank of Japan, is in fact less powerful than MoF and by no means independent. Former MoF officials are regularly appointed to head the Bank of Japan. MoF and the Bank of Japan are sometimes at loggerheads over either financial or economic policy and capital markets development. For example, MoF has fought a long battle opposing the development of the short-term capital markets in Japan, especially for shorter-dated government securities, a development that has been strongly supported by the Bank of Japan. The Bank of Japan has gradually won in this battle, although progress has been slow.

Often criticised as a bulwark against change, MoF has shifted progressively

Budgetary indicators of the major industrial countries

	Deficit/ total expenditure		*Interest payment/ total expenditure*		*Long-term government debt outstanding/ GNP*		*Long-term government debt outstanding per capita*	
	Year	*%*	*Year*	*%*	*Year*	*%*	*Year*	*US$*
Japan ('86)	1986	20.2	1986	19.6	1986	50.0	1986	5,800
US	1987	14.4	1987	14.9	1985	36.5	1985	6,000
UK	1985	4.0	1985	7.0	1984	47.2	1984	3,600
W. Germany	1986	9.1	1986	11.5	1985	20.8	1985	2,100
France	1986	13.7	1986	9.1	1984	9.9	1984	880

Note: US: The figures in FY1987 are from Budget of the US government, FY1987.

Government income and expenditure budget, FY1986 (¥bn)

	FY1986			*From initial FY1985*	*From revised FY1985*
	Initial	*Revised*	*Budget*		
Revenue					
1. Tax revenue	38,550.0	38,145.0	40,560.0	(5.2) 2,010.0	(6.3) 2,415.0
2. Non-tax and other revenue	2,269.6	2,639.9	2,582.6	(13.8) 313.0	(−2.2) −57.3
3. Government bond issues	11,680.0	12,438.0	10,946.0	(−6.3) −734.0	(−12.0) −1,492.0
of which Deficit-financing bonds	5,730.0	6,135.0	5,246.0	(−8.4) −484.0	(−14.5) −889.0
Construction bonds	5,950.0	6,303.0	5,700.0	(−4.2) −250.0	(−9.6) −603.0
Total	52,499.6	53,222.9	54,088.6	(3.0) 1,589.0	(1.6) 865.7
Expenditures					
1. National debt service	10,224.1	10,180.5	11,319.5	(10.7) 1,095.4	(11.2) 1,139.0
2. Local allocation tax grants	9,690.1	9,690.1	10,185.0	(5.1) 494.9	(5.1) 494.9
3. General expenditures	32,585.4	33,352.3	32,584.2	(0.0) −1.2	(−2.3) −768.1
Total	52,499.6	53,222.9	54,088.6	(3.0) 1,589.0	(1.6) 865.7

Note: The figures in parentheses indicate the percentage change from the previous fiscal year.
Source: MoF.

Government financial balance (revised budget), 1972-86

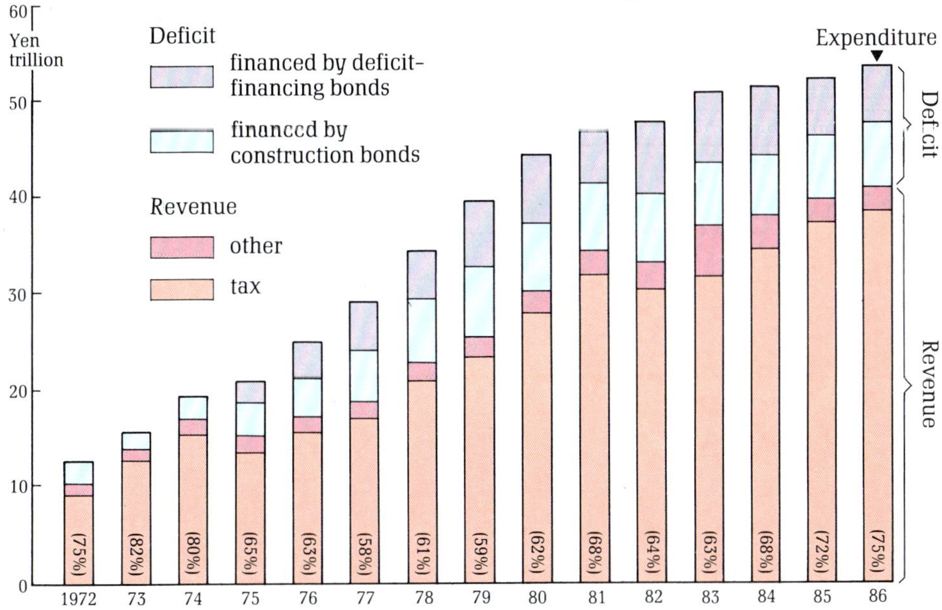

Figures in brackets show tax revenue as percentage of total revenue

over the past five years as it has become increasingly appreciative of the need to change the financial system if it is to ensure that Japanese institutions continue to be allowed to expand offshore.

The decision to speed up the approval process for foreign borrowers wishing to tap yen markets is tangible evidence of the change of heart, as are the decisions to adopt a shelf registration system and to simplify filing procedures for new bond issues.

In the regular audits of the activities of the foreign securities houses with seats on the Tokyo Stock Exchange, MoF officials adopted what some of the foreign brokers referred to as a 'godfatherly' approach to their operations as they checked operating systems and procedures, and offered advice on the need to expand the brokers' operating base in Japan. MoF maintains its control through regular and extensive discussions with all institutions operating within the financial system.

Any new product can be introduced only after approval is received from MoF. Any new entrant to the marketplace also needs to obtain approval. If the change involves something that has not been done before, the approval process can be excruciatingly slow, since MoF officials will painstakingly assess all aspects of the proposal before giving approval. When Lumbermans Mutual Casualty, part of the Kemper Group, sought approval to introduce a new variety of fire insurance policy, known as 'highly protected risks' (HPR) involving complex engineering specifications, it took eight years from the initial application until final approval to introduce the policy in 1986. Such difficulties are not unusual, attesting to the fact that MoF is slow but thorough in assessing all aspects of the proposed new policy, instrument or venture.

The degree of moral suasion MoF holds over the finance sector can work with stunning effect. In late April 1987, for example, when the yen was peaking against the US dollar, MoF put strong overt pressure on Japan's financial institutions to stop the heavy selling of US dollars – a move that had a fundamental influence in effecting the turnaround of the exchange rates at that time.

When foreign banks were proposing to introduce yen/yen swaps products, MoF and the Bank of Japan held exhaustive discussions to clarify exactly what the full implications of the proposal were before allowing these deals to be marketed to domestic financial institutions in 1986.

Often criticised for deregulating too slowly, MoF can move quickly to head off potential structural difficulties emerging in the finance and banking system. For

General account budget by major expenditure programmes, FY1984–86 (¥bn)

	1984 initial	*1985 initial*	*1986 initial*	*'83–'84 %*	*'84–'85 %*	*'85–'86 %*
National debt service	(18.1)	(19.5)	(20.9)			
	9,155.1	10,224.1	11,319.5	11.7	11.7	10.7
Local allocation tax	(17.5)	(18.5)	(18.8)			
grants	8,886.4	9,690.1	10,185.0	21.5	9.0	5.1
General expenditure	(64.4)	(62.1)	(60.2)			
	32,585.7	32,585.4	32,584.2	−0.1	0.0	0.0
Of which						
Social security	(18.4)	(18.3)	(18.2)			
	9,321.1	9,573.7	9,834.6	2.0	2.7	2.7
Education and science	(9.5)	(9.2)	(9.0)			
	4,832.3	4,840.9	4,844.5	0.7	0.2	0.1
Pensions and others	(3.7)	(3.5)	(3.4)			
	1,885.9	1,863.7	1,850.1	−0.2	−1.2	−0.7
Local finance	(0.4)	(–)	(–)			
	182.9	–	–	−51.1	–	–
National defence	(5.8)	(6.0)	(6.2)			
	2,934.6	3,137.1	3,343.5	6.6	6.9	6.6
Public works	(12.9)	(12.1)	(11.5)			
(General public works)	6,520.0	6,368.9	6,223.3	−2.0	−2.3	−2.3
	(6,313.9)	(6,207.6)	(6,135.9)	(−0.9)	(−1.7)	(−1.2)
Economic cooperation	(1.1)	(1.1)	(1.2)			
	543.9	586.3	623.3	7.9	7.8	6.3
Small business	(0.5)	(0.4)	(0.4)			
	229.2	216.2	205.2	−5.5	−5.7	−5.1
Energy measures	(1.2)	(1.2)	(1.2)			
	603.2	628.8	629.7	0.9	4.2	0.1
Foodstuff control	(1.6)	(1.3)	(1.1)			
	813.2	695.4	596.2	−11.0	−14.5	−14.3
Miscellaneous	(8.6)	(8.2)	(7.6)			
	4,369.4	4,324.4	4,083.7	−1.1	−1.0	−5.6
Reserves	(0.7)	(0.7)	(0.6)			
	350.0	350.0	350.0	0.0	0.0	0.0
Total	50,627.2	52,499.6	54,088.5	0.5	3.7	3.0

Note: The figures in brackets indicate the percentage change from the previous year.
Source: MoF.

instance, as they followed market demand for longer borrowings, the city banks began lending longer term, leading to severe mismatching of their portfolios. Even though they were restricted to borrowing funds for a maximum of two years, MoF allowed the city banks to access long-term funds through swaps involving Euroyen fund raisings. This move highlights the flexibility of the authorities in sidestepping existing lines of demarcation within the financial system if deemed necessary. Together with closely controlling the development of the financial system, the primary roles of MoF are setting economic policy and drawing up the national budgets.

Budget and taxation policy

In the budget forming process, political force weighs more heavily than economic necessity or rationale in Japan, the same as in most advanced countries.

Japan's fiscal policy of the 1970s has created a massive overhang of public debt, which MoF is trying, with limited success, to bring under control. The debt service ratio exceeded 20 per cent of the total budget in fiscal 1986, indicating the strain placed on fiscal policy. In addition, government bonds outstanding represent 42.5 per cent of GNP. So debt servicing has risen by 10 per cent annually and exceeds the annual payment for social security. By the end of fiscal 1986, total outstanding debt reached ¥143 trillion, with 60 per cent financed through construction bonds and the balance through normal deficit-covering bonds.

But the fears that the high level of government bond issues would crowd out the domestic debt markets have proved to be largely illusory, thanks to the excessive liquidity of the corporate sector and its easier access to alternative financing techniques, especially during the 1980s.

The budget process

Usually in May, soon after the start of the new fiscal year, each government ministry and agency begins estimating its revenues and expenses for the budget of the following fiscal year. In June or July, the Cabinet Council sets guidelines for the budget requests being made, which are then taken into account by the various ministries and agencies, and incorporated in their final submissions which are lodged with MoF by 31 August.

From September, the Budget Bureau holds hearings into the requests and a draft budget is compiled before the end of the calendar year. Typically, in January there is intense lobbying by each ministry and agency seeking to obtain its initial request.

The budget is submitted to the House of Representatives of the National Diet (parliament) in late January and subsequently to the House of Councillors. Once the budget has been approved, details are given to the heads of the ministries and agencies. Provisions in the national budget cover all the standard areas of government spending, from defence to public works and social welfare programmes. In addition to the national tax, there is also a local ward tax paid by residents, which covers the provision of local government services.

The government has generally run a restrictive fiscal policy since the late 1970s, after a significant increase in government spending in the wake of the two oil crises sparked fears that the growing debt would be almost impossible to bring under control.

Between 1972 and 1975, for example, general budget expenditures increased by an annual average of 22.5 per cent. A high rate of growth was maintained until 1980, when the budget increase was cut to 5.1 per cent. Since then, the belt has been progressively tightened. Prime Minister Yasuhiro Nakasone has in particular held to a highly restrictive fiscal policy, even when faced with severe external pressures to boost government spending to take pressure off the US economy's role in fuelling world economic growth.

As part of this there have been various 'administrative reform' measures, aimed at making the various bureaucracies more efficient. Ceilings have been put on budget allocations for most ministries, with regular cuts each year of a projected 10 per cent. The significant development in 1985 was the cut in national health insurance coverage by 10 per cent; this proportion of medical expenses would have to be borne by the patient. Further reductions are probable.

The national budget is usually passed by the Diet by May each year, although in recent years this schedule has varied slightly, with the opposition parties delaying approval of the budget as they try to block the successive increases in military spending. The budget for fiscal 1987 planned for a 0.02 per cent rise in spending – the lowest in 32 years – to ¥54.1 trillion, with defence spending rising 5.2 per cent and public works spending declining 2.3 per cent. In 1987, as in 1986, the government introduced a supplementary budget following strong US pressure on Japan to reflate its domestic economy. Subsequently, a ¥5 trillion package was introduced, but it is likely to boost GDP by only an estimated 0.5 per cent. A similar ¥3 trillion package was introduced in 1986, which also had only a minor impact on increasing GDP growth.

The most notable feature of the national budgets during the 1980s is that, following the spending spree of the 1970s, servicing the national debt has exceeded 20 per cent of total budget outlays. In the budget for fiscal 1987, it was anticipated that the debt servicing ratio would slip back below the 20 per cent level, to 19.4 per cent of GDP, for the first time since the budget began to grow in the later 1970s.

The government under Mr Nakasone, and especially MoF, is determined to hold down the general budget in order to remove the need to issue 'deficit-covering bonds'. The initial plan was for these bonds to be redeemed by fiscal 1990, but the pressure on the government to maintain spending levels is likely to result in an extension into the early 1990s.

From 1948, no government bonds were issued in line with the Public Finance Law. This formed a key part of the Dodge Plan, which was imposed on Japan in the aftermath of high post-war inflation. The basic aim was to balance budgets without subsidies. The impact went beyond this, however. Without the need to finance a budget deficit through household savings, these savings could be directed towards financing the reconstruction of industry. In the light of the ill-formed nature of international capital markets at that time, this step was fundamental in achieving basic financial efficiencies in Japan.

The concept of balanced budgets was adhered to until 1965, when a national bond issue was made to make up for declining tax revenues. After that, issues of construction bonds began and, in the mid-1970s, so-called 'deficit-covering bonds'. Once the government discovered how easy it was to issue bonds to finance new programmes, it quickly became addicted.

As part of the broad government policy of rolling back the budget deficit, the government made its first attack on agricultural subsidies with the decision in fiscal 1987 to cut the ceiling on the domestic rice price, reducing the amount paid to rice farmers by 5.95 per cent – the first cut in 31 years, setting the scene for further reductions in the future.

The Fiscal Investment and Loan Programme

The real point of interest in the budget-setting process is not the national budget, which will remain under pressure for some time to come, but the so-called 'second budget', administered directly by MoF through the Fiscal Investment and Loan Programme (FILP).

Despite the steady pressure on the national budget and the large cuts in construction spending, MoF has maintained a significant rise in FILP – a 22.2 per cent increase was budgeted for in fiscal 1987, following a 6 per cent rise in fiscal 1986. The rate of increase budgeted for in fiscal 1987 is the highest since 1978. In terms of total outlays in fiscal 1987, FILP was budgeted to reach ¥27.08 trillion – half the size of the national budget.

FILP, which is administered by the Trust Fund Bureau within MoF, effectively operates as a bank within the ministry. The Post Office savings system, the largest pool of small deposits in any advanced country, is compelled by law to deposit all funds raised through its nationwide network with MoF for investment. This system was first adopted in 1875, was reformulated during the occupation and was the subject of new legislation in 1953.

In recent years, postal savings have accounted for 60 per cent of all funds lodged with the Trust Fund Bureau of MoF. Funds invested in postal life insurance policies and annuities accounted for an additional 1.6 per cent. Other funds are generated through a borrowing programme and funds from the national pension plan. Of the funds deposited with the Trust Fund Bureau of MoF, 29.6 per cent are invested in government bonds and other low-risk securities, with the balance lent to specified corporations and provided as loans to general and special accounts.

The bulk of the funds utilised through FILP are used to finance a variety of government activities. In addition, FILP finances the activities of a range of other institutions, such as the Export-Import Bank of Japan, the Japan Development Bank, the People's Finance Corporation, the Housing Loan Corporation and a number of others of lesser importance.

Private sector banks and savings institutions have complained long and loud about the competitive advantage that the Post Office savings system enjoys, and the opposition of the Ministry of Posts and Telecommunications (which controls the Post Office savings network) to change is the largest remaining stumbling block to the reform of Japan's interest rate structure. For political and financial reasons, it is not necessarily in the interest of the government or the Ministry of Posts and Telecommunications to contemplate any change in the present structure. The Post Office savings system has emerged during the mid-1980s as the pre-eminent savings institution in Japan, accounting for 30 per cent of total savings.

Tax reform

From relying on land taxes for more than 80 per cent of its revenues in the 1880s, Japan's tax system has progressively changed. Property taxes now make up a minor proportion of tax revenues, with the bulk raised through direct taxes. One result of this is that a far larger share of the tax burden rests on the shoulders of the salaried employees.

In the 1930s, individual income tax and corporation taxes each amounted to 10 per cent of national tax revenues. By fiscal 1986, this weighting had changed, so that individual income tax accounted for 40.5 per cent and corporate taxes for 30.6 per cent. The weighting of indirect taxes, which made up 65.2 per cent of tax revenues during the 1930s, had been cut to only 26.2 per cent.

Direct income tax forms the base of Japan's taxation revenues, but when compared with other advanced countries, the overall tax burden is comparatively light. The ratio of the taxation burden – both national and local tax – to national income in Japan stood at 23.1 per cent in 1983. At the same time, it was 26.6 per cent in the US, 41.9 per cent in the UK, 31.0 per cent in West Germany and 33.5 per cent in France. By 1985, the tax burden in Japan had risen to 25.1 per cent. There is a common phrase that is used when discussing the tax burden of the salaried employees: 'ku-ro-yon'. That is, 90 per cent of a salaried

Summary of medium-term fiscal projection, 1986-89

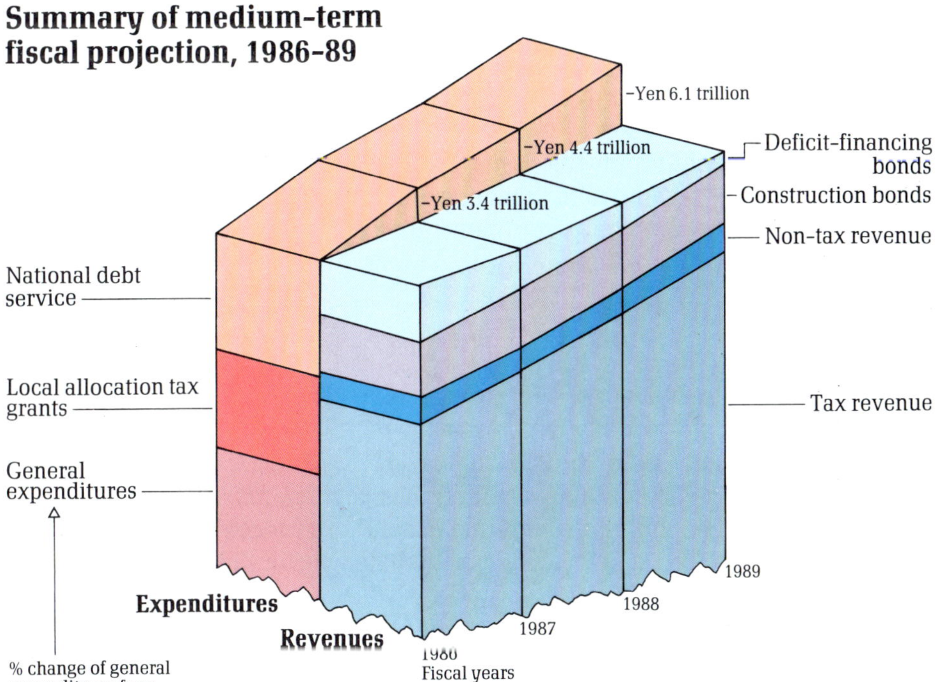

% change of general expenditures from previous fiscal years:
FY 1987 : 3.8%
FY 1988 : 4.2%
FY 1989 : 6.8%

Notes:
Medium-term fiscal projection is based on the estimates of obligations in ensuing fiscal years which are projections of programmes and activities in the fiscal year 1986 budget under specific assumptions.

Assumptions: Tax revenue: nominal GNP growth 6.5% × elasticity ratio 1:1. Deficit-financing bonds: ¥1,310 billion of issues are to be reduced in each year after 1986.

employee's income is taxable, 60 per cent of that of professionals and those independently employed, and only 40 per cent of farmers' income.

For an average family of four, an annual income of less than ¥2.35 million is free from national taxation. For the corporate sector, the tax rate is 33.3 per cent on distributed profits and 43.3 per cent on undistributed profits. There are variations for corporations with a capital of less than ¥100 million. Closely held family corporations are usually subject to an additional tax on retained earnings, in order to maintain the tax equity between incorporated and unincorporated ventures.

Direct taxes – both national and local – account for almost 75 per cent of all tax revenues. For national taxation, revenues from direct taxes have risen, accounting for 55 per cent of national tax revenues in 1950, 66 per cent in 1970 and 71 per cent in 1980.

Substantial change was proposed in 1979, when the government, at the urging of MoF, opted to introduce a broadly-based Value Added Tax. Faced with strong public opposition, and the prospect of defeat in the general elections in 1979, the government was forced to back down. After that defeat, the government introduced sizeable tax increases during 1981 to try and bring the deficit under control. Later, the government was forced to abandon the proposed introduction of the 'green card' system. Under the 'maruyu' savings system individuals are allowed tax free savings deposits of up to ¥3 million, and the usual practice is to have several accounts with different savings institutions, which easily avoids the taxation liability. The government proposed to issue a green card, with a code number, to all bank and postal savings depositors, and to introduce a nationwide computerised system to prevent the holding of multiple savings accounts. The proposal failed due to stiff public opposition.

In an attempt to control the growing dependence on direct taxation, in 1986 the government, again pressed by MoF after a study by the Tax Commission, unveiled a new tax scheme, aimed at boosting sales taxes and abolishing the maruyu savings system in return for sizeable direct tax cuts.

The government mishandled the tax reform proposal politically, and it resulted in strong opposition, especially from the powerful small business lobby which stood to lose out heavily with the introduction of a broadly-based sales tax. The government argued that the proposed changes were revenue neutral but failed to muster popular support for the proposal and was forced, again, to back down. Even so, the government is still seeking to introduce cuts in direct taxation, along with scrapping the maruyu system, as the first step towards introducing a broad sales tax.

The loss of momentum on this issue means that it could now take several years before there is any meaningful change in the present taxation system. This limits the policy options of the government, and of MoF in particular, in trying to correct the large budget deficit.

Privatisation

One policy being pursued which will restore some fiscal balance is privatisation of a number of state-owned corporations which will give the government greater fiscal flexibility in the future.

In privatisation the Japanese government has perhaps more experience than most, since it engaged in a massive round of sales of government enterprises in the latter part of the 19th century, which paved the way for the emergence of the large zaibatsu earlier this century.

This time, the government is moving more cautiously, although with the same overall intent. In the 1880s, the aim was to rid the national account of loss-making concerns that could be operated profitably through private ownership. This time, the need is more urgent. The rapid ageing of Japan's population will begin putting severe strain on the national budget during the second half of the 1990s.

Although MoF was confident that it would be able to reduce spending sufficiently to cease making new issues of construction bonds by 1990, this is looking increasingly remote. Consequently, with a continued high level of government spending, few options to boost tax revenues and the burden of an ageing society, one of the few options for raising cash is to privatise existing assets.

The most notable move so far is the privatisation of the national telecommunications monopoly, Nippon Telegraph and Telephone (NTT). With a turnover of ¥5.35 trillion and post-tax earnings of ¥358 billion, it ranks as the second largest telecommunications group worldwide after AT&T of the US.

The government has also taken preliminary steps to privatise the Japan National Tobacco Corporation and the deficit-ridden Japan National Railways. The national railways lose an estimated ¥6.3 billion a day. In addition, the government intends to sell its remaining one-third shareholding in Japan Airlines, the national air carrier.

A range of other public corporations could also be privatised, although the government has yet to clarify fully its intentions. These corporations include the Japan Highways Corporation, the Japan Railways Construction Corporation, the Japan Export-Import Bank, the Japan Development Bank, the Electric Power Development Corporation and the Japan Nuclear Fuel Research Corporation.

For the time being, the government is moving cautiously, waiting for the complete privatisation of NTT, and especially the disposal of Japan National Railways, which will bring with it some regional dislocation and potential opposition.

Nippon Telegraph and Telephone

NTT was privatised in April 1985, although the first tranche of stock was not sold until the next year. A limited tender for 200,000 shares was held in November 1986, with an average price bid of around ¥1.2 million per share. Based on the tender prices, MoF decided to offer an additional 1.75 million shares in January 1987 at ¥1.19 million per share, which was well received. The total raised through sales of NTT scrip in 1987 was ¥2.37 trillion. Even though there were considerable doubts about how well the scrip would be received when it hit the market, it was strongly bid, and the NTT share price regularly reached its one-day stop limits in the first week of trading. NTT's share price was quickly pushed above the ¥2.5 million level, reaching a peak price of ¥3.18 million. The lowest sale price was ¥1.6 million. To bolster initial trading liquidity in the stock,

Government-owned corporations that could be privatised

	Capital (¥m)
Agricultural and Fisheries Finance Corp	16,823
Small Business Insurance Corp	39,488
Housing Loan Corp	9,720
Japan Export-Import Bank	96,730
Japan Development Bank	23,397
Central Commerce Credit Association	19,560
Forestry Development Corp	20,070
Japan Railways Construction Corp	48,090
New International Airport Corp (Narita)	11,005
Japan Highways Corp	52,704
Metropolitan Highway Corp	15,649
Kobe Highway Corp	10,650
Honshu Shikoku Bridge Corp	36,103
Japan Tobacco Corp	10,000
Nippon Telegraph and Telephone	78,000
Japan Railways Group	46,400
Japan Nuclear Research	69,279

Source: MoF.

MoF sold a small amount of additional equity into the market. An additional tranche of 1.95 million shares is to be sold in late 1987 to an underwriting syndicate at a slight discount to the market price. The aim of MoF is to sell 70 per cent of NTT's shares held by the government over a four-year period. At present, the company has 15.6 million shares on issue, mainly held by the government.
MoF sold a small amount of additional equity into the market. An additional tranche of 1.95 million shares is to be sold in late 1987 to an underwriting syndicate at a slight discount to the market price. The aim of MoF is to sell 70 per cent of NTT's shares held by the government over a four-year period. At present, the company has 15.6 million shares on issue, mainly held by the government.

Initially, foreign investors were barred from investing in NTT scrip, although this ban may be lifted eventually. In mid-1987, the Ministry of Posts and Telecommunications removed a ban preventing foreign trust banks from holding NTT scrip on behalf of clients. Similarly, foreign stockbroking houses were expected to be able to participate in the underwriting syndicate for the second offering of NTT scrip provided that they eventually sold it on to Japanese investors.

When completed, the sale of NTT scrip is expected to gross over ¥10 trillion and, while MoF is seeking to utilise the proceeds to whittle down the accumulated debt, some of the funds raised will be used to finance new government spending.

Japan National Railways

The Japanese have long complained about the 'three Ks': kome (rice), kokumin kenko hoken (health insurance) and kokuden (national railways). During Prime Minister Yasuhiro Nakasone's administration, the first steps in more than 30 years have been taken to lower the rice subsidy and to cut the health insurance deficit. Stemming the national railways' drain on the national budget, however will not only prove difficult, but will also take considerable time.

Privatisation of Japan National Railways, renamed JR, began in April 1987. The government divided the company into six regional carriers prior to offering it for sale. Progress may be slow, however, since there are a number of significant issues that remain to be clarified, in particular, whether the new companies will be forced to assume additional responsibility for JR's accumulated debts, since it is unlikely that the funds raised through the sale of JR will be sufficient to meet its outstanding liabilities. JR has an estimated ¥41.5 billion of capital investment, 58,500 hectares of land and ¥25 trillion of accumulated debt. It is provisionally planned that ¥10.4 trillion of the debt will be transferred to the new companies. Resolution of the JR privatisation would free the government's hand to turn to other corporations, of which there is no shortage although, unlike in some European countries, most of the electricity and gas utilities are privately held. Beyond JR, there has been no positive statement of which government corporations are likely to be put up for sale.

The private Research Institute on the National Economy has estimated that ¥171 trillion could be raised through the privatisation of public corporations and enterprises – an amount equal to Japan's outstanding national debt. This figure was arrived at by assuming a multiple of 20 times the capital of government corporations if they were taken public. Many of these public corporations would, however, be unsuitable candidates for public flotation because of their poor financial position, or because the services they perform could not be undertaken by the private sector.

The Research Institute on the National Economy argues that, if an aggressive programme of privatisation is carried out, this would enable the level of outstanding debt to be wound back significantly by the turn of the century – from an estimated ¥160.68 trillion in 1990 to ¥87.34 trillion by the year 2000.

The Institute also maintains that an extensive privatisation programme would reduce the need to continue issuing construction bonds in the late 1990s, aiding the improvement in the budget.

Opposite: Will MoF's deregulation attract foreign investors to the bright lights of Tokyo?

あさ五時まで
心の居酒屋
北の家族
4F
居酒屋
玄海灘
3F
炭火ろ
心の居酒屋
B1.2
大小宴会
北の家族
7F
ろばた焼
大漁船
6F
焼肉バイキング
COFFEE
LOUNGE
ボン
くまくら
B1
石塚ビル

大蔵省
一時停止

CHAPTER FOUR

The Bank of Japan

Established in 1882, the Bank of Japan is the country's central bank. As such, it is the sole note issuer, with the task of controlling the currency and supporting the credit system. Not only does it act as the bank of issue, but also as the bankers' bank and the government bank.

Its primary role is to achieve the stability of the value of money, and in accordance with this basic policy, it regulates money and credit, and supervises the operation of the financial system. Unlike its equivalent in most countries, it is not independent, as it is directly controlled by the government and forced to act, in many instances, as an extension of government policy. This occasionally leads to friction with the Ministry of Finance (MoF), in particular over the setting of monetary policy and the development of capital markets.

With MoF at the centre of deregulatory moves, the Bank of Japan has been responsible for handling much of the extraordinary changes to Japan's external financial position since September 1985, when the decision was taken to push for a devaluation of the US dollar.

Charged with implementing government policy, the Bank of Japan played the pivotal role in forcing the revaluation of the yen in currency markets both in Japan and, on occasion, by intervening in other currency markets in tandem with other central financial authorities. In addition to this, it lowered domestic interest rates to encourage capital outflows. Usually limited to either 'window guidance' or direct intervention in domestic money markets, events since late 1985 cast the central bank in an unusually prominent role. Not only was it successful in increasing the value of the yen against the US dollar, but it then had to cope with the rising domestic pressures stemming from the deflationary impact of the currency shift on the domestic economy.

History

When it was established in 1882, the Bank of Japan was modelled on the Banque Nationale de Belgique. In line with this, half of its equity was held privately, and half by the government, to give it nominal independence. Lending was mainly through discounting commercial bills and its main source of funds was the issuance of bank notes.

Even with its nominal independence, the first Governor and Vice-Governor were former MoF officials, establishing a precedent that later became entrenched.

In its first 50 years, the Bank of Japan operated as the central bank domestically, with the Yokohama Specie Bank (now Bank of Tokyo) effectively acting as its external arm in overseas transactions. In 1942, with the expiry of its founding charter, the Bank of Japan's operations were remodelled along the same lines as the Reichsbank in Germany. With this change, the Bank of Japan was to assume the task of controlling currency and finance and promote the credit system. Its sole guiding principle was the accomplishment of national aims. It was authorised to make unlimited advances to the government without security, and to subscribe for and absorb government bonds. At the same time, government control over the bank was tightened, with the government able to nominate, superintend and give orders to the president and the directors.

In addition, many activities of the bank, such as the setting of bank rates, note issues and accounts were subject to government approval. An amendment to

The Bank of Japan's traditional building (opposite above) and the entrance to MoF (below), the two pinnacles of power in Japan's financial system.

the Bank of Japan Law was enacted in 1949, which established a policy board separate from the board of directors to formulate monetary policy. The board consists of seven members – the Governor of the Bank of Japan and one representative each of MoF, the Economic Planning Agency, the city banks, the local banks, commerce and industry, and agriculture.

The board makes most of the key decisions about the bank's policy and activities. It is responsible for setting the official discount rate, regulating market operations and reserve ratios of payments reserves, as well as controlling advances to security dealers by financial institutions.

Reform

The lack of independence from MoF remains a sore point. In the mid-1950s a Financial System Research Council was set up to prepare for a revision of the Bank of Japan Law. But agreement could not be reached over exactly how the independence of the bank should be developed.

An interim report of the standing planning committee of this council opted for independence of the bank, planting the seed which forced MoF to enter the fray to prevent any substantial change.

As unanimous recommendation was not possible, the committee offered two alternatives. If MoF considered that the policy of the bank was at variance with the policy of the government, and if agreement could not be reached to adjust policies after consultation with the government, then the Finance Minister could either issue a straightforward directive to the central bank, or demand that the decision of the Policy Board be delayed for a set period of re-evaluation. Although it had two policy options, the government failed to make a decision.

Progress on this issue remained slow, and in the mid-1960s MoF released its own draft of a revision of the Bank of Japan Law, which kept the central bank firmly under MoF's control. Subsequently, the Radcliffe Report into the working of the British monetary system was released, which supported the argument that the central bank should be subordinate to the government of the day. This report was used to some effect by MoF in its lobbying.

The lack of independence of the Bank of Japan is evidenced by the fact that appointments to the position of Governor of the bank rotates between officials of the Bank of Japan and MoF. The present incumbent, Satoshi Sumita, is a former senior official of MoF. The previous Governor, Haruo Maekawa, was a Bank of Japan official.

However, being tied to government policy has not prevented the Bank of Japan from pursuing a markedly different strategy to that of MoF. Specifically, the bank has long supported the market setting of interest rates, including the substantial expansion of the short-term money markets to achieve this, together with expanding the market for short-term government paper. Both moves have been strongly opposed by MoF, since it has held to the tenet that any such liberalisation would lead to a higher cost of financing the government debt.

Organisation

The highest policy-making body of the Bank of Japan is the Policy Board. This board directs the overall activities of the bank in regulating money and credit. It is this body which makes the specific decision on expansion or contraction of lending limits, the decisions about market intervention in both money market and foreign exchange market and the decisions on reserve deposit requirements.

With the Governor and Deputy-Governor appointed by the government, and MoF nominating directors put forward by the Governor, as well as appointing the auditor of the bank, the real power over the Bank of Japan's activities lie outside the Policy Board. If there are disputes between the two organisations which cannot be resolved, then there are specific provisions which enable MoF to resolve the issue in question.

The Minister of Finance, for example, holds the power to issue general directives and may also give supervisory orders to the bank. The Minister also appoints the Comptroller of the Bank of Japan, who superintends its business. The Minister also can dismiss the officers of the bank.

In addition to these broad powers, the Finance Minister can determine, permit and approve the various individual matters of the bank's business. As a result, all activities of the central bank are directly under the control of MoF.

And, at the end of the day, MoF is the dominant shareholder in the Bank of Japan, which is traded through the over-the-counter market in Japan.

Functions

The Bank of Japan is the bank of issue and is responsible for controlling the currency. It also performs the key role of the bankers' bank. At the heart of these operations are its activities in lending to the commercial banks, which typically takes the form of discounting bills held by the commercial banks and making advances against those bills. It also holds current deposits for the main financial institutions, which are mainly used for clearing accounts and the usual financial settlements.

The Bank of Japan also has a specific role in financing the government debt, as it acts as the agent of MoF in issues of national bonds. And, along with its role in the buying and selling of gold, it plays a role when thought necessary in intervening directly in currency markets, a notable feature of its activities since the second half of 1985.

But these various functions are subordinate to the pivotal role of the bank, which is to regulate the monetary system, for which it has an array of policy options.

Through its lending policy, it can move the ceilings it imposes on the main lending institutions, acting to limit or expand credit depending on the underlying monetary situtation.

Such credit controls used to be exercised monthly, but since the latter part of the 1960s, they have been set quarterly. Nonetheless, there is significant scope for short-term variations, if the bank deems it appropriate in the light of underlying market conditions. More important, however, is the bank's direct control over interest rates in the official short-term money market, where it can readily influence market conditions through its close links with the limited number of short-term brokers, or 'tanshi'.

Similarly, it can move to reduce or expand the volume of credit in the official market, and also the unofficial market, through issues of short-term government debt. It can also decide to alter the reserve requirements which are set for all the banks. All financial institutions must lodge a proportion of their deposits with the central bank for safe-keeping. The reserve controls are changed from time to time, although in the post-war period rather infrequently. This partly reflects the fact that for much of this period most of Japan's financial institutions were cash-hungry, but also the fact that with the bank's range of other official and unofficial controls, repeated changes to the reserve controls are not considered necessary.

Supervision

The main interaction between the Bank of Japan and the various financial institutions is through direct supervision of their activities. The bank meets and consults regularly with representatives of the banking system, and requires regular reports of lending and investment activities that have been undertaken.

The close scrutiny of the financing activities of the banks is aimed at ensuring that excesses are held in check before they get out of hand, although this is not always reliable, since cases such as the near collapse of Heiwa Sogo Bank in 1986 do occur from time to time. With the increasing complexity of financial markets, the Bank of Japan has stepped up its monitoring activities, and, more recently, has begun to assess off-balance sheet liabilities as well.

Japan's banks have a notably lower exposure to the third world debt crisis than their international competitors, largely because their main international lending has been in the Asian region where debt risk has been lower. Even so, all the big city banks have some exposure. The largest is the Bank of Tokyo, followed by Sumitomo Bank.

The Bank of Japan has been the main conduit for negotiations with the US Federal Reserve and the Bank of England over the poor capital adequacy ratios of Japanese banks when compared with their international competitors.

It has held long and hard to the argument that a substantial portion (70 per cent) of the hidden value of shares held by each of the banks should be included in the calculation of capital adequacy ratios. If included, the capital ratios of Japanese banks would be about 10 per cent; if excluded, the average is around only 3 per cent. (See Chapter 5 for further discussion.)

The Bank of Japan and MoF

Relations between the Bank of Japan and MoF, responsible for different areas of economic policy, have been mixed. MoF has control of fiscal and monetary policy; the Bank of Japan controls monetary policy and foreign exchange rates.

Conflict between the two institutions over economic policy options is inevitable, and has been seen regularly over the past decade. In addition, difficulties have arisen over the development of the domestic capital markets.

The first significant disputes were over the independence of the Bank of Japan. More recently, the two institutions were at odds over proposals to allow Japan's banks to issue commercial bills as an extra means of raising funds, in the light of the difficulties the banks face with increased competition for deposits, and to give them more flexibility. Additionally, there has been tension over the development of a market for short-term government paper.

Economic policy formulation and interest rate policy

It is in the formulation of interest rates that the complexities of the present organisation of the regulators of Japan's financial system come into full play.

Under the Temporary Money Rates Adjustment Law ceilings are in place covering most main interest rates. When setting interest rates, MoF may take the initiative in proposing appropriate ceilings to the Policy Board of the Bank of Japan which, after consulting with the Money Rates Adjustment Council, fixes maximum rates. Once the basic rate, or prime rate, is agreed, most other main interest rates are set in relation to the prime rate according to a strict structure. The actual implementation of a discount rate change is made by the Bank of Japan.

Similarly, the bank has other means of influencing interest rate developments through, for example, its 'window guidance' covering the activities of the money market brokers. With such moves it can influence short-term interest rate trends.

In addition, it can offer for sale short-term bills, as a means of reducing excess liquidity, or sell bills to the market if monetary conditions are becoming tight.

Equally, MoF can, and does, intervene in the bond market to influence market movements. In July 1987, for example, when the market was signalling a rise in long-term interest rates, MoF intervened to inject liquidity through the Bond Liquidation Fund. Such a move is, however, unusual. The last occasion on which MoF intervened in this fashion was in July 1984.

The two institutions work closely together in determining new issues of government bonds, with the Bank of Japan acting as the agency bank to MoF for such issues. The broad details such as the timing and size of issues and decided by MoF in consultation with the Bank of Japan, although it is the Bank of Japan, through the underwriting syndicate, that determines the actual pricing of the bonds to be offererd. Even though the system, in operational terms, works smoothly enough, there are significant policy differences between the two institutions.

The Bank of Japan has, for some time, sought to expand the market for shorter-term government paper, a development that has been strongly opposed by MoF.

Negotiations over this have taken place for several years with little progress, although the Bank of Japan now appears to have the upper hand since there has been a steady expansion of the volume of short-term paper issued by the government, which has helped to give the short-term money markets additional depth.

The other issue where the two institutions were at odds with each other is the issuance by the banks of certificates of deposit (CDs) as a means of expanding their deposit base, and overcoming some of the pressures stemming from the gradual loss, especially by the city banks, of their share of the savings base.

The issue was first raised prior to 1970 through the Committee on Financial System Research. With only limited support within the banking system, and some opposition from regional banks and the securities houses, no move was ultimately made. It was decided, in 1972, to allow banks to issue CDs offshore, so that the city banks in particular could finance their international expansion more cheaply, putting them on an equal footing with their international competitors. The argument in support of issuing CDs revolved around accessing the rising cash surplus of the corporate sector, together with aiding the move towards deregulating interest rates.

The issue was raised for discussion again in the second half of the 1970s, although the banking sector was itself split, since the long-term credit banks were opposed to any such move, arguing that it would adversely affect their issues of debentures which form the basis of their fund-raising efforts.

Gradually, MoF changed tack and began to support the introduction of CDs with deregulated interest rates, and final approval was given in 1979 for the start-up of the proposed market.

The Bank of Japan supported the introduction of CDs since it argued that a more developed short-term money market would aid the effectiveness of monetary policy by intervention in monetary markets. For the city banks, the introduction of CDs was important since it enabled them to offset the pressures on their operations caused by the continuing decline in their proportion of deposits.

The issue of the development of a short-term market for government paper again highlights the opposing attitudes of the Bank of Japan and MoF. In a bid to facilitate the absorption of the large amount of government debt, the bank strongly supported the development of a market for short-term government paper. Also, a proper development of the short-term capital markets would increase the central bank's influence over the market.

The opposition of MoF stems directly from its fears that, if interest rates on small deposits were boosted to market levels, it would impact directly on the cost of the government's debt, at a time when any meaningful decrease in government borrowings is still far from certain.

To all intents and purposes, the Bank of Japan has won in this dispute. The expansion of short-term government paper has been limited, but progress has been made.

The bank as trader

It is the central bank's role in setting interest rates and in monitoring currency developments that has put it into the spotlight since 1985. The Plaza Hotel agreement in September 1985 to continue the trend of depreciating the US dollar against other major currencies has focused the attention of capital markets on the role of the Bank of Japan.

The bank was forced to monitor closely interest rate differentials between Japan and the US, in seeking to encourage capital outflows to restrain the strength of the yen, while at the same time lowering the official discount rate to revive the flagging domestic economy.

After successfully pushing the yen higher against the US dollar, the bank has had to cope with the latent inflationary pressures stemming from the successive cuts in the official discount rate, which it reduced to an all-time low of 2.5 per cent, while maintaining an easy monetary policy at a time of surplus liquidity within the financial system.

The prospect of latent inflationary pressures within the financial system caused concern in fiscal and monetary policy circles during 1986 and 1987. Tight limits on new bank lendings were introduced in order to ensure that inflationary pressures would not get out of hand.

With a period of somewhat greater currency stability in the first half of 1987, the Bank of Japan and MoF became more cautious about the lending policies of the banking sector, and held a number of closed-door hearings with representatives of the leading banks to assess accurately their lending portfolios. This was to keep them under control as well as to ensure that lending for speculative purposes, such as for property or stockmarket speculation, was kept in check.

In addition extensive controls covering the foreign investment policies of the insurance companies and the trust banks were either removed completely or substantially relaxed to promote capital outflows – a policy that achieved singular success.

The success of the Bank of Japan's push to revalue the yen against the US dollar had unfortunate side effects. For example, the newly formed government bond futures market was thrown into confusion when trading commenced in October 1985.

More important, the Bank of Japan had to contend with strong criticism from the domestic manufacturing sector, whose success depended on the cheap yen policies of earlier periods.

It was argued increasingly that the yen's strength would cause a large-scale collapse of Japan's manufacturing sector, with the 'kudoka', or hollowing out, of Japan's industrial base. Notable was the release in 1986 of a report by an advisory committee to Prime Minister Nakasone, headed by Haruo Maekawa, former Governor of the Bank of Japan. This report urged that government policies be implemented to force the shift of Japan's economy away from a heavy reliance on exports for growth, in favour of boosting domestic demand. That report, initially promoted by the government to sidetrack any foreign criticism of Japan's burgeoning trade surplus, was, however, not acted upon.

The Bank of Japan, while successful in launching the revaluation of the yen against the US dollar, was not so successful in reining in the yen when it moved above ¥150 to the dollar. Large-scale direct intervention in foreign currency markets failed to have much effect. It was not until MoF stepped in, and summoned the heads of the various banks to specifically instruct them to stop selling US dollars, that there was evidence of at least an initial turnaround in currency markets.

CHAPTER FIVE

Japan's banks

A massive deposit base, lower asset ratios, limited domestic demand for new funds and stiff domestic competition have turned Japan's banks increasingly to overseas markets, catapulting them to the fore of the world banking system. A much lower exposure to LDC debt and to problems in the energy and agricultural sectors – unlike their North American counterparts – has insulated them from many of the difficulties confronting the world banking system during the 1980s.

And with the continuing squeeze on domestic earnings, they have pushed hard into international financial centres, bidding aggressively for new fund raisings, making it increasingly difficult for many competitors. Hamstrung by the division between the securities and banking sectors at home, they have taken full advantage of liberalisation abroad to expand the range of services on offer.

Changes in world capital markets, combined with deregulation of Japan's financial system, have squeezed earnings which they have not been able to offset by moving into the domestic securities industry. Some concessions, however, such as access to full dealing in government bonds and active foreign exchange trading, have boosted profits in the short term.

Japanese banks include some of the most powerful, and some of the weakest, in the world. The big city banks have some of the most aggressive management, equal to the best in North America and Europe. Equally, there are slow-moving colossi uncertain of their future direction, following competitors' moves closely in offering new services.

A number of the smaller regional banks and mutual banks are locked into narrow deposit bases, with little chance for any significant improvement in their outlook or operating environment.

In the background, the heavy hand of the Ministry of Finance (MoF) lies firmly on the banking sector, closely monitoring and controlling its every action. There is no banking secrecy in Japan. MoF can demand, and obtain, full details of securities transactions by the securities companies, along with access to all the information it may deem relevant from the banks.

The securitisation of debt markets from the mid-1980s, combined with meagre demand by the corporate sector for new funds, has shifted the focus of attention away from the banks, at least within the domestic market.

Interest rate deregulation, combined with threats to change the taxation system by abolishing the 'maruyu' tax-free savings system, has cut, and will cut further, into the cheap funding base of the banks. Confronted with rising costs and the need to boost deposit bases, the earnings of the banks are progressively being squeezed. Most are fighting to redefine their role, although, within the highly structured banking system in Japan, their options are limited.

The city banks are emerging as universal banks, very much along the lines of the larger West German and Swiss banks. The trust banks become fund managers and the long-term credit banks wholesale banks, with the regional and mutual (sogo) banks remaining ostensibly savings associations.

Much of this natural evolution is being hampered by the controls of MoF and the Bank of Japan, together with the highly structured nature of the financial system within Japan. Quick change is unlikely, although many of the lines of segregation are becoming blurred. The major banks are, for example, allowed to trade in government bonds and have become much more open in showing the links with their affiliated securities companies. In addition the banks, together with the securities companies, have been given approval to trade in the domestic commercial paper market.

More substantial change must await any move to abolish Article 65 of the Securities Exchange Law. Abolition is inevitable, although when it will happen is open to conjecture.

Many of the difficulties confronting Japan's banking system could be overcome if mergers and acquisitions were possible, although, given the staunchly independent nature of all companies and banks within Japan, such moves are usually fraught with difficulties.

There has been a number of mergers among Japan's smaller credit associations, which are very exposed to deregulation. The last prominent merger within Japan was between the failing Heiwa Sogo Bank and Sumitomo Bank. Prior to that, there had been occasional mergers of sogo (mutual) banks to form regional banks, as well as the earlier mergers of Dai-Ichi Bank and Nippon Kangyo Bank to form Dai-Ichi Kangyo Bank, and Kobe Bank and Taiyo Bank to form Taiyo Kobe Bank.

It is in the international arena, however, that Japan's banks have made their mark during the 1980s. Cautious to move offshore in the intitial stages, their push gathered pace during the first half of the 1980s. The first wave was the bigger city banks, which have been progressively followed by the trust and long-term credit banks, the larger regional banks and, from 1985, the sogo banks.

Typically Hong Kong, New York and London form the initial axis, with a comprehensive branch network radiating out from these three centres into Asia, North America and Europe. Most of these operations are focused on wholesale banking, the main exception being the US, where there is a heavy concentration of Japan's city banks in retail and commercial banking on the west coast, reflecting its regional role as the prime entry point for most of Japan's trade with the US, and the absolute size and growth of the Californian economy.

Indicative of the changes underway in capital markets was the decision by Sumitomo Bank to acquire a stake in Goldman Sachs for US$500 million. The subsequent tight controls placed on this purchase by the US regulatory authorities have reduced the immediate impact of the purchase for Sumitomo Bank, although in the longer run, relations between the two institutions are expected to broaden.

The cheap deposit base of Japan's banks, together with lower capital adequacy ratios and their aggressive pricing policy, has underwritten much of their success in new fund raisings in capital markets, causing rising criticism from their international competitors and increasing pressure from both the Bank of England and the US Federal Reserve Board for a tightening of capital controls.

The increasing competitive pressure from Japanese banks in the international arena has taken place against further change in their operating position within Japan. Trading income from government bonds and foreign exchange dealings is now a significant source of earnings, offsetting the profit squeeze caused by the deregulation of interest rates.

New areas have been progressively targeted for expansion during the 1980s. The growth of lease financing, consumer credit, mortgage securities trading, housing finance and the like have all attracted increasing attention from the larger banks. Some areas can be entered directly, others indirectly. The rapid penetration of credit card services in Japan has resulted in all the big banks offering a range of such services to clients; they also offer mortgage securities trading and debt factoring. In other areas, the banks are allowed to enter only through affiliates of which, even though they are clearly controlled by the bigger banks, the banks' direct level of ownership is limited, usually to a maximum of 5 per cent. Included here are securities trading, lease financing, venture capital, investment advisory services and information networks.

In this regard, there has been significant change since the mid-1970s. The much greater freedom of US banks in moving into many of these areas in the US has been studied closely by most of the big Japanese banks; they monitor the shift of assets and changing mix of business of the US banks as they take advantage of shifting demand for banking services. In many of these new areas of growth within Japan's financial sector the banks (either directly or through their affiliates) are engaged in head-to-head competition with either specialist firms in each field, for example, in consumer financing or leasing, or with affiliates of the securities houses. A particular battleground is mortgage securities trading, where the traditional dominance of the banks has been successfully challenged by Nomura Securities. Equally, venture capital is dominated by the Nomura affiliate, Jafco, although its leadership in this industry is coming under challenge from a range of affiliates of the big banks.

The same pattern applies to leasing where, even though the banks can only participate through affiliates, they have aggressively pushed for new business to make up for shortfalls in traditional lending.

Interest rate deregulation

One of the most significant changes that has occurred in the banking system has stemmed from the liberalisation of interest rate controls over large deposits, which has occurred gradually since 1985. The limited interest rate deregulation

Satoshi Sumita, Governor of the Bank of Japan, speaking to the influential Foreign Correspondents Club.

that has already occurred has brought about a significant rise in the level of liberalised interest rate products such as CDs, money market certificates (MMCs) and so-called 'large deposits', which by mid-1987 accounted for 30 per cent of deposits of the city banks, with smaller shares for the regional and mutual banks.

The progressive introduction of the broader range of products directly linked to market rates has given the city banks in particular much greater operating flexibility, although by the same token there has been a significant cut in their operating margins. And the introduction of these products has resulted in the bigger banks adopting spread lending techniques – common in most major banking centres but, given the controls on domestic interest rates, new to Japan.

The big change occurred in late 1985, when MMCs were introduced. Initially, they had a fixed interest rate ceiling at a discount of 0.75 per cent to the ruling CD rate. In March 1987, that was reduced to a 0.5 per cent discount. There has also been a steady reduction in the minimum unit size of MMCs from the initial ¥50 million to ¥20 million, and the maturity has been extended from the initial period of one to six months first to one year, and in 1987 to two years.

Over the same period, the maximum size of large-scale deposits has been cut from ¥1 billion in 1985 to ¥100 million. The maturity varies between three months and two years.

The progressive liberalisation has meant that all banks have steadily increased the size of funds raised through both MMCs and large-scale deposits. By the end of June 1987, large-scale deposits held by the city banks had expanded to ¥17 trillion, with the regional banks holding ¥7.3 trillion, the sogo banks ¥3.61 trillion, the trust banks ¥1.8 trillion and the long-term credit banks ¥539.9 billion – a total of ¥30 trillion. At the same time, MMCs stood at ¥10.6 trillion. For the larger city banks, around 30 per cent of all deposits are now raised through deposits with liberalised interest rates.

To offset the squeeze on earnings stemming from interest rate liberalisation, most of the major banks have pushed aggressively to expand their bond dealing capabilities, and are also keen to obtain official approval to trade bonds on behalf of clients, which they are now specificially prohibited from doing.

There has also been a sizeable increase in the volume of consumer lending provided by the city banks in particular, which carries with it higher margins. In fiscal 1986 (to 31 March 1987), city banks expanded their housing lending by 31 per cent to ¥11.89 trillion and consumer lending up by a large 53 per cent to ¥1.07 trillion. Included in their consumer lending activities is financing through their credit card services, which accounts for almost half of total consumer lending. The largest provider of finance through its credit card services is Dai-Ichi Kangyo Bank, which enjoys the biggest savings network, although Sumitomo Bank has the clear lead for overall consumer finance, due to its purchase of Heiwa Sogo Bank.

By 1987, however, interest rate deregulation had largely ceased. A longstanding political dispute between the Ministry of Posts and Telecommunications (MPT), which operates the Post Office savings system, and the banks resulted in the liberalisation programme for small-scale deposits becoming much less clear than originally expected.

The Post Office savings system – the largest such savings system in the world – competes with other savings institutions in Japan which must comply with reserve requirements, carry deposit insurance and earn a profit on operations. Also, the nationwide network of the Post Office savings system gives it a strong advantage over its rivals. MPT is jealous of its role and has consistently fought against an independent policy in the financial services sector, as well as in the communications sector generally. Its persistent refusal to allow more than one international competitor to Japan's international telecommunications monopoly, Kokusai Denshin Denwa (KDD), resulted in an at times bitter international dispute during 1987, with foreign governments pressing Japan to abide by its own legislative moves to free international competition in this vital telecommunications area. The intransigence of MPT has slowed the pace of financial deregulation. As a result of the moves undertaken to date, most of the impact of deregulation has been felt by the commercial banks, as their larger clients have taken maximum advantage of freer interest rates to shift surplus funds from the banking sector to a variety of money market instruments, in a bid to boost rates of return.

Confronted with the slide of margins in this area, the banks have been looking much more closely at generating greater fee income from their consumer banking divisions to overcome higher operating costs. Clearance difficulties, combined with a natural aversion to cheques and preference for cash, have resulted in a much more advanced development of automatic payment systems. Most simple utility payments, as well as simple bank transfers, which in most countries would be completed by using cheques, are conducted by direct bank transfers in Japan, many of which, particularly for utility payments, can be completed automatically. Gradually, bank charges for these services have increased, with charges even for a funds transfer to another account in the same branch of the bank. All the banks have targeted increased fee income from consumer banking services as a means of offsetting higher operating costs. Such moves have met with little consumer resistance.

International expansion

Hemmed in by limited growth potential and tight controls in the domestic market, Japan's banks have made their mark over the past decade in the international market, in both commercial banking and underwriting. Since they have been involved offshore for a longer period, the city banks have both the largest international earnings and the largest network of branches and offices. All have networks of operations centred on Hong Kong for Asia, London for Europe and New York for the US.

The US, as the largest economy in the West, is where most of their overseas commercial banking is concentrated. The west coast is a logical regional centre for many of the bigger city banks, such as Mitsubishi Bank and Dai-Ichi Kangyo Bank, since Los Angeles and, in particular, San Francisco are the main points of entry for Japanese exports to the US.

In addition, the south-west of the US has enjoyed significantly higher growth during the 1980s than the rust belt of the north-east, notwithstanding the adverse effect of the slump in oil prices. There is also the added advantage that holding a bank licence in California gives banks the opening to advance into 11 neighbouring states from 1991.

The international commercial banking activities of Japanese banks initially revolved around the needs of their Japanese corporate clients as they moved offshore and have gradually expanded from this base.

Japan's official foreign exchange bank, the Bank of Tokyo, has the most extensive international branch structure of any Japanese bank, since its specific purpose was to serve the national need by expanding abroad to aid the growth of Japan's trade. The city banks have developed an increasingly international network of branches, resulting in a decline in the relative importance of the Bank of Tokyo, with much of its former activities taken over by rival Japanese banks. Typically, retail banking is only undertaken overseas where it forms a natural adjunct to existing operations, such as on the west coast of the US, or where it is a condition of obtaining a banking licence. Even though retail banking may have its advantages once operations in a foreign country achieve a certain size, until that point is reached Japanese banks avoid developing any comprehensive deposit base, since it would add substantially to their cost structure.

Both New York and London are of critical importance, due to their role as centres of world capital markets. The growth of the Euroyen market in London has acted as a magnet for Japanese institutions, both banking and securities houses, keen to become active. Similarly, and more recently, they see the start of Japanese government bond futures trading on London's International Financial Futures Exchange as an opportunity for future growth. Switzerland offers a similar attraction for Japanese institutions, particularly in light of the continued active fund raising by Japanese corporations in Swiss francs.

The first Japanese bank to venture offshore was the Bank of Tokyo, under its former name of the Yokohama Specie Bank, with an extensive network in operation in the pre-war period.

Tight foreign exchange controls limited Japan's banks to the domestic market until the second half of the 1960s but by the mid-1970s, Japanese banks had 106 foreign subsidiaries and 106 representative offices overseas. By the end of 1986, they had 178 foreign subsidiaries and 362 branch offices.

The recent spate of overseas acquisitions by Japanese banks came in two waves – the first in 1984 and the second in 1986. In early 1984, Fuji Bank bought Walter Heller and Co for US$425 million, Sumitomo Bank bought 52.7 per cent of Banca del Gottardo for US$140 million, Sanwa Bank bought Continental Illinois' leasing division for US$50 million and Mitsubishi Bank finalised its purchase of the balance of Bank of California.

During 1986, Sumitomo Bank paid US$500 million for a stake in Goldman Sachs, Sanwa Bank US$263 million for Lloyds Bank of California and Dai-Ichi Kangyo Bank ¥10 billion for 62 per cent of the Hong Kong bank Chekiang First Bank, giving it control of 97 per cent of the capital; Industrial Bank of Japan, through its 75 per cent owned US subsidiary J. Henry Schroder Bank and Trust, bought US primary dealer Aubrey G. Lanston and Co, among others.

The divergent overseas acquisition strategy of Japan's bigger banks points to the basic differences in approach. The most aggressive has been Sumitomo Bank, with its purchase of a controlling stake in Banca del Gottardo of Switzerland and its investment in Goldman Sachs. Mitsubishi Bank has two subsidiaries in the US, the Bank of California and the Mitsubishi Bank of California. Mitsubishi Bank has pursued a clearly defined strategy of expanding in a cohesive manner in the Asia-Pacific Basin, in line with the common perspective in Japan that this region will be one of the strongest areas in the world economy in the next century.

Not all the overseas acquisitions by Japanese banks have been successful. The most notable disappointment is Sumitomo Bank's investment in Goldman Sachs. Sumitomo Bank envisaged close cooperation between the two institutions following this move, but the US Federal Reserve Board adopted a much more conservative view of the link and has severely constrained the benefits that will flow to Sumitomo from the deal. While disappointed, Sumitomo Bank has taken a long-term view and is confident that relations between the two institutions will be strengthened in time.

This other embarrassment was Fuji Bank's decision to buy Walter Heller – an acquisition that has been slow to produce results. Walter Heller was one of the largest independent debt factoring organisations in the US, an area of business that has been targeted by several of the big Japanese banks as promising strong growth, since it provides an entrée to the middle market. All of Japan's big banks complain that they find it hard to get in the door to write business with medium-sized US companies, along with the difficulty of accurate debt and cashflow assessment.

Fuji Bank has refrained from discussing the difficulties that have been encountered with this acquisition, although it has injected additional capital, through equity and loans, of more than US$700 million, taking its total investment in the company to well over US$1.1 billion, for a negligible return.

Notwithstanding the difficulties here, Japanese banks have a sizeable presence in the US. The Bank of Tokyo, for example, is estimated to be the second largest foreign bank in the US, with total assets exceeding US$20 billion. It operates through the Bank of Tokyo Trust Bank and the California First Bank, with offices in 11 cities. Given the very nature of its operations, the Bank of Tokyo has the greatest offshore exposure of any Japanese bank, with at least one-third of its lendings focused offshore.

The best indication of the rapid expansion of Japanese banks internationally is provided by statistics from the Bank of International Settlements, which show

Assets and liabilities of financial institutions, 1982-86

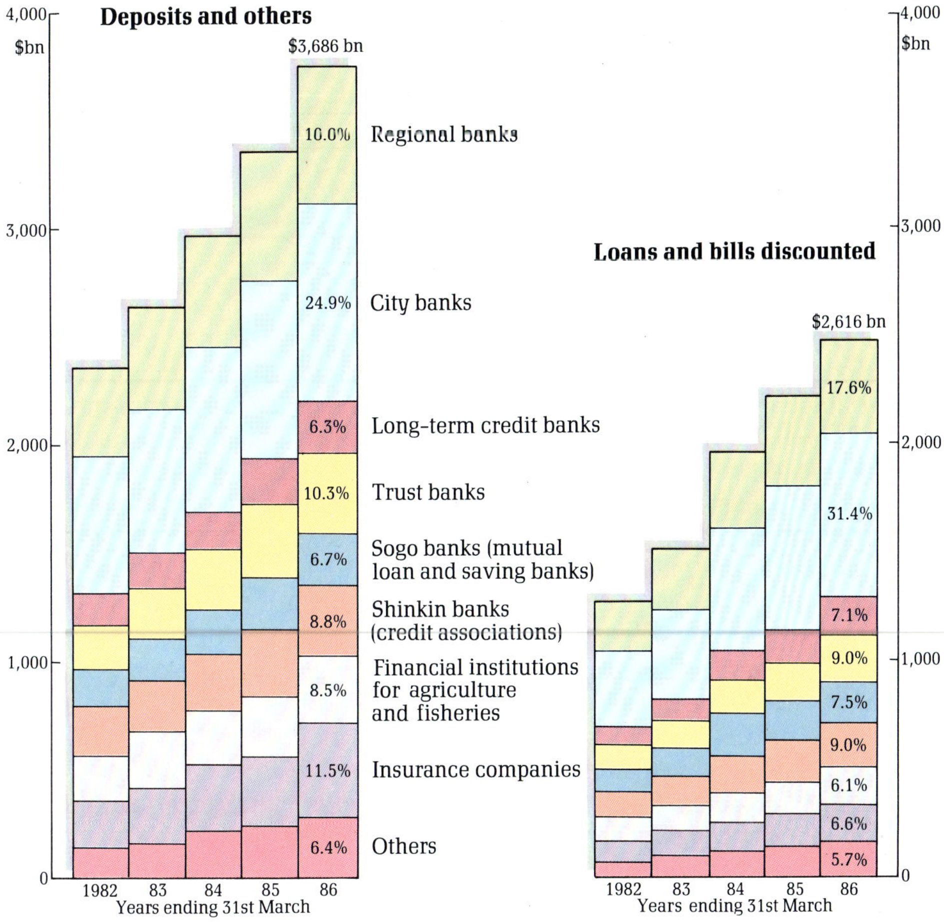

Notes: 1. The US dollar amounts are based on an exchange rate of ¥156.05 to $1.00
2. Deposits and others include CDs, bank debentures, trust funds and instalment savings
3. Figures for insurance companies include all operating assets
4. Loans and bills discounted include trust account

that in 1986, the share of Japanese banks in global banking surged to 33 per cent, up from 27 per cent the previous year. The rise in the fortunes of Japan's banks occurred while the US banks' share fell from 22 to 17.6 per cent.

Increasingly during 1987, however, Japanese banks became sensitive to what they termed 'over-presence' in foreign capital markets, which was leading to difficulties with regulatory authorities in the US and the UK.

There was extensive speculation, for example, that the Long-Term Credit Bank was frustrated in its ambition to buy a US primary dealer, Greenwich Securities, claiming that the US Federal Reserve Board threatened to remove its dealer's licence if the purchase was completed. That may have been due more to sensitivities ruling at that time, since Sanwa Bank was subsequently negotiating to acquire another US primary dealer.

Given the divergent strategies of Japan's banks in moving offshore, the one that has aroused the greatest interest is Dai-Ichi Kangyo Bank, the largest in Japan, which has yet to make a significant offshore acquisition. Company officials argue that they have been offered a number of deals which were bought subsequently by their domestic rivals, although they have decided for the time being simply to build on existing offshore assets. Dai-Ichi Kangyo Bank's offshore lendings are estimated at 12 per cent of total outstandings, which is broadly in line with those of the other major city banks.

But speculation surrounds the fact that Dai-Ichi Kangyo Bank is yet to make a large offshore move, with the common perception that the bank has yet to determine an appropriate strategy. In early 1987 it was approached to take up a stake in Hill Samuel of the UK, but turned it down. The purchase of control of Chekiang First in Hong Kong, while representing the first purchase of an Asian bank by a Japanese bank, gave it a multibranch operation in a market where foreign banks are restricted to a single outlet.

This was followed in January 1987 by Mitsubishi Bank's purchase of the business rights of Mercantile Bank, also in Hong Kong, for US$8 million from Citibank. This bank also holds a multi-branch licence. In the same month, Mitsubishi Bank also acquired control of Bank of California New York Trust, bringing it into the securities market.

Overseas assets

For all the big city banks and long-term credit banks, international lending accounts for about 10 per cent of their total portfolios. For the mutual banks, which began overseas operations much more recently, the proportion is much lower, although the Bank of Yokohama, the largest regional bank, has lent about 10 per cent of its funds abroad. The second largest regional bank, Hokuriku Bank, has lent an estimated 2 per cent of its funds overseas. Without the strong commercial banking base enjoyed by the big city banks, the smaller regional and mutual banks have found it much harder to expand their US dollar-based assets, although special instruments, such as synthetic floating rate notes, may gradually help them overcome some of these difficulties.

For any analysis of Japan's banks, assessing the profit contribution from their overseas activities is not easy, since it includes profits from foreign exchange trading which has been especially active since September 1985. This renewed activity has also helped offset the lower overseas profit contribution stemming from the currency revaluation. For the city banks, the gross contribution from international operations is estimated at 20 per cent of earnings, a figure that is unlikely to expand significantly in the immediate future.

With their aggressive move offshore, Japanese banks are estimated to hold at least 8.4 per cent of commercial loans in the US. And with their concentration in California, they control assets of US$22 billion.

In the UK Japanese banks controlled 22 per cent of total assets of the banking system in 1985, according to Bank of England statistics.

One of the keys to the success of Japanese banks has been their very low capital ratios in comparison with other international banks, although with the pressure being exerted during 1987 by the Bank of England and the US Federal Reserve, this advantage may be weakened. While strengthening their position in commercial banking, Japanese banks have also become significant players in capital markets. The continued strong level of interest in US Treasuries by Japan's life insurance companies in particular has prompted continued interest in buying US primary dealers, although there is some sensitivity in the US to this move.

In early 1987, the US government and the foreign securities houses in Tokyo pressured MoF to boost the participation level of foreign securities houses in the bond underwriting syndicate. MoF ultimately gave ground, although there was still sensitivity about further purchases of US primary dealers by Japanese banks.

Along with the high level of purchases of US government paper, Japanese banks are also estimated to have acquired half the municipal bonds issued in the US in recent years. Their activity in primary capital markets is increasing, as is evidenced by the high level of activity of Japanese banks in the swap market in London, where they swap Euroyen raisings for US dollars, giving them access to long-term funds in significant quantities.

The earlier decision by MoF to allow Japanese banks to float unsecured bonds in Switzerland was followed by the gradual expansion of the overseas offices of the city banks into underwriting.

Capital adequacy

The biggest, and most difficult, issue to resolve between Japanese banks and their overseas competitors is capital adequacy ratios. With substantially lower capital bases than other international banks, Japanese banks have an enviable edge in writing new business in capital markets, leading to continued criticism from North American and European banks that Japanese banks have an unfair advantage.

One of the most fundamental differences between Japan's financial system and others is the definition of capital ratios. Japanese banks are allowed to include a large proportion of the unrealised capital profit of their shareholdings in other corporations in calculating the value of their reserves.

As most North American and European countries do not allow their banks to hold direct shareholdings, this distinction is fundamental. In Japan, up to 70 per cent of the hidden profit of these shareholdings can be included in banks' capital adequacy ratios – a high figure, especially in the light of the highly speculative rise in share prices in Japan since 1984 and given the fact that the market for most stocks in Japan is extremely illiquid.

At the heart of much of the response in Japan to foreign criticism was the argument that while foreign banks are usually not allowed to hold equity investments, Japanese banks are, so due consideration should be given to this basic difference.

In determining their capital adequacy ratios, Japanese banks sought to include 70 per cent of the 'hidden' market value of their extensive shareholdings, which would boost their capital ratio to an average of about 7 per cent and would help them meet even the most rigorous standards.

As Japan's overheated stockmarkets continued their upward spiral during 1986 and 1987, the 'hidden assets' of the banks rose accordingly. The Japanese authorities argued that 70 per cent of the hidden value should be included when assessing capital ratios, because even if Japan's equity markets do undergo a major correction, the market would not fall by more than 30 per cent.

The negotiations with both the US Federal Reserve and the Bank of England have proved to be a sticking point for the Japanese authorities, and by the latter part of 1987, there was a growing feeling that an element of the banks' hidden profits from their shareholdings could be included in their capital adequacy ratios. However, this would fall far short of the 70 per cent sought, and could be perhaps a five-year average of the net value of their assets, or somewhat less than 40 per cent of the so-called 'hidden value'. As a result, extensive capital raisings are necessary.

In broad terms, the net worth ratio of most large Japanese banks is on average 3 per cent. Historically, under MoF guidelines, the banks were to have a capital adequacy ratio of 10 per cent. This ruling was ignored by the banks and in 1984, MoF moved to draw up new guidelines. In 1986, it recommended that by 1991 banks achieve a minimum ratio of equity to assets of 4 per cent, and 6 per cent

Capital ratios of Japan's city banks (%)

	A	*B*		*A*	*B*
DKB	2.87	9.66	Taiyo Kobe	2.77	9.00
Sumitomo	3.11	9.09	Kyowa	2.81	10.61
Fuji Bank	3.31	9.70	Daiwa	3.59	10.82
Mitsubishi	3.22	11.39	Saitama	3.09	8.84
Sanwa	3.02	9.36	Hokkaido Takushokin	2.59	8.73
Tokai	2.92	9.70	Bank of Tokyo	3.53	9.19
Mitsui	2.97	10.94			

A: Excluding book profits on shareholdings. B: Including 70% of unrealised profits.

for those with foreign subsidiaries. In addition, the ceiling on the ratio of foreign net worth to foreign assets was cut from 3.5 to 2.5 per cent in a bid to force the larger banks to improve their capital base. Even with the low ratio, there is little chance that the bigger Japanese banks will be able to comply easily.

In 1985, there were strong suggestions that all of Japan's big commercial banks intended to make large share issues aimed at improving their capital ratios. In the event, no new capital raisings occurred. During 1987, however, a number of the bigger banks began to move. Taking advantage of an earlier MoF decision to make it easier for them to issue convertible bonds both offshore and domestically, a number of issues were signalled. It is now possible for foreign subsidiaries of Japanese banks to make subordinated bond issues, which are usually counted as capital by foreign financial authorities.

In September 1987 alone, well over US$2 billion was raised by Japanese banks in a variety of currencies. A larger volume of yen-denominated capital raisings are expected from early 1988, once the sale of the second tranche of equity in Nippon Telegraph and Telephone, due in November 1987, has been absorbed by the domestic capital markets.

However, it will take some time for Japanese banks to boost their capital bases sufficiently to comply with tougher standards in the US and Europe. In June 1987, for example, the Long-Term Credit Bank of Japan signalled that it intended raising fresh capital of ¥92 billion. When completed, this will boost its shareholders' funds from 3 to just 3.5 per cent. Similarly, Mitsubishi Bank also intended to raise an estimated ¥90 billion, which would boost its net worth ratio from 3.22 to 3.54 per cent.

If the market value of the extensive shareholdings of Japan's banks is ignored, then their capital ratios are dismal, averaging 3 per cent. If 70 per cent of the market valuation were included, it would boost their ratio to an average of about 7 per cent, at least for the city banks.

With the increasingly risky nature of international banking, particularly in view of the problems that have been experienced with some of the more sophisticated markets that have evolved, such as perpetual floating rate notes, the need for stronger capital bases has been clear for some time. Given the massive volume of funds needed to correct the present imbalance, Japan's bigger banks have put off the inevitable for so long that, by the second half of the 1980s, the amount of funds needed to correct the situation is so large that it will be difficult to raise quickly or easily.

The growing perception of the pressures on the world financial system was one reason why some of the larger Japanese banks decided to move quickly, especially if there was a threat to some of their international operations.

In late August 1987, Moody's announced the downgrading of long-term debt ratings of the Bank of Tokyo, the Long-Term Credit Bank of Japan, Mitsubishi Trust and Banking Corporation and Sanwa Bank. It also signalled a possible future downgrading of the long-term debt of the Dai-Ichi Kangyo Bank, the Industrial Bank of Japan, Sumitomo Trust and Banking and Mitsui Trust and Banking.

The Moody's downgrading came at a time when the Bank of Japan was locked in an extended dispute with the US Federal Reserve Board and the Bank of England over the capital adequacy ratios of Japanese banks. It also took place against the backdrop of the large round of write-downs made by a number of the big US banks, such as Citibank and Chase Manhattan, against the book values of their country debt exposure.

The exposure of Japanese banks to the debt crisis is not as great as that of US banks as they entered the international financial markets later than the big US banks. None of the Japanese banks have confirmed their country debt exposure. The Bank of Tokyo has the largest exposure, estimated at over US$4.5 billion, and the exposure of most of the other large city banks is commonly put at around US$400 million.

Of particular note in Moody's downgradings is the fact that it includes a number of Japan's trust banks but excludes big city banks such as Sumitomo

Dai-Ichi Kangyo Bank: its zaibatsu was only formed in the late 1970s, but it is now ranked, by assets, as the world's largest bank.

Bank, Mitsubishi Bank and Fuji Bank – banks that have pursued perhaps the most aggressive international expansion of any of Japan's banks in recent years.

It was Moody's view that the 'credit culture' of the Japanese banks has yet to develop an appropriate degree of sophistication for the new, riskier trading environment. Moody's saw that the asset quality of the Japanese banks is essentially sound, but their adaptation to the changing market and their sometimes aggressive business goals will put increasing pressures on internal credit disciplines. Equally, the profit squeeze following interest rate deregulation has propelled the banks towards non-traditional markets which involve added risks that may not be fully understood. In particular, the short positions on the funding side of the city banks have boosted profits while interest rates have fallen, but leave them equally exposed once interest rates begin to rise.

With the quickening pace of change, and the greater emphasis on trading for new income, the banks have yet to change their training systems or their approach to employment to enable them to capitalise on this shift. In addition, their poor capital base will become a greater impediment in the future given the rise in risks. Unrealised capital profits from securities held have underpinned the position of the banks for much of the post-war era. Moody's argued that this was supportable when the unrealised gains of the portfolio investment were based on the rising economic worth of the corporate sector during the 1960s and 1970s. During the 1980s, however, the growth has been more dependent on increases in stock multiples, rather than increases in the true economic worth of the companies.

The words of caution from Moody's were largely overlooked, as the Bank of Japan was more concerned with forcing the point that some proportion of the unrealised capital gains of the portfolio investments should be included when assessing the capital bases of the banks.

Many of the fundamental issues remain, and it will need a sustained round of capital raisings and more accurate asset–liability management by the banks to put their operations onto a more even keel.

Mergers and acquisitions

One of the thorniest issues surrounding the future of Japan's banking sector is mergers of banks. The limited interest rate deregulation that has taken place by mid-1987 has had the greatest effect on the city banks, which were faced with a higher cost of funds which lowered their spread. The impact of this was offset by allowing them to trade in government securities. If interest rate deregulation proceeds to the smallest deposit levels, then there is the prospect that some of the weaker banks and savings associations will fail. To avert this, a round of forced mergers is likely.

The last merger that occurred was between the Heiwa Sogo Bank and Sumitomo Bank. Heiwa Sogo Bank, which was ruled as the private fiefdom of the founding Komiyama family, was split by personal feuds and had mounting bad debts. The decision to force a merger caused enormous surprise in finance circles in Japan since previously the authorities had endeavoured to maintain the independence of banks that had run into financial difficulties.

The tougher attitude of MoF and the Bank of Japan was interpreted as a clear signal that Japan's banks faced a more difficult future if they ran into financial problems. Government officials concede that mergers of Japan's weaker savings institutions are inevitable but at the same time there is already marked concern about the power of the largest city banks and their concentration of financial muscle.

Even among the city banks there is a large gap between the five largest, the middle three or four and the remainder. Equally, there are sizeable differences between the biggest and the medium-sized regional and mutual banks.

The mergers that occurred during the 1970s and 1980s have largely been among the fringe savings institutions. Deregulation and a tougher competitive environment have increased the pressures on the smaller regional savings institutions but mergers have been limited.

MoF tried to pave the way for mergers in the late 1970s with the release of various reports calling for a degree of merger activity to help prevent failures of weaker institutions but the attempts fell largely on deaf ears.

In this context, the forced merger of Heiwa Sogo Bank with Sumitomo Bank forms a useful case study, although the real stimulus to merge the failing bank was to avoid the collapse that could have occurred even if a rescue package were put in place, since it would have been difficult for Heiwa Sogo Bank to maintain public confidence.

A longstanding power struggle on the board of directors ultimately led to the demotion of the son of the founder of Heiwa Sogo Bank, Eichii Komiyama, from executive director to director in early 1985. The increasingly public board struggle and the growing round of litigation resulted in MoF bringing forward a scheduled inspection of the bank to mid-1985.

Engulfed in litigation, and with bad debts of an estimated ¥180 billion, the only way to stave off a serious run on deposits was by merging it with a stronger bank – a clear break with the past, when an institution's independence was protected at all cost.

In the light of the stringent MoF and Bank of Japan controls over all banks, just how the difficulties remained undetected for such a long period of time has not been adequately explained. Many of the problems surrounding the bank date back to the second half of the 1960s, when a variety of companies affiliated with the Komiyama family were established to engage in fringe areas such as golf course management, housing development, tourism and trading. Much of the funds lent to these companies were ultimately claimed to have been spent on land speculation.

The full extent of the bank's problems did not become apparent until mid-1985, when both MoF and the Bank of Japan carried out exhaustive studies into the bank's operations. Among other things, the studies found that one of the companies in the group, Sobu Tsusho, had been unprofitable since its founding in 1968, yet it continued to borrow funds from the bank, raising a total of ¥46 billion. The MoF study found that most of the group affiliates were unprofitable, yet total loans extended reached ¥530 billion, of which an estimated ¥390 billion were termed problem loans, which did not yield interest payments. As a result, total problem loans were estimated at over ¥500 billion, with bad loans put at ¥180 billion.

The authorities reacted quickly once they realised the full extent of the problems. Senior advisers from MoF and the Bank of Japan were installed to monitor and control the bank's activities. A special credit line of ¥200 billion was put in place, of which ¥70 billion with an interest rate pegged to the official discount rate was provided directly by the Bank of Japan. The balance of the funds was provided by the three long-term credit banks – the Industrial Bank of Japan, the Long-Term Credit Bank of Japan and Nippon Credit Bank – together with Fuji, Sumitomo, Mitsubishi, Sanwa, Mitsui and Dai-Ichi Kangyo Banks.

While these plans were being pursued, the authorities were moving quickly behind the scenes, seeking suitable merger partners, so as to stave off collapse.

A variety of potential banks were suggested as likely suitors, such as the Tokyo-based regional bank affiliate of the Industrial Bank of Japan, Tokyo Tomin Bank, Citibank and some of the leading city banks. Heiwa Sogo was a good fit for Sumitomo Bank, which had already completed an extensive study of its difficulties before merger prospects became likely, which included building up a substantial indirect shareholding of 34 per cent in the bank. Sumitomo Bank was anxious to get control, even with the difficulties that would be encountered, since a merger filled some strategic gaps in its operations.

For Sumitomo, its base in Osaka was beginning to act as a drain on earnings, as that area's economic growth had lagged behind Tokyo since the second half of the 1960s. Heiwa Sogo, as a Tokyo-based savings institution with 101 branches, and MoF approval for 115 branches, would give Sumitomo Bank much greater access to the Tokyo market, helping to broaden its deposit base. The short-term earnings dilution stemming from the merger was not a serious impediment for Sumitomo Bank, which admitted that the proposed merger would impact on the bottom line, although the medium-term prospects for the merged group were sufficient to see it anxious to conclude the deal quickly. Sumitomo Bank was, however, cautious, since an earlier proposal to merge with the Kansai Sogo Bank was thwarted due to stiff staff opposition, even though it is part of the Sumitomo group. As a result, lengthy discussions were held with employees to convince them that they would stand much greater opportunities for advancement if a merger was achieved, and that they would not be penalised by their association with Heiwa Sogo Bank, since the difficulties the bank had encountered were due primarily to the former directors' autocratic ways. Specific undertakings were given to bring staff salary levels into line with Sumitomo Bank's and not to transfer staff outside Tokyo against their wishes, a particularly touchy domestic issue.

Along with the extensive branch network, which would have been impossible for Sumitomo Bank to duplicate in the light of stiff administrative controls, Sumitomo Bank was also able to maintain the same trading hours for the former Heiwa Sogo Bank branches, which remained open until 7 p.m., instead of the usual bank closing time of 3 p.m. Also, the bulk of the bank's branches were located adjacent to major railway stations, giving it access to the large number of commuters. Even though Sumitomo Bank was forced to assume additional bad loans stemming from the merger, the actual cost of the purchase, never confirmed but put at ¥100 billion, will be largely offset by the sale of duplicated outlets.

Mergers of any groups in Japan are difficult, due to the extreme loyalty of employees and concern about reduced prospects for promotion after a merger. For Sumitomo Bank, the merger has been a success notwithstanding the subsequent earnings dilution, since a broader retail base helped overcome structural difficulties restraining its growth.

The largest merger in Japan's banking history was between Nippon Kangyo Bank and Dai-Ichi Bank, to form the Dai-Ichi Kangyo Bank, the largest bank in the world. Merged in 1971, the two organisations are still not fully integrated, and it may take another generation before this is achieved. From the outset it was decided to operate the two former banks along parallel lines, with detailed undertakings to ensure that the clients of the two banks still received access to the same volume of funds as they did previously.

More than 15 years on, there are scant signs that any significant progress has been made. Whether the paralysis runs deeper is hard to evaluate, although the fact that of all of Japan's major banks, Dai-Ichi Kangyo Bank is yet to make a significant overseas expansion points to an overall lack of direction, even though it has an unrivalled deposit base in Japan – almost nine million individual regular accounts, one million more than Fuji Bank.

A more successful merger was between Taiyo Bank, based in Tokyo, and Kobe Bank, based in Kobe. Given the two banks' widely separate regional spread of operations and differing strengths, this merger has gone much more smoothly. The heads of both banks had traditionally been retired MoF officials, and this ensured that the merger proceeded with few problems.

One of the benefits of merging banks in Japan is that it may enable an upgrading of bank status from, say, mutual bank to regional bank, which can facilitate future growth. There have been examples of this in the post-war period, although the last involving the formation of a city bank was the merger of four regional banks to form Saitama Bank soon after the war.

The last merger of two banks that resulted in an upgrading of status occurred in 1984, when the Nishi-Nippon Sogo Bank and the Takachiho Sogo Bank agreed to merge, and the new bank was upgraded to regional bank status centred on Kyushu, with total assets approaching ¥2.5 trillion at that time. Nishi-Nippon Sogo Bank, the largest mutual bank, had earlier merged with a credit bank.

Such a change of status is rare. There have been a number of mergers of credit associations which were then upgraded to community banks. The last merger to form a mutual bank was in 1970, with the creation of the Nagano Sogo Bank.

The concentration of banking activities between the big city banks and the handful of large regional banks has made MoF officials wary of actively promoting mergers of existing large institutions, although they concede that with the weaker community savings associations and banks they have little choice, if failures are to be prevented.

Unlike the post-war experience in the US, there has been no bank failure in Japan since before the war and MoF and Bank of Japan are anxious to avoid any possibility of such an event. Ministry officials do concede that further deregulation will bring additional pressures on the management of many smaller institutions which may not be well prepared to cope.

As a result, controls on bank reserve funds have been tightened and there has been a steady stream of mergers of smaller savings associations in order to improve their operating bases. In 1985, for example, 11 credit associations in

Kumamoto prefecture merged to form the Kumamoto Prefecture Credit Association with deposits of ¥80.68 billion. In the same year, three credit associations in Miyagi prefecture merged and there were separate mergers of two groups in Tokyo and another two in Osaka.

There has been a noticeable increase in merger activity among these smaller savings institutions during the 1980s. There was regular merger activity during the 1970s, usually with one or two mergers a year. So far this decade, even though there may only be two or three mergers a year, the number of institutions involved has expanded dramatically. Typically, all such mergers involve credit associations in a single prefecture.

Such mergers on a regional basis are likely to increase steadily in the future, as the authorities continue to bring pressure to bear for mergers of the weaker associations to avoid possible collapses. In Fukuoka prefecture, south of Tokyo, successive mergers over the past 20 years have reduced the number of credit associations from 37 to just 12. In Gunma prefecture the local authorities have worked steadily at building up a consensus aimed at merging its various credit associations into 10 – a move that, while taking several years to achieve, indicates a broadening perception that mergers need to be promoted.

There are significant gaps appearing in the growth of the big city banks, with the big four widening their lead over the smaller banks, such as Saitama Bank and Hokkaido Takushoku Bank. Mergers of some of the smaller city banks with large regional banks would be logical, and would allow some to achieve a better mix of business, enabling a more stable expansion in the future.

The only way foreign banks can expect to boost their presence in Japan is through mergers with or acquisitions of smaller financial institutions. The size of the larger institutions and their close relationship with the industrial sector, combined with their close and extensive links with both the Bank of Japan and MoF, would make it all but impossible for a foreign bank to merge with any of the larger financial institutions.

Smaller savings institutions, such as some of the weaker regional and sogo banks, would provide the best opportunity. When Heiwa Sogo's problems were publicised, Citibank expressed interest in making a move but Sumitomo Bank quickly seized the golden opportunity to boost its network base substantially.

Citibank formed a link in April 1987 with one of the larger sogo banks, the Tokyo Sogo Bank, to cooperate in the field of credit cards and foreign exchange. Whether this initial link will enable the two banks to move closer together in the future is a moot point but forming such a link is, in the Japanese context, the first step to closer links in the future.

In preparation for the increased difficulties that Japan's banks will face in the future in the light of deregulated interest rates and the rise in the level of risks stemming from many of the instruments presently being traded, in 1986 the Deposit Insurance Corporation increased cover for individual depositors from ¥3 million to ¥10 million; at the same time it boosted the deposit insurance paid by the banks by 50 per cent to cover this increase, as well as raising the funding available to the corporation from the central bank, the Bank of Japan. And, as part of this package of measures, additional powers were sought to force bank mergers.

CHAPTER SIX

City banks

Japan's premier financial institutions are its city banks. A nationwide branch network and favoured treatment by the Ministry of Finance (MoF) have created some of the largest commercial banks in the world. Originally focused on the big industrial combines, or zaibatsu, their fortunes grew in line with their industrial base. Dai-Ichi Kangyo Bank (DKB), Fuji Bank, Sumitomo Bank and Mitsubishi Bank are usually ranked the four largest banks in the world by either net assets or total deposits. Others, such as Sanwa Bank and Tokai Bank, are usually also ranked in the top 10.

As Japan's industrial base expanded, so too did the activities and size of the city banks. Those at the hub of the big zaibatsu, such as Mitsubishi Bank, Mitsui Bank, Sumitomo Bank and Sanwa Bank, grew rapidly during the post-war period. Others, such as DKB, Kyowa Bank and Tokai Bank, have relied on the growth of second-tiered industrial groups for their expansion of assets and activities. The growth of many of these smaller companies, particularly in newer industries such as communications and services, has resulted in these city banks servicing some of the biggest companies in Japan. DKB, for example, claims it is the main bank to a variety of industrial groups, from trading house C. Itoh and Co and Kanematsu-Gosho, Fujitsu, Kawasaki Steel and Showa Shell Oil to Asahi Chemical and Asahi Life Insurance. Its zaibatsu, termed the Sankin-kai, was formed only in the 1970s.

The introduction in 1985 of money market certificates (MMCs), which have interest rates at a slight discount to those of CDs, has resulted in a large amount of funds raised through these new instruments. With MMCs and the commercial paper market, due to start in late 1987, the proportion of funds raised by the city banks through the money markets will continue to rise, and is likely to exceed 35 per cent of the city banks' total liabilities in the near future, up from about 20 per cent in 1984.

With their web of inter-connecting shareholdings, the city banks have significant securities holdings which are carried in their books at cost. For DKB, for example, these holdings are valued at ¥3.09 trillion, which is only a fraction of their market worth.

Being the main bank to a corporation carries with it considerable responsibility, since if the client faces financial difficulties, the main bank is charged with taking the necessary steps to get the company back onto the rails. Also, the city banks are caught up in the deregulation of Japan's financial system.

Stiffer competition for deposits has resulted in a continuing decline in the city banks' share of total deposits, forcing a progressive increase in their reliance on short-term capital markets for funding.

As well as financing the expansion of Japan's capital base during the post-war era, the city banks played a vital role in funding the expansion of government debt that began in earnest in the mid-1970s, as public spending was boosted to stave off recession in the wake of the oil price rises. The city banks are responsible for taking up 30.7 per cent of all government bonds issued through the bond underwriting syndicate. For much of the 1980s, this has been profitable, as long-term interest rates have tended downwards although during the late 1970s, when the Bank of Japan quickly raised interest rates to reduce inflationary pressures, the city banks were badly exposed and ran up large losses on their bond investments.

Mitsubishi Bank carried out a restructuring in 1986 to increase operating flexibility.

Funding

The continued long-term decline in the share of savings deposits held by the city banks has forced them to finance an increasing proportion of their activities through the short-term money market. The success of the insurance companies and the postal savings system in boosting their share of total deposits has resulted in the city banks' share declining to 15.85 per cent by the end of 1986. Until there is either total interest rate deregulation, or the competitive advantage of the postal savings system is reduced or offset, the share of deposits held by the city banks will continue its gradual, but sure, decline. As a result, the reliance on the short-term capital markets for funds will continue to grow. In the call market, for example, the city banks have traditionally been the biggest borrowers although, with the expansion of this market over the past decade, their share as a percentage of the total has declined.

In 1976, for example, the city banks accounted for almost 90 per cent of all fund raisings through the call market. By 1986, it was a more modest 45 per cent. In absolute terms, the city banks more than doubled their borrowings to ¥4.4 trillion by the end of 1986, although the total size of this market had more than quadrupled over this period.

Equally, the city banks are the largest borrowers through the discount market where they account for 85 per cent of total borrowings. In addition to these two markets, the development of the CD market has been a boon to the city banks, and their use of this instrument now outstrips their funding through the call market. Establishment of the CD market in Japan took over a decade to achieve and its steady development has benefited the city banks in particular, since it gives them an alternative funding source to offset their dwindling share of saving deposits.

The banks had been pressing for the establishment of this market since the early 1960s and, while MoF was not opposed to their tapping this market offshore to help fund their overseas expansion, it was reluctant to allow a CD market to be established in Japan.

By the end of 1986, the balance of CDs issued by the banks stood at ¥8.4 trillion, up from just ¥2.73 trillion four years earlier. Since its start-up, the city banks have accounted for 50 per cent of all funds raised through this market, with the regional banks taking a much more modest 20 per cent. The balance is spread across the other financial institutions.

With the segmentation of Japan's financial system, the city banks have been limited to raising short-term funds domestically, although this is gradually changing as they have been able to build up their portfolio of longer-term borrowings.

The city banks have for some time borrowed through the Eurodollar markets, which gave them access to longer-term funding, although often not long enough to allow them to match adequately both sides of their portfolio. More recently, with the start-up of the Euroyen market in late 1984, the city banks have been actively engaged in the swap market, taking yen funds, which has given them access to long-term yen funding for the first time. Again, this has been of enormous benefit in enabling them to match their portfolio more evenly, as well as contributing further to the deregulation of the domestic capital markets.

Earlier, the long-term credit banks had lobbied hard, and successfully, to prevent the city banks from being allowed to raise longer-term funds in Japan. The significant expansion of new fund raising activity through the Euromarkets has enabled the city banks to overcome this restriction.

At the same time as the city banks have gradually increased their access to longer-term funds, the long-term credit banks have increased their portfolio of shorter-term funds. Gradually, one of the more irrelevant lines of demarcation in Japan's financial system is being broken down. In 1965, for example, mismatching – long-term lendings less long-term borrowings – stood at ¥2.53 trillion. By the end of fiscal 1985 it had reached ¥27.9 trillion, rising to ¥33.3 trillion in March 1987.

As a proportion of net assets, the level is broadly unchanged, but the growth in absolute terms has been large enough to cause significant difficulties stemming from short-term interest rate movements, as well as potentially severe liquidity risk.

Against this backdrop, the rise in longer-term funding by the city banks is striking, although insufficient to stave off difficulties if there is a sudden change in external conditions. By March 1986, 39.7 per cent of the funding of the city banks was long-term, up from 28 per cent a year earlier. And by March 1986, the short-term funding of the long-term credit banks had risen to 26.4 per cent of their total funds supply, up from just 6.7 per cent a decade earlier. The change in the mix of business of both sectors lies behind the change in their funding mix.

During the 1960s, the city banks lent almost exclusively to big industrial groups. The slowdown in their demand for new funds has resulted in a steady increase in the city banks' reliance on small and medium-sized companies, especially in the services and real estate sectors. In 1965, for example, these two sectors accounted for 19.8 per cent of advances by city banks. By 1985, it had reached 38.2 per cent and by the end of calendar 1986 43.2 per cent, helping to fuel much of the increase in both new construction activity and property prices in Japan from the mid-1980s. By the end of 1986, 39.4 per cent of total domestic advances were to small and medium-sized corporations, compared with 18.4 per cent in 1965. At the same time, lending to individuals, which accounted for a marginal 3 per cent of total advances in the mid-1960s, rose to 39.6 per cent by the end of 1986.

There are clearly large differences between the 12 city banks in their access to personal deposits. To boost its retail base, as well as its activities in Tokyo, Osaka-based Sumitomo Bank took on the troubled Heiwa Sogo Bank in 1986. The merger expanded Sumitomo Bank's branch structure in Tokyo and lowered its percentage of assets tied up in the slower growing Kansai region around Osaka. Similarly, the semi-government DKB, as the banker to the National Lottery, enjoys a massive infusion of funds in the lead up to the holding of these events, which typically involve huge financial flows.

Source of profits

The progressive deregulation of interest rates on large-sized deposits, most of which have been switched out of the banks directly into the short-term capital markets, primarily MMCs, has hurt the city banks the most.

To offset this, they have been given direct access to trading in government bonds, which has proved to be a lucrative new source of income. With the volatility of domestic interest rates during 1986 and 1987, access to government bond trading has been a boon to the bottom line, accounting for over 3 per cent of total gross profits soon after the city banks were given access, according to the Federation of Bankers' Associations of Japan. Since then, earnings from bond trading have continued to increase. Some banks were cautious at first but most moved quickly to take full advantage of their new profit stream in a bid to offset pressures on their lending activities.

While banks are permitted to trade in government bonds, they are restricted to trading on their own account. The banks' pressure to be permitted to trade bonds on clients' behalf is being strenuously opposed by the securities houses. Equally, the banks are strongly opposed to the securities houses being allowed direct access to foreign exchange markets.

In general terms, bond dealing now accounts for 10 per cent of pre-tax earnings, with some of the larger city banks, for example Sumitomo Bank, claiming that earnings from bond trading now rival those of the bigger securities houses. It is estimated that in the 1986 financial year (to March 1987), Sumitomo Bank earned ¥27.1 billion from bond trading, the largest earnings from bond trading of any city bank. It led Fuji Bank which earned ¥26 billion, Sanwa Bank (¥21.6 billion), Mitsui Bank (¥21.5 billion) and DKB (¥20.6 billion). The subsequent bearish trend in bond markets, however, is likely to reduce considerably the income from bond trading in fiscal 1987.

In addition to this, the city banks' growing international operations contribute, on average, another 20 per cent of earnings. The contribution from international activities is bolstered by the inclusion of foreign exchange trading, which has been extremely profitable in the wake of foreign exchange market volatility since late 1985.

All of the city banks have aggressively pursued computerisation programmes and cut excess staff to keep overheads under control. Attention has also been focused on their branch structures and they are progressively moving to close or relocate unprofitable branches. Of Japan's major deposit-taking banks, the city banks have been the most aggressive, and successful, in reducing costs. Personnel and non-personnel costs have been reduced steadily, with their cost ratio declining to 1.12 per cent during 1986 – the lowest of any sector of the banking industry, reflecting their much larger wholesale operations. Against this, their profit margin has also declined, although their earnings have continued to show growth thanks to rising offshore earnings, higher-income trading activities and the sale of securities.

To make up for the lack of demand for new funds by larger corporations, the city banks have pushed hard to boost lending to medium-sized and small companies, which typically carries better margins; there is also the prospect of a further expansion of new lending in the future, as these companies grow. Lending to medium-sized and small corporations has emerged as a battle ground between the city banks, regional banks, mutual banks, trust banks and the insurance companies, so margins are coming under pressure.

The overall decline in demand for new funds by the industrial sector, together with the steady rise in indirect funding by corporate borrowers, has resolved one of the thorniest problems of Japan's capital markets for much of the post-war

Sumitomo Bank is ranked one of the four largest banks in the world.

period, when they were overlent. Strong demand for funds during the era of fast growth in the 1950s and 1960s forced the city banks in particular to rely heavily on short-term funding from the Bank of Japan to solve their chronic cash shortage. As a result, for much of this period lendings exceeded borrowings, forcing them to turn to the Bank of Japan to cover the shortfall, which made implementing monetary policy difficult for the central bank.

This has changed since the second oil crisis and the volume of funding provided by the Bank of Japan to the city banks has declined to around 2.4 per cent of total deposits. With their rising cash surplus, the city banks have emerged as large buyers of securities, as well as investing funds in tokkin investment trusts. An estimated 70 per cent of the funds in tokkin accounts are deposited by financial corporations, with most of these funds coming from insurance companies and banks.

Direct purchases of securities by banks is also rising. Net purchases of securities by banks rose by ¥4.26 trillion in calendar 1986. Net purchases in the first quarter of 1987 totalled ¥1.18 trillion.

One penalty for the city banks is their dominant role in the syndicate for subscribing to new issues of government bonds. In total, the city banks take up 30.7 per cent, with the first-ranked banks forced to take up 4.1 per cent each, the second-tiered banks 2.9 per cent, and the smallest 2.1 per cent. The quick upturn in interest rates in 1979 and 1980 hit the city banks hard, as they incurred massive paper losses on their uptake of recently issued government paper. Their position was compounded at that time, since they were forced to hold the bonds for a 12-month period before they could be sold on – a restriction that has since been relaxed. The government's inability to reduce the budget deficit has meant that construction bonds issued in the second half of the 1970s are progressively falling due for rolling over in the second half of the 1980s, adding to the volume of government paper the city banks are forced to take up.

Even though the debacle of 1979 and 1980 cost the city banks dearly, the progressive slide in interest rates since the mid-1980s has been a boon for profits. The positive interest rate trend has increased competition from the foreign securities houses, in particular, for a larger share of the bond syndicate. Along with this, there has been mounting pressure for MoF to boost the proportion of government bonds offered for competitive tender, which has been adopted increasingly for shorter-dated government paper since 1978.

Reorganisation

To cope with the rapidly changing business environment, most of the leading city banks have undergone reorganisation. The most notable was the complete reorganisation of Sumitomo Bank in the wake of the collapse of trading company Ataka and Co in the mid-1970s. It called in management consultants McKinsey and Co to advise on changes in the organisation and operating procedures following that failure, which resulted in Sumitomo Bank absorbing ¥113.2 billion and Kyowa Bank ¥7.5 billion of losses. Other banks absorbed smaller amounts.

More recently, other banks have followed suit in adopting new structures aimed at boosting their capital markets activities. Mitsubishi Bank completed a reorganisation in 1986, which resulted in the creation of two new divisions – capital markets and merchant banking division. The changes it implemented were part of an overall shake-up of the bank which, as part of the Mitsubishi group – the leading industrial combine in Japan which accounts for around 10 per cent of GDP – had lost direction when compared with the single-minded determination of others such as Sumitomo Bank.

Mitsui Bank also carried out a restructuring in 1986, creating a range of smaller working units to increase operating flexibility. Along with this, an overhaul of loan limits imposed on its managers was carried out, giving them greater flexibility. It also implemented a system whereby the same group of officers would be responsible for the bank's contact with, and lending to, large

Japanese corporations on a worldwide basis, which was intended both to speed up servicing clients' needs and to create much closer evaluation of clients on a worldwide basis.

While preparing for the increased emphasis on dealing activities, the city banks also face longer-term difficulties due to their role as the main banks to many old-line manufacturers. With the main bank system, the banks must usually play a key role in forcing through a restructuring or reorganisation of an ailing client to avoid collapse.

Many of these problems have been exacerbated by the harsher business environment stemming from the appreciation of the yen, which has cast a cloud over the future of Japan's 'smokestack' industries. The collapse of the Sanko Shipping group in 1985, for example, cost a number of the city banks dearly, especially Daiwa Bank which was forced to make provisions of ¥62.68 billion. Similarly, there have been write-offs stemming from the reorganisation of the Japan Line which has cost both city banks and the long-term credit banks. The reorganisation of the shipbuilding industry and other shipping lines will force all the city banks to make provisions or write-offs, although the final impact will be offset by the sale of securities so that there will be no impact on the bottom line. Many of these problems will only become apparent from 1988 on, once these companies realise that the changed competitive environment is a long-term phenomenon, rather than just short-term.

Mismatched portfolios

There is little doubt of the international power of Japan's city banks. Built on a massive deposit base in Japan, they have expanded dramatically internationally since the early 1970s. The fundamental difficulties they face lie with domestic restrictions which pose significant problems for their overall activities.

The largest potential problem is the steady rise in their mismatched portfolios – basically borrowing short and lending long – which is a classic prescription for operating difficulties as soon as interest rate volatility emerges, in particular when interest rates begin rising.

Technically prevented from borrowing long-term, yet forced to lend long to meet borrowers' needs, the city banks are faced with a considerable conundrum. They have managed, however, to boost their long-term funding, mostly through offshore capital markets. Longer-term borrowings have increased steadily, and have reached the point where they account for almost half of their total capital supply. But this growth has continued to lag behind their overall increase in longer-term lending.

The strong demand by the city banks and trust banks for long-term funding fuelled the growth of the Euroyen market, underpinning all of the increase in activity during the first two years of its operation. As the city banks' demand for longer-term funds has slowed, so too has new issue activity in the Euroyen market.

With the development of the swap-driven Euroyen market, an increasing sophistication of swap structures developed during 1985 and 1986 until MoF cracked down, making it known that the amount of activity was excessive and that, with many of the structures being pursued, risks were not fully understood. Almost all of these products were developed to fill the specific needs of Japanese institutional investors, such as the trust banks and life insurance groups. Many of these products carried attractive returns but equally there was virtually no marketability so that, if the institution needed to liquidate some of these investments, severe difficulties would be encountered.

Although city banks were allowed to take advantage of this opening in the market, the long arm of MoF has prevented them from making full use of market liberalisation internationally.

The 'big bang' in the UK market presaged a great deal of merger activity as foreign banks and other financial institutions moved in. There has been a notable lack of activity by Japanese banks, especially the city banks, whose

Opposite above: Daiwa Bank, the only city bank with a trust bank division.

Opposite below: Sanwa Bank has grown rapidly in the past two decades: its earnings from bond trading are beginning to rank with the bigger securities houses.

DAIWA BANK
大和銀行

三和銀行
Sanwa Bank

ambitions in this area are well known domestically. The lack of activity was largely due to MoF making it clear that it would not countenance Japanese institutions expanding their influence in the UK capital markets, for the time being at least.

Being prohibited from moving directly into the securities market offshore has not stopped the city banks from stepping up their links with domestic securities houses. All the major banks have formed, or strengthened, links with Japanese securities houses, even though under existing regulations they are not allowed to hold more than 5 per cent of the equity. Even with this limit, there has been an extensive transfer of staff between the banks and their affiliated securities house.

Along with this, typically the president and chairman of affiliated securities houses are nominated by the bank. The most notable links are between DKB and one of the larger securities houses, Kangyo Kakumaru Securities, and between Sumitomo Bank and Meiko Securities. IBJ also has very close links with both Wako Securities and New Japan Securities.

The city banks have become increasingly public about links with their affiliated securities house and, even though their direct shareholding is limited to 5 per cent, indirect influence through large shareholdings of other companies within their 'keiretsu' typically gives them control.

The Bank of Tokyo

The Bank of Tokyo is in fact Japan's only specialised foreign exchange bank. As such it has grown largely thanks to the patronage of the government. With the growing international network of most of Japan's other commercial banks, the special role the Bank of Tokyo played during much of Japan's development has passed, although its close links with MoF and the Bank of Japan will continue for some time to come.

Established as the Yokohama Specie Bank in 1880 with a capital of ¥3 million, which was equal to 7 per cent of the capital of all Japan's banks in operation at that time, its specific charter was to serve as the official foreign trade bank of the government. Growth was rapid and by 1885 it had assets of ¥23 million. It developed as the dominant short-term financing bank, with assets equal to over 15 per cent of all commercial banks by the year 1900. Its primary objective was to act as an intermediary between foreign and domestic traders, to facilitate finance and to prevent the rise in the premiums on silver. (At the time the Yokohama Specie Bank was established, Japan was still seeking to stay on the silver standard, while most other major powers were switching to the gold standard.) The main reason for establishing the Yokohama Specie Bank was to ensure that Japan's foreign trade transactions were financed by a Japanese bank and not by some of the big foreign mercantile banks that had made inroads into India and China during the 19th century.

The Yokohama Specie Bank was helped on its way by the Bank of Japan making special low-interest loans to the bank from the Treasury reserves, and subsequently by rediscounting foreign bills held by the bank. With access to such cheap financing, it could expand its lending and develop a comprehensive overseas network quickly.

During the occupation after World War II, it was transformed into the Bank of Tokyo, a commercial bank. Subsequently, in 1954, the Foreign Exchange Banks Law was passed under which the Bank of Tokyo became a specialised foreign exchange bank. Under this legislation, the number of domestic branches that it could operate was severely limited and therefore branches could only be justified in centres where there was extensive trading. Accordingly, with the expansion of Japan's trade during the 1950s, it found it increasingly difficult to expand its deposit base; so legislative action in 1962 gave it the right to issue debentures. This right was enjoyed only by the long-term credit banks, the Norin Chukin Bank and the Shoko Chukin Bank.

Additional legislative change in 1982 gave it the right to issue debentures up to 10 times its capital and reserves, up from the previous level of five times.

The Bank of Tokyo, classed as a city bank, still has a special relationship with MoF and the Bank of Japan.

The distinction of being Japan's foreign exchange bank has been gradually reduced, however, as the international networks of the rival commercial banks have expanded, although usually the Bank of Tokyo gets preferential treatment in being the first Japanese bank to open a representative office or branch in an overseas country. With its traditional function becoming increasingly irrelevant, the Bank of Tokyo has evolved as an important wholesale bank, with a range of functions similar to the long-term credit banks and the city and trust banks.

Its historical role as a quasi-government bank continues, with close and extensive links with MoF and the Bank of Japan.

In large offshore fundings that involve the Export-Import Bank of Japan, the Bank of Tokyo is typically lined up alongside the Export-Import Bank, and well ahead of any of the other commercial banks. Equally, when the Chinese government became more active in tapping international capital markets in

1985, the Bank of Tokyo was involved in handling many of the issues made by the Bank of China or the China International Trust Investment Corporation. The Bank of Tokyo led the bulk of the yen-based issues, which were preferred by the Bank of China at that time as these borrowings were regarded as government-to-government transactions.

Given its large international network and the extensive offshore financings, it is only natural that the Bank of Tokyo has the most exposed position of any of Japan's banks to the debt difficulties of LDC countries. Neither the government nor MoF has disclosed the true level of exposure of Japan's banks to the debt crisis, although it is estimated that the exposure of the Bank of Tokyo is over ¥700 million, which is equal to 4 per cent of total assets and exceeds its equity and loan loss reserves. At this level, the Bank of Tokyo's exposure is twice that of other leading city banks, such as Fuji Bank or Sumitomo Bank. However, as over 80 per cent of the Bank of Tokyo's earnings are derived offshore, it is not surprising that it has a much higher exposure to the debt difficulties than its major city bank rivals.

As for overseas activities, the Bank of Tokyo is estimated to have the second largest operation of any foreign bank in North America, with total assets put at more than US$20 billion. Its prime vehicles are California First Trust and Bank of Tokyo Trust. It has 11 offices in the US, including those of its affiliates, compared with just 42 in Japan. In all it has 250 overseas offices.

As the bulk of the Bank of Tokyo's operations are offshore, deregulation of the domestic financial system has had little effect on either expanding or limiting its potential share of the domestic market. Rising foreign exchange rate volatility has underpinned the bottom line since, given its substantial foreign exchange related financing, its forex exposure is large. In recent years, foreign exchange trading income has accounted for about 20 per cent of gross income, well down on the figure in former years when it occasionally exceeded 40 per cent of gross income.

CHAPTER SEVEN

Long-term credit banks

The long-term credit banks are the banks most exposed to change through the progressive deregulation of the financial system. As specialised banks to provide long-term loans to industry, their role has become less important. In the mid-1960s, they provided 15 per cent of all equipment loans to industry. With the increased sophistication of borrowing alternatives for industry, their provision of equipment funds has fallen to less than 5 per cent. The declining demand for new borrowings by industry left them free to absorb large quantities of government bonds which were issued from the latter part of the 1970s.

The three long-term credit banks, especially the Industrial Bank of Japan (IBJ), enjoy close relationships with both the Ministry of Finance (MoF) and the Bank of Japan. They are emerging as sizeable wholesale banks and are increasingly aggressive in international capital markets.

Tracing their roots back to the turn of the century, their role was to provide long-term funds for the development of industry and infrastructure. At that time, there were three banks, the Industrial Bank of Japan, the Hypothec Bank and the Hokkaido Colonial Bank. Originally, these three banks were intended to relieve the Bank of Japan of the role of providing industrial finance, and to ensure development of the long-term financing markets. A key part of their initial role was to provide real estate financing but market developments changed this.

Before World War II, IBJ was the leading underwriter in Japan, although with the split between banking and underwriting activities during the post-war occupation, it decided to give up its securities functions.

During the occupation, the Hypothec Bank and the Hokkaido Colonial Bank went through a change of status, becoming commercial banks. The Hypothec Bank became the Kangyo Bank (which subsequently merged with Dai-Ichi Bank) and the Hokkaido Colonial Bank, the Hokkaido Takushoku Bank. In 1950, the system of specialised banks was abolished, and IBJ was also converted to a commercial bank. Subsequently, legislation was approved allowing all banks to issue debentures under certain conditions. This legislation was soon repealed, although not before a number of banks had taken advantage of the change, since it was thought that such a development would cause confusion between the long-term and short-term capital markets.

Established after special legislation was introduced in 1952, there are now again three long-term credit banks – IBJ, the Long-Term Credit Bank of Japan and the Nippon Credit Bank. IBJ is the largest and most prestigious. The Nippon Credit Bank is the smallest and also the weakest of the three. It was the last established, opening in 1957.

Along with the Bank of Tokyo, the Norin Chukin Bank and Shoko Chukin Bank, they are the only banks allowed to issue bank debentures. They are specifically precluded from accepting bank deposits other than from governments, public authorities and loan customers, which are comprised of Japan's blue chip companies.

Unlike the city banks, which are restricted to raising funds short-term, the long-term credit banks can raise funds for up to five years, to extend to industry.

With the development of Japan's infrastructure and also the expansion of the size and liquidity of the corporate sector, the traditional role of the long-term credit banks has become largely redundant.

Funding

Most of their funds are raised through short- and long-term debentures which are issued at regulated interest rates, although the expansion of short-term capital markets has given them an additional funding option. For much of the 1950s and 1960s, debentures accounted for 70 per cent of their liabilities but during the 1980s this has declined slightly, standing at 64 per cent by the mid-1980s. Deposits make up an additional 12 per cent and funding through call markets another 4 per cent. In contrast to the city banks, which are gradually increasing their longer-term borrowings, the long-term credit banks have substantially boosted their short-term funding since the mid-1970s, at a time when their overall borrowings have continued to expand. By the end of March 1986, their short-term funding accounted for 26.4 per cent of the total.

In line with the changes in demand for funds, loans and bills discounted have

IBJ, a semi-government institution, used to be the leading underwriter in Japan.

fallen progressively over the past three decades. In the mid-1950s, loans and bills discounted made up over 80 per cent of assets. By the mid-1980s, this had fallen to less than 63 per cent. Continuing subdued demand for new borrowings by the corporate sector is likely to result in this share continuing to fall. With the decline here, the securities holdings of the long-term credit banks have risen, accounting for 19 per cent of assets, reflecting the deepening of credit markets, together with the large funding programme of the national budget. With this shift, income from securities trading by the long-term credit banks has risen steadily, although interest income remains the dominant source of gross earnings.

Reflecting the change in Japan's industrial structure, lending to the manufacturing sector has declined as a proportion of total outstandings, from over one-third for IBJ in the early 1980s to less than 25 per cent today, with a steady expansion of new lending to service sector companies and also smaller companies. Overseas lending has also risen and is estimated to make up approximately 10 per cent of all outstandings.

Since they have a much more defined nature of operations, the long-term credit banks have only a limited branch network, so that lending per employee exceeds ¥2 billion.

Corporate financing

The critical feature of the activities of the long-term credit banks over the past decade has been their role as the lead commissioned banks for new corporate bond issues. As the lead commissioned banks, the long-term credit banks collect the interest and principal repayments, and forward them to the bond holders.

Since all bond issues are made with collateral, the long-term credit banks hold lieu over the collateral until the bond issue is redeemed. They also perform a vital function in determining the issue details. As a result, they are placed in a powerful position, being partly commercial banks in their provision of long-term loans to industry, and partly merchant banks in their role of negotiating issue details.

They have been loath to see their controls over the corporate bond market weakened and their attitude has been an important element in restraining the development of this market within Japan. They played a key role in limiting the relaxation of rules covering unsecured domestic bond issues in the early 1980s, and again in 1987, when controls over the issuance of corporate bonds were a target of criticism by the Securities Exchange Commission.

The long-term credit banks are likely to continue to be a conservative force, until they can either negotiate direct access to the securities industry, or Article 65 of the Securities Exchange Law is abolished, allowing both banks and securities houses to move into each other's field.

Industrial policy

In the post-war period, the long-term credit banks played a vital role in shaping and building Japan's industrial structure. With the big electricity utilities among the limited number of corporate groups that were permitted to issue domestic corporate bonds, IBJ in particular emerged as an independent source of advice on many of the details of Japan's power development programme – both the funding and overall forecasting.

Equally, in the establishment and structure of the steel industry, the shipping industry and the shipbuilding industry, the long-term credit banks played an important role not only in funding the necessary developments but also in undertaking independent research to encourage expansion and product development. They also played a part in making raw commodity forecasts on the inputs needed by large basic industries, such as the energy and steel sectors, and in financing some overseas developments needed for Japanese industry.

IBJ was the prime mover behind the merger of the Yahata Iron Works and Fuji

Iron and Steel to form Nippon Steel, the world's largest privately owned steel producer. The two companies had been one before their demerger by the occupation government in the immediate aftermath of World War II.

More recently, with the difficulties that have plagued the shipbuilding and shipping industries in the wake of the currency appreciation, IBJ has played an important mediation role in trying to streamline existing capacity, as well as in advising existing groups on possible extensions to their areas of activity, which may promise greater returns in the future. IBJ is also involved in large domestic developments, for example, the construction of Tokyo Disneyland.

In 1987, IBJ began playing a key, behind-the-scenes role in reorganising the shipbuilding and shipping industries, although at some cost. With the problems confronting the shipper Japan Lines, for example, IBJ was forced to write-off ¥22.6 billion and to extend new assistance of ¥39.7 billion.

In line with its close connections to the government, IBJ has also steadily, but

The Long-Term Credit Bank of Japan has been especially active by dealing in government bonds, in Samurai issues and in swaps.

quietly, stepped up its role as an adviser to the Chinese government and some of its key departments, utilising its accumulated knowledge and expertise in developing Japan's basic industry and infrastructure.

As lending to new sectors expands, all the long-term credit banks are faced with a reappraisal of their advances to many of Japan's long-established industries, especially shipbuilding and shipping, two industries that are finding it difficult to refocus on new ideas for expansion.

New areas have opened up for the long-term credit banks which promise further profit growth. Full dealing in government bonds is the most important, with the Long-Term Credit Bank in particular playing an active role in this market. With full dealing in government bonds, the long-term credit banks more than trebled their trading in 1986, compared with 1980, the Long-Term Credit Bank being easily the most active trader.

Offshore activities

In fiscal 1985, IBJ was the most active of any Japanese bank in lead managing and co-lead managing Euroyen bond issues in London, and its activity in overseas bond issues by non-Japanese and Japanese borrowers ranked second only to that of Nomura Securities.

The Long-Term Credit Bank has also increased in activity in offshore and domestic markets. In 1986, it was the commissioned bank in 17 out of 21 Samurai issues and lead or co-lead manager of 28 yen loans and 19 foreign currency loans.

Even with the existence of the 'three bureaux' agreement which excludes Japanese banks from competing for foreign currency issues by Japanese entities, the long-term credit banks have been particularly successful in expanding their international lending and securities activities. They complain at length about the 'three bureaux' agreement which, with their extensive links with Japanese industry, gives the securities houses a degree of activity in the offshore raisings by Japanese industry that they could not otherwise command.

Swaps is another area that the long-term credit banks have targeted for expansion. The two largest, IBJ and the Long-Term Credit Bank, have been especially successful, although the profit margins on these deals have dwindled since they first became popular in the mid-1980s. They have also become much more active in cross-border leasing, and in aviation leasing in particular.

Future developments

Given their historical role within Japan's banking system, the long-term credit banks are the nearest financial institutions within Japan to wholesale, or merchant, banks. In their moves offshore over the past decade, they have fitted easily into the deregulated environment of Europe. Also, they have been closely involved with the expansion of the Euroyen market since its liberalisation and the swap market as it has become better established.

Faced with a decline in demand for funds, and full access to bond dealing, they have a clear idea of their future direction, as they seek to evolve into wholesale banks, along the lines of those active in North America and Europe. Indicative of their future direction is the diversification strategy undertaken by IBJ in North America. Its first acquisition was a controlling interest (75.1 per cent) in J. Henry Schroder Bank and Trust Co, which was used as a vehicle to buy the US primary dealer Aubrey G. Lanston.

IBJ in particular has increased the pressure on MoF to allow some relaxation of Article 65 of the Securities Exchange Law. It took legal advice on the prospect of its UK securities subsidiary, IBJ International, opening up a branch office in Tokyo but kept these plans on hold after extensive unofficial discussions with MoF. Eventually a licence was granted for Aubrey G. Lanston to open a representative office in Tokyo, primarily for advising its Japanese clients on market developments for US Treasuries. This move represents the first meaningful crack in the wall between the banking and securities sectors in Japan.

The earlier move by Sumitomo Bank to open a representative office in Tokyo of its Swiss subsidiary, Banca del Gottardo, attracted some publicity, given this bank's extensive security dealings in that market.

Along with this, the long-term credit banks have also applied whatever pressure they could for foreign banks to be given access to the domestic securities market, since they foresaw any development here as aiding them in their campaign to move directly into securities.

There were also rumours that the Long-Term Credit Bank of Japan was seeking to purchase another US primary dealer, Greenwich Securities, in early 1987 but nothing happened. There was speculation that the US Federal Reserve had threatened to withdraw this company's dealer's licence if the acquisition went ahead, due to the feeling that Japanese institutions were building up too large a presence in the US primary market at a time when US institutions were effectively barred from a similar level of access to Japan's primary market in government bonds. There are some doubts about this, however, as Sanwa Bank was negotiating to buy control of another US primary dealer, BGK Securities, in mid-1987.

In moving towards wholesale banking, the big long-term credit trust banks are taking as their models some of the bigger US institutions such as Bankers Trust, as well as buying into areas for specific expertise. The Long-Term Credit Bank of Japan, for example, has acquired small equity stakes in two foreign entities, M&A specialist Peers and Co and aircraft leasing group GPA.

CHAPTER EIGHT

Trust banks

The changing emphasis of capital markets worldwide, combined with the difficult outlook for traditional lending, has pushed Japan's trust banks to the centre of its banking sector.

They have experienced the strongest growth of any part of the banking sector, with earnings of the largest eclipsing all but the leading city banks. Their exceptional growth has been predicated on the rising liquidity within Japan, with earnings rising in tandem with the strength of the stockmarket. Profit growth has been so impressive that there is little chance that other banks will be able to close the gap of earnings growth, unless there is a significant change in, or outright abolition of, Article 65 of the Securities Exchange Law.

The key change in the fortunes of the trust banks stemmed from the introduction of share trusts – tokkin and kingai – which have been very popular with both the industrial and the financial sector. The massive expansion of these trusts has underwritten the substantial rise in profits of the trust banks, with little sign of any short-term slowdown.

With the shift in capital markets, the trust banks now regard themselves more as fund managers than as trust banks. Along with the rapid growth of funds under their control held through these two main varieties of trust funds, the trust banks, together with the life insurance companies, have sole access to managing pension funds, one of the areas of strongest growth of Japan's financial system. The rapid ageing of Japan's population will ensure that this expansion will continue well into the 1990s.

History

The trust banks trace their origins to 1905, when the Secured Debenture Law was passed, which allowed banks to handle collateral securing corporate debentures on behalf of the owners of security. Subsequently, there was a rush of new groups established in this area, although legal controls were tightened in the early 1920s, when new legislation was passed, the Trust Law and the Trust Business Law. The industry went through a fundamental reorganisation at that time and trust banks closely affiliated with each of the big zaibatsu came into being.

Gradually, through mergers forced by the government, the number of trust banks was reduced to seven. In 1954, the Loan Trust Law was enacted, which laid down the areas of activity for the trust banks. Soon after, the Ministry of Finance (MoF) attempted to force a strict separation of commercial and trust banking. It was generally successful, although Daiwa Bank refused to comply, and it has emerged as the only city bank with a trust bank division.

The most recently formed trust bank is Chuo Trust Bank, which was established in 1962, taking over the trust bank activities of Tokai Bank and Dai-Ichi Trust Bank. In addition, Daiwa Bank has extensive trust bank activities, and there are two small regional institutions, the Bank of Okinawa and the Bank of the Ryukyus, which can carry out trust banking operations, although on a limited scale since their trust business is of a different nature and is basically money in trust.

The biggest of the trust banks are broadly affiliated with the main zaibatsu, as is the case with all other sections of the banking industry. The largest trust bank in terms of both assets and earnings is Mitsubishi Trust Bank, followed by

Sumitomo Trust, Mitsui Trust, Yasuda Trust, Toyo Trust, Chuo Trust, which went public in the latter part of 1987, and Nippon Trust. Their ranking in terms of assets also reflects their command over kingai and tokkin funds, except for Yasuda, which has been more successful in building up its presence in this sector, managing to outdistance Mitsui Trust.

Between them the trust banks control approximately 20 per cent of all funds of the banking system in Japan and they have been the only sector to show any growth over the past decade, rising from 14.6 per cent to 18.5 per cent by the end of 1985.

Fund raising

The bulk of their funds are raised through so-called loan trusts, which are used primarily by small investors for lodging term deposits with the trust banks, although earlier maturity is provided for. Loan trusts, together with money trusts, were instituted as a means of raising long-term funds necessary to fuel the industrial sector's demand for funds. In addition, the trust banks also accept large-size deposits, also a growing area of funding during the 1980s.

Although the trust banks were initially formed as vehicles for raising long-term funds to be lent to industry, with the city banks concentrating on short-term fund raising, they were established under general banking legislation. So they can raise funds through ordinary deposits although their limited branch network restricts them to raising large deposits. In other words, they can carry out all the functions of the city banks and have the added advantage of conducting trust banking activities.

The trust banks prefer to concentrate on lending the funds they raise to industry, although with the slowdown in the demand for new funds, it has become increasingly difficult for the trust banks to place all of the funds at their disposal. As a result, they have pushed further into lending to small and medium-sized companies, as do the city banks and insurance companies. The changing mix in demand for new funding led to a revision of the Loan Trust Law in 1971, giving the trust banks approval to lend to a broader range of industries as the demand for funds by the manufacturing sector slowed. With this change, they were allowed to lend to the wholesale industry, small and medium-sized manufacturers, property companies and the like. Lending to small and medium-sized companies now comprises one-quarter of total outstandings, with housing loans to individuals comprising a further 10 per cent.

At the same time as freeing their lending activities, the trust banks were also given approval to boost their international presence, including offshore lending, where they have been increasingly active.

Fund management

In line with the shift in Japan's financial system, the trust banks have geared themselves more towards fund management, away from their original role of providing long-term funds to industry. Even so, their total lending has continued to rise, as has their level of deposits.

The rapid increase of their trust funds has fuelled their earnings growth over the past five years and will continue to provide the strongest increase over the coming decade.

Until recently, the life insurance companies were able to point to a superior performance. But the recent heavy foreign exchange losses run up by the insurance companies with their big investment in overseas securities have reduced their overall returns on managed funds. The trust banks, in contrast, were told by MoF that they had to hedge their offshore investments, to offset the impact of any currency fluctuations. Although the cost of that hedging cut into their potential returns on funds under management, the subsequent currency shift resulted in their coming out ahead of the life insurance companies in returns on pension funds under their management.

Ranking of trust banks by deposits, March 1986

	¥m
Mitsubishi Trust	6,819,630
Sumitomo Trust	5,804,427
Mitsui Trust	3,800,601
Toyo Trust	3,145,610
Yasuda Trust	3,091,178
Chuo Trust	1,607,529
Nippon Trust	500,574

Source: MoF.

The foreign trust banks are fighting to take market share from Yasuda Trust (left) and the other leading Japanese trust banks.

Each of the big trust banks has established internal merchant bank divisions which form the core of their fund management activities. The importance of the trust banks also figured heavily in the creation of special Eurobond issues that were brought to market in the latter part of 1986, with a variety of issues aimed at evening out their tax liability.

The trust banks have also been successful in generating new products which promise to maintain their earnings growth in the future. For example, they introduced so-called property trusts, where a property owner signs over control of a property to a trust bank for a specified period for redevelopment. The trust bank carries out the full redevelopment, in consultation with the owner, financing, organising and supervising the construction of the proposed new building. In return, it manages the building for a set period after construction is completed, during which time it generates its return on the initial funds laid out

Mitsubishi Trust's headquarters. The trust banks control some 20% of all funds in Japan's banking system.

in financing the development. After the expiry of the agreed period, the ownership of the property reverts to the original owner. This scheme was devised, and introduced, as a means of promoting property redevelopment which often faces hurdles not encountered in western countries.

The potential of property trusts received an added fillip when it was decided that local governments and government authorities could also take advantage of these schemes to redevelop their property holdings.

Foreign trust banks

The most notable recent development in the structure of the trust banking sector was the decision to allow the entry of a limited number of foreign trust banks in 1985, after a battle of wills between MoF and the domestic trust banks, which were strongly hostile to any suggestion that foreign trust banks be given access to domestic industry.

The strengths of foreign institutions in fund management caused grave concern to the domestic banks and they reacted harshly to the prospect that foreign trust banks would enter Japan with the sole aim of trying to win away the most lucrative parts of the business. Initially MoF indicated that only eight foreign trust banks would be allowed to enter Japan. Eventually, after stiff last-minute pressure from Switzerland, the ministry yielded, and allowed nine in. Switzerland's influence was due to the fact that there had been a bitter dispute between the two governments earlier over the issue of reciprocity, which resulted in a large number of Japanese banks entering the Swiss market, even though there were only three Swiss banks large enough to enter Japan at that time.

After the trust banks' initial fears and criticism of foreign banks entering the cosy domestic trust bank industry, relations have improved considerably, largely because the Japanese banks realised the enormous difficulties that foreign trust banks would have in making much headway in the domestic market. Most of the foreign trust banks have been able to expand their presence and generate

After Mitsubishi Trust Bank, Sumitomo Trust (above) is the second most powerful of the trust banks.

revenues sufficient to cover their start-up and operating costs, thanks to the boom in tokkin and kingai investment trusts. Moving beyond that into pension fund management will take several years before any of the foreign banks has accumulated a sizeable portfolio.

Conclusion

The burst in earnings of the trust banks that began in earnest in fiscal 1984 has resulted in a startling transformation of the sector. In particular, it has enabled the unlisted Chuo Trust Bank to raise capital, and in the process improve its balance sheet significantly, as well as paving the way for it to go public.

The weakest is still Nippon Trust and Banking, which has been propped up by Mitsubishi Trust Bank for several years now. Its earnings have risen strongly, in line with the rest of the industry, although it still has a considerable way to go if it is to reach a position where it can survive independently.

The stagnant demand for new loan funds has kept pressure on this side of the trust banks' activities, with most of the sharp rise in earnings coming from fee-based income, combined with an improvement in margins, as interest rates have fallen. As a result, the trust banks are the largest lenders to the call market. Earnings growth has, for example, outstripped the expansion in funds available since 1983.

Along with funds management, the trust banks have pushed other fee-earning business. Proxy services to foreign companies listing in Tokyo, for example, is seen as not only providing a source of additional revenue growth, but also as a means of getting the foot in the door with foreign companies active in Japan, so that they can potentially write other business, such as pension funds management.

The trust banks are also actively pushing new forms of business such as property trusts. All have reported a sizeable increase in such ventures since they were first launched in 1985.

The long-term threat confronting the trust banks stems from any moves to liberalise pension fund management. All the fund management companies active in Japan consider that steps will be taken to broaden the number of groups that can manage pension funds, which are at present limited to the seven trust banks and the life insurance companies.

The size of pension funds under management has grown at a compound rate of 24 per cent during the 1980s, with similar strong growth anticipated well into the 1990s. Other fund management groups argue that it does not make sense to limit pension fund management to such a small group. There have been few positive indications from the government or MoF that it intends giving any ground on this issue, although there is a general optimism that change will come, even if slowly, in light of the overall shift in favour of deregulation. Liberalisation of pension fund management will result in loss of revenues and earnings for the trust banks.

Foreign trust banks have yet to make a significant impact. They manage only a very small proportion of the tokkin or kingai funds and, due to the organisation of pension fund management, it will take them several years before they will build up a sizeable portfolio of funds under management. The overall growth of the pensions area will restrict the impact their entry will have on the big Japanese trust banks.

CHAPTER NINE

Specialised banks

The Norinchukin Bank

The largest specialised bank in Japan is the Norinchukin Bank. It is owned by the agricultural cooperatives and acts as their central bank. Each agricultural cooperative (nokyo) is required to deposit over half of its surplus funds in the various agricultural federations (shinnoren) which are, in turn, required to deposit over half their surplus funds with the Norinchukin Bank.

Between them, the Norinchukin Bank and the agricultural cooperatives control 11 per cent of all deposits in Japan, a share that has been largely static in recent years.

While it collects deposits from the agricultural sector, lending to this sector accounts for a declining share of Norinchukin's activities. In 1982, lending to affiliated organisations (agricultural and fishery groups, and so on) made up 27.6 per cent of total advances, with the balance lent to the manufacturing and services sectors. By 1986, lending to affiliated organisations had declined to 24 per cent, while lending to the manufacturing and other sectors had risen to 76 per cent.

By the end of fiscal 1986, Norinchukin's total assets stood at ¥24.75 trillion, ranking it as one of the largest financial institutions in Japan.

The bank has played a key role in taking up government bonds, and it forms an important part of the underwriting syndicate. By the end of fiscal 1986, total securities holdings reached ¥10.36 trillion, up from ¥5.84 trillion in 1982, with over half of that held in national bonds. Foreign securities now form a rising part of the bank's portfolio, making up over 15 per cent of total securities holdings by the end of fiscal 1986, compared with less than 6 per cent four years earlier.

Source of funds

The steady growth in the bank's assets reflects the rising affluence of Japan's agricultural sector, which is buoyed by extensive, and generous, government subsidies. Equally, Norinchukin Bank is caught up in the conservatism of this sector and, while it boasts a Triple A rating from overseas credit agencies, it has been cautious in developing its offshore interests.

However, it has now established a branch in New York, relying heavily on the support of the Bank of Tokyo, which seconded a number of its staff to Norinchukin to help with the move. In return, Norinchukin Bank supplies a considerable volume of short-term funds directly to the Bank of Tokyo, bypassing the official short-term money market, despite the fact that this is usually prohibited by the Bank of Japan, which insists that all short-term funds be provided through the money market.

Foreign banks have tried to get access to some of the Norinchukin Bank's cash hoard, but they have been forced to borrow it through the short-term money market, which involves brokerage fees, as well as running the gambit of the implicit credit controls levied by the Bank of Japan over the short-term money market brokers.

Along with the Bank of Tokyo and the long-term credit banks, Norinchukin Bank is allowed to raise funds through bank debentures, although given its cash-rich status, it raises only a minor volume of funds in this manner.

By the end of fiscal 1986, Norinchukin Bank debentures stood at 15.9 per cent of total liabilities, a level which has been unchanged for some time. The bank can issue either one-year discount debentures, known as 'warino', or five-year interest-bearing debentures, 'ritsuno'. Of the debentures on issue, half are one-year debentures and half five-year debentures. The bank is a modest issuer of debentures, but may become more active in the issuing market if its international activities continue to expand.

In addition to slowly moving to broaden its international activities – the New York office was opened only in 1984 – the bank has also become much more active in foreign exchange markets. By the end of fiscal 1985, total foreign exchange trading reached US$49.9 billion, almost double the fiscal 1984 level of US$26.77 billion.

The entire agricultural cooperative sector is likely to undergo a slow, but nonetheless dramatic reorganisation over the coming decade, which will force the Norinchukin Bank to focus on its future strategy. The national government has signalled that it intends to reduce some of the privileges of the agricultural sector, primarily through its decision to cut the domestic price support for rice from fiscal 1987 – the first step in what is likely to be a major reduction of the subsidies provided to the agricultural sector. The extensive protection afforded to Japan's agricultural sector has been a source of constant friction with foreign countries.

Norinchukin Bank's decision to formalise its international activities, even if it means tapping the expertise of other domestic institutions, is indicative of its future direction.

The Export-Import Bank of Japan

The Export-Import Bank of Japan plays the dominant role in financing exports, particularly of large items of plant and equipment, and overseas projects of interest to Japan. However, the decline of many of Japan's large, long-established manufacturing industries has altered the bank's financing role.

Annual credit commitments have stagnated at between ¥900 billion and ¥1,000 billion since the early 1980s, although there has been a recent increase after a decline in the mid-1980s. But export financing still forms the bulk of the outstanding finance provided by the bank.

The slowdown in exports has meant that the Export-Import Bank has shifted its emphasis to providing direct overseas loans, in the form of both government loans and buyers' credits, and also to providing import credits in line with the government's policy of boosting import levels. Overseas investment credits have also expanded sharply over the past five years.

There has also been a shift in credit commitments by area, with Latin America making up a much larger portion of total commitments, although typically the size of each new commitment is comparatively small. However, the biggest shift in exposure since the early 1980s has been to China, where the steady economic liberalisation led to a sharp burst of trading activity with Japan. Investment funding by the Export-Import Bank, a government agency, has made up for some of the poor response by Japan's industrial sector to consistent pressure to boost investment levels in China, a recurring political issue between the two countries.

The most important change in the activities of the Export-Import Bank over the past five years has been the decision to extend and expand import credits in line with the government's attempts to be seen to be actively supporting a higher level of imports. As a result, import credits are now the second largest form of financing provided by the bank, accounting for 25 per cent of all financing undertaken in fiscal 1986, involving 97 cases.

The largest form of financing is now untied direct overseas loans, primarily to finance resource developments.

Funding

The Export-Import Bank derives most of its funding from the Fiscal Investment Loan Programme (FILP) operated by the Trust Fund Bureau of the Ministry of

Finance (MoF). In addition, the bank occasionally borrows through international markets directly.

With its foreign currency denominated bond and note issues, it usually taps either the Swiss franc market or the Eurodollar market.

The key to the cheap funding provided by the bank stems from its access to funds available through FILP. If MoF agrees to further financial deregulation, this will entail moves to free deposit rates on small savings, which form the bulk of the funding source for FILP. Consequently, further financial deregulation would make it much more difficult for the Export-Import Bank to maintain the present level of cheap funding.

Lending

The rise of the yen during fiscal 1985, and the subsequent slowdown in export volumes, resulted in export credits provided by the bank being almost halved, dropping to ¥228.7 billion. This decline was offset by a large boost to direct overseas loans, which more than doubled to ¥243 billion, with a growing proportion of untied loans, principally to China.

Of equal significance was the decision to begin providing import credits. The first import credits for manufactured goods were provided in late 1983 but were an insignificant portion of the bank's portfolio until fiscal 1985, when there was a large increase. Import credits have been used to finance aircraft purchases, and also some imports of telecommunications equipment. During fiscal 1986, import credits exceeded export credits for the first time, accounting for 25 per cent of all credit commitments, with further growth underway.

There has been a sizeable increase in Japan's exposure to South East Asia, as well as a continued high level of involvement with the Chinese government, with funding for both infrastructure developments and energy project developments.

During the first half of the 1980s, the bank provided a large portion of its credit commitments to Latin America, although this weighting has shifted as more attention has been paid to China and the US. There has also been a decline in the importance of Africa but Europe remains prominent in the bank's activities.

The most important area of financing now is untied direct loans, which formed a negligible part of the bank's activities in the first half of the 1980s. This form of financing will continue to expand as the Export-Import Bank continues to recycle Japan's trade surplus through cheap loans extended by the bank.

Part of the large growth that occured in fiscal 1986 is due to the involvement of the bank in its first project financing, an LNG gas project being developed in Australia solely for gas sales in Japan. The project financing followed an amendment to the legislation covering the Export-Import Bank's activities in 1984, which permitted it to provide import financing directly to foreign companies.

Terms and conditions

Similar to the criticism levelled increasingly by South East Asian countries over government-to-government yen-based development funding extended previously, a number of countries that have received finance from the Export-Import Bank have complained about issue terms and conditions, especially following the revaluation of the yen.

The problems are similar to those encountered by borrowers through the Samurai bond market, who have moved in rising numbers to opt for early redemption. The principal difficulties were encountered with China, although there has been criticism by other countries including Indonesia. The Export Import Bank of Japan provided two jumbo loans to the Chinese government, principally to finance domestic energy project developments.

Because of the rapid fall of interest rates in Japan during 1986 and the appreciation of the yen, the Chinese government brought strong pressure to bear on the bank for a renegotiation of the terms and conditions of the loans. The bank resisted this pressure at first: it was extremely wary of being seen to give in to pressure, which would result in a rash of similar moves by countries that had obtained funding through the bank.

Conceding that little could be done about the repayment of principal, the Chinese government sought a revision of the interest rates ruling on the loans. Lengthy negotiations in the later part of 1986 resolved the issue, up to a point, with a reduction of the interest rates to a level much closer to Japan's long-term prime rate.

The bank is therefore likely to step up the provision of foreign currency loans, first undertaken in 1986, especially those denominated in US dollars. When the bank first began to tap offshore capital markets, it moved first into the Swiss market, attracted by the low coupons and the currency stability between the Swiss franc and the Japanese yen. More recently it has become a borrower of US dollars, with regular raisings since 1984, usually in June of each year. It has signalled that it will continue to tap US dollar markets with the decision in early 1987 to adopt shelf registration for future bond raisings.

The Japan Development Bank

The biggest of the Japanese government's financial institutions, the Japan Development Bank, has steadily broadened its operating base over the past decade and its earnings are now on a par with some of the richer city banks. Acting as a conduit of government policy, the bank has steadily boosted its fund raisings through international capital markets. A revision of its operating charter has also given it a new lease of life.

Its primary role is to lend, in accordance with government policy, to develop Japan's infrastructure. The initial funding for the establishment of the bank came from the US government, and subsequently, during the 1950s, the bank also obtained additional funds from the World Bank, all of which have now been repaid.

The basic policy of the bank is to co-finance projects in cooperation with Japanese and foreign banks.

Funding

The biggest change in the bank's funding operations over the past five years has been the steady rise in borrowings through offshore markets, in order to take some of the strain off the government's budget. The Japan Development Bank, like the Japan Export-Import Bank, sources most of its new funding from FILP, the internal bank of MoF. Five years ago the government provided over 85 per cent of the bank's new funding but this has steadily fallen as the Japan Development Bank has gradually boosted the volume of funds it has raised through offshore markets. By fiscal 1986, the Japan Development Bank had raised 22 per cent of its new funding needs offshore, with 32 public offerings and six private placements, raising a total of ¥538.1 billion (US$2.98 billion). The steady increase in offshore fund raisings has been coupled with a continuing reduction in new funds raised from the government.

In fact the dominant source of funds for the Japan Development Bank is loan repayments. In fiscal 1985, for example, total funding of the bank was ¥1.1 trillion. Of this, ¥803.9 billion came from loan repayments, with net borrowings accounting for ¥317.9 billion.

Lending

As a direct instrument of government policy, lending by the Japan Development Bank falls within the broad parameters of government planning.

Following the oil price rises of the 1970s, lending for energy development projects has become the priority for the bank. During the 1980s, 40 per cent of new lending has been allocated for energy projects, primarily for the development of Japan's nuclear programme, and also for energy diversification.

By the end of fiscal 1985, resources and energy-related projects accounted for 43.2 per cent of all loans outstanding. Urban development, basically lending to private railway networks in Japan and also some redevelopment in the major cities, was the second most active area, making up an additional 17.6 per cent of all advances. Shipping, transport and regional development projects followed, making up a further 9.4 per cent.

The mix of the bank's lending has changed substantially over the past two decades. At the end of the 1960s, for example, shipping was the biggest area of lending, accounting for 35 per cent of total advances. Electricity development was second, making up a further 21.3 per cent. The balance of lending was to industry.

Now, the only specific industrial lending is for the development of new technology, which the bank has emphasised over the past five years. The main area of attention for the bank is lending for information processing technologies, especially the development of semiconductor production and software development.

Funds are lent at the long-term prime rate, which makes them attractive for companies that cannot access long-term funding easily, and are typically for between one and 10 years, although the bank can lend for as long as 30 years.

Operations

The biggest change in the bank's operations in recent years was due to the revision of its charter when The Japan Development Bank Law was amended in mid-1985, the first revision in 13 years. The main areas of change involved giving the bank far more flexibility in investing in equity and allowing much greater financing of personnel and other costs related to boosting Japan's research and development effort. This latter point has attracted some attention, since it exemplifies the direct role the Japanese government plays, at all levels of policy, in fostering Japan's technological success.

The bank has also stepped up its lending to foreign firms active in Japan. Since its financing is provided at the long-term prime rate, it is a sought-after source of funds. The amount advanced in line with this programme is so far limited, having reached ¥66.99 billion. It will always be a minor part of the bank's portfolio, but having this in its array of lending programmes makes it easier to deflect foreign criticism about the bank's role.

The bank also provides loan guarantees to Japanese companies for overseas purchases, guaranteeing only the foreign currency obligations of Japanese companies, including loans from foreign banks and credits from foreign suppliers. Its first foreign credits were aircraft purchases, and this remains the principal area of funding that is guaranteed. The other area is overseas equipment purchased by domestic electricity utilities.

The bank charges between 0.2 and 0.3 per cent annually on the outstanding principal of the credit guarantees. This service is used only erratically by Japanese corporations, but it is a useful form of additional income for the bank, as it trades off its government guarantee. At the end of fiscal 1985, total guarantees oustanding were ¥137.24 billion, with approximately 70 per cent of this for aircraft purchases and the balance for electricity utilities.

Small business financing

Concessional financing for small businesses is provided through the Shoko Chukin Bank and the Small Business Finance Corporation (SBFC). The Shoko Chukin Bank has outstanding loans of ¥8.28 trillion and SBFC ¥5.2 trillion.

While both organisations were established to fund small businesses, they are fundamentally different: one is a bank, the other a specialised financial organisation. Finance for small businesses is also a specific part of the activities of the sogo (mutual) banks (see Chapter 10).

With financial institutions concentrating on providing funds for the bigger corporations, smaller groups have historically found it much more difficult to raise funds. Many of these difficulties have been overcome with the maturing of the economy.

The Shoko Chukin Bank

The Shoko Chukin Bank was established in 1936, following the passing of special legislation. The new organisation was to provide specialised assistance to small businesses by providing finance to the nationwide organisation of cooperatives, to help avoid the large-scale bankruptcies that occurred during the great depression. The government, through MoF and the Ministry of International Trade and Industry, directly controls the operations of the bank, holding 69 per cent of the capital, and has absolute command over its board composition.

The bank accepts deposits from its affiliated organisations and specified public bodies, as well as from non-profit making organisations. It also raises a considerable proportion of its funding requirements through bond issues.

The bank was originally established under a 50-year charter which expired in 1986. The Shoko Chukin Bank Law passed in 1986 gave permanency to the bank's operations.

Like most of the bigger banks in Japan, the Shoko Chukin Bank has been active in stepping up its foreign exchange dealing capabilities, and has also moved into government bond trading. Total foreign exchange dealing has risen by an annual rate of 50 per cent in recent years. In fiscal 1986, it reached US$19.67 billion, more than double the US$8.3 billion level in fiscal 1984.

The primary aim of the bank's activities is the provision of finance to member cooperatives and small companies. For much of the 1980s lending expanded at an annual rate of around eight per cent.

There has also been a steady increase in the volume of short-term financing provided, which rose to 46 per cent of loans outstanding by the end of fiscal 1986, with long-term funding static at around 33 per cent of outstandings. Manufacturing accounts for the bulk of lending.

Most of the bank's funds are raised through debenture issues. It is one of the few banking institutions permitted to do so and it raised ¥7.18 billion in fiscal 1986. Typically around 7 per cent of these debentures are placed with the government, with the balance sold to the public. Two types of debentures are issued – 'warisho', or one-year discount debentures, and 'rissho', or five-year interest-bearing coupon debentures.

The revision of the Shoko Chukin Bank Law in 1986 gave the bank approval to make loans to the overseas subsidiaries of existing customers, and to form joint ventures with foreign partners, as well as to take part in loan syndications to overseas financial institutions. As part of this, the bank has started to participate in the swap markets.

The Small Business Finance Corporation of Japan

Established in 1953, SBFC is an independent government institution, established specifically to fund the operations of smaller corporations. Initially its lending was through private financial institutions which served as its agent but this gradually changed, and SBFC began to lend directly through its own office network.

The organisation broadly extends two forms of loan – general purpose loans and special purpose loans. General purpose loans are for the usual business development programmes such as funding working capital increases and general investment. This lending accounts for the bulk of SBFC's activities. In fiscal 1986, general purpose lending reached ¥1,847.4 billion.

Special purpose loans were just ¥260.3 billion. Even so, special purpose lending can play an important role in helping to achieve the national objectives. For example, in the after-shock of the two oil price rises of the 1970s, the government embarked on aggressive policies to both cut energy requirements and diversify energy sources. As part of this, concessional loans were provided to small companies for the purposes of reducing energy consumpton. These loans, for a 15-year term, carried a concessional interest rate of 6.3 per cent.

Most of the corporation's funding is provided either directly or indirectly by the government. In fiscal 1986, SBFC borrowed ¥1.4 billion directly from the government and had a further ¥2 billion capital subscription from the government; small business bond issues raised another ¥174 billion and loan repayments ¥505 billion. But, along with most other government and semi-government institutions, SBFC is gradually beginning to diversify its funding sources. In late 1985 it made a small Sfr100 million bond issue.

The corporation lends at a small margin of 0.35 per cent above the interest rate for its borrowings from the government, this rate moves in line with the long-term prime rate.

CHAPTER TEN

Regional banks

Japan's regional banks include some of the most innovative groups in the country, as well as some of the sleepiest. The largest, the Bank of Yokohama, is the same size as the smallest of the city banks, Hokkaido Takushoku Bank. At the end of March 1987, the Hokkaido Takushoku Bank had total assets of ¥9.03 trillion while the Bank of Yokohama had total assets of ¥9.06 trillion – surpassing its city bank rival for the first time.

This trend can only continue, as the larger of the regional banks, especially those in regions neighbouring Tokyo, such as Chiba Bank, Bank of Yokohama and others, are pulled along by the stronger growth of the Tokyo region when compared with all other parts of Japan, especially the northern island of Hokkaido, which is the home base of the Hokkaido Takushoku Bank.

There are 64 regional banks in Japan, compared with just 13 city banks (including the Bank of Tokyo), a figure that has remained static for several years. Regional banks offer basically the same range of services as the city banks, although their regional deposit base puts them at a disadvantage when compared with their big city cousins. As regional banks, their geographic spread of operations is heavily proscribed by the Ministry of Finance (MoF) and they were not allowed to establish offshore branches until comparatively recently.

Limited largely to individual savings deposits, most of the larger regional banks have gradually increased the sophistication of their operations over the past decade. They are now, for example, the second largest issuers of CDs after the city banks, accounting for 12 per cent of all notes on issue, although their usage of this facility has declined since the mid-1980s.

A number have instituted aggressive policies aimed at consolidating their position among savers in their region. Some have teamed up with the bigger security houses to offer cashing facilities for securities holdings or for cashing investments in medium-term government bond funds or investment trusts. The more active have formulated business plans aimed at boosting their share of local savings, in an attempt to consolidate existing allegiances and prepare for future expansion ahead of further deregulation of savings deposits.

Some, such as the Bank of Fukuoka, have forged links with financial groups in China as a means of expanding future business. Musashino Bank, which is based near Tokyo, has developed Swiss franc time deposits and gold investment accounts as a means of encouraging an increase in deposits.

The links between many of these banks and either MoF or the Bank of Japan are strong. For example, Bank of Japan officials have retired to senior positions with Chiba Bank, and both the President and the Chairman of the Hokkaido Bank are ex-MoF officials.

Developing regional industry

Given their strong regional orientation, the regional banks are usually expected to play a prominent role in developing industry in their region. For some regional banks located in the more remote parts of Japan this is all but impossible. Others have aggressively fostered schemes, in conjunction with the local or regional government, to attract new start-up businesses, or medium-sized and small companies seeking to expand.

Success in expanding the industrial base of the region adds further to the growth potential of the regional bank involved. Indicative of some of the moves

Opposite above: Hokkaido Island. Its resident bank, Hokkaido Takushoko Bank, is the smallest city bank. Opposite below: Japan's commercial life still leaves time for the maintaining of tradition.

that have been undertaken, the Hyakugo Bank set up a research institute in conjunction with the Nomura Research Institute and the Mitsubishi Research Institute, two of the top research groups in Japan, with the aim of fostering local industries as well as trying to attract industries from other areas.

The Bank of Kyoto has an especially strong reputation for its work in aiding venture capital businesses as part of the overall policy of the local government of encouraging such businesses to move to the area.

Many regional banks have close links with the bigger city banks. For example, Tokyo Tomin Bank is closely associated with IBJ, and Chiba Kogyo Bank has close links with Fuji Bank, Musashino Bank with Daiwa Bank and the Bank of Osaka with Sumitomo Bank, which is headquartered in Osaka.

At the heart of the operations of all regional banks is the role they play as banker to the local government and its various instrumentalities, which typically gives them a solid business base from which to expand. Building up their region's industrial base naturally fosters additional growth, as well as offering special incentives to local residents. With the regional banks' franchise on local government financing, city banks find it all but impossible to make serious inroads into most local areas. Regional loyalties run deep and the city banks would find it difficult to justify the cost of operating an extensive nationwide network, quite apart from the fact that MoF tightly controls the number of branches banks can operate.

Nonetheless, most regional banks are limited to growing in tandem with growth in their region, making it difficult for many to expand at a rate that will enable them to avoid difficulties, unless there are extensive mergers.

Offshore presence

To capitalise on new areas for growth, as well as to offset the slowdown of new opportunities in their region, many have moved to boost their offshore presence – usually in London, New York and Hong Kong. However, it has been much harder for the regional banks to move offshore than for the city banks, since regional banks have had a ceiling for foreign currency loans of five per cent of capital, compared with 14 times capital for the city banks.

With their smaller capital bases, and the natural difficulty they face in building up deposits overseas, particularly US dollar-denominated deposits, a number of regional banks have opted for developing their business links with various financial groups in China, and other foreign specialised financial institutions.

In line with the progressive expansion of their offshore branches, there has been a significant increase in their foreign currency deposits, which were negligible until the mid-1980s. In 1982 they stood at just ¥2.07 trillion, rising to ¥6.5 trillion by the end of 1986.

With much lower levels of wholesale banking activities than the city banks, the regional banks are faced with a higher cost structure, which they are gradually seeking to reduce. At the same time, they have a slightly fatter profit ratio, which gives them more room to manoeuvre. At the end of 1986, for example, the cost ratio of the regional banks stood at 1.96 per cent, showing a steady reduction. This compared with just 1.12 per cent for the city banks. At the same time, the regional banks' profit margin was 0.21 per cent, compared with 0.15 per cent for the city banks.

Like the city banks, the regional banks also play an important role in financing government debt, taking up a total of 14.6 per cent of bonds offered through the underwriting syndicate, the second largest portion after the city banks' share of 30.7 per cent. And, like the city banks, the regional banks have been given approval to begin trading in government bonds. Starting in 1984, they were cautious traders at first but it is estimated that bond dealing accounted for 7.8 per cent of earnings in 1986, with their offshore operations accounting for just 2.8 per cent – a share that will be difficult to increase substantially due to their smaller capital base and their rather late move into the international arena.

10 largest regional banks ranked by deposits, July 1987

	¥bn
Bank of Yokohama	5,415.0
Chiba Bank	3,675.5
Hokuriku Bank	3,624.5
Joyo Bank	3,613.9
Shizuoka Bank	3,545.3
Ashikaga Bank	3,348.6
Bank of Fukuoka	3,013.9
Hiroshima Bank	2,956.8
Hachijuni Bank	2,856.6
Gunma Bank	2,691.0

Lending

Regional banks account for 21.7 per cent of all lending to small business, the second largest of any of the bank sectors after the city banks, which lend 27.7 per cent of all advances. The regional banks' share has been broadly static for several years, although it has shown a slight decline since the end of the war. Typically, 80 per cent of their funding is from term deposits of individuals, giving them a much stabler funding base than the city banks.

Lending by regional banks has grown in line with the rest of the industry, although their share has remained static in recent years at 11.7 per cent of the total. They, too, have lost some ground in their overall share of deposits due to the incursions of the Post Office savings system. Regional banks accounted for 10.7 per cent of total deposits in the financial system at the end of 1986, down from 11.3 per cent a year earlier.

One yardstick for determining the prospects, or the management sophistication, of the regional banks is to assess the volume of funds obtained from CDs. For many of the smaller, and weaker, regional banks, time deposits and ordinary deposits account for well over 80 per cent of their funds on hand, with funds raised through CDs playing a negligible role. For the larger, more aggressive, regional banks such as the Bank of Yokohama and Chiba Bank, CDs may make up around 15 per cent of deposits on hand. The higher reliance on CDs by the larger regional banks also points to the much stronger demand for funds they enjoy, compared with some of the banks in more remote regions. Most of the regional banks have stressed increasingly their consumer banking and credit card services, aimed at capitalising on one of the few areas of growth in the banking sector. By shifting further into consumer lending, they are cutting into the ranks of the smaller community banks and savings associations, which has resulted in steady merger activity in this area. Among regional banks, mergers have been few, the last most notable being in 1984, when two smaller financial institutions merged to form the Nishi-Nippon Bank, which was promoted to regional bank status in the process.

Sogo banks

Established under different legislation, the sogo (mutual) banks form mirror images, although necessarily on a smaller scale, of the regional banks. Established under the Sogo Bank Law of 1951, they are specifically limited to lending to medium-sized and small companies, originally companies capitalised at less than ¥200 million, although this has since been raised to ¥400 million.

Similar to the regional banks, the largest of which have surpassed the smaller of the city banks, the biggest of the sogo banks rank well up in the list of Japan's financial institutions. The Tokyo Sogo Bank, with total assets of ¥5.9 trillion, is ranked as the 32nd largest bank in Japan in terms of funds available, exceeding the smallest of the long-term credit banks, the Nippon Credit Bank. The Hyogo Sogo Bank, with funds available of ¥2.72 trillion, is ranked number 34. The two largest sogo banks rank well ahead of the rest. The third largest, the Kinki Sogo Bank, has funds available of only ¥1.52 trillion.

Based strongly in their own geographic region, the sogo banks are usually the main savings association of a particular area. But with their much narrower capital bases, and limits on their lending to small and medium-sized business, the sogo banks, along with the community banks and credit associations, are perhaps the section of the financial system most exposed to interest rate deregulation. Over the past 20 years there has been little overall change in the composition of their balance sheets, with 81 per cent of their liabilities stemming from simple deposits, and 67 to 69 per cent of their assets being loans. There has been a steady increase in their securities holdings, which stood at 13.7 per cent of total assets at the end of 1985, up from just 7 per cent in the mid-1960s.

The more active of the mutual banks have significantly boosted the volume of funds raised through CDs. The Hyogo Sogo Bank, for example, sources over 20

10 largest sogo banks ranked by deposits, July 1987

	¥bn
Hyogo Sogo Bank	2,584.4
Tokyo Sogo Bank	2,085.5
Fukuoka Sogo Bank	1,536.5
Kinki Sogo Bank	1,461.7
Nagoya Sogo Bank	1,458.7
Kofuku Sogo Bank	1,347.6
Fukutoku Sogo Bank	1,197.0
Chuo Sogo Bank	1.163.2
Hiroshima Sogo Bank	1,118.4
Chiba Sogo Bank	1,099.2

per cent of its funds through CDs.

The sogo banks are running into much stiffer competition from all the other major sections of the banking and finance industry which have targeted this market sector for growth, since it carries much fatter margins.

The share of deposits held by the sogo banks has declined to 4.4 per cent by the end of 1986, down from 4.7 per cent a year earlier, and they account for 4.8 per cent of all advances, down from 5 per cent. Like the regional banks, the more aggressive of the sogo banks have worked hard to implement new programmes aimed at consolidating their position within their region, by developing special savings policies or inducements for individual savers to remain loyal.

The sogo banks have the advantage of existing business links with medium-sized and small groups in their area. But with the greater research capacity and financing muscle and techniques of the larger institutions, the sogo banks will find it increasingly difficult. In the mid-1960s, they accounted for one fifth of all lending to these smaller companies; by 1985 this had fallen to 14.5 per cent due to mounting competition among lenders. With the difficulty of expanding their lending, many have opted to boost their level of housing loans, along with consumer lending, and to expand their credit card activities. Many of the sogo banks have affiliations with the bigger city banks, which give them access to expertise and personnel transfers. By shifting further into consumer lending, they are cutting into the ranks of the smaller community banks and savings associations, which has resulted in steady merger activity in this area.

Indicative of the greater exposure of the sogo banks to deregulation, the two biggest banking crises of the past decade have involved sogo banks; first the extensive run on Taiko Sogo Bank in 1978 which resulted in emergency action by the authorities to prevent its failure, and then the near collapse of the Heiwa Sogo Bank in 1986, staved off thanks to a merger with Sumitomo Bank. Moral pressure for mergers has been markedly unsuccessful to date although, if the Bank of Japan and MoF stepped up their efforts, moves could be effected quickly.

Credit associations and credit cooperatives

The credit associations and co-operatives are, like the regional banks and sogo banks, based on their own defined region, with a limited deposit base. They are also limited to lending to smaller businesses and to members.

The credit associations also have their own central organisation: the Zenshinren Bank which, while one of the largest banking organisations in Japan, has a restricted role (see Chapter 9). The total volume of funds held by the credit associations – sometimes called community 'shinkin' banks – is roughly double that of the labour savings associations. Both groups have gradually expanded their volume of funds on deposit over the past decade, with the labour associations growing much faster than the community banks, although from a much smaller base. However, both groups are extremely exposed to interest rate deregulation and to the more demanding needs of depositors as they seek out ever higher returns.

Locked into a difficult position in the banking system, the combined power of the community banks is deceiving. Total assets are ¥12.57 trillion, and total deposits with the Zenshinren Bank are ¥18.4 trillion, which puts it on a par with the Bank of Tokyo. The heavily regional orientation of the community banks, however, gives them a far less important role than these figures suggest.

The Zenshinren Bank borrows funds from member credit associations, and can, in turn, lend back to member groups, with a ceiling of 20 per cent of the member's capital and reserves. Total assets of the 455 credit associations have expanded moderately, reaching ¥637.7 trillion by the end of calendar 1986, up from ¥591.2 trillion a year earlier.

The number of credit associations and credit cooperatives has gradually declined over the past decade, and is likely to continue to fall in the future. Various schemes are being pursued to reduce the number of groups operating in each region still further in an attempt to improve their operating efficiency.

10 largest credit associations by deposits, July 1987

	¥bn
Jonan	1,453.67
Kyoto	1,237.37
Cifu	1,077.60
Kyoto Chuo	1,063.57
Okazaki	1,060.14
Amagasaki Naniwa	878.85
Hachiyo	868.41
Sugamo	642.89
Saitama-ken	591.19
Oji	588.94

CHAPTER ELEVEN

Corporate finance

The corporate sector was desperate for funds until the mid-1970s. But now its rising cash surplus is one of the prime reasons behind the extraordinary surge in Japan's capital flows since 1984. Funds are being raised to invest not in new capital equipment, but in new instruments as the corporate sector strives to boost overall returns.

Since 1985, earning profits from active fund management has been of increasing importance to overall corporate health and profitability. Previously, senior management's emphasis was on constantly upgrading equipment to keep abreast of state-of-the-art technology. With profits for many long-established manufacturers under pressure due to currency shifts, the aim now is to restrict new spending as far as possible in order to stem losses.

'Zaiteku', which loosely translates as financial engineering, has taken hold, with corporate treasurers keen to maximise financial returns. For many, this involves little more than moving deposits out of low-interest time deposits with the banks into money market certificates. The moralists argue that this trend will be ultimately self-defeating, since it will reduce interest in investing in new plant and equipment, thus jeopardising the viability of Japan's manufacturing base in the long run.

Senior managers reply that, unless they earn additional profits by aggressively managing surplus corporate cash, earnings will fall, threatening their survival.

The net effect is that fund management has taken hold, although there are very real concerns that senior management is not fully aware of the risks that have been incurred with some investments. The surplus cash position of the corporate sector is evidenced by the surge of funds in special investment trusts, or 'tokkin'.

The continuing liberalisation of domestic financial markets has resulted in a wider variety of instruments for corporate fund raising and asset management techniques which provide attractive rates of return. Even though new demand for funds for capital investment has been at a low level since the revaluation of the yen began in earnest from late 1985, new borrowings from banks and, increasingly, directly from capital markets have continued.

By early 1987, the short-term prime rate, which is charged by the big commercial banks to their important corporate clients, was cut to just 3.375 per cent, with some forecasters projecting that it will decline further. For many corporations, even cheaper funds could be raised offshore through convertible bond issues or issues with warrants attached, where new issue activity remained strong for much of 1987.

The low cost of new fund raisings, which usually involve an all-in cost of less than 5 per cent, increased the attraction of pursuing investment alternatives which offer better than 7 per cent, providing a real incentive to many corporate treasurers seeking to boost earnings from playing the various financial markets. With the alternative of cheap offshore fund raisings, around half of all raisings since 1986 were conducted outside Japan. There has been substantial diversification of currencies as well. Typically, most foreign currency raisings were denominated in US dollars, although with currency uncertainty, particularly from the mid-1980s, many corporations opted for other currencies. For example, Swiss francs became popular as corporate treasurers pursued either cheaper funding options or currencies and markets where reporting requirements were not as onerous.

Investment diversification increases

Along with this, there has been a swing of the corporate sector's surplus financial assets out of bank deposits into a wide variety of instruments, both domestic and international, with the larger companies increasingly trading on their blue chip reputation to raise funds cheaply in one market for reinvestment in another.

As part of this trend, the number of companies establishing offshore finance subsidiaries has risen continuously since 1985. Typically based in London, these affiliates trade a variety of instruments in different markets. Most companies that took this step are engaged in export markets and, by utilising an offshore finance affiliate, can increase their range of financing options, as well as match foreign exchange risks. The stimulus for much of the increasing emphasis on financial management since the mid-1980s was the easing of credit, after the tight monetary policy pursued in 1979 and 1980, when the authorities were concerned about the inflationary pressures stemming from the second oil price rise. Since then, monetary conditions in Japan have been easy.

The liquidity of the corporate sector increased markedly following the export boom of 1984–85, which resulted in record profits. The more active financing activities of the corporate sector also received a boost from the progressive financial deregulation policies following the yen/dollar committee accord reached in early 1984. More attractive domestic investment alternatives have encouraged more active fund management in order to boost returns. In turn, this has increased the volume of funds released by the corporate sector chasing higher rates of return.

In addition, the successive reductions of the official discount rates since the beginning of 1986 have significantly affected the easy monetary conditions and have increased the competition to maintain returns on funds invested.

Since the start of the period of easy monetary policy, there has been a steady increase in the level of corporate liquidity, when compared to nominal total demand, from a low of less than 35 per cent in 1980 to almost 50 per cent by 1986.

This growth has been in financial assets and land, with a slide in the proportion of real assets (plant and equipment, plus inventory, minus property) to total assets held by the corporate sector. By the end of 1985, for example, the proportion of real assets had declined to 56 per cent, down from 60.2 per cent five years earlier, with the increase split between the rise in land assets and financial assets.

In line with this, the growth of financial assets has increased faster than the growth of real assets in the corporate sector.

This increase in corporate assets has continued while overall borrowings of the corporate sector have increased, highlighting the drive to boost earnings from financial activities. In particular, there has been a large increase in non-yen-based investments, which account for almost one-third of the total, and also a big shift of funds from regulated interest rate deposits in favour of unregulated interest rates. Much of these funds have flowed into high-risk, high-return investments, which represents a significant shift of attitude on the part of Japan's corporate investors.

Zaiteku

Indicative of the changing perceptions to financial speculation within Japan was the boom in so-called 'zaiteku' as companies rushed to use their surplus cash to offset the downturn in traditional operations following the rise in the yen against the US dollar.

The word was first coined in 1985, following the rapid rise in financial speculation by most large companies. Trading companies in particular became increasingly active in making Eurobond issues in minor currencies, such as Australian or New Zealand dollars which carried the prospect of very high rates of return at that time.

Along with establishing affiliated finance companies offshore to engage in speculation, many of the trading companies also organised their foreign exchange dealing into more organised units, with the specific aim of profiting from hedging the company's foreign exchange exposure. For most of the ailing industrial groups, a growing portion of their profits from the mid-1980s came from zaiteku activities, with additional profits booked from the liquidation of long-held securities. Some, such as the fiercely independent small specialist trading company Hanwa Industries, harboured ambitions of boosting portfolio management services following its successful track record in financial speculation. But for many corporations, zaiteku involved little more than devoting a portion of their surplus funds to investing in so-called 'tokkin' share trusts, through which funds were mainly invested in equity and bond markets.

As a result, Chiyoda Chemical Engineering, for example, managed to offset the heavy pre-tax losses of around ¥10 billion from its traditional operations to generate small profits. Others, such as the big electrical group Hitachi, earned as much as 40 per cent of parent company pre-tax earnings from financial investments, thus helping earnings to overcome the worst effects of the currency shift. In Hitachi's case, the investments were of a far less risky nature than tokkin or bond futures speculation.

Zaiteku was viewed by many in the government and also by the conservative business elite with considerable disapproval since, it was argued, too much indulgence in financial speculation would result in a running down of manufacturing activities, presaging Japan's decline as an industrial power.

For much of 1986, profiting from zaiteku activities was comparatively straightforward. The yen was moving up against the US dollar and domestic and international interest rates were trending down, which also sent equity markets firmly higher. That scenario changed during 1987, however, when currency markets and domestic interest rates became much more unpredictable.

Companies that had profited from earlier trends found it more difficult to maintain their position in the tougher investment climate ruling during 1987. Short-term interest rates had begun to trend upwards, creating havoc in domestic bond markets and also clouding the short-term outlook for equity markets. Future trends of currency markets also became harder to predict. Nervousness increased greatly in the wake of enduring speculation about heavy losses.

Japanese corporate financing in capital markets, 1965–86 (all industries)

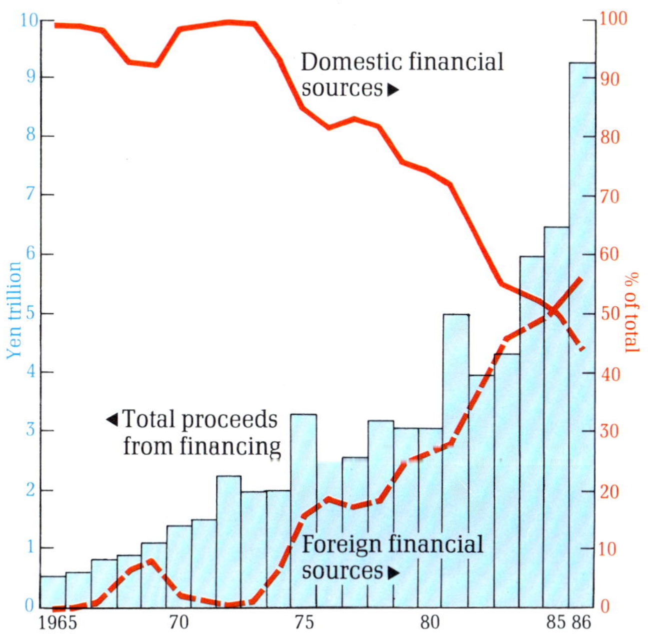

Source: Nikko Securities

Breakdown of assets held by the corporate sector, 1975–86

All enterprises in all industries

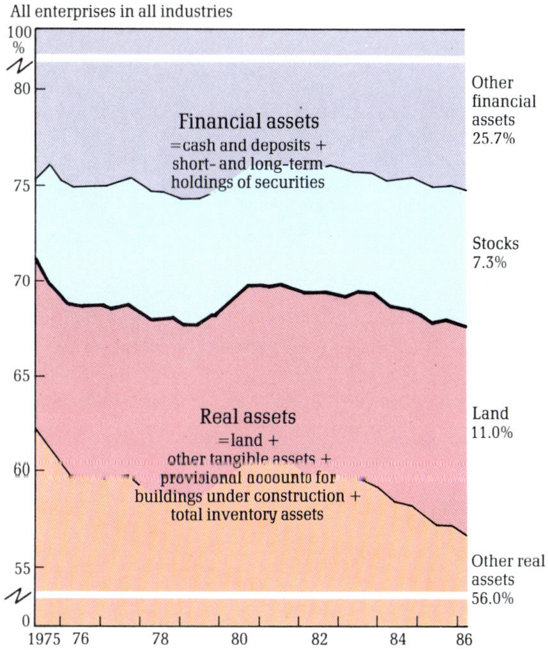

Source: 'Quarterly Financial Statement of Incorporated Enterprises', MoF

Some of the largest investors in tokkin and kingai were the biggest trading houses, with C. Itoh, for example, said to have invested ¥270 billion by the end of March 1987, and Mitsubishi Trading ¥281 billion, Sumitomo ¥248 billion and Marubeni ¥176 billion.

The near collapse of a small specialist chemical company, Tateho Chemical Industries in early September 1987 drew attention to the fact that zaiteku could result in losses as well as profits.

The company's pre-tax earnings from traditional activities fell heavily, declining to just ¥186 million in fiscal 1986, and income from zaiteku made up virtually all of the pre-tax profit of ¥2.65 billion posted in that year. At that time, the company was confident of generating larger profits from zaiteku, as earnings from its traditional chemical operations slowly recovered.

The turmoil in domestic bond markets during 1987 had a disastrous effect on the company, especially since it had been heavily involved in bond future markets. With the bearish bond market, the company incurred losses initially estimated at ¥20 billion. Total losses were later put at ¥28 billion against net assets at the time of just ¥16 billion.

Disclosure of the company's difficulties had impacted on domestic and international bond markets for a time. Like a large number of Japanese concerns, Tateho Chemical had raised funds through Eurodollar bond issues, and also some warrant issues. In the short term, these markets were severely affected. The collapse of the company was staved off thanks to support by its main bank, the Taiyo Kobe Bank, and others such as the Chugoku Bank.

As a result of the company's difficulties, the Ministry of Finance (MoF) stepped in to conduct investigations. The authorities were keen to limit the fall-out from this incident, and there were vigorous denials that more companies would also be posting heavy losses from ill-judged zaiteku investments. The attention of the authorities was particularly focused both on the role of the company's banks in providing it with funds, and also on its broker for the futures transactions, Nikko Securities.

There were also extensive reappraisals of companies that were active in financial speculation. Most broking houses circulated internal lists of the biggest zaiteku players, and there was heavy selling of many of these stocks. The difficulties of Tateho Chemical also resulted in heavy foreign selling of Japanese

Ratio of outstanding corporate sector liquidity to nominal total demand, 1970–85

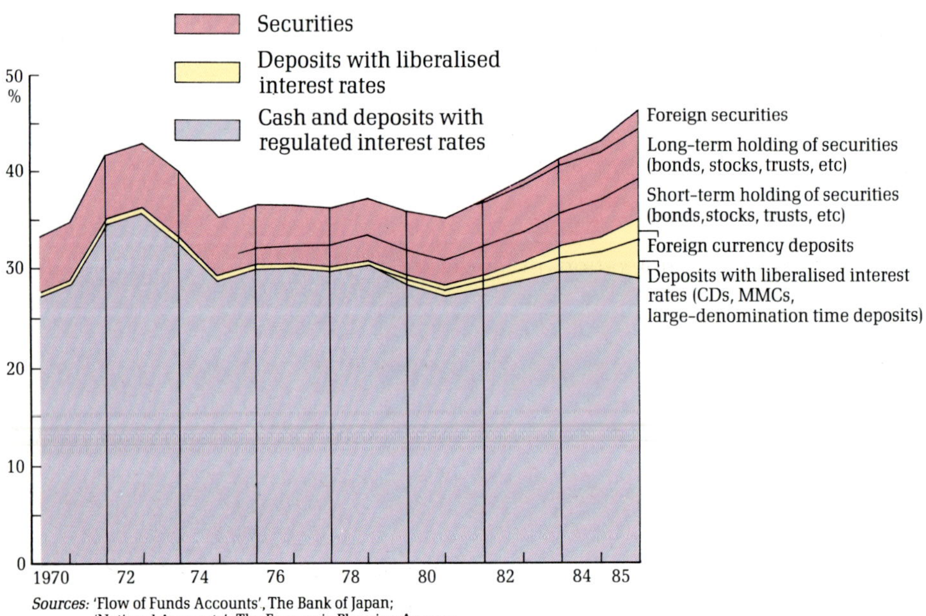

Sources: 'Flow of Funds Accounts', The Bank of Japan;
'National Accounts', The Economic Planning Agency;
'Quarterly Financial Statement of Incorporated Enterprises', MoF

equities for a time. But, even with the enormous publicity that was given to this incident in Japan, the shift towards zaiteku is largely irreversible. More adept financial investments has been an integral part of corporate management in the US and Europe for many years. It was slower to catch on in Japan, but it has become an important part of most large company's operations. However, more stringent internal controls will progressively be adopted by many companies to limit the extent of losses in the event of sharp market shifts.

Fuji Bank, one of the world's largest banks, sits at the centre of a web of inter-connecting shareholdings.

The move offshore

The proportion of funds raised through overseas markets more than doubled from just 8.1 per cent in 1980 to 17.5 per cent in 1985, with foreign bond issues accounting for half of the total funds raised offshore in that year. The drive to raise funds in offshore markets has been in response to easier issuing terms and, for many corporations, the need to offset the foreign exchange risk of foreign trade and earnings. This move offshore has also been fuelled by the growing sophistication of swap markets, particularly in Eurodollar markets.

Against the backdrop of the steady drift offshore for fund raising, there has been a progressive relaxation of domestic bond issuing conditions. In the convertible bond market there has been a reduction in the size of unsecured bond issues, together with a number of other changes, such as broadening the discretion of the underwriter in setting coupon rates, and a lengthening of the terms of issues to a 10-year period.

For straight domestic bonds there has been some relaxation of the restrictions on which groups can access the market, and an easing of conditions for totally unsecured bonds, together with an extension of maturity periods. With easier access to debt markets, the corporate sector has decreased its reliance on bank borrowings to less than one-third of funding requirements, with a corresponding rise in the issuance of securities, which now exceeds 30 per cent of financing needs.

Capital market growth

In line with the shift that has taken place in corporate financing, funds raised through capital markets have grown at an annual rate of over 40 per cent since 1983, reaching a record ¥9.3 trillion in fiscal 1986.

Included in this figure are convertible bonds floated domestically, which more than doubled the 1985 level to reach ¥3.47 trillion, and bonds with warrants issued offshore, which also more than doubled to ¥1.99 trillion.

During the 1970s, domestic capital markets fed the industrial sector's demand for funds; but during the 1980s, more relaxed fund raising conditions in international capital markets, combined with the fact that Japanese corporate names are now better known in international credit markets, have made offshore funding much more popular, comprising in value approximately half of all issues. As well as taking advantage of easier fund raising conditions, by 1985 the corporate sector had raised a larger volume of funds through capital markets in order to retire more expensive bank debt, thus minimising net interest costs as it locked into historically low interest rates.

Companies such as Nippon Yusen KK, for example, survived the downturn in Japan's shipping industry better than most of the domestic competitors by instituting centralised fund management operations as well as offshore financial affiliates to service both the parent company and its myriad subsidiaries – a significant break with previous operating methods, when simple service functions were the key to its activities.

A similar shift has occurred in a range of groups across the breadth of Japan's industry.

Decline in bank lending

More active fund management by the corporate sector, together with increased interest rate sensitivity, has had clear consequences for Japan's banks. Specifically, there has been a reduction in long-term loans extended by all parts of the banking sector, especially the city banks. From ¥8.22 trillion at the end of 1982, this had declined to ¥6.37 trillion by the end of 1986. During 1987, it fell month by month, reaching just ¥5.77 trillion by the end of May 1987. Mutual banks, credit associations and regional banks have all faced a similar decline in demand for funds.

Against this backdrop, the volume of funds raised through bonds with warrants through overseas markets stood at US$4 billion in May 1987, US$5 billion in June, and an expected US$7 billion in July – at a time when domestic investment has been stagnant, with the corporate sector taking maximum advantage of historically low interest rates to boost liquidity.

The switch in borrowings by the corporate sector comes at a time when its financial position is the healthiest ever, even with the impact of the currency shift which has cut export profitability. Record earnings in 1984 and 1985, following the export boom to the US, resulted in a significant improvement in the financial position of the corporate sector. Between 1980 and 1985, for example, the ratio of net interest burden to sales decreased from 1.67 per cent to 0.58 per cent. In that period, the recurring profit of the manufacturing sector grew by ¥830 billion, and net interest payments declined by ¥915.5 billion.

The ratio of net worth to total assets has risen consistently over the past decade, from less than 20 per cent in the first half of the 1970s to over 30 per cent by the mid-1980s. The decline in bank borrowings has been coupled with a substantial rise in direct borrowings through capital markets. Convertible bonds, which accounted for just 14 per cent of fund raisings by the corporate sector in 1975, totalled 43 per cent in fiscal 1986, with bonds with warrants reaching 23 per cent. The rise in borrowings through such issues occurred as straight bond issues declined, dropping from 56 per cent in 1985 to just 28 per cent in 1986. Similarly straight equity raisings have declined from 29 per cent in 1975 to just 7 per cent in 1986.

With the changing structure of borrowings by the corporate sector, the dependence on borrowed funds has fallen to 35 per cent, down from 47 per cent in the mid-70s.

The strong links between the banks and the industrial sector has meant that for some time it was difficult to reduce bank debt, but with the balance of power shifting for the first time markedly from the banks to the corporate borrowers, there has been a sizeable reduction in debt, which contributes significantly to the volume of liquidity. Much of the improvement in the debt burden of the corporate sector was due to not only the decline in net bank borrowings, but also the steady decline in interest rates. Thus, as soon as interest rates begin to turn upwards, there may be some reversal of the improvement that has occurred since 1985. This may be compounded by the investment policy pursued by the industrial sector, since much of the funds raised since the start of 1986 have, in turn, been reinvested in domestic equity markets which would be vulnerable to any rise in interest rates.

The changes in corporate financing since the mid-1980s have underscored the disparities between the large companies and the medium-sized and small ones. With their better known names, the big corporate borrowers have naturally been able to borrow funds at much more attractive rates than most others, and achieve a much greater improvement in their financial position in the process. For smaller companies, the net financial position has worsened, due to their greater exposure to the shift underway in the Japanese economy as more manufacturing is moved offshore. As a result of the reduction in demand for funds by heavy industry, smaller companies have been able to obtain access to bank finance much more easily than was ever possible before.

In addition, the risks carried by the finance sector have risen enormously as it began investing in a greater range of paper and using much more complex techniques than was possible until recently. There are doubts as to how sophisticated their risk management techniques are, particularly if there are further strong currency and interest rate fluctuations. With greater knowledge of Japanese corporations in foreign capital markets, the rise in offshore capital raisings has been significant. In the mid-60s, when international capital markets were much less developed, and when there were still stiff controls over offshore capital raisings by Japanese corporations, over 99 per cent of all capital raisings were made domestically. Since then, there has been a steady move offshore.

In 1980, 74 per cent of all fund raisings were completed domestically. Since then the figure has declined to a low of 49.8 per cent in fiscal 1985, rising slightly in fiscal 1986. The slight reversal in fiscal 1986 was due to the extreme popularity of domestic convertible bond issues.

The percentage of funds raised domestically will receive an added impetus from the second half of 1987 with the start-up of the proposed commercial paper market, which will result in a further shift away from foreign markets and bank borrowings in favour of the new market for some corporations.

Corporate bonds

Tussles over regulations surrounding the domestic corporate bond market are symptomatic of the broader dispute between securities companies and banks within Japan's financial system. With banks barred from underwriting all but government and semi-government bonds, their role is that of the lead commissioned bank, to negotiate the terms of the proposed issue with the securities houses. The banks, especially the long-term credit banks, are increasingly vocal in their opposition to this system, arguing that even though they do all of the issue preparation, they are unfairly prohibited from acting as lead underwriter, a position reserved for the securities houses.

'The securities houses are protected by the Ministry of Finance, yet the banks are controlled by the Ministry of Finance', is the common saying.

Given the overwhelming size of the national bond issuing programme, domestic issues by the corporate sector, excluding the electricity utilities and

NTT, of straight bonds are modest, accounting for just 0.5 per cent of all domestic bonds issued in 1986.

This attests more to the absolute size of the government borrowing programme and its growth, than to the size of the corporate borrowing programme.

Smaller companies are largely unable to tap domestic markets, so they have tapped with increasing regularity the Swiss market, where the minimum limit on the size of offerings is low, while larger corporations go to the Euromarkets.

The pressure of the move offshore and the implications for the domestic corporate bond market resulted in the securities companies, via the Securities Exchange Council, an advisory body to MoF, lobbying hard for a relaxation of the restrictions on domestic bond issues in an attempt to bring some of the offshore borrowing back onshore. This is but the latest in a long-running dispute surrounding the domestic bond market.

Market history

In the early part of the century, most of the bond issues in Japan were unsecured, although, after a spate of bankruptcies, the authorities demanded stiff collateral requirements.

This protected and entrenched the role of the long-term credit banks, since they generated useful collateral commissions from the operation of the present system.

Nonetheless, by the early 1970s, the corporate sector was beginning to press for approval to be able to issue unsecured bonds. In this, they naturally had the full support of the securities houses.

The long-term credit banks were obviously opposed, arguing that the collateral system ensured that investors were adequately protected from loss of their investment, and that the existing system maintained an orderly organisation of the market.

The issue was argued throughout the 1970s and finally, in 1977, a committee of the Securities Exchange Council released a report supporting the introduction of a system of unsecured bonds.

The debate hotted up the following year when the US retailer Sears Roebuck said that it intended to seek approval to issue unsecured yen bonds. In mid-1978, the Japanese retailer Ito-Yokado made an unsecured bond issue in the US. This bond issue enabled external pressure to be brought on the Japanese government, since it was confronted with the fact that domestic companies had open

Bond issues by Japanese corporations, fiscal 1979–86, in ¥100m

	Ordinary bonds			*Convertible bonds*			*Total*		
Fiscal year	*Domestic*	*Overseas*	*Total*	*Domestic*	*Overseas*	*Total*	*Domestic*	*Overseas*	*Total*
1979	15,042	2,930	17,972	3,310	1,820	5,130	18,352	4,750	23,102
	(83.7)	(16.3)	(100.0)	(64.5)	(35.5)	(100.0)	(79.4)	(20.6)	(100.0)
1980	9,935	1,680	11,615	965	5,149	6,114	10,900	6,829	17,729
	(85.5)	(14.5)	(100.0)	(15.8)	(84.2)	(100.0)	(61.5)	(38.5)	(100.0)
1981	12,690	491	13,181	5,460	10,690	16,150	18,150	11,181	29,331
	(96.3)	(3.7)	(100.0)	(33.8)	(66.2)	(100.0)	(61.9)	(38.1)	(100.0)
1982	10,475	6,812	17,287	4,645	6,933	11,578	15,120	13,745	28,865
	(60.6)	(39.4)	(100.0)	(40.1)	(59.9)	(100.0)	(52.4)	(47.6)	(100.0)
1983	6,830	4,039	10,869	8,780	15,145	23,925	15,610	19,184	34,794
	(62.8)	(37.2)	(100.0)	(36.7)	(63.3)	(100.0)	(44.9)	(55.1)	(100.0)
1984	7,200	11,345	18,545	16,145	16,606	32,751	23,343	27,951	51,296
	(38.8)	(61.2)	(100.0)	(49.3)	(50.7)	(100.0)	(45.5)	(54.5)	(100.0)
1985	9,435	14,393	23,828	16,405	18,142	34,547	25,840	32,535	58,375
	(39.6)	(60.4)	(100.0)	(47.5)	(52.5)	(100.0)	(44.3)	(55.7)	(100.0)
1986	6,150	8,600	14,750	16,475	17,668	34,143	25,873	26,274	52,147
(4–11)	(41.7)	(58.3)	(100.0)	(48.3)	(51.7)	(100.0)	(49.6)	(50.4)	(100.0)

Source: MoF. (Annual percentages are shown in parentheses)

access to US capital markets but foreign companies could not obtain the same access to Japan. Later that year, Matsushita Electric announced that it, too, intended seeking approval to make an unsecured domestic yen bond issue. The Industrial Bank of Japan, as the leading long-term credit bank, was asked to draw up a set of proposals to resolve the impasse. It did so by putting forward suggestions that allowed only a highly restricted number of Japanese companies to tap the domestic market.

In 1982, Dow Chemical sought approval to tap the market through an issue of unsecured bonds which, after some delay, was finally given, thus setting the scene for further change.

Since Dow Chemical was allowed to make an unsecured issue, other Japanese groups of equal or better financial standing, which could not tap the domestic unsecured market, were in a position to move. Headed by the securities companies, a campaign was launched to liberalise issuing conditions. This included a halving of the minimum net assets required by an issuing corporation to ¥55 billion, which would have lifted dramatically the number of corporations that could tap the market. Once more a compromise was reached, which broadened, slightly, the number of domestic corporations that could tap this market to an estimated 70.

With the rising volume of offshore bonds, the securities houses began a further lobbying campaign in 1986. Alarmed by the drift of domestic borrowers offshore, the Securities and Exchange Council in late 1986 recommended that MoF abolish the commissioned bank system, with negotiations undertaken directly between the borrower and the underwriter. In addition, it sought a liberalisation of the private placement market, to put it on an equal footing with the public bond market.

An overhaul of issuance qualifications was carried out, with final agreement reached between the securities houses and the banks in early 1987. With this agreement, it was decided to implement the new system from mid-1987.

The new criteria will approximately double the number of companies that can access this market to around 170 – still a far cry from complete liberalisation. An estimated 330 companies will be able to issue convertible bonds, almost double the number that were allowed to issue such bonds previously.

Interestingly, the new system goes half way towards incorporating a ratings system. One continuing difficulty is that bond issuance will still be restricted to twice a month, rather than once a month as was previously the case. All parties agree that they are moving cautiously at this point, although by including elements of a ratings system, the potential for significant deregulation in the future has been dramatically expanded.

Bond ratings

In the light of the tight prudential requirements imposed on borrowers accessing Japan's domestic bond markets, the role of ratings agencies has been historically negligible. The security of most bonds issued has been absolute, and investors do not need additional independent assessments before making their decision to invest.

Gradually the role of ratings of bond issuers has been broadened, and was given further importance in mid-1987 with the decision to incorporate more fully ratings for domestic corporate bond issues.

There are now five ratings agencies in Japan – three Japanese and two US. The three Japanese agencies are the Japan Bond Research Institute, an affiliate of the Nihon Keizai Shimbun which publishes daily business and financial newspapers, the Japan Credit Ratings Agency, established jointly by a number of Japanese financial institutions, and Nippon Investors Service. The other two agencies are Standard & Poors and Moody's.

Bond ratings have been used in Japan for several years, although primarily for foreign borrowers seeking to tap the yen market. Not all had to fulfill ratings requirements, since there was also provision for potential borrowers complying with a range of other financial yardsticks which could also be used to determine whether access to the yen bond markets for foreign borrowers would be granted.

Moody's and Standard & Poors were the first agencies recognised for rating Euro-yen, private placement paper and Samurai issues. The Japan Bond Research Institute is also active in rating Samurai issues. Competition became more intense in early 1986 with the decision to admit also the Japan Credit Rating Agency and Nippon Investors Service.

The critical factor was allowing ratings to be attached to domestic bond issues for the first time, which was part of the changes incorporated to the domestic bond market in 1987.

Moving beyond this, to only using ratings to assess credit worthiness, will take time since it is usually argued that domestic investors are unfamiliar with the role of bond and company ratings in determining prices.

The signal from MoF that it may approve from late 1987 the issuance of domestic straight bonds secured only with a bank guarantee may encourage a further shift in favour of ratings.

Further progress

The key to future moves will be trade-offs that will go some way towards eroding the present commissioned bank system, while giving the long-term credit banks direct access to the underwriting sector. The three big long-term credit banks – the Industrial Bank of Japan, the Long-Term Credit Bank and the Nippon Credit Bank – all have sizeable overseas operations involved in the full range of merchant bank and underwriting activities, although they are specifically prohibited from moving into this area in Japan at present.

The Industrial Bank of Japan lifted the stakes when it decided to apply for permission for its US affiliate, Aubrey J. Lanston, to open a representative office in Tokyo. Similarly, the long-term credit banks were actively lobbying behind the scenes for foreign banks to gain access to the domestic securities industry through independent investment advisory companies.

Dismantling the present commissioned bank system could cause some pain, since it would cut off a sizeable source of income for the trust banks. If implemented, it would cut borrowing costs for the corporate sector, which would provide additional incentive for domestic borrowers to move from foreign capital markets to domestic markets. The commissioned banks claim that they are forced to include securities companies in bond issues, due to the 'three bureaux' ruling of MoF.

Under this system the three bureaux of securities, banking and international finance have indicated the real point of divide between the securities companies and the commissioned banks. The commissioned bank can advise and negotiate with the borrower on issue details, but the issue must be taken to the securities house for lead underwriting. Since the bank cannot act as lead underwriter, the securities house gets greater prominence in the tombstone advertisement. The only exception is government guaranteed bonds, for semi-government corporations and the like. Even though the controls over the domestic corporate bond market are largely in place to protect the antiquated commissioned bank structure, for much of the 1970s the authorities were more concerned with ensuring that the market for the massive government debt programme was developed adequately, with scant concern for the needs and demands of the corporate sector.

At the same time there were fears that the large government debt programme would crowd out corporate sector borrowings, although this was again of only peripheral concern, since the dominant national need was to ensure adequate absorption of government debt and an orderly expansion of the market as much of that debt began to be rolled over.

That fear may have been real enough during the early and mid-1980s, when the government debt programme was at its peak, although fears of a 'crowding out' have proved to be largely groundless. By 1986, total outstanding government debt reached 51.8 per cent of all bonds on issue, and with the expansion of domestic bond markets, this proportion was not expected to rise any higher, so the earlier caution proved unwarranted.

The 1987 measures

With corporate fund raising moving offshore in increasing volumes since the early 1980s, the securities houses had stepped up their campaign to loosen the controls on domestic bond issues with considerable success.

Under the new formula agreed between the banks and the securities houses, and implemented in mid-1987, a complete overhaul of the restrictions covering issuing corporations for domestic bonds has been undertaken.

The driving force has been to bring the new rules, especially in terms of issue size, broadly into line with those governing issues in Switzerland, which has been a particularly attractive market for many smaller Japanese borrowers since the mid-1980s.

For straight bonds, net assets must exceed ¥3 billion, and dividends of more than ¥5 per share must have been paid continuously for the three previous periods. In addition, the issuing corporation must satisfy three of the following four conditions: the ratio of shareholders' funds must exceed 30 per cent, net assets must be covered three times, the gross profit rate must exceed 8 per cent and interest must be covered more than three times.

For trading companies, slightly looser conditions apply. Here, net assets must exceed ¥25 billion.

There are also provisions for ratings criteria for the first time for issues of straight bonds. Corporations rated BB or better must have net assets of more than ¥106 billion, with shareholders' funds of more than 15 per cent.

For B rated companies with net assets of ¥3 billion, shareholders' funds must exceed 30 per cent, with an interest cover of three times.

Similarly, with convertible bond issues, the minimum size of net assets has been reduced to ¥3 billion, with shareholders' funds of more than 15 per cent, gross profit rate of more than 7 per cent, and other criteria. For trading companies issuing convertible bonds, net assets must exceed ¥25 billion.

For unsecured issues, the minimum size of net assets has been set at ¥55 billion, an interest cover of more than five times and shareholders' funds of more than 50 per cent, among other criteria. As a result, these tight controls will limit access to these issues to all but the largest, most secure corporations.

The toughest controls relate to unsecured convertible bonds, where the corporation's net assets must exceed ¥20 billion, with net shareholders' funds exceeding 50 per cent and an interest cover of more than five times.

Even with the latest liberalisation moves, and the incorporation of ratings criteria, issuing domestic bonds, either secured or unsecured, will remain problematical for most Japanese companies, forcing them to continue to raise funds offshore. Along with the complex set of issuing guidelines to be complied with, the issuing company cannot freely determine when bonds will be issued, since they can be issued only twice a month, a considerable handicap during times of rapidly changing external conditions. A full relaxation of the present terms and conditions requires a fundamental change of approach by both the long-term credit banks and MoF. The ministry has long adopted the approach of ensuring that investors were fully protected which meant that, in effect, there was virtually no prospect of corporate failure affecting bondholders. Even if a corporation fails, the banks that guaranteed the issue are forced to step in and buy up all of the outstanding bonds at par. With the guarantees provided for convertible bonds, the banks received a fee of ¥0.20 per ¥100 guaranteed. For unsecured bonds it was pegged at a similar level. When Sanko Steamship filed for corporate reorganisation in 1985, for example, the banks that guaranteed its various issues were forced to step in and bail out the bond holders.

With the extremely tight issuance criteria that are applied, together with the guarantees provided by the banks, the risk carried by the general investor in buying domestic corporate paper in Japan is virtually nil.

New legislation

As part of the general overhaul of issuance criteria implemented from mid-1987, MoF also intends to introduce a shelf registration system for both domestic bond issues and overseas issues denominated in yen.

The government is keen to match closely developments in the US, where a shelf registration system has been successfully implemented, giving corporate borrowers much greater flexibility in the timing of any proposed issues. The registration procedures for new bond issues were relaxed from April 1987, to provide for much easier and faster processing of applications.

Under the old system, there was a 30-day validation system, which has been shortened to 15 days. Also, much of the information sought in the original registration has been simplified. The proposed shelf registration system is intended to have an even easier procedure with intended issuers simply filing information about previous bond issues.

The ministry made the principal decisions on the proposed changes to be implemented during the first half of 1987, after exhaustive discussions with the securities houses in particular, as well as interbureau negotiations. MoF officials were working on drafting the necessary legislative changes to consolidate most of the proposed changes during the second half of 1987. As part of this, a substantial amendment to the existing Securities and Exchange Law is being drafted, said to be the most thorough since 1971. Officials anticipate that the detailed amendments will be considered by the Diet in the first half of 1988.

Commercial paper

The shift of corporate sector borrowings away from commercial banks will receive an additional incentive once the proposed commercial paper market is operational from the end of 1987. Progress with the start-up of this market was delayed, pending the settlement of the dispute over which financial institutions would be able to trade in the paper. The securities companies were determined to retain full control over the market, although the banks argued that since the commercial paper market will increase the shift away from bank funding, it was only fair that they also have direct access to trading in commercial paper, to help offset the loss of profits that will occur once the market is operational. Eventually it was decided that both the securities houses and the banks could trade in commercial paper. But, as with the start-up of most new markets in Japan, initially only a modest number of Japanese corporations will be allowed to tap the market. Principally, access to this market is limited to those corporations which can issue unsecured straight bonds; this, with the changes in eligibility criteria which were introduced from mid-1987, indicates that around 170 of the larger corporations will be able to tap the market.

With the highly restricted number of Japanese corporations that can access the domestic commercial paper market, growth will be slow. MoF is hoping that this new market will grow to a size roughly equal to the French commercial paper market in its initial stages. In its first year of operation, the total outstandings in France's commercial paper market were ¥1 trillion.

Total short-term loans from the banks to the industrial sector are an estimated ¥10 trillion, which indicates the potential size of the market in Japan once a broader base of companies is allowed to access this market. Few formal requirements have been issued as to which Japanese companies will be permitted to access the market, although administrative guidance will limit the potential issuers to those which can issue unsecured straight bonds, so as to avoid any possibility of default.

Eventually, commercial paper in Japan will be rated along the same lines as in the US, but developing the ratings system fully to cover corporations in Japan is likely to take some time, several years at least, although the move to broadly include ratings in the latest revision of domestic bond issuer criteria will help to start the process.

International comparisons
In the US, the commercial paper market accounted for 28.6 per cent of trading in short term capital markets at the end of 1986, compared with 18.6 per cent in 1980, with the bulk of the paper issued by finance companies, usually affiliates of manufacturing concerns. In Japan, even though the market will be subject to onerous restrictions when trading first begins, it is commonly anticipated that it will grow rapidly, and that many of the present restrictions will be lifted over the next three years.

Most of the major Japanese corporations are well acquainted with commercial paper, since their subsidiaries have often actively tapped the US and the Eurocommercial paper markets. In Japan, bank guarantees will not at first be necessary, although back-up lines will be required. The development of this market will bring with it a potent force for change in domestic capital markets and it may provide the key to unlock the difficulties that continue to surround domestic corporate bond markets. If the commercial paper market does expand in the way commonly expected, it will help to foster the wider usage of ratings systems and a further loosening of the unnecessarily tight controls surrounding the domestic corporate bond market. Change here will hinge heavily on the attitude of the long-term credit banks, which will depend in turn on their gaining access to the domestic securities market.

Venture capital

With the high level of liquidity in the financial system, one area where there has been a significant increase in new activity is venture capital financing. Following the boom in the US that began in earnest in the early 1980s, activity in Japan began to quicken in 1983, in line with a sharp growth in the number of venture capital financing companies in operation, and after new initiatives were taken by the Ministry of International Trade and Industry (MITI).

In 1973 MITI had launched a series of studies into the venture capital area, as it realised that the needs of such start-ups were fundamentally different from those of already established small and medium-sized companies.

MITI moved cautiously, although in 1975 it launched its own limited programme of guaranteeing debt of a small number of venture capital companies in a bid to help them over the initial hurdle of moving from the research and development stage into full-scale production. The cautious move by MITI into this area followed the realisation that employment growth among the big, listed companies was stagnant, and that new policies needed to be developed to foster start-up companies, to ensure adequate employment growth.

After a period of moderate activity in the 1970s, its work flagged and it was not until 1985 that there was a significant increase in new guarantees provided by MITI.

Most of the venture capital financing companies that began expanding their activities are affiliated with or controlled by the big Japanese securities houses, while more recently a number of the banks have moved in as well. For the securities houses, the move into venture capital financing was a logical extension of their existing activities, since they have formed a variety of investment trusts targeted specifically at venture capital companies. There is also the added incentive of fostering close links with newly emerging companies in the hope of taking them public, and thus generating additional fee income. The increase in venture capital financing was also partly an extension of activity to revive interest in Japan's over-the-counter market, which has not been particularly successful since its reorganisation in the late 1950s.

Prior to 1982, there were some seven venture capital financing companies active in the market, although by the following year there had been a significant increase as a number of bank-affiliated companies moved in. Now, about half of the bigger financing groups are associated with securities houses, and the balance with banks. The biggest is Japan Associated Finance Co (Jafco), which is an affiliate of Nomura Securities. Other large participants include Japan

10 largest private venture capital finance companies by total investment outstandings

	¥m
Japan Associated Finance (Jafco)	66,067
Nippon Investment Finance	19,209
Yamaichi Univen	10,407
Japan Enterprise Development	10,197
Tokyo Venture Capital	9,057
Nikko Venture Capital	9,000
Sanyo Finance	8,982
Diamond Capital	7,835
Kangyo Kakumaru Investment	6,407
New Japan Finance	6,000

Investment Finance (Daiwa), Yamaichi Univen (Yamaichi), Nikko Venture Capital (Nikko Securities), Japan Enterprise Development (Long-Term Credit Bank), Tokyo Venture Capital (Dai-Ichi Kangyo Bank), Sanyo Finance (Sanyo Securities), Diamond Capital (Mitsubishi Bank) and Kangyo Kakumaru Investment (Kangyo Kakumaru Securities). Others include affiliates of government agencies, such as the Small Business Financial Corporation. The largest, Jafco, accounts for almost half of all advances to and investments in venture capital companies. Jafco went public in early 1987, listing on the OTC market.

Direct financing accounts for about 65 per cent of the total capital raisings. Organising funds for venture capital investments is quite lucrative for the financing companies, which typically generate management fees of 3 per cent annually of the capital raised. The total raised by these investment unions exceeds ¥160 billion. By the end of 1986, 59 such investment unions had been formed. The bulk of these funds, over 80 per cent, is invested directly in the equity of start-up companies.

Intense competition between the venture capital financing companies resulted in a boom in new lending and investment in 1984 and 1985, with predictable consequences. Many small venture capital businesses were offered new funds far in excess of their needs. This, combined with often inadequate management, resulted in a large number of failures from late 1985, which continued into 1987.

A number of well publicised venture capital companies were among those that failed, including Sord Computer, Chescom, Dainichi Kiko and Cosmo 80. Some were partly absorbed into other groups, and others simply disappeared. The most commonly stated reasons for their failure were lack of adequate management systems, too easy access to finance, over-investment in plant and facilities, poor attention to marketing products and weak financial controls. The initial failures revolved around poor management; the collapses from the latter part of 1986 were due to a more complex mix of factors, including the sharp appreciation of the yen against the US dollar.

Until early 1987, the total losses on investments in venture capital companies that had failed was ¥225 billion, with the majority of that incurred in 1986, when the number and scale of failures rose sharply. On average, two venture capital companies failed a month between 1982 and 1985; but in 1986, 60 companies collapsed, with losses totalling ¥164.9 billion. As a result, most of the venture capital financing companies have changed their lending practices, and lay out a much smaller amount of funds and are generally more circumspect in evaluating prospects of new start-ups. Some of the more spectacular failures involved companies that were flooded with cash, resulting in senior management undertaking a variety of speculative investments unknown to their financial backers at the time. Consequently, some of the venture financing groups have added management consulting functions to their range of services, as well as boosting their general market research, so that they can more carefully assess a potential client and form a clearer idea of the likely success or failure of processes or technology under development. As a result, the total number of new financings has declined significantly since mid-1986, which may force some of the present participants out of the market altogether.

Bullishness about the industry's prospects continues, particularly among those financing companies affiliated with the securities houses, since they stand to profit much more than the banks from their involvement in this area. Their primary motivation is to take start-up companies public so that they can generate fee income from underwriting, particularly if these companies can graduate to the main board of the stock exchanges.

MITI's overall involvement is now fairly tangential. It monitors developments but does not play a particularly aggressive role in trying to limit the industry from some of the excesses. Through its Venture Enterprises Centre MITI provides various financial guarantees, although it puts potential candidates through a rigorous testing procedure. It limits its involvement to those companies which are most likely to succeed, so it carefully assesses proposed research work, along with management strength. It limits the guarantee it provides to 80 per cent of the total size of the loan sought by the venture capital company, with a maximum guarantee of ¥80 million per project, for which it charges a fee of 2 per cent pa. The maximum guarantee term is eight years.

A company such as Jafco typically generated most of its income through its lending to venture capital companies, although as the formation of investment partnerships expanded, this, together with capital gains from direct investments, began to generate significant profits. A similar pattern of developments is clear with the other affiliates of the securities houses. As a result, the three principal earnings streams are interest on loans, capital gains from investments and investment management fees. Other areas, such as consultancy, which forms a natural adjunct to existing services in other areas, generate useful, although limited, fee income. Jafco's experience to date is fairly typical of the industry. By mid-1987, it had invested in a total of 360 companies since it began operating. Of this total, over 50 have gone public, 21 have failed and 29 companies have merged or have been sold.

Jafco has tightened up its internal controls covering new investments, and is generally acting far more cautiously than was the case since the boom got underway in earnest in 1984. The company's bottom line mirrors the boom–bust cycle of venture capital seen over the five years to 1987. Earnings peaked at ¥1.33 billion in fiscal 1984, dropped to ¥800 million the following year and rose to ¥922 million in fiscal 1986. Even though there have been further failures during 1987, it believes that the worst is now over, and that the industry will advance steadily from now on. Overall, there has been a modest increase of Jafco's total assets, which reached ¥181.92 billion at the end of fiscal 1986. The company claims to have US$785 million at its disposal, representing 40 per cent of the total of Japan's venture capital.

OTC trading

Part of the revival of the venture capital sector hinges on the future development of the OTC market and whether it can maintain the active trading that has emerged over the past three years. For the OTC market to break out of its present vicious circle of limited expansion, it needs to increase the liquidity of the market, which can really only be achieved if it manages to increase significantly the number of listed stocks. Forecasts drawn up by Jafco demonstrate its optimism that the number of companies listed on the OTC will increase to 2,000 by the turn of the century.

This figure is an estimate, although it is based on the fact that the total size of the Japanese economy is about half that of the US; therefore the OTC market, which in its view is modelled on the NASDAQ market, will manage to boost the number of traded stocks to half that of its US equivalent, that is 2,000 companies.

Even with the increase in trading activity on the OTC market over the past 18 months, this really only brings it back to volume levels traded in the late 1970s, when the market went through a burst of enthusiasm, before the actively traded stocks graduated to the main boards and overall trading in the OTC market trailed off. Boosting liquidity of the OTC market may also help overcome the big margins that stocks are often traded at, which is largely a reflection of the thinness of the market at present. Overall trading figures this year and next will be boosted significantly by the addition of Toa Domestic Airlines, although this company, by listing on the OTC, will achieve a sizeable reduction in interest charges, which should enable it to graduate quickly to the second board of the stock exchange. Given the fact that Toa has been profitable now for four years, it should be in line to comply with main board listing requirements, enabling it to move up sometime in 1988.

Leasing finance

With the progressive decline in corporate sector funding by the commercial banks, other alternatives, apart from tapping debt markets directly, have experienced strong growth. In particular, Japan's leasing industry has grown from a minor section of the finance industry in the mid-1970s to one of considerable size, with total new leasing contracts exceeding ¥4 trillion annually. For much of the industry's development it has been dominated by a handful of specialised leasing groups. That is now changing, with the increasing incursions by affiliates of the big commercial banks. Of the 10 largest leasing groups, seven are affiliated directly to the large banks.

The newcomers to the field have been attracted by the strong growth of this form of financing over the past five years, with continued bullishness within the leasing industry that total outstandings will double again by the early 1990s.

Japan's banks are unable to undertake leasing transactions directly due to limitations imposed by MoF which prohibit banks from directly owning plant and equipment. As a result, the banks are involved through affiliated financing companies, such as Diamond Lease (Mitsubishi Bank), Kogin Lease (IBJ and others), Sumitomo Lease (Sumitomo Bank), Tokyo Lease (DKB) and so on.

While the big commercial banks have been flexing their muscles in this form of financing in recent years, most of the original leasing companies have also experienced strong growth. Many of these early starters were formed by trading companies and manufacturers, keen to bolster sales through leasing affiliates. One of the earliest independent operators was Nippon Lease, founded at the behest of office machinery group Ricoh. Fuyo General Lease, one-third owned by Marubeni Corporation, one-third by Citicorp and the balance by Fuyo Group companies, is typical of many other operators in this sector.

The strong growth of the industry since the early 1980s has attracted a number of new entrants, although a slowdown since 1985 is evident. The industry has undergone two bursts of rapid expansion of the number of leasing finance companies – the first between 1973 and 1975, and more recently between 1980 and 1982.

For the leasing companies themselves, lease financing has been profitable, since they effectively borrow short-term and lend slightly longer-term, so that with declining interest rates they have been typically locked into healthy operating margins since 1984. Nearly all of the leasing companies fund their commitments by borrowing from the call markets, which are refinanced regularly, yet nearly all of their lease commitments are fixed for periods much longer than one year. Since domestic interest rates have been falling since the early 1980s, this has assured leasing companies of good margins. As soon as interest rates rise, however, this could lead to severe difficulties for a time for some leasing companies, until they can adjust their leasing contracts.

Even with the relatively easy operating conditions over the past five years, however, business conditions have become tougher. Industrial concerns such as steel manufacturer Nippon Steel Corporation and construction group Kajima Construction have decided to enter the leasing sector. Also, some of the banks' affiliated groups have become much more aggressive in seeking new business in the light of the continued strong growth of this industry during the 1980s.

Users of leasing finance

In the early 1970s, the bulk of new lease financing was provided to the industrial sector for plant and equipment. This sector of industry accounted for 40.8 per cent of total outlays, with office equipment comprising a further 28.5 per cent.

There has been a progressive change, however, with office equipment making up 42.0 per cent of total demand in 1985, and industrial machinery declining to 25.6 per cent. Much of the 'other' classification is composed of communications equipment which has grown rapidly as a result of office automation.

The bulk of the users of leasing finance are service sector companies, accounting for the much larger demand for office automation and communications equipment. Much of the relative decline in demand for lease financing of industrial machinery follows the slowdown in demand for new machine tools, which surged with the introduction of automatically controlled equipment. The downturn in economic activity due to the high yen, combined with the very high penetration of these more sophisticated machines, has resulted in a drop in new lease financing.

Part of the decline is also due to the increasingly competitive market in lending to small and medium-sized corporations. With the larger industrial groups' overall decline in demand for new funds, lending to smaller companies has become an intense battle ground for all banks and finance companies. Consequently these smaller industrial groups, which were usually cash-starved and found lease financing an attractive means of funding new capital spending, now have a variety of alternatives at much more attractive interest rates than previously.

Most lease financing to date has been for communications and computer equipment purchases, with only fragmented demand for other items of equipment. Detailed figures are not available, although leasing industry officials estimate that as much as half of all domestic sales of office and computer equipment are financed through leasing contracts. Movement of the big players overseas has been limited, although Orient Lease has established subsidiaries or joint ventures in a limited number of countries. Much of its initial activities was in financing the shipping industry, especially in Hong Kong, which has proved problematical.

The recent history of the industry has not been one of uninterrupted growth, however, with the largest operator, Orient Leasing Co, among others, forced to write off large amounts outstanding to the shipping industry over the past three years. Attracted by the ever present argument that the shipping industry was about to turn the corner, it accumulated an exposure to shipping concerns in Hong Kong, which cost the company heavily. In fiscal 1983, exposure to shipping accounted for 16 per cent of Orient Leasing's total asset portfolio. Provisions and write-offs cut that back to less than 10 per cent by the end of fiscal 1985 and to 5.5 per cent by the end of fiscal 1986.

Another area that provided some growth until recently was cross-border leasing, occasionally termed 'samurai leasing', although there has been a steady decline in new business written since 1985. Industry estimates put the total amount of cross-border leasing transactions by Japanese groups at over US$1 billion in fiscal 1985, but it declined to less than US$600 million in fiscal 1986. Country risk is the usually cited reason for the decline of interest in this form of financing.

The big leasing concerns, like most parts of Japan's financial system, have progressively expanded their operations to include consumer financing, housing loans, mortgage securities and venture capital financing. Some have also formed links with small independent securities houses; for example, Orient Lease bought a 58 per cent stake in Akane Securities in 1986, as it prepares for further financial deregulation. Most of the diversification of activity is to hedge against the growing competition within the leasing industry itself, as well as to become more fully integrated financial service companies.

Even with the rapid expansion of lease financing in Japan, its penetration lags well behind that in other advanced countries. Lease financing is estimated to account for 24 per cent of all capital spending financing in the US, 20 per cent in the UK, 7.6 per cent in West Germany and 7 per cent in France; yet in Japan it accounts for only an estimated 6 per cent.

Lease financing in Japan does not attract the same tax incentives as in either the US or Europe, which is a natural limitation on the future expansion of the industry.

Along with the lack of any tax incentive to using lease financing, few expect it ever to reach the size of lease financing in the US due to the much closer links between the banks and their corporate clients in Japan, although lease financing will still prove attractive in specialised funding areas.

CHAPTER TWELVE

Stock markets

The Tokyo Stock Exchange emerged in the first half of 1987 as the largest stockmarket in the world, with the combined capitalisation of listed stocks finally eclipsing the New York Stock Exchange. Whether it retains that mantle of course depends on future stock prices in both markets and future currency movements. Apart from some minor corrections, the Tokyo market has been in a sustained bull market since early 1984, as interest rates have fallen worldwide. In that time, the Nikkei index of leading issues has risen from a low of 9,703 points to reach a peak of more than 25,000 points by mid-1987.

In the process, the capitalisation of the Tokyo stockmarket rose from ¥154.8 trillion at the end of 1984 to ¥394.2 trillion by the end of August 1987. At the same time, the average price/earnings ratio was more than 70, compared with an average of 31.4 in 1984.

Aided by currency movements over the two years from 1984, the Tokyo market, which was ranked at less than one-third the size of the New York Stock Exchange, finally moved ahead in the second quarter of 1987.

In addition to the staggering price movement, particularly since early 1986, there has been an explosion in trading volumes, which almost doubled to reach 238.35 trillion shares traded in calendar 1986, up from 146.3 trillion in 1985. In the first half of 1987, daily trading volumes were more than double previous levels. The value of shares traded has also more than doubled. In the first six months of 1987, the average daily volume of shares traded was 1.04 billion shares with the average value of turnover ¥1,158 billion.

Despite being the largest equity market in the world, Tokyo remains comparatively unsophisticated. The liberalisation of trading in equities markets worldwide is yet to touch Japan, with commissions, for instance, still tightly controlled. Insider trading rules are ignored and short selling is impossible. Frequently share price movements bear little relationship to fundamentals and dividend policies no relation to earnings. In addition, apart from the very low pay-out rate (dividends are taxable in the hands of shareholders), any surplus profits generated are rarely distributed to shareholders.

In spite of the size of the Tokyo sharemarket, the power of the big four securities houses – Nomura, Daiwa, Nikko and Yamaichi – is unrivalled. Between them they directly control 45 per cent of total turnover on the Tokyo stockmarket. When adding in the indirect control each of the big four hold over a range of smaller firms, then their power is even greater. Their view of market movements and of a particular company's prospects, and their ability to place stock and promote rumours which can materially affect stock prices, puts them in a powerful position in the Tokyo market.

Growth of the market

The most common theory for the rapid expansion of the Tokyo market over the past three years is the 'weight of money' argument. This states that since there is so much surplus liquidity in the financial system, combined with falling interest rates, the stockmarket has been the logical place to invest.

Even with the rapid expansion of the Tokyo market over the past five years, it remains fundamentally different from most other markets. The traps for the unwary investor are extensive. Stock prices move totally unpredictably, frequently because of a good rumour spread by one of the big security houses.

Opposite above: The floor of the TSE, the largest stockmarket in the world by early 1987 in terms of capitalisation of listed stocks.

Opposite below: Activity is not always as gentlemanly as on some of the European exchanges.

Good research, while occasionally available on listed stocks in Tokyo, is not used by domestic fund managers, who simply follow the big four. Fundamentals have little bearing on stock price movements.

One key feature which is often overlooked is that equity markets in Japan are remarkably illiquid. Typically, of the blue-chip companies, at least 35 or 40 per cent of the shares on issue are locked up in long-term holdings which, for a variety of reasons, are unlikely ever to come onto the market.

Investment institutions, apart from banks, own just 21.8 per cent of shares in issue on the Tokyo Stock Exchange. Banks hold an additional 18.9 per cent, with corporations holding a further 25.6 per cent. Neither the banks' nor the corporations' holdings are readily traded, so that over 40 per cent of the shares on issue are not on the market, whatever the price.

Longstanding links between banks, the corporate sector and company affiliates result in a complex web of cross-shareholdings which rarely come on the market. These stockholdings are included in the balance sheet at purchase price, not market value. If a company, or a bank, wishes to improve its below-the-line profit, it will sell a small portion of its holding.

Capital gains taxes are part of the reason underlying the formation of various trust accounts by mainly corporate investors over recent years, primarily to invest in equities. By the very nature of these trusts, the income derived is not taxable. Called 'tokkin' and 'kingai', the trusts have been a primary force in many of the developments that have occurred in the stock markets in Japan over the past three years. The secret behind the success of these trusts is that they are purely share trading vehicles, and thus lie outside the web of corporate loyalty.

Due to the low interest paid on funds on deposit during the era of controlled interest rates, surplus cash was often invested in the stockmarket, rather than placed in other outlets. With liberalised interest rates, this appears to be gradually changing, and corporate finance directors are willing to seek a diversity of outlets for surplus fund seeking attractive yields. As part of this, Japanese investors are increasingly moving funds into equity markets internationally for the first time. The preference of most Japanese investors for holding foreign bonds is well known, although that has steadily shifted over the past four years, with a sharp increase in interest in equity markets, in line with the trend of falling interest rates worldwide.

Shareownership by market value, all listed companies, 1983–86

	¥bn				*%*			
	1983	*1984*	*1985*	*1986*	*1983*	*1984*	*1985*	*1986*
Central & local government	357	468	667	1,136	0.3	0.3	0.4	0.5
Financial institutions	40,996	58,617	69,600	93,685	38.6	37.4	38.0	39.7
All banks	19,112	27,021	31,909	45,353	18.0	17.2	17.4	18.4
Investment trusts	1,726	2,298	2,695	3,945	1.6	1.5	1.5	1.7
Annuity trusts	388	871	996	1,809	0.4	0.6	0.5	0.8
Life insurance Cos	12,626	18,431	22,086	29,114	11.9	11.7	12.1	12.3
Non-life insurance Cos	4,750	6,524	7,554	9,671	4.5	4.2	4.1	4.1
Other financial institutions	2,393	3,473	4,361	5,593	2.4	2.4	2.4	2.4
Business corporations	26,985	43,316	54,015	67,887	25.4	27.6	29.5	28.8
Securities companies	1,830	2,720	3,335	4,365	1.7	1.7	1.8	1.8
Individuals & others	27,919	38,001	42,081	52,465	26.3	24.2	23.0	22.2
Foreigners	8,081	13,750	13,504	16,536	7.6	8.8	7.4	7.0
Total	106,168	156,872	183,208	236,075	100.0	100.0	100.0	100.0

Source: MoF.

Historical development

The Tokyo and Osaka stock exchanges trace their origins to stock exchange legislation that was passed in 1878. It took some time for the markets to become established, and much of the early trading was in bonds, both government and corporate. Also, since much of the industrial sector was organised around the 'zaibatsu' which had their own bank at the centre, its need for external financing was limited. However, between the First and Second World Wars, a number of the zaibatsu began to issue stock, although the bulk of funds for new investments came from bond issues.

With the end of World War II, trading on the stock exchanges was suspended from August 1945 and did not resume until 1949. With Japan under the control of the occupation forces, fundamental changes were made to its securities trading system. The most basic change was the decision to split the banking and securities businesses.

Prior to World War II, the quasi-government Industrial Bank of Japan was the dominant underwriting house of both bonds and securities. However, after the war it opted to continue with its banking operations, vacating the securities industry altogether. Even so, it has very close links with several of Japan's larger second-tier securities houses such as New Japan Securities and Wako Securities.

The occupation resulted in a reorganisation of the stock exchanges, which during the war had been consolidated into one. As part of the post-war change, the stock exchanges were established as independent non-profit exchanges, futures trading was banned, margin trading was eventually introduced, and subsequently new legislation was introduced controlling the establishment of investment trusts.

One of the critical changes that were implemented prior to the resumption of stock exchange trading was the dissolution of the zaibatsu, with large volumes of stocks offered to individual investors.

The markets gradually expanded, fuelled for much of the 1950s by a large flow of personal savings into investment trusts, although equity markets did not succeed in becoming a useful source of funds for the big industrial concerns – a bias in Japan's capital markets that lasted until recently.

Under the Securities and Exchange Law which was implemented in 1955, the various securities financing companies were reorganised into three main concerns in an attempt to aid the overall strengthening of the securities markets.

As the post-war recovery continued, strong economic growth in the late 1950s brought about a balance of payments crisis. This led, in mid-1961, to the Bank of Japan raising the official discount rate, and gradually introducing a tough deflationary policy. Later that year, as stock prices fell, margin requirements were relaxed, and the loan ceiling set by the Securities Finance Company was raised.

In a bid to stabilise prices, the Japan Joint Securities Company was formed by a number of the big institutions, with the sole aim of bolstering market prices. And for much of the latter part of 1964, it was largely the only buyer. A second company, the Japan Securities Holding Company, was organised in early 1965 to help in buying up stock to prop up the market after the Japan Joint Securities Company's funds were exhausted. The market remained jittery, especially after it emerged that Yamaichi Securities needed special assistance from the Bank of Japan. A smaller securities company, Ohi Securities (later Wako Securities) was bailed out by the central bank at the same time.

The Industrial Bank of Japan was called upon to play the main role in reorganising Yamaichi Securities, and key personnel were transferred from the bank to the securities company to aid in the reconstruction. The securities market gradually recovered from the panic, although it took several years for all the difficulties to be overcome.

Before 1962, investment trusts accounted for almost 10 per cent of all holdings of listed stocks; by 1967, that had fallen to less than 2 per cent. Similarly, there was a decline in the direct participation of individual shareholders. This was partly due to the liquidation of some positions as the markets in Japan went through the usual gyrations, although it was perhaps mainly due to the growth of funds in the market from overseas investors, institutional investors and the corporate sector.

Stock exchanges

Even though Japan has eight stock exchanges – Tokyo, Osaka, Nagoya, Hiroshima, Niigata, Fukuoka, Kyoto and Sapporo – nearly all of the business is written through the Tokyo Stock Exchange.

In 1986, the Tokyo Stock Exchange accounted for 82.9 per cent of all transactions by volume and 82.8 per cent by value. Osaka was a distant second, with 12.2 per cent of trading by volume and 13.0 per cent by value, followed by Nagoya with just 4.4 per cent of trading by volume and 3.8 per cent by value.

Tokyo, Osaka and Nagoya have first and second section markets, with the first section being for blue-chip corporations, and the second sector for comparatively smaller companies. Listing on the second section has slightly easier criteria.

At the end of 1986, there were 1,075 stocks listed on the first section of the Tokyo Stock Exchange (1985: 1,052), with another 424 second-section stocks. In Osaka, there were 782 (1985: 776) first-section stocks and 268 second-section stocks.

Nearly all of the first-section stocks in both Osaka and Nagoya are listed on the first sections of more than one exchange, although slightly more than one-quarter of stocks on the main board in Tokyo do not have a second listing in either Osaka or Nagoya.

In broad terms there has been a steady increase in the number of new listings which has more than offset a minor number of delistings of issues over the past decade.

The dominance of the Tokyo market is evidenced by the fact that out of the 139 full members of the stock exchanges in Japan, 86 (including Saitori) are members of the Tokyo Stock Exchange, with 35 members of the Osaka Stock Exchange, and 14 members of the Nagoya Exchange. Tokyo's dominance is highlighted by the fact that bond market trading is also concentrated there. In calendar 1986, straight bond trading on all stock exchanges was ¥58.5 trillion, with Tokyo accounting for ¥53.7 trillion.

With the steady consolidation of all of Japan's financial markets in Tokyo, the Osaka Stock Exchange is fighting a rearguard action to boost its position. It pressed for the start of trading in stock futures which, after delays due to changes pending to Japan's taxation system, finally commenced in June 1987. Similarly, the Osaka City government is seeking to consolidate the various small commodities markets in Osaka and Kobe into one unified market in an attempt to increase trading interest in these markets. The Osaka Stock Exchange boasts that by market capitalisation it is the third largest stock exchange in the world, after Tokyo and New York, although in terms of the volume of equities traded it is well down the list. In calendar 1986, total trading on the Tokyo Stock Exchange reached ¥159.8 trillion. Osaka, on the other hand, had total turnover of ¥25.18 trillion.

Stock trading volume (millions of shares) and value (¥bn) on all exchanges, 1982–86

	All exchanges		*Tokyo*		*Osaka*		*Nagoya*		*Kyoto*		*Hiroshima*		*Fukuoka*		*Niigata*		*Sapporo*	
	Volume	*Value*	*Volume*	*Value*	*Volume*	*Value*	*Volume*	*Value*	*Volume*	*Value*	*Volume*	*Value*	*Volume*	*Value*	*Volume*	*Value*	*Volume*	*Value*
1982	91,241	42,668	78,474	36,571	9,179	4,576	2,564	1,148	201	79	297	108	130	47	319	110	78	27
1983	122,320	65,333	104,309	54,845	13,469	8,350	3,375	1,665	244	104	331	149	149	61	341	120	102	39
1984	124,346	83,122	103,737	67,974	16,247	12,448	3,331	2,097	219	116	268	151	140	159	294	130	109	47
1985	146,302	94,640	121,863	78,711	18,295	12,536	5,151	2,885	245	123	156	82	152	93	329	155	110	55
1986	238,354	193,059	197,699	159,836	29,028	25,181	10,394	7,307	363	221	117	71	190	119	437	249	124	76

Source: MoF

The sharp slowdown in economic growth in the Kansai region surrounding Osaka when compared with the Kanto region around Tokyo lies behind the steady decline in Osaka's economic fortunes.

Foreign stocks

The liberalisation of listing requirements for foreign stocks in 1984 has resulted in a steady increase in the number of foreign stocks listed on the Tokyo Stock Exchange. At the same time, there has been an increase in the volume of foreign equities traded in Japan.

A small number of listings in the early 1970s was seen at the time as representing the internationalisation of Japan's capital markets, although it subsequently became an embarrassment, as the number of foreign stocks listed in Tokyo dwindled due to the stiff reporting requirements.

An overhaul of the requirements was carried out in 1984, specifically removing the requirement that the accounts of foreign firms had to be independently audited by a Japanese accounting firm. In addition, the Tokyo Stock Exchange extended the time period for registering financial statements to six months, from the former standard of three months which had been difficult for many foreign companies to comply with. And as the Tokyo market was perceived to be emerging as a truly international capital market, there has been an aggressive drive by Japan's big securities houses to boost the number of foreign listings.

Foreign companies come to Tokyo for many reasons. Those with large operations in Japan, such as IBM, McDonald and Eastman Kodak, seek to raise their profile in the Tokyo market. Other companies have extensive trading links with various groups in Japan. And companies who find it difficult to place equity in their home markets want to tap the considerable surplus liquidity in Japan.

With the cost of listing in Tokyo now lower than before, the rising strength of Japanese investors in international markets has led to an increase in the interest of foreign corporations to list. The total more than doubled to 52 in calendar 1986. Japanese houses were predicting that a minimum of 50 companies would come to the market during 1987, with most of those listings occurring in the second half of the calendar year.

Typically, a foreign company seeks to list existing securities, with only a small number aiming to raise funds through a listing.

Of the foreign stocks listed on the Tokyo Stock Exchange, 32 have offered equity to Japanese investors. Of the 52 stocks listed in calendar 1986, for example, eight companies raised funds. The largest amount, ¥190 billion, was raised by British Petroleum in 1987.

The cost of an initial listing which includes a share offering, is estimated at over ¥20 million on average. In addition, the annual cost of maintaining a listing is estimated at over ¥10 million. For a listing that includes with it a public offering, it takes 150 days from the time the original decision is taken to completion; without an offering, it takes 120 days.

Usually, the volume of the foreign stock traded in Tokyo is only a fraction of that traded on its home exchange; for US-based Waste Management Inc, trading in Tokyo totalled 10 per cent of that on its home exchange during 1986. For many of the stocks that are listed in Tokyo, the volume of shares allocated is small, making it virtually impossible to maintain an adequate market in Japan. As a result, the leakage of stock back to the home market for most listings has been large. A listing on the Tokyo Stock Exchange is usually judged a success if the flowback is no higher than 50 per cent.

Apart from the annual fees involved, the cost of maintaining an informed market in the stock can be expensive. The easiest way, and the one adopted by most foreign companies eager to maintain interest in their stock in Japan, is to hold annual presentations for stockholders, since the dissemination of information to Japanese shareholders is usually difficult through the financial press.

All the big Japanese houses have competed aggressively to sponsor new listings, with Daiwa Securities the most successful to date. When a listing is sponsored, usually no fee is earned by the securities house. Rather, it is taking a longer-term view, aiming to encourage the foreign company either to raise funds in the future through a placement with Japanese shareholders, or to set aside for Japanese investors a proportion of any offering made to shareholders.

In line with the active interest in new foreign listings, the volume of trading of foreign securities has continued to grow. Trading volume in 1985 was 131.4 million shares, rising to 309 million shares in 1986. During 1987, the daily average of foreign stocks traded has exceeded that registered during 1986. If new listings in 1987 run at near the level predicted by the Japanese houses, then foreign trading on the Tokyo Stock Exchange will continue to expand rapidly.

Under the Tokyo Stock Exchange's listing requirements, net assets must exceed ¥10 billion, with a pre-tax profit of at least ¥2 billion in each of the three years prior to listing. Also, a company must have more than 1,000 shareholders to maintain the listing on the TSE.

The role of the securities houses

The grip of the big four securities houses – Nomura, Daiwa, Nikko and Yamaichi – on Japan's equity markets is unlike anything that exists in other large capital markets. Directly and indirectly they control over half of all equities trading on Japan's stockmarkets. Driven by the need to constantly move stocks, in order to maintain revenue and build up trading commissions, their approach is strictly short-term, aimed at making trading profits for clients as quickly as possible. Active share traders, who are keen to make a profit, have little choice but to follow the suggestions of their brokers, and trade in and out of positions.

Even though the actual proportion of equities turnover controlled by the big four houses has been on a steady decline over the past 20 years, improved communications and automation systems together with more centralised management has resulted in even greater cohesion of their sales pitches to clients over the past decade, thereby increasing their influence over market movements.

These problems often make it difficult for investors not affiliated with the big four houses to generate profits if they decide to actively trade their accounts.

Often rivalling the big four are well organised consortia of investors which will try to corner stocks, leading to some aggressive on-market dealings between the big four and these independent consortia.

The excesses of the trading floor are compounded by the activities of the several daily or weekly stockmarket newspapers which also encourage rumours. So, most investors spend their time trying to determine what stocks are being pushed by the bigger brokers, or which ones are likely to become recommendations in the not too distant future.

Nevertheless, some of the excesses are being whittled away. For example, the introduction of new legislation covering investment advisers in late 1986 points to a new era of competition among fund managers. And, increasingly, the US government has raised the issue of allegations of insider trading in Tokyo, arguing that it is time that tougher controls were introduced to bring Tokyo in line with the other major capital centres.

Many Japanese brokers argue that allegations of insider trading are irrelevant in Japan, since it only occurs with mergers and acquisitions activity. As there are no takeovers and acquisitions in Japan, so the argument goes, insider trading does not exist either.

The role of research

The foreign brokers that have moved into the Japanese market over the past five years have all highlighted research in trying to carve out a niche in the market. The foreign houses believe that, as Japan's institutional investors become used to quality research in foreign markets, they will begin to demand similar work on

Japanese stocks. For this to occur, the power of the big four in moving stock prices needs to be broken, since this has become the principal means of the fund managers and institutions to buoy rates of return on their investments, especially with the introduction of 'tokkin' and 'kingai' investment trusts since 1984.

The large increase in funds flowing into Japan's equity markets since the tokkin and kingai funds were created has served to consolidate the power of the big securities houses, since the subsequent rise in stock prices has been due to the much greater role of institutional trading than has been seen before. It has also meant that the trading on Japan's stockmarkets has become much more institutionally based than was previously the case.

Efficiency of the market

Over the past decade, the primary role of raising funds through equity markets was to finance new plant and equipment, which accounted for over 60 per cent of all such fund raisings. Smaller amounts were raised to cover operating costs and the retirement of expensive debt. Typically, in a bull market, companies seek to capitalise on their strong share price to raise cheap equity finance, although this has not necessarily been the case in Japan. The amount raised from shareholders peaked at ¥1.7 trillion in 1981, and has since fallen to around half that level. In the bull market underway since 1984, the corporate sector has tapped the interest in equity markets worldwide by issuing a massive quantity of bonds – typically either bonds with warrants or convertible bonds. Issues with warrants are almost exclusively offered outside Japan, while most convertible bond issues are offered domestically, although the amount raised offshore is still sizeable. In 1986, ¥1.86 trillion was raised through domestic convertible bond issues, with a further ¥1.29 trillion raised offshore. The continued high level of fund raising has enabled a progressive improvement in corporate balance sheets so that the ratio of net worth of corporations to total assets has steadily risen over the past decade and now exceeds 30 per cent.

Until the end of the 1960s, most secondary equity issues were organised so that shares were offered to existing shareholders at par. Those shares not taken up by shareholders were then offered for public subscription. But obviously there was a much higher cost, particularly opportunity cost, of raising funds through share issues at par.

The dispute heated up in the mid-1960s. Immediately prior to that, new fund raisings had been banned, while the equity markets overcame the worst of their difficulties. Initially, a limited number of issues of convertible debentures were made but it was not until late 1966 that the first announcement of an intended issue of scrip at market price was made. Even though this proposed issue, by Oki Kensetsu, was finally shelved, the debate raged for some time. The securities companies argued that existing shareholders should be compensated for the difference between the face value of the scrip and the market price by either a free issue of scrip, or higher dividends.

Volume ('000s of shares) and value (¥m) of foreign stocks listed on the Tokyo Stock Exchange, 1982–86

	No. of trading days	No. of listed companies at year-end	Volume		Value	
			Total	*Daily average*	*Total*	*Daily average*
1982	285	12	1,271	4.5	18,257	64.1
1983	286	11	4,974	17.4	126,858	443.6
1984	287	11	4,522	15.8	93,118	324.5
1985	285	21	131,424	461.1	853,336	2,994.2
1986	279	52	309,701	1,110.0	1,151,863	4,128.5

Source: MoF.

Institutional shareholders also entered the debate, arguing that if stock is issued at market price, then dividends should be paid on the basis of earnings per share, not on the par value of stock on issue. They also claimed that if shares were issued at market price, it would absorb too much of their investment funds, forcing them to divest parts of their investment portfolio.

The first offering at market price was made by musical equipment maker Nippon Gakki in 1968. It softened the blow by making a large bonus issue straight after the rights issue which helped to overcome most of the objections.

After considerable debate, a compromise was finally worked out, and the Governor of the Tokyo Stock Exchange proposed that if too many issues at market prices were made, then the exchange had the right to suggest that adjustments be made, and also that the shares issued through these issues be non-par scrip and that dividends be expressed in yen. However, these rules, which were ultimately included in new regulations of the exchange, have basically been ignored.

The number of issues at market price gradually increased and by 1971, for example, 71.8 per cent of all share issues were offered to existing shareholders, with 18 per cent offered for general subscription at the market price, the balance being private placements.

By 1974, 58.1 per cent of issues were offered at par to existing shareholders, and 40.7 per cent were put up for general subscription at market prices. By 1982, 79.3 per cent of all issues were put up for general subscription, and this reached 87.2 per cent in 1984. And in 1986, the total raised through stock markets was dominated by public offerings, together with the exercise of warrants. The amount raised through straight offerings to shareholders was negligible.

Not only does pitching a new issue at market price give directors greater flexibility in fully maximising that price, but it is also a much quicker procedure than making a full issue to existing shareholders at par. A share issue at market price typically takes up to 70 days to process, but a full-scale rights issue at par will often take up to 150 days, with much of that taken up with submissions of registration statements to the relevant authorities.

This change has proved fundamental in enabling Japanese corporations to capitalise on their market value, and has enabled a steady improvement in the corporate sectors' balance sheet.

The aggressive fund raisings in recent years, as more and more corporations take maximum advantage of convertible bond issues and those with warrants, has added to the liquidity of Japan's corporate sector. Much of the funds raised through these issues have, in turn, been reinvested in domestic equity markets, either directly or indirectly.

In the late 1970s bonus share issues were a sizeable source of new shares listed on the Tokyo Stock Exchange, although in the first half of the 1980s this

Convertible bond trading on the Tokyo Stock Exchange, 1977–86

During or end of	*No. of listed issuers*	*No. of listed issues*	*Amount listed (¥bn par value)*	*Total market value (¥bn)*	*Trading volume (¥bn par value)*	*Trading value (¥bn)*	*Turnover ratio (%)*
1977	205	282	1,032	1,202	1,509	1,800	147.0
1978	211	297	1,233	1,558	4,244	5,879	374.6
1979	209	306	1,308	1,419	1,520	1,887	119.6
1980	198	275	1,134	1,211	2,178	2,614	178.4
1981	206	289	1,224	1,406	3,102	4,423	263.0
1982	223	307	1,569	1,744	2,331	2,680	166.9
1983	221	296	2,072	2,616	6,510	8,012	357.6
1984	249	350	2,925	3,584	11,612	14,619	464.8
1985	306	437	4,286	5,251	22,131	28,926	613.8
1986	362	545	5,882	8,714	52,816	84,345	1,038.9

Source: MoF.

The Tokyo Stock Exchange looks sedate enough from the outside.

changed in the light of the rising number of convertible bond issues that were made. In 1986, for example, the number of shares converted from convertible bond and warrant issues totalled 3.7 billion, compared with bonus issues of 3.33 billion.

Given the size of some of the issues that can hit the market, there are special provisions in place for various 'stabilisation transactions' to be carried out, as the underwriter to an issue tries to ensure that the underlying stock price is not unduly depressed by a proposed issue. The aim of these transactions is to prop up the share price of the company undertaking a new issue through direct share purchases.

These provisions, put in place in mid-1971, limit the broker to such activities as listed in the registration statement for the new offering. In addition, stabilisation purchases can only be carried out if specifically provided for in the prospectus covering a new issue.

For a new offering, price stabilisation transactions are approved for the period shortly prior to the issue being opened for subscription, and extending until subscription is closed and payment due. When an issue price is set before price stabilisation begins, it continues until subscription is closed. If an issue price is not set before price stabilisation, then stabilisation purchases are allowed from the day after the issuing price is set, for a 10-day period until subscription closes.

There are other variations, depending on the pricing of an issue. Under the rules surrounding stabilisation purchases, the broker is not allowed to make purchases for its own account, apart from stabilisation purchases. Since these provisions have been in operation, there was a peak of 142 cases where they were applied in 1979, with 64 cases occurring in 1984.

Stock financing

Central to the financing activities within Japan's securities industry are the three securities finance companies, of which the Japan Securities Finance Company is the dominant force.

The securities finance companies play a key role in financing particularly the smaller and medium-sized securities houses. The banking sector was not geared to finance securities dealing until comparatively recently, and as many of the securities houses were unable to fund clients' activities, they had to rely on the established securities finance companies to provide the necessary credit.

In broad terms, the proportion of shares traded on margin financing is declining although, with the sharp upturn in the markets, there has been a significant increase in the value of margin financing in 1986, after several years of steady decline. It rose from ¥36.12 billion at the end of 1985 to ¥67.81 billion a year later. The total for 1987 may well exceed the ¥80 billion level. As important as their financing function is the role the securities finance companies play, in conjunction with the securities houses and the government, in establishing margin limits, particularly at times when stock prices are over-heated.

Background

Securities finance companies were first formed in the mid-1920s with the largest, Japan Securities Finance, established in 1927. Their main role at that time was to finance short-term stock futures dealings.

With futures trading prohibited in the aftermath of World War II, the securities financing companies were reorganised as general securities financing companies.

The entire industry was reorganised in 1955, when the Securities and Exchange Law was amended. The following year, the nine securities finance companies were reorganised into three groups. Japan Securities Finance is restricted to financing transactions on the Tokyo, Sapporo, Niigata and Fukuoka exchanges; the Osaka Securities Finance covers Osaka, Kyoto, Kobe and Hiroshima, with Chubu Securities Finance covering the Nagoya exchange.

Japan Securities Finance in Tokyo is dominant, accounting for well over 70 per cent of all margin trading financing. The company is also gradually expanding its operations. It has large shareholdings in a money market dealing company, as well as in the listed Japan Securities Agents, which is rapidly expanding in the securities transfer area.

The basic activities of the securities finance companies revolve around loans for margin trading, general loans using security as collateral and financing securities companies' trading activities in bonds. Japan Securities Finance is also actively trying to boost direct lending to individual investors to overcome the steady decline in new funding needs of the securities companies.

Japan Securities Finance's main activity for much of the 1980s was financing bond transactions, accounting for 48 per cent of revenue, with margin financing making up 35 per cent and general securities financing most of the balance.

Typically, securities financing transactions cover deals where securities houses needed to borrow either stock or funds to allow settlement of a deal for a client.

Given the large size of the major participants in Japan's securities industry, their need to rely on the securities finance houses has declined steadily, particularly since they can obtain competitive financing elsewhere. The major securities houses finance their operations primarily through the call market, with additional funds raised from the banking sector through syndicated loans.

For Japan Securities Finance, for example, the outstanding balance of loans for margin trading has expanded, reaching ¥267.1 billion in fiscal 1985, with the value of stocks lent reaching ¥99.7 billion. This has been on a gradual rise over the past five years, moving from 23 per cent of total margin financing outstandings to 37 per cent in 1985.

The big increase in activities occurred in the 1960s, when the securities finance companies began to boost their bond financing activities. The overall increase in bond issue size has meant that the burden on the securities houses in financing their purchases of bonds held for resale has increased sharply. To fund these holdings, the securities houses raise most of their funds through the gensaki market, with additional amounts sourced from the securities finance companies or through the call market.

Apart from their margin and general financing activities, the securities financing companies also play a key role in establishing the margin requirements.

In line with the overall tempo of stockmarket activity, the margin requirements are moved in order to prevent the market from over-heating. In mid-1987, for example, the margin requirement was at a peak of 70 per cent, of which 20 per cent has to be lodged in cash, with the balance in stocks or bonds. Of the stocks or bonds lodged as collateral, only 50 per cent of the face value is accepted. No other form of collateral is acceptable. From early 1986, both the cash requirement and the nominal value of the collateral requirements have been raised, although with little material effect on overall stockmarket activity.

Even though the net outstandings of the three securities finance companies show continued growth, their role in securities financing has declined as the finances of the securities companies in general have improved. Progressively the role of the securities finance companies as the lender of last resort to the securities houses has been taken over by the banks.

The gradual reduction in the role of the securities finance companies is highlighted by the fact that they are seeking to increase their financing to individual investors.

The securities houses themselves play an active role in funding clients' transactions, with rates set at the same level as by the securities finance companies.

As an additional step to overcome their reduced role, the securities finance houses intend to expand the number of stocks that are available for margin trading, although progress with this may be slow due to the overheated trading on the exchanges during 1987.

Securities trading

Even though there are four forms of transaction approved for dealing in shares by the stock exchanges, virtually all dealing is carried out through 'regular-way' transactions, where settlement is on the fourth day after the transaction is completed. Transactions are automatically regular-way unless otherwise stated when the order is given to the broker. In recent years, regular-way transactions accounted for 99.99 per cent of all transactions carried out on the exchanges.

Three variations are provided for – cash transactions, special agreement deals and 'when-issued' transactions. With cash transaction, settlement is made with the delivery of cash and shares through the clearing department of the exchange on the day of the contract. Special agreement deals allow settlement 14 days after the day of the contract, while when-issued dealings are made for deals in new issues, where the scrip has not yet been issued.

Trading hours are 9–11 a.m. and 1–3 p.m., although in the bull market during 1986, the Tokyo Stock Exchange restricted trading hours for a time to enable the processing of stock to keep pace with the frantic volume of turnover. At that time, the average volume traded exceeded 1 billion shares a day.

All trading must be done through regular members of the exchanges. In addition to the regular members, there are what are termed 'saitori' in the Tokyo market and 'nakadachi' in Osaka, which perform the same function. Their role is to act as intermediaries between the regular members. The saitori members have an additional role prior to the opening of the morning and afternoon trading sessions. Using the 'itayose' trading method, all buy and sell orders are matched to arrive at a market price. After trading begins, trading switches to the 'zaraba' method where the highest buy order and the lowest sell order is treated on a first come, first serve basis.

The number of saitori/nakadachi needed in the markets has gradually dwindled, largely due to the mechanisation of trading. On the Tokyo Stock Exchange, for example, all dealing is computerised, apart from trading in the 250 most active issues.

Plans for completely electronic trading are remote, since share traders argue that a physical market is preferable for assessing market mood, which would be hard to establish if trading were fully computerised. Complete electronic trading would also remove one of the historical features of the exchanges, where all dealers on the floor communicate through sign language, with a different hand signal for each of the listed stocks.

Dealing commissions on transactions in Japan's stockmarkets are still fixed, making Japan the only large equities market worldwide that refuses to consider switching to negotiated commissions.

In their fight against the introduction of negotiated commissions, the Japanese houses have been joined by the foreign houses active in Japan, which are pleased to see rates pegged at comparatively higher levels than those operating in other major markets in Europe or the US, since it helps offset the high cost of operating in the Tokyo market. Even so, commissions on large-lot transactions (¥10 million and above) were cut by approximately 10 per cent in late 1986, with larger-sized deals cut much further. The average commission reduction hit some of the foreign houses by as much as 25 per cent. An additional cut averaging approximately 10 per cent was implemented in the second half of 1987. This second cut was strongly resisted by the foreign houses, since they argued that it unfairly impacted on their business. Since all their clients are institutional (none of the foreign houses in Japan are trying to develop a private client base, apart from a limited number of high net worth individuals), cutting commissions on larger transactions hits the foreign houses proportionately much more than the Japanese houses, which have extensive retail brokerage activities.

The Japanese houses are also more insulated because they have enjoyed the significant expansion of activity of their investment trusts, which have seen a large amount of new funds flowing in over the past two years.

Along with the general reduction in commissions, it was also decided to reduce the amount of the commission retained by member firms for processing transactions on behalf of non-members. Formerly, this was set at 27 per cent, although it was reduced in the latter part of 1987 to 20 per cent.

Securities depository system

As part of the overall efforts to improve the operations of the stock exchanges, the government, after lengthy and detailed study, has moved to establish a central depository system which, when operational, should have a considerable impact on reducing the cost of both transferring and issuing securities.

The present system largely operates through Japan Securities Agents, a public

The Osaka Stock Exchange is fighting a rearguard action to protect its position. It now accounts for only 12 per cent of trading by volume.

company controlled by Japan Securities Finance, with a number of securities houses depositing stock certificates with this organisation. To date, however, the stock clearance system has been inefficient, since deposited certificates had to be returned at the end of each accounting period to reflect the change in ownership that had occurred in the previous period, making it difficult for the certificates to be used in a co-mingled manner. The prime difficulty, however, is that this system applies only to stocks listed on the Tokyo Stock Exchange.

Under the new system, which has been the subject of special legislation, the scrip will be deposited with the depository organisation, where it will remain in custody. Thus, instead of transferring the underlying scrip when transactions are carried out, book entries will be made by either the clearing house or the affiliated securities companies, so that a central registry will be updated, with the actual scrip remaining in deposit.

The new system was originally due to be operational from 1987, but it has been delayed and may not be operational until 1989 at the earliest.

Problems associated with stock clearance present perhaps the biggest difficulty for the foreign houses. Japanese houses have a large pool of scrip in-house, held on behalf of clients, over which they have absolute discretion. Already some of the foreign houses, which do not have this bank of scrip under their control, have run into several clearance problems, and a number of fines have been levied. This should gradually be rectified as the role of foreign houses in the market expands.

Stock index futures

The introduction of stock index trading in Japan came after the start of a contract based on the Nikkei stockmarket index contract on the Singapore International Monetary Exchange.

After lengthy planning, and delays, the Osaka Securities Exchange began trading in the Osaka 50 Stock Futures contract from 9 June 1987. This contract suffers from the fact that although the most widely used yardstick when assessing the movement of Japan's stock exchanges is the Nikkei index of the leading 225 stocks – unchanged in make-up since it was first introduced – the Osaka Exchange took a basket of 50 stocks using the Osaka Exchange as their home exchange. While there has been some debate about its weighting, and whether it fully reflects underlying market movements, the start of trading has been judged a success.

Much of the focus of attention of those traders interested in stock index futures in Japan may shift to the Tokyo Stock Exchange (TSE) when trading commences in the TSE's proposed new stock index contract based on the TSE Stock Index. However, the start of trading may have to wait for the overhaul of the Securities Exchange Law, which is planned for the first half of 1988.

Once legislative changes are in place, there is likely to be a substantial diversification of futures and options contracts in Japan. The groundwork was laid in early 1987, when the Securities Futures Committee of the Securities Exchange Council released a report calling for the introduction of a broader range of contracts in Japan. The Federation of Bankers Association has also sought the introduction of a broader range of contracts, covering futures and options for both interest rates and currencies.

Of particular note is that when trading began in bond futures, Japan's banks were admitted to the market as special participants, with approval to trade on their own behalf but precluded from acting on behalf of potential clients. With the expected expansion of the variety of futures and options markets in Japan, it is anticipated that banks would be given similar trading rights in these markets. This would leave them well poised to move quickly if more substantive change to the present lines of demarcation between banking and broking is permitted.

Regulation

Control of the securities industry is primarily through the Securities and Exchange Law of 1948, which was introduced by the occupying military authorities, and modelled on existing US legislation and attitudes. Section 65 of this Act, which provides for the separation of banking and securities businesses, was added to the legislation as an afterthought.

The legislation has been regularly amended to take into account various changes, for example, simplification of corporate reporting systems and new provisions for banks dealing in government bonds. The last major overhaul of the legislation occurred in 1971. At that time changes in the corporate reporting system were made along with making provision for 'tender offers'.

A further extensive revision of the legislation is being planned for the first half of 1988. This revision is expected to include provisions for a shelf registration system for bonds issued in the Tokyo market.

In addition to this legislation are the direct and indirect controls wielded by the Ministry of Finance (MoF) which, through the usual 'administrative guidance', provides an additional layer of control of industry activity, although its main role is largely to monitor activity through regular consultations with the industry, as well as scrutiny of detailed financial information that has to be supplied by all securities companies to MoF.

These additional controls are at least as important as the overall legislative controls and, even though they have force through only 'moral suasion', are very potent.

Central to MoF's and the Securities Bureau's attitude is the protection of investors. This attitude, while ensuring that investors do not suffer unduly from normal market movements, is difficult to understand fully, given the fact that insider trading and extensive stock manipulation are the order of the day, which means that smaller investors are regularly exposed to unscrupulous business dealings and are less than adequately protected.

By and large, the activities of the Securities Bureau amount to little more than monitoring industry developments, although it acts to safeguard the securities industry if it comes under threat from other sections of Japan's financial system.

Japanese bankers regularly complain in private that the Securities Bureau wields much more power than the International Bureau or the Banking Bureau within MoF, as it ensures the securities companies maintain their position within the industry.

Additional monitoring is carried out by the stock exchanges themselves on the activities of members, and also through an independent body, the Securities Exchange Council, which advises the ministry directly on matters of importance to the industry.

This advisory group played a role in pressuring for the setting up of a futures market in Japan and, more recently, it has been pressing a campaign for changes in many of the controls of the issuance of domestic bonds. With the present onerous controls, there has been a dramatic increase in the number of Japanese companies going offshore to raise funds.

International equities

The biggest difference between Japanese and foreign investors is their differing perception of the outlook for the sharemarkets in Japan.

After being heavy net buyers of stock in the early 1980s, following the freeing of most of the major remaining foreign exchange controls, foreign investors have been consistent net sellers since 1984 – just at the time when the bull market in Tokyo was getting underway.

At about the same time, Japan's big institutional investors started moving cautiously into foreign equity markets for the first time. Japanese investors have had a traditional aversion to foreign equity markets, preferring the security of bond markets which were much easier to understand.

Nonetheless, in 1984, some of the big institutions made an initial foray into the West German market which proved highly successful. More recently they have invested heavily in other equity markets in Europe, but especially in North America, as their level of confidence and understanding of these markets has broadened. Mostly they limit their buying to blue-chip equities, where they feel on safer ground and where the level of information is high enough to resolve any qualms they may have.

For some Japanese institutional investors, foreign bonds will still be preferred over equities, due to domestic legal and administrative requirements. Life insurance companies, for example, cannot access capital gains in determining overall returns to policy holders, since they must be allocated to a separate reserve. Even though no immediate change is expected on this point, there is a general view that this policy will be eased progressively. In any case, the overall interest in equity issues is gradually on the rise.

The increasing activity of Japanese investors in non-Japanese equity markets is in line with the broad increase in activity of foreign investors in most major equity markets worldwide.

Foreign investors

Even though foreign investors have been net sellers of their Japanese holdings over the past two years, and well into 1987, the overall volume of trading has risen significantly. Total trading – buying and selling – stood at ¥6.7 trillion in 1981. By 1986 this had risen to ¥34.99 trillion. Foreign investors' level of participation in Japan's equity markets remained largely constant over that period. They accounted for 10.2 per cent of total trading in 1981 and 10.9 per cent in 1986. Over this period, the percentage of shares held by foreign investors has grown from around 4 per cent to 6 per cent – well ahead of the total equity holdings of the investment trusts.

Foreign investors now hold a significant position in a range of Japanese stocks, the most popular in the first half of 1987 being domestic demand related issues, in line with the clouded outlook for most of Japan's big export groups. Consequently retailers, food stocks, pharmaceutical issues, machine tool and property sectors stand out. In addition, foreign investors have long had a large holding in Japan's general insurance companies, which are among the most profitable in the world.

Of the foreign investors participating in Japan's equity markets, the most active are European, with US investors only entering in a significant way since 1982. The role of US investors in the Japanese market is surpasssed by that of Asian investors, primarily overseas Chinese, who have been active players in the Japanese market for several years, mainly through Hong Kong and, to a lesser extent, Singapore. There is a large residual presence of Middle East investors as well, stemming from the prosperity of the late 1970s and early 1980s.

Europeans account for half of the total activity of foreign investors in Japan. Purchases and sales of Japanese equities by foreign investors reached ¥35.04 trillion in calendar 1986, with European investors accounting for ¥18.5 trillion, Asian investors for ¥7.21 trillion and US investors for ¥5.4 trillion. All three groups have been net sellers of Japanese equities since 1983. For Japanese investors buying stocks offshore, their net purchases stood at just US$133 million in fiscal 1984, rising to US$1.74 billion the following year. In fiscal 1986 (to 30 March 1987), Japanese investors were net purchasers of US$7.05 billion of foreign equities according to official statistics. This figure understates the real level of their activity to a significant degree, since it does not include the purchases undertaken by the growing number of foreign affiliates of Japanese investors, both corporate and institutional. The total amount traded by Japanese investors rose to US$4.5 billion in fiscal 1984, US$12.6 billion in fiscal 1985 and US$34.78 billion in fiscal 1986. These figures are inevitably distorted by currency movements, but the underlying trend is clear.

The level of activity on the Tokyo Stock Exchange, combined with the increasing purchases by Japanese investors of international equities, has acted as a magnet to foreign securities houses. The first foreign house to move into Japan was Merrill Lynch, which established a branch in Tokyo in June 1972. It was followed by Vickers da Costa in August 1978 and Bache Halsey Stuart Shields in December 1979.

By the end of 1985, there were 12 foreign houses with branches in Tokyo, more than doubling to 34 groups with 36 branches, and a further 120 representative offices, by the end of 1986.

Japanese representation overseas

At the same time, there has been a steady rise in the number of Japanese securities houses with overseas representation. The big four securities houses have been active internationally for some time, although the most notable feature since 1985 has been the rush offshore by the second tier of security houses, as the big four houses have consolidated their international network.

By the end of 1986, 25 Japanese securities houses had offices in London, 20 in

Hong Kong, 15 in New York, nine in each of Paris and Geneva, eight in Sydney and Bahrain, seven in Los Angeles and Beijing, six in Frankfurt and Seoul and five in Singapore. With the steady increase in interest in foreign equities, there has been a large rise in the number of investment funds offered to Japanese investors – six in 1983, and five in 1984. In 1986 a total of 20 trusts was offered, up from nine in 1985, which raised ¥285.4 billion (US$1.90 billion) from Japanese investors.

With the rise in the number of trusts offered for offshore investments, there has also been a broadening of both the diversity of offerings and the range of brokers acting as the sales agents.

One of the largest trusts offered during 1986 was by Merrill Lynch, which launched the First Convertible Securities Fund. Of the total of ¥26.47 billion raised, ¥12.75 billion was from Japanese investors.

The OTC market

Japan's over-the-counter (OTC) market, with only 160 companies traded, is a dwarf compared with the main boards of the stock exchanges. After languishing in the backwater of the securities markets in the early 1980s, it has been trying to take on a new lease of life, although with only limited success to date.

New listings have been active since 1985, and the indications are that it will remain buoyant for the medium term, although the burst of new activity could easily run out of steam.

The OTC market was revamped in 1983, in a bid to revive interest, and it has taken some time to make any progress. With only three companies listed in 1983, it is easy for any growth to look exceptional. At that time, listing requirements were relaxed; since then there has been a steady increase in new listings, with 22 companies going to the market in 1986, and with the prospect that around 40 will be listed in 1987.

Along with the increase in listings, trading activity has steadily increased, with trading volume topping the 200 million mark in 1986 – historically high, but still a minnow compared to the daily volumes of more than five times that amount on the main board of the Tokyo Stock Exchange.

The OTC market likes to model itself on the NASDAQ exchange in the US, which boasts over 4,000 actively traded companies. A more appropriate comparison for the OTC market in Japan is the unlisted securities market in London.

Historically, Japan had a very active OTC market, which was subject to extensive trading excesses. Before World War II, trading on the main board was mainly in futures, with the OTC market functioning more as a spot market.

With futures trading outlawed after the war, OTC dealings were more in stocks not listed on the main boards. Partly as a means of cleaning up this

20% of capital held by foreign portfolio investors

Stock	*%*	*Stock*	*%*
Amada	26.2	Marui	23.3
Arabian Oil	20.2	Mitsui Real Estate	23.4
Canon	21.6	Nichei Construction	22.4
Daifuku	24.4	Nishimatsu Construction	23.1
Dai-Ichi Seiyaku	20.4	Orient Leasing	39.3
Daikin Industries	20.8	Raito Kogyo	22.8
Dainippon Screen	22.0	Royal	22.3
Danto	25.2	Santen Pharmaceutical	22.9
Eisai	20.7	Tokyo Denki Komusho	26.8
Kashiyama	21.6	Tokyo Style	27.4
Kobori Juken	33.4	Yasuda Fire	20.3
Makino	20.6		

market, the authorities established a second trading board on all of the big exchanges in 1961, which assumed the bulk of the OTC market stocks, leaving a small number of mostly sickly stocks out in the cold.

While trading on the main boards is regulated by the stock exchanges themselves and the Securities Exchange Law, the OTC market is controlled by the Securities Dealers Association of Japan. The quality of the companies traded is modest, with most of them being small groups operating regionally and tightly controlled by their founders. A number of the OTC stocks are managed, that is, they are in financial straits, although trading is still permitted. Not all of the companies listed on the OTC market are small, however, since the list includes one of Japan's largest domestic airlines, Toa Airlines, and, ironically, the Bank of Japan, Japan's central bank. Toa Airlines has annual revenues of around ¥150 billion but, due to its erratic profit history, has been unable to comply with listing requirements to list on the main markets.

The Bank of Japan is one of the most profitable in Japan. The bulk of its capital is held by the government through MoF. Its share price traded at a low of ¥18,000 in 1984, reaching a peak of ¥200,000 in 1986.

The burst of new listings activity has breathed some life back into the OTC market, although it is likely to be some time before it is established on a firm footing and taken seriously by investors.

Trading requirements

The overhaul of the OTC market that occurred in November 1983 included removing or relaxing a number of requirements. Rules insisting that a dividend be paid to shareholders and that a company be in operation for more than two years were scrapped, together with a reduction in the minimum number of shares on issue from 400,000 to 300,000, institution of an electronic trading system (prior to this trading had been haphazard, often with a wide discrepancy between traded prices), and other changes, including a reduction in listing fees. There are no annual listing fees. As a result, the usual cost of listing on the OTC market is now put at up to ¥60 million, compared with up to ¥350 million for a listing on the main boards of the stock exchanges.

These changes were aimed at broadening the attraction of the OTC market for smaller companies aiming to go public, although interest has been slow to catch on.

Additional changes implemented during 1987 may help the market to develop further. The first mutual funds have been launched, based on smaller stocks in the OTC market, together with those on the first and second boards of the stock exchanges. These funds will help to expand investor interest in this section of the market, although long-term success hinges on the quality of new paper that comes to market. In addition, MoF is likely to make it easier for OTC companies to issue convertible bonds, which will help to broaden the funding options of these companies, as well as investor interest.

At present there are large differences between the OTC market and the second board market of the stock exchanges.

For the OTC market, the authorised number of shares is a minimum of two million, compared with six million for the second board. Net assets of only ¥200 million are permitted on the OTC market, compared with ¥1 billion for the second board. No minimum requirements on the net tangible assets per share apply to the OTC market, compared with ¥100 for the second board. No profit history is necessary and net earnings per share of just ¥10 are allowed for the OTC market, compared with ¥20 for the second board. On the OTC market no trading history is required, compared with a five-year history for the second-board companies. A company needs to have only 200 shareholders for the OTC market, against 1,000 for the second-board companies.

The OTC market as a proving ground

Most companies going to the OTC market do so with the ultimate aim of graduating to the second board of the stock exchanges, which marks a major point of contrast with the NASDAQ market in the US. One of the reasons for the smaller size of the OTC market in Japan is the fact that companies regularly graduate to the second board; small companies go to the OTC market simply for cheap equity funds.

One of the pecularities of the corporate scene in Japan is that small, privately-held companies find it very hard to attract and retain competent staff, who prefer the security of working for larger organisations. Going public, even if to the OTC market, not only provides access to cheaper equity finance, but also enables much broader public attention, which often helps the small company to boost the scale of its activities, attract better personnel and generally achieve faster growth.

Against this background, the OTC market, even though it may succeed in expanding the number of new listings, will in the longer term continue to be a proving ground for companies waiting to graduate to the second board of the main exchanges. Even with this inherent limitation to its operations, the market has been successful in attracting one foreign company, Shaklee Corporation of the US, which decided to float off a small stake in its Japan affiliate. Avon Products also floated off a 40 per cent stake in its Japanese subsidiary in late 1987, raising an expected US$200 million.

In addition, AM International of the US has a controlling stake in Nippon AM, Sando AG has a stake in S.D.S. Biotech, Merck in Torii Pharmaceutical, Alcoa of the US in Shibasaki Seisakusho and Dopa Corporation has a large holding in Japan Dopa.

From the former policy of basically ignoring the OTC market, leaving it as a resting home for weaker companies or as a loosely organised market for trading in the myriad regional stocks, the authorities have begun to take a more active interest in trying to develop the market, although substantial limitations are faced.

Since the changes introduced to the OTC market in 1983, 16 stocks have graduated to the second board of the stock exchanges, with eight during 1986 alone. Development of the OTC market is being strongly pursued by the Nomura Securities affiliate Jafco, which sees an active OTC market as a natural adjunct to its activities in venture capital financing. An active OTC market will provide a greater inducement to small ventures to go public quickly, and enhance capital gains all round, particularly for the investors in the partnerships organised and managed by Jafco which invest in smaller venture capital businesses. A look at the companies that have come to the OTC market in recent years indicates that they are primarily service companies. However, a number of electrical machinery and other industrial groups have entered this market over the past 18 months.

An important aspect of listing on the OTC for smaller companies is that the value of the listing can be used as collateral for lending, which can also help to reduce funding costs.

Commodity markets

Although Japan is the largest single importer of a wide range of commodities, the development of its commodities exchanges lags far behind the level expected in most advanced countries. Ironically, Japan established the first recognisable futures exchange, in rice futures, in 1730. But with strict domestic price controls there has been no need for a rice exchange for several decades.

Japan boasts 16 commodity exchanges, ranging from rubber and eggs to dry cocoons, but most of the exchanges are small and inefficient. There are regular complaints from investors alleging that they have suffered at the hands of unscrupulous dealers.

The commodities futures industry is also poorly regulated and most of the big broking houses are reluctant to become involved.

Of the 16 exchanges, four are under the control of the Ministry of International Trade and Industry (MITI) and the balance under the control of the Ministry of

Agriculture, Forestry and Fisheries. MITI in particular has played a key role in seeking to reorganise the industry to put it onto a firmer footing. It engineered the merger of the Tokyo Gold Exchange, the Tokyo Rubber Exchange and the Tokyo Textile Commodities Exchange in November 1984. The merged exchange, known as the Tokyo Commodity Exchange for Industry, is Japan's largest, with most of the trading in gold and platinum.

The government's, especially MoF's, strong opposition to financial speculation has restrained the development of commodities futures markets in Japan, but official attitudes are slowly changing. After its success in putting the various Tokyo exchanges under its control onto a firmer footing, MITI has been seeking to merge the smaller Osaka Textile Exchange and the Kobe Rubber Exchange, although this has run into difficulties due to strong local loyalties.

There have also been calls for a revamping of the organisation of Japan's commodities exchanges into one body under more uniform controls, although these steps are unlikely to be taken rapidly.

There are two categories of member of the Tokyo Commodity Exchange for Industry – general members who are limited to transactions on their own accounts, and ring members who take orders on a commission basis. Foreign traders or companies involved in business in any of the commodities traded through the exchange may be able to participate as associate members.

The method of price setting is unusual. When a price has been set in each commodity, the Exchange's staff mark this by clapping traditional 'hyoshigi', a pair of wooden clappers used during Shinto religious ceremonies. There are six calls a day for gold, ranging down to four a day for cotton and woollen yarn and two for platinum. Delivery is usually to be completed by the last day of the contract month.

CHAPTER THIRTEEN

Japan's securities houses

Buoyed by the strength of the yen and their exceptionally powerful domestic base, Japan's 'Big Four' securities houses have begun to establish a major presence in international capital markets.

A substantial push into both London and New York during the 1980s has focused international attention on the breadth and power of their operations. But even with their ambitious international development programmes, their fortunes are inextricably linked with their domestic operations, where a nationwide network of branches and aggressive sales staff gives them extraordinary placing power.

The expansion abroad

The securities houses' move abroad is not new, although it has gained impetus in recent years. Nomura Securities, for example, first established an overseas branch in 1927. With its expansion in the 1920s, Nomura had begun marketing US dollar-denominated paper to domestic clients, and decided to establish a New York office to process the paperwork involved. After the tightening of domestic controls during the 1930s, the office was closed down in 1936. In line with Japan's post-war reconstruction, the big securities houses began establishing offshore representative offices and branches from the early 1950s.

The securities houses' expansion offshore followed the increasing international exposure of Japan's giant institutional investors and large corporations. Moving beyond that base has been less easy.

For some years the houses' most significant overseas presence was in Hong Kong. Instead of trying to penetrate the local market, however, they established a niche advising overseas Chinese on investments in the Japanese market. Gradually they expanded into Singapore for largely the same reasons, although Daiwa Securities, in conjunction with local groups, played a role in helping the Singapore government develop the Asia dollar market, based in Singapore.

In London, the openness of the Euromarkets has made expansion there comparatively straightforward. The rise of the Japanese houses to the top of the Euromarket league tables, for instance, has been largely due to their dominance in Euroyen issues since this market was liberalised in late 1984. The subsequent explosion of activity pushed Japanese groups to the fore.

The move by Nomura Securities to begin market making in a restricted number of securities in the UK from the second half of 1987 signalled its determination to penetrate the London markets. And Nomura was the first Japanese house to obtain a banking licence to operate in the UK; the other three top houses will follow.

New York is a key market for the big Japanese houses, largely due to the attraction of the US government bond market. Sanyo's decision in the early 1960s to list its ADRs in New York brought home to the Japanese houses the importance of establishing a presence in this market, so that they could continue servicing their domestic corporate clients as they moved offshore.

The increasing importance of Japan's big institutional investors in the market for US government paper helped the big securities houses into this market. The importance of Japanese investors to the success of US Treasury auctions resulted in Nomura and Daiwa obtaining primary dealer status; Yamaichi Securities and

Nikko Securities are expected to follow in due course. Now, with Japanese institutions becoming increasingly interested in equities, especially in the large US market, the Japanese securities houses are being compelled to establish their strength in this market, if they are to prevent foreign brokers obtaining access to their Japanese institutional clients.

But, just as they face competition from foreign financial institutions penetrating the domestic market in Japan, the Japanese securities houses have found fierce competition overseas. In particular they have found it difficult to advance from the base of selling Japanese stocks to local institutions, to the marketing of local stocks, although their efforts are gathering pace. The rapid increase in the houses' staffing levels is seen as part of a major commitment to garner a large share of the markets in both New York and London.

The securities houses are also keen to establish a broader base, especially in the US where Japanese investors are active traders not only in government

Nikko Securities: the push into London and New York has focused international attention on the breadth and power of the Japanese houses.

securities and equities, but also, since 1986, the property market. The securities houses have signalled that where they lack the necessary in-house experience, they will buy it or forge strategic alliances to obtain it.

In 1986, for example, Nomura bought a half interest in Eastdil Realty Inc, a US investment house that specialises in property transactions. It also bought into a US leasing company, Babcock Brown, to increase knowledge of leasing within the group.

But despite the expansion during the 1980s, international earnings account for substantially less than 20 per cent of consolidated profits of the bigger houses, which have the largest representation.

Nomura, the biggest and the most aggressive internationally of the'Big Four', is ambitiously pursuing a strategy of boosting profits from overseas related operations to half of group profits by the mid-1990s. But the difficulties involved in ceding independence to its overseas operations are proving to be a significant hurdle.

The proportion of income generated from international activities for all houses may be slightly understated in terms of the overall volume of business, since in most major international markets all the big houses are charging negotiated commissions which are typically far lower than the margins generated from domestic business, based on fixed commissions.

The major Japanese houses want to be involved in all aspects of international securities dealings, with the capability of providing a full range of services to clients.

In typically Japanese fashion the securities houses closely watch each other's expansionary moves, and any new service or product offered by one is quickly followed by the others, depending on the attitude of the Ministry of Finance.

The foreign houses in Tokyo

Much of the spurt of activity by the biggest Japanese broking houses to strengthen their presence in London and New York has been fuelled by the entry of foreign security houses to the Tokyo market.

Given the tough competition in Japan, few doubt that the foreign houses will find it difficult to expand their operations rapidly, although the force of their latest push is a clear indication of their intentions. Salomon Brothers, for example, in early 1987 boosted the paid-up capital of its Tokyo subsidiary from ¥5.1 billion to ¥51 billion, giving it the fifth largest capital base of any securities house in Japan. In the second half of 1987, Shearson Lehman decided to increase the capital of its Tokyo affiliate by US$85 million to over US$100 million.

The rapid expansion of the number of employees of the foreign securities houses in Tokyo has given rise to speculation over just how long it will be before one of the foreign firms emerges as large enough to rival one of the big four Japanese houses.

Earnings

Buoyed by fixed commissions, Japan's big securities houses have emerged not only as the most profitable financial groups in Japan, but also as the most profitable companies overall. Even the gradual reductions in commission rates have not slowed the sharp growth of their earnings, since their fortunes have been built on their massive retail base.

The volume of stocks traded on the first and second boards of the Tokyo Stock Exchange, which covers over 80 per cent of all trading in Japan, has increased steadily in recent years, with a 62 per cent rise in calendar 1986 to 197.69 billion shares traded. Trading volumes will grow further in 1987. In addition, bond and convertible bond markets have also been extremely active.

Japanese securities houses have traditionally derived the bulk of their earnings from commission on stock and bond transactions carried out on behalf of clients. Income from this source is usually balanced by earnings from

富士商品
野村證券

大和證券
ダイワカード
コーナー

underwriting, together with interest income and trading gains. The bull market underway in Japan since 1984, however, has changed that, with commission income accounting for over half of earnings since late 1985. This will continue while Japan's equity markets maintain their record volume and price levels.

For the biggest securities houses, commission income accounts for over 50 per cent of income, with the balance spread across underwriting, dividends and interest income.

With commission income making up the bulk of the securities houses' earnings, the pressure constantly to turn over stock can only continue. Since a large proportion of a corporation's stock is tied up in the hands of a number of large, long-term shareholders, liquidity in any one issue is limited. Consequently, to maintain trading volumes, the broking houses have little choice but to trade stock actively for their clients if they want to buoy their bottom line performance.

For medium-sized firms, such as Yamatane Securities and Cosmo Securities, commission income can account for over 70 per cent of income. Typically the smaller the firm, the greater is the proportion of income derived from trading commission. The larger securities houses with their much broader financial capability are gradually evolving as more general finance companies, with a range of services available or offered through affiliated companies.

But while moving into the fringe financing areas, the strength of the strong retail base of the securities houses will continue to propel the bigger houses forward, and will continue to form the key to their future earnings.

The 'Big Four'

Due to their sheer strength in the Japanese market, few professional investors can afford to move far from the 'Big Four' – Nomura Securities, Daiwa Securities, Nikko Securities and Yamaichi Securities.

In many respects, equity markets in Japan are far less professional than major equity markets internationally. The market responds not to research and intelligent assessment, but to speculation about which stocks are about to be listed as buy recommendations of the bigger securities houses. Inclusion means a certain rise in stock prices. Knowing what is on the buy list of the big houses is very important to the foreign houses and the smaller Japanese houses.

Buying on independent research has less to do with market movements than the ability of the more aggressive traders to sell their clients a 'story' justifying why a stock's price is likely to rise.

If anything, the improvement in communications systems during the 1970s has enhanced the power of the Big Four, enabling much greater coordination of buying and tighter control over client recommendations than was the case for much of the post-war period.

The near collapse of some of the larger stockbroking houses in the market crisis of the early 1960s and the big increase in domestic bond markets during the 1970s signalled the changing fortunes of the industry.

Until the 1960s, the dominant forces among the securities houses were Yamaichi Securities and Nikko Securities. The near collapse of Yamaichi Securities together with the problems faced by Oi Securities, renamed Wako Securities, resulted in a decline in their fortunes for a time.

Daiwa Securities and Nomura Securities, both with origins in Osaka, had a much stronger presence in the bond markets. As a result, the surge in government bond issues from the second half of the 1970s enabled them to entrench their positions as the leaders of the securities industry.

Notwithstanding the concentration of power of the Big Four their overall share in equities trading in Japan has gradually declined, and the medium-sized broking houses now have a gradually growing share of the business. The Big Four now account for 47 per cent of all trading in equities in Japan, down from well over 50 per cent a decade ago.

In a sense this reduction is misleading, since all of the Big Four have strong

Opposite above: Nomura Securities: it first established an overseas branch in 1927 when it began marketing US dollar-denominated paper to Japanese investors.

Opposite left: Daiwa Securities, along with Nomura, has obtained primary dealer status in the US Treasury market.

links with a number of medium-sized and smaller houses. If the share of those houses is included, the total trading position of the Big Four may be unchanged.

Even so, the changing nature of capital markets, and particularly the growing sophistication of the big institutional investors, are likely to underwrite a further expansion of the role of the medium-sized and smaller houses which can often offer better services and execution than the bigger houses.

Much of the growth of the big houses has stemmed from their sheer spread of operation and the lack of serious competition in the race for returns on clients' funds.

The growing sophistication of smaller investors in particular, who have become much more adept in the search for higher rates of return, and the pressure from pension fund managers and other professional investors seeking better returns have placed the securities houses under increasing pressure to improve their performance.

It has often been alleged that with their extensive operations, the bigger securities houses could shift stock in and out of their 'in-house' investment trusts, and also use clients' holdings held in trust at whim, allowing them to shift underperforming stock and minimise the adverse effect of poor investments.

But increasing performance pressures have made this option less feasible. Now, with a rising number of international fund managers seeking to carve out a niche in the overall funds management market in Japan and the greater focus on returns of funds invested as interest rates decline, it has become harder for the bigger houses to hide their mistakes.

The securities houses also face a longer-term threat from the domestic banks. All the major banks have close and long-term associations with a number of medium-sized and small broking houses, the most notable being between Dai-Ichi Kangyo Bank and Nippon Kangyo Kakumaru, the sixth largest securities house, and the Industrial Bank of Japan and New Japan Securities and Wako Securities. Usually, staff are seconded to, or rotated between, the bank and its

Opposite right: The view towards Uchisaiwaicho from the Kasumigasi building.

Below: Yamaichi Securities – the Big Four now account for 47 per cent of all trading in equities in Japan.

TOTO
OMEGA
TOTO

securities affiliate, and the board of the affiliate is dominated by representatives of the bank.

Even though the Ministry of Finance maintains a strong public image of refusing to allow any significant breaking down of the barriers between the banking and securities sectors, the banks have become increasingly open about their links and affiliations with securities houses. Equally, the bigger securities houses have close links with a number of smaller regional banks through which they obtain clearing services, although the authorities have refused to allow same-day clearance from their investment trusts, which would also mark a substantial breaking down of the existing lines of demarcation.

It is a common assumption in Tokyo's financial circles that any future significant liberalisation would quickly bring about a merger of Nomura Securities and Daiwa Bank, which had been a single organisation in the past. Interestingly, Daiwa Bank is the only city bank which has retained its trust bank operations. Also, it is the largest pension fund manager in Japan and is in a powerful position to capitalise on any future liberalisation measures, either in terms of greater freedoms for banks and securities houses or relaxation of the controls over pension fund management.

CHAPTER FOURTEEN

The foreign factor

A major change in Japan's financial system over the past five years has been the rapid growth in the participation of foreign financial groups. Attracted by the rising capital outflow from Japan, the pressure from foreign banks and securities houses to expand their presence in Tokyo has been intense. Surging equity markets and the progressive deregulation of the domestic financial system have given the foreign institutions a much stronger position than ever before, even though it is still tiny compared with the giants of Japan's financial sector.

Over the past five years, there has been a dramatic change in the degree of foreign participation in the Japanese financial system. Foreign broking houses have been granted membership of the Tokyo Stock Exchange, foreign trust banks have been given access to the domestic trust banking sector and foreign banks have been allowed to open security company affiliates, with some foreign banks also likely to have their own securities dealing operation in the near future. Along with this, some foreign securities houses have been granted permission to open banking affiliates in Tokyo and foreign investment advisory firms have been granted licences to operate in Japan.

In other sectors of the financial system foreign participation is still severely limited, however. In the insurance field, for example, foreign participation is marginal, and likely to remain so. In life insurance, foreign companies find it hard to achieve the critical mass to challenge the army of direct sales representatives employed by the giants of the industry. Nonetheless, the growth enjoyed by some of the foreign firms has been impressive in recent years, albeit from a modest base.

In the banking and securities sectors, access to the financial system has improved for foreign companies, but they still find it difficult to establish a sufficient presence in Japan's capital markets to be able to compete on an equal footing with the domestic institutions. Foreign companies are hampered by the longstanding and close links between the domestic financial institutions and Japan's industrial and commercial sectors.

Even so, the critical feature of the past few years is that many of the structural constraints limiting the degree of participation of foreign firms have been either removed or relaxed.

Much of the present advantageous position of some of the foreign banks may prove to be only temporary, until Japanese banks are given similar freedom, which will bring with it progressive pressures on the operations and activities of the foreign banks and securities houses. Most of the foreign banks are fully aware of the fact that they have only a temporary window of opportunity, and are moving to take full advantage of the present opening before the giants of the Japanese financial system begin to compete on a directly equal footing.

The speed of development in granting foreign financial institutions a greater role in Japan's financial system was mainly due to the realisation in Japan that if its big banks and securities houses were to be guaranteed continued access to foreign markets, then foreign groups had to be given greater access to the Japanese markets. In early 1987 the British government threatened to restrict access of Japanese institutions to the London markets unless UK securities houses were given greater direct access to the floor of the Tokyo Stock Exchange. Although there was common agreement that if the UK were to carry out its threat, London would be the loser in the long run, the dispute served to crystallise feelings within Japan that steps needed to be taken to boost the level of participation of foreign groups.

Just as foreign banks have found it difficult to build up a sizeable domestic client base, so too have the foreign securities houses. Developing the power to place securities domestically when competing with the strength and financial muscle of the dominant Japanese houses is a major task, and one that cannot be achieved overnight. Even so, in spite of the, at times, inordinate difficulties, foreign securities houses are slowly but steadily making progress.

The Ministry of Finance (MoF) has made it clear, for example, that foreign securities houses will continue to be given a role in underwriting future issues of Nippon Telegraph and Telephone scrip, the next sale of which is to take place in November 1987, and future sales at approximately twelve months' intervals.

Foreign securities houses have also established a strong presence in underwriting convertible bond and warrant issues for Japanese clients in European markets, but to develop their business with Japanese investors in the domestic market will take time.

The concessions made by MoF in increasing steadily the number of issues of government bonds put up for tender, despite entrenched opposition both from within the ministry and from banking circles, points to MoF's sensitivities to foreign pressure. For much of 1986 and 1987, Japanese banks and securities houses have been wary of what they term 'over-presence' – emerging as too strong a force in foreign capital markets – which has resulted in increased foreign criticism and pressure for greater access to Japan's domestic capital markets.

By giving foreign banks access to the trust banking sector, and the ability to establish their own security branches, the authorities moved to take much of the sting out of the foreign allegations. In addition, Merrill Lynch, for example, was given approval for its London bank affiliate to establish commercial banking operations in Tokyo, which will be primarily centred on foreign exchange dealing. This points the way to future developments. At present, foreign exchange trading is denied to Japan's securities houses, although it is likely to be only a matter of time before they are given access to this market.

MoF has also agreed to grant investment advisory licences to 17 foreign firms, out of the total of 56 licences to be granted in the initial stage of this opening.

The much greater flexibility adopted by the authorities when dealing with the foreign banks and securities houses points the way for future developments within Japan, although making the same changes for the domestic institutions is unlikely before there is significant erosion of the Glass-Steagall Act in the US.

CHAPTER FIFTEEN

Foreign banks

Restrained by uncompetitive financing conditions and the securitisation of capital markets, the role of foreign banks in Japan has a marginal one. Impact loans, the provision of US dollar loans for an unspecified purpose to corporate customers, proved to be a profitable niche during the 1970s. But the relaxation of foreign exchange controls in 1980 took away that advantage, pitting the foreign banks in head-on competition with the giants of Japan's banking system.

Indeed, one of the ironies of deregulation of Japan's financial system is that as it has proceeded, the position of the foreign banks has been reduced steadily with little prospect of any significant improvement in the short term.

The business of the foreign banks

The foreign banks' share of assets in the banking sector has been gradually squeezed from 3.15 per cent in the early 1980s to under three per cent by the mid-1980s.

By the end of 1986, there were 115 foreign banks with branches in Japan. The number has shown only a gradual increase over the past five years, with a steady trickle of newcomers offsetting some who withdrew due to the difficulty of developing sustainable commercial bank operations.

The principal difficulty for the foreign banks was the impediment to full access to the short-term money market. The existence of collateral requirements means that foreign banks cannot obtain funds on an equal basis to the domestic banks, even though overall creditworthiness is usually the same, and often better. This has become less of a burden with the securitization of capital markets as the foreign banks have steadily reduced the role of their traditional lending activities.

The development of the unsecured call market, which was started specifically to help the foreign banks overcome their funding problems, has resulted in easier access to funds. The foreign banks have become the dominant users of this market. Even so, foreign banks are at a disadvantage to Japanese banks, which can obtain marginally cheaper funding through the secured call market.

The difficulty of funding has been compounded by the shift of corporate borrowers worldwide away from indirect financing in favour of direct financing, which reduced what demand there has been for funds from foreign banks. One result is that several foreign banks have also closed some of their regional offices, in order to concentrate business in Tokyo and reduce their operating expenses.

Securities licences

Due to the difficulties of buiding up a sizeable domestic book some foreign banks, for example American Express and Marine Midland Bank, decided to surrender their banking licences. American Express took this step because it decided that its interests would be better served if it applied for a securities company licence, as it anticipated that the securitisation of debt markets would make it more worthwhile to move into Japan's securities sector.

With the deregulation of Japan's financial markets, most of the foreign banks have moved to establish a securities company affiliate as soon as possible. As a result, 10 of the 16 securities company branches established during 1986 were affiliated with European or US banks. Banks can hold only a 50 per cent interest in these affiliates, although usually the other partners are 'sleeping' partners. The West German and Swiss banks have relied on other industrial corporations, with which they have close links, to participate.

This circuitous shareholding requirement is likely to be dropped once Article 65 of the Securities Exchange Law is repealed, although this could take time. Indicative of the shareholding mix that has occurred, Bankers Trust, for example, has Exxon holding half of its securities company affiliate.

Foreign exchange trading

Apart from Japan's securities sector, the other main source of earnings for the foreign banks stems from the burgeoning level of activity in the domestic foreign exchange market. Daily foreign exchange trading volume in Tokyo now rivals New York, and during active trading often exceeds New York.

The increase of trading volumes in Tokyo has made it an essential centre for most banks operating internationally. And earnings from foreign exchange trading has fuelled much of the earnings growth of the foreign banks since 1985, when foreign exchange trading became markedly more active in the wake of the Park Plaza Hotel agreement of September 1985.

Foreign exchange activity made it comparatively easy for foreign banks to earn profits during fiscal 1985, when the US dollar was falling against the yen and most other major currencies. But during fiscal 1986, forecasting market movements was more difficult.

Bond markets

Along with foreign exchange trading, foreign banks have been given greater access to trading in public bonds, which has helped to offset the profit squeeze from other operations. Foreign banks had been part of the underwriting syndicate for government bonds, but had only a minor share.

Then, in early 1984, three foreign banks – Citibank, Chase Manhattan and Bank of America – were allowed to begin bond trading, and a larger number of foreign banks was approved from mid-1985.

The rapid growth of the Euroyen market since 1984, fuelled by activity in the swaps market, has meant that those banks with special capabilities in financial engineering have been able to boost their volume of business substantially. For example, whereas most Japanese banks undertake swap transactions directly only if they have an offsetting transaction, some of the larger foreign banks are willing to take on a swap transaction and hold the risk on their own book before matching it into ancillary transactions.

Profits

Against the backdrop of the rising cash surplus in Japan, total assets of foreign banks expanded by 5 per cent in fiscal 1986 to ¥16.59 trillion. The largest is Citibank, with total assets of ¥1.29 trillion, followed by Société Generale at ¥805.9 billion. Profits, however, are low. For example, Citibank generated pre-tax income of ¥1.6 billion and net earnings of just ¥940 million. The largest profit was posted by Bankers Trust, which declared net income of ¥1.15 billion.

Profit figures on the performance of foreign banks are not particularly meaningful, however, since the foreign banks disguise earnings in Japan because of the comparatively high level of corporate taxes. Even so, profits from their Tokyo operations are typically marginal at best.

Investment banking

The bigger foreign banks have substantially strengthened their investment banking divisions in Tokyo as they seek to widen the range of financial engineering services offered to clients. Included here is swap dealing, cross-border leasing and the like, as the foreign banks promote their greater experience with more sophisticated financial engineering and products to woo potential clients.

Most of the foreign banks realise that unless they have specialised services to offer clients in Japan, they will find it all but impossible to compete against the bigger Japanese banks with their close, and long-term, links with the corporate sector.

Trust banking

The introduction of foreign banks to the domestic trust bank sector, as well as the decision to allow a number of European and American banks to establish securities affiliates, has given greater flexibility to the foreign banks. So some of the bigger foreign banks now have commercial bank and trust bank arms which, together with their securities affiliates, give them a far broader spread of activities than Japan's major city banks.

The bigger Japanese banks have largely supported this development, since they see it as helping to contribute to the eventual liberalisation of many of the barriers surrounding the domestic banking and securities industries in the future.

Acquisitions

The other way for foreign banks to dramatically expand their presence in Tokyo is through acquisition. The continuing round of international acquisitions by Japanese banks has resulted in the Ministry of Finance (MoF) indicating that it would not block any move by a foreign institution to take over a domestic bank.

Acclimatising: foreigners practising zazen in a zen temple in Tokyo.

The only move made so far was by Citibank suggesting it was interested in buying control of the failing Heiwa Sogo Bank, although it was beaten to the post by Sumitomo Bank. Subsequently, Citibank took initial steps in forging an alliance with the large mutual bank Tokyo Sogo Bank, which have been read in Japan as the preliminary steps to a merger.

Acquisition of this bank would fit in with Citibank's strategy of building up its retail base. Tokyo Sogo Bank would bring only a modest amount of corporate business since, as a sogo (mutual) bank, it is restricted to lending to medium-sized and small companies.

No other foreign bank has yet indicated serious interest in taking a similar step, probably due to the difficulty of effecting a successful merger in Japan. In particular, there is the residual suspicion in Japan that foreign institutions may not be in the market for the long term, that they have come in to take advantage of present market opportunities and if conditions change in the future, they may move out of Japan again.

MoF's stated lack of opposition to any foreign bank takeover has yet to be tested, although any hostile takeover would stand little chance of success. This is not due to the opposition of the regulatory authorities, but due to a lack of support from the targeted institution.

Far East headquarters

Due to the high costs of operating in Japan, only a limited number of foreign banks have, so far, signalled a shift of their regional headquarters from Hong Kong to Tokyo, although all have significantly increased their representation in Japan.

One of those to shift regional headquarters was Bankers Trust, which has keenly pursued investment banking opportunities in Japan. To date, Japan Bankers Trust, the group's trust bank arm, has been the most successful of the foreign trust banks, quickly winning the management of the pension fund of Heiwa Sogo Bank from Sumitomo Bank, aided by its connection with Sumitomo Trust and Banking.

Foreign trust banks

The decision in 1985 to allow a restricted number of foreign banks to enter the domesic trust banking sector was the most significant liberalisation move for foreign banks in Japan made over the past decade.

Initially, MoF intended limiting to eight the number of foreign trust banks allowed to enter the domestic market, so that there would be an equal number of Japanese and foreign trusts banks.

But the Swiss government stepped in late in the negotiation process to argue its case. Swiss banks had been disadvantaged during earlier negotiations over entry of Japanese banks into Switzerland and Swiss banks' entry into the Japanese market, and many more Japanese banks entered Switzerland than Swiss banks entered Japan. MoF therefore felt morally obliged to give additional representation to Swiss banks, which accounted for the sudden shift to allow nine foreign trust banks to enter Japan, instead of the original target of eight.

Although officially there are only eight Japanese trust banks, one city bank, Daiwa Bank, has extensive trust bank operations. In addition, two small Okinawa institutions, the Okinawa Bank and Bank of the Ryukus, have limited trust bank businesses.

From 1985, Bankers Trust, Chase Manhattan Bank, Chemical Bank, Citibank, Manufacturers Hanover Trust, Morgan Guaranty Trust, Crédit Suisse, Union Bank of Switzerland and Barclays Bank were permitted to move into the domestic trust bank sector. All have formed associations of various degrees with domestic trust banks, to help them establish their position in the market.

For most, initial profitability has been easy to achieve. But expanding their trust bank divisions to the point where they achieve a strong presence in the industry will take several years. Most of the foreign trust banks have been successful in obtaining a portion of the tokkin funds trust management. This has required them to develop their back office systems but has given them only minimal chance to demonstrate their funds management skills.

Penetrating the pensions sector is the ultimate goal of most of the foreign banks, but most concede that due to the very nature of this sector in Japan, it will be a slow process.

By the end of 1986, foreign trust banks were acting as custodians for US$2.6 billion of tokkin accounts, managing US$1.1 billion of fund trust money and handling US$64 million in pension accounts. The long-term goal of managing pension funds assets, a more stable source of funds than tokkin accounts, remains elusive.

Corporate pension funds are estimated to total about ¥25 trillion (US $140 billion). According to Mitsubishi Trust figures, corporate pension funds are expected to reach ¥35 trillion (US$195 billion) by 1991 and ¥60 trillion by 1996. Some estimates put them at US$560 billion by the year 2000. That means that between now and the end of the century, over US$420 billion of business will be handed to fund managers. Of that, at least US$80 billion are earmarked for overseas markets, where foreign banks believe they can perform better than their Japanese competitors.

Pension funds management in Japan is organised through a syndication system, and even though foreign banks may be permitted to bid for a portion of the funds management, it will take time to demonstrate their claim that they have much higher funds management capabilities than domestic trust banks.

The future

The foreign banks, with neither the extensive retail deposit base of the Japanese banks which provides very cheap funds, nor equal access to the call market, have often been forced to lend to lower-quality customers. So whenever there is a large corporate collapse in Japan, foreign banks tend to be among the groups with greatest exposure. For instance, the failure of medium-sized groups such as J. Osawa and Co and Riccar had a greater impact on foreign than domestic banks. On the other hand, the failure of big groups such as the Ataka and Co debacle of the late 1970s or Sanko Steamship of 1985 has less impact on the foreign banks. The large, mainstream Japanese companies have ready access to funds from Japanese banks.

The funding costs of the foreign banks remain an acute issue for many. Although given limited access to the Euroyen market, new issues by foreign banks have been sparse. Access to this market was granted with the provision that any yen funds so raised would not be utilised in Japan. The funding should be improved in the future if the foreign banks can gain access to the yen commercial paper market, scheduled to be operational from the latter part of 1987. This issue was pushed strongly by foreign banks during 1987, once the decision to establish a commercial paper market was taken.

However, for foreign banks to be able to make better inroads into the domestic banking sector, there needs to be a further erosion of the present concept of relationship banking. In Japan, strong personal and corporate links remain the order of the day. This serves as a natural constraint to the ability of foreign banks to penetrate the domestic market, a constraint that has been exacerbated by the huge surge in surplus liquidity in Japan's financial system, and the maturity of large sectors of its industry, which has reduced the corporate sector's demand for new funding.

CHAPTER SIXTEEN

Foreign securities houses

The rapid expansion of trading in Japan's equity markets since 1985 has been a beacon to the larger international securities houses, which have aggressively sought a role in helping to recycle Japan's abundant trade surplus.

The expansion of foreign banks opening branch offices or representative offices in Tokyo tapered off during the 1980s, but the growth in the number of securities companies moving into Japan has continued, although rising from a comparatively low base.

By the end of 1986, there were 36 foreign securities houses with branches in Japan, and a further 125 had representative offices. During 1987, an additional 10 foreign houses were granted operating licences.

It is unlikely that there will be any slowdown in the level of interest in the short term, especially as the Tokyo Stock Exchange is moving to expand the number of foreign member firms from the present six to probably more than double that number. The attraction is not only the surge in trading levels of equity and bond markets worldwide, but also the fact that the capitalisation of Tokyo's equity market is equal to New York's.

Foreign houses have also been successful in obtaining a larger presence in the primary government bond market. After consistent pressure, foreign securities houses were given a larger share of the underwriting syndicate for government bonds. In addition, some of the bigger foreign houses' aggressive bids for stock in the limited number of bond tenders, on occasion outbidding the larger of the Japanese houses, has been a signal of their determination to carve out a sizeable stake in the market for government debt in Japan. On one notable occasion, Salomon Brothers bid for 40 per cent of the stock offered in a short-term bond tender. Morgan Stanley has also been extremely aggressive. The level of activity of the foreign houses has also been fuelled by the rising volume of trading of US Treasury bonds in Japan, following the sharp increase in the exposure of Japan's institutional investors to these securities over the past two years. Trading is miniscule compared with volumes dealt in New York, but it has expanded, and on an active day turnover has often reached US$5 billion – well above the average daily volume of US$2 billion.

The growth in volume traded by the foreign houses has been impressive, although in terms of equity volumes they rank well below Japanese houses.

The largest of the foreign member firms on the Tokyo Stock Exchange, Morgan Stanley, is ranked about number 30 in equities trading according to its estimates, and the company is optimistic of boosting its position further in the medium term. However, since the four big Japanese securities houses alone directly control 45 per cent of the trading in equities, building up a significant presence in Japan will be very difficult for the foreign houses.

The seats bought to date by foreign houses cost an estimated US$5 million each, and the second round of seats to be offered from late 1987 are assumed among the foreign securities houses to cost close to US$9 million each.

Foreign member firms have, however, found it easier to attract quality staff, since holding a seat gives an air of permanence to their Japanese operation, which was lacking while they still operated solely as branches and were not well known among Japanese investors.

The first foreign house to open a branch in Tokyo was Merrill Lynch, and it was gradually followed by others. Now, with 46 foreign houses licensed to operate branches, the competition is intense. The six foreign houses that gained membership of the Tokyo Stock Exchange in 1986 were Morgan Stanley, Jardine Fleming Securities, Merrill Lynch, S. G. Warburg, Goldman Sachs and Vickers da Costa (now part of Citibank).

The dominant foreign firm, in terms of the volumes traded, has been Morgan Stanley. Occasionally, when the Tokyo market is in a sustained rise, Jardine Fleming emerges as the most active foreign broker, but there is speculation that much of this volume may in fact represent trading conducted on behalf of the group's extensive investment trusts. The other foreign firms rank much further behind, although Merrill Lynch is quite active.

With their strong international links, the foreign member firms have established their operations on the back of dealing for overseas clients, while trying to enlarge their domestic client base. For most, domestic clients account for around one-quarter of their trading volume, although Morgan Stanley has been able to boost this to around 40 to 50 per cent. Ministry of Finance (MoF) officials are keen to encourage the foreign houses to boost their volume of domestic business.

Salomon Brothers is one of the foreign firms most keen to obtain a seat on the Tokyo Stock Exchange, and has made it clear that if it is successful in obtaining a seat, it intends to rank along with Jardine Fleming and Morgan Stanley in the daily volume of equity trading handled.

The Nankai railway incident

After the six foreign firms received their membership of the Tokyo Stock Exchange, there was endless speculation around 'kabutacho', Tokyo's version of Wall Street, that it was only a matter of time before one of the foreign houses was taken advantage of by one of the more unscrupulous investor groups active in Japan.

Nankai Electric Railway is one of the regional railway companies in Japan. There was strong investor interest in railway stocks during 1986 because of the extensive property holdings of all railway companies, but the Nankai stock had the added speculative attraction of benefiting from the construction of a new international airport near Osaka.

A client of Merrill Lynch Japan emerged as a strong buyer of the stock, but when the company's share price fell, the client refused to pay, and Merrill Lynch Japan was forced to offload the accumulated stockholding onto a falling market, resulting in a loss of US$17.3 million for the parent company.

MoF subsequently launched an investigation into the incident, and in particular targeted Merrill Lynch's internal operating systems. Senior staff at the broker were replaced and overall operating systems were tightened up. Merrill Lynch subsequently reached a settlement with its wayward client, and claims to have ultimately covered most of its costs.

Clearance difficulties

One of the major difficulties facing foreign brokers in Japan is the quirky domestic securities clearance system. Even though trading in all but the largest issues is fully computerised, the clearance system still relies on physical delivery. In addition, the time limit for clearance is set at three days which, while perhaps appropriate for Japanese investors, creates difficulties when dealing with overseas investors. As the bulk of the clients of the foreign broking houses are primarily foreign investors, difficulties ensue constantly, compounded by the lack of a computerised clearing system.

Japanese houses faced with potential clearance problems usually have a large inventory of stock in hand held on behalf of clients, and which they can use to avoid clearance difficulties. All member firms of the stock exchanges can borrow stock from the securities finance companies, primarily the Japan Securities Finance Company in Tokyo, to overcome clearance problems, but the cost involved eats into revenues, a sore point particularly for the foreign houses. There have also been several instances to date of foreign firms being fined for failing to comply with clearance limits.

As a result, some of the foreign houses are pressing for an extension of clearance to seven days, given the difficulties of physically clearing within the presently prescribed three-day limit. These calls, however, have largely fallen on deaf ears.

Plans are well advanced for the installation of a computerised clearing system, operated by the Japan Securities Depository Corporation, which will enable book entry settlement and may go some way towards getting around clearance difficulties, but the strict three-day clearance limit will still pose difficulties for foreign houses.

Operating costs and commissions

The cost of locating suitable office accommodation, installing appropriate computer systems and building up a strong research team is high. With the rush of foreign firms into Tokyo since 1985, there has been a severe shortage of qualified staff, and salaries have continued to rise.

The requirement that 40 different reports are compiled each month for MoF and the Japan Securities Dealers Association adds to the cost of operations. Some reports have to be completed on a daily basis, some weekly, and others monthly. This can mean up to three employees working full time just compiling and filing these reports.

Other significant costs include annual membership fees, fees for trades completed through the 'saitori' members on the floor and fees for computer-matched trades.

Operating costs, and the costs incurred in borrowing stock, would be reduced if the foreign houses built up a large retail base, but given the high costs involved, none of the foreign houses have moved in this direction, preferring to concentrate on institutional clients. The rising number of 'high net-worth individuals' in Japan, and especially in Tokyo, is an attraction and some of the more aggressive of the foreign houses have targeted this market for attention.

With the high overhead costs of doing business in Tokyo, foreign firms have emerged at the forefront of those opposing moves to reduce commission rates on transactions.

Commissions on larger transactions were reduced in late 1986, and a number of the foreign firms estimated that this cost them around one-quarter of their revenues. For the bigger Japanese houses, with their very large retail base, it is estimated that the reduction in commissions cut their revenues by around 18 per cent.

New stock exchange members

After the first six foreign firms joined the Tokyo Stock Exchange during fiscal 1986, the exchange, after lengthy pressure, indicated that a second round of foreign firms would be approved for entry during fiscal 1988.

There was a bitter dispute over the matter, and the Tokyo Stock Exchange held out for some time, arguing that there was insufficient space available to accommodate more traders on the floor of the exchange. In early 1987, the UK government applied strong pressure on the Tokyo Stock Exchange, requesting that three UK houses – Baring Brothers, J. Henry Schroder-Wagg and Kleinwort Benson – be allowed to buy seats on the exchange from late 1987.

Eventually, the Tokyo Stock Exchange backed down, and made it clear that it would expand membership of the exchange, including a number of foreign houses, but left the precise number unspecified. It is commonly assumed that the membership will be increased by more than 10 seats. A number of Japanese firms are also likely to apply for newly created seats.

CHAPTER SEVENTEEN

Japan's bond markets

Japan's dominant capital market by far is in government bonds: both primary and secondary market activity tower over all domestic financial markets. It is now the second largest market for government debt in the world after the US. And, with the approval of Euroyen bond issues by non-Japanese corporations, this market, too, is now the second largest after the Eurodollar market.

In other financial markets, however, Japan lags well behind North America, Europe and other capital markets around the globe, although plans are steadily advancing to expand trading opportunities in many of these. A limited market for trading in government bond futures has been established, steps are underway for a broader range of futures and options contracts and moves have been initiated to revamp the poorly organised commodities markets.

Japan's financial institutions have also been given approval to trade directly in offshore futures markets and contracts in Japanese government bond futures have commenced in London, giving Japanese investors alternative markets in which to hedge their risks.

Government bonds

A massive increase in government spending in the 1970s to offset the recessionary impact of the first oil price rise has resulted in Japan's level of gross government debt exceeding that of all OECD member countries except Italy. By 1985, it stood at 68 per cent of GDP, compared with 46 per cent for the US, 33 per cent for France, 54 per cent for the UK, 41.7 per cent for West Germany and 96.9 per cent for Italy.

At the net level, i.e after including net social security assets, Japan's level of government debt is a more modest 26.5 per cent, in line with the US.

But the level of government debt has hampered government moves to expand domestic spending since the overall aim of the government and the Ministry of Finance (MoF) is to bring the level of accumulated debt under control.

Approximately one-fifth of government spending is to finance the accumulated debt, which exceeds ¥143 trillion. The original government target was to stop issuing deficit-financing bonds by fiscal 1984 but because of the weakness of the economy in the early 1980s and a shortfall of tax revenues this target had to be postponed. The revised target, set in 1983, was for all new issues of government bonds to be eliminated by fiscal 1990. In line with this, MoF has endeavoured to reduce issues of deficit-financing bonds by ¥1 trillion annually, with construction bond issues also held down as far as possible.

The renewed pressure on the government to expand spending both to boost imports and to take some of the pressure off the US economy makes this revised target again look doubtful.

Consideration for both the financing of the debt programme and the need to limit the cost of carrying this heavy accumulated debt has been the cornerstone of much of MoF's policy over the past decade, accounting for its various moves – so far largely unsuccessful – to revise the taxation system, as well as its general reluctance to deregulate interest rates fully.

MoF's highly cautious policy has also restrained the government's flexibility in changing the present archaic syndication system for distributing the bulk of new bonds, an issue of some contention for foreign securities houses anxious to boost their presence in Tokyo's bond markets.

Redemption of the massive 10-year bonds issued during the second half of the 1970s has resulted in the development of a market for short-term government paper, even though MoF has been ideologically opposed to this development, in an attempt to even out the financing flows for the government.

The sheer size of the national debt programme created fears in the late 1970s that this could lead to a 'crowding-out' effect during the 1980s, with non-government borrowers finding it increasingly difficult to raise sufficient levels of funds through bond issues. These fears have proved to be largely illusory, as the rise in government borrowings has occurred at a time when the corporate sector's demand for new funds has declined. There has also been an expansion of alternative funding sources.

The massive increase in the government's bond issuance programme has had other ramifications as well. It has largely underwritten the emergence of the big broking houses Daiwa Securities and Nomura Securities at the top of the securities industry, giving them a lead over their main rivals, Yamaichi Securities and Nikko Securities.

Historical background

The 'Dodge line' policies adopted in fiscal 1949 required that Japan run a balanced budget, as part of a general set of policies aimed at stamping out inflation then running rampant.

The government managed to run a small budget surplus for much of the 1950s, and the only bond issues were made by the corporate sector and local government. The 'Dodge line' was held until 1966. Economic growth fuelled national tax revenues, enabling the government to achieve spending increases without incurring debt. But an economic slowdown in 1965 led to the rejection of the 'Dodge line' and the government decided to begin issuing bonds in a limited fashion to finance rising public spending levels.

An underwriting syndicate was formed, with 40 per cent of all issues being allotted to the city banks, 20 per cent to regional banks, 11 per cent to securities companies and the balance spread among other financial institutions. To ensure adequate absorption of the bond issues, the Bank of Japan made special advances to the short-term money brokers (tanshi brokers).

The total volume of bonds issued in the first year reached ¥230 billion, of which ¥110 billion was absorbed by the Trust Fund Bureau of MoF. It primarily financed this out of the funds deposited through the Post Office savings system and the national pension funds.

From this small start, public bond issues gradually increased. By 1969, the level of national debt was a modest 7.9 per cent of GNP. But the first oil crisis of the early 1970s threw the Japanese economy into a lengthy recession, heavily cutting tax revenues. To bolster economic growth, the government began a large-scale increase in spending levels in fiscal 1975. In fiscal 1974, national bond issues slightly exceeded ¥2 trillion; by 1979 they topped ¥13 trillion. In the late 1970s the potentially adverse impact of the unrestrained increase in government spending became a major point of debate, not only over the crowding-out effect, but also because of the latent inflationary pressures stemming from such a large and sustained increase in government spending.

By 1980, the turning point had been reached. In fiscal 1980, bond issues as a proportion of the national budget financing declined to 34 per cent, down from 39 per cent the previous year, and there has been a progressive reduction since.

The reduction in new bond issues lowered the ratio of bond issues to the national budget to less than 25 per cent by 1985. However, with the need to roll over bonds becoming increasingly urgent as the volume of redemptions of earlier issues continues to rise, this ratio is likely to begin increasing again in the late 1980s. Long-term projections of MoF, for instance, indicate that total outstanding of government bonds will exceed ¥19 trillion by 1999.

Part of the success in handling the rising volume of government bonds has stemmed from the limited growth of bond issues by other authorised entities.

Local governments, for example, account for only around 2 per cent of all bonds issued domestically, with corporate bonds approximately equal to that.

Further large volumes of funds are raised through financial debentures, which have traditionally accounted for just less than 50 per cent of all public issues. And, even with the high level of government bond issues, there has been a steady increase in the volume of financial debentures and corporate bonds outstanding, helped by a steady decline in the volume of regional bonds.

Securities companies have tried to market government bonds aggressively to individual investors but with only limited success. By the end of fiscal 1985, for example, individuals accounted for only 12.1 per cent of all holdings of long-term government bonds, although a further proportion is held through the highly successful 'chuki kokusai' funds – medium-term government bond funds – which the securities houses began marketing from 1979. Discounted government bonds are much more popular, with individual investor holding over 60 per cent of those bonds on issue.

Government bond issuance

The preferred method for issuing public bonds is through the large bond syndicate originally formed in the 1960s. Tenders are usually restricted to shorter-term public offerings. The standard practice is for the Bank of Japan, as the agent of MoF for national bond issues, to meet with the leaders of the underwriting syndicate to determine issuing conditions for the forthcoming bond issue. The chairman of the syndicate is the head of the Bankers Federation, a position which rotates between a limited number of city banks headquartered in Tokyo.

Usually, proceedings are smooth, although during periods of rapidly changing conditions in bond and capital markets it can take some time for agreement to be reached.

The syndication system has been a very profitable arrangement for the banking sector for much of the 1980s, and has helped to offset the losses incurred in 1979 and 1980 when the Bank of Japan quickly forced up interest rates, leaving the banks with sizeable capital losses on their recently acquired bond holdings.

The general downward trend of interest rates during the 1980s made the banks very reluctant to accept any reduction of their share of the syndicate or any increase in the quantity of government bonds being put up for tender.

Notwithstanding their attitudes, MoF felt increasingly exposed following the decision of the US Federal Reserve to permit both Nomura Securities and Daiwa Securities to act as primary dealers in US government debt markets. Consequently, MoF put pressure on the Japanese securities houses to give a greater role in the syndicate to foreign securities houses.

For some time, MoF officials argued that there was little demand for Japanese government bonds among foreign investors and hence little need to change the bond issuing system. Some of the big foreign brokers threw the ball back into the court by bidding aggressively for large volumes of short-term government stock put up for tender; two brokers in particular, Salomon Brothers and Morgan Stanley, made their presence felt. There was also some severe criticism of the cost to the government in issuing bonds through the unwieldy syndication system rather than through a much simpler tender system.

This argument has not yet swayed MoF to any significant extent, since it is still wary of the fact that it is easy to bed down large volumes of stock when bond markets are bullish, but not easy when they turn bearish.

Ultimately, MoF began to put pressure on the large domestic securities house to make further way for the foreign firms. Subsequently, in April 1987, the domestic securities houses decided to expand the number of foreign houses that could participate in the syndicate to 23, so they share 5.72 per cent of the security industry's allocation of 26.2 per cent of national bonds. The largest foreign interest went to Salomon Brothers, which garnered 1 per cent, and S.G.

Warburg, Goldman Sachs, Jardine Fleming, First Boston, Merrill Lynch and Morgan Stanley each received 0.5 per cent, with the remainder receiving smaller interests.

In addition, MoF has signalled that it intends to implement a new system through which a proportion of the 10-year bonds will be issued through a so-called 'non-competitive' bidding system, whereby each member of the syndicate can submit a tender for only the amount of bonds it intends to purchase, up to a limit of 1 per cent. This should theoretically boost the position of the foreign broking houses.

MoF also signalled that it would put up for tender a larger proportion of government debt. MoF has put a rising volume of short-term discount bonds up for tender, but has been cautious about any additional increase in the proportion of long-term government debt put out to tender. However, there are indications that the government is considering boosting the quantity of paper put up for tender, including 10-, 20- and possibly 30-year paper – a move which, if implemented, will mark a distinct break with the past.

Bond trading

Bond trading in Japan is dominated by dealing in government bonds, which has steadily expanded to reach over 90 per cent of all dealing during 1986. Almost all of this is handled through the over-the-counter market.

The only other area to show any real growth is convertible bonds, which during 1986 accounted for 4.3 per cent of all dealing.

Dealing in government bonds has expanded from approximately ¥300 trillion in 1983 to ¥2,592.58 trillion in 1986, with declining interest rates fuelling much of the trading during 1985 and 1986. This sharp increase in trading activity is unlikely to be sustained at the same pace, although trading volumes during 1987 remained at extremely buoyant levels. The value of dealing in the first half of 1987, for example, exceeded that of the whole of 1986.

Apart from interest rate volatility, trading has been boosted by the decision to give banks full dealing rights, which has generated an enormous volume of trading.

Between 1981 and 1986, the volume of dealing has grown 10 times. The largest increase stemmed from the bond dealers, whose activities expanded by over 30 times. The next largest increase in trading was due to the trust banks, whose trading volume rose 9.9 times over this period.

While giving banks full access to dealing, MoF has also progressively expanded the ability of banks and other institutions to sell national bonds over the counter. The Banking Law and the amendments to the Securities Exchange Law of 1981 permitted banks to sell national bonds in some circumstances, but it was not until 1983 that approval was given to sell long-term government bonds, including long-term interest-bearing government bonds, government-guaranteed bonds and local bonds. It was subsequently decided to allow banks to sell also outstanding medium-term and discount government bonds over the counter from October 1983. Full dealing commenced the following year, and some foreign banks have also been given approval to participate.

The growth of dealing in government bonds has swamped all other bond trading in Japan, due largely to the massive volume of bonds issued. In 1977, for example, the most actively traded bonds were financial bonds, with trading in government bonds accounting for just 3.6 per cent of total volumes. By 1980, however, government bonds accounted for over half of total trading volume. Even so, there was still healthy dealing in financial bonds, which made up an additional 17 per cent. By 1986, trading in national bonds made up 95 per cent of all bond dealing. Most of the trading interest is focused on one 'bellweather' government bond issue.

In a move aimed at giving the trading in other bond issues some additional depth, it was decided in September 1986 that two-way prices be quoted by bond traders for recently issued regional government bonds, government guaranteed bonds and corporate bonds for the first time. It is expected to take some time before this move begins to have any particular effect on trading.

The other trading change was the move to tighten up settlement periods. Following the confusion caused in the New York market in 1985 after the failure of the Bank of New York computer, the Bank of Japan became concerned over the impact of a similar failure on trading in Japan, since settlements have traditionally been on the twentieth and the final day of the month.

The issue was discussed at great length in early 1986, with the security houses seeking to retain a 30-day settlement period and the Bank of Japan adamant that it be reduced to four days. Initially, agreement was reached on a 20-day settlement period, adding the 10th of the month as a settlement day. The Bank of Japan raised the issue again in 1987, and it was decided to add settlement days on the fifth, 15th and the 25th days of the month. This move reduced the entire 'futures' element from trading in the physical market of government bonds. It will also reduce the premium that the bellweather bond issue will command over other issues, and could reduce the volume of physical trading, although this will not become apparent for some time.

Bond futures

A remarkable feature of Japan's capital markets has been their comparative lack of sophistication. Trading has been primarily limited to stock and bond markets, with traditionally no futures or options markets and only limited commodity markets.

The most important development in recent years was the decision to begin trading in bond futures, which commenced in October 1985. Trading is, however, restricted, with contracts limited to 10-year government bonds. The authorities are committed to extend the range of instruments available for trading in futures markets, but they are, as usual, cautious and it may take some time before a substantial variety of instruments is available.

The minimum size of each trading lot, ¥100 million (US$650,000), is also a hurdle for traders, limiting the market primarily to the big institutional investors. There appears to be little desire on the part of the authorities to reduce this limit to bring it within the reach of smaller investors.

Trading in the early months was volatile, not only due to traders' inexperience but also because the Bank of Japan decided to drive up short-term interest rates in the final quarter of 1985 as part of its efforts to force the yen higher against the US dollar. Notwithstanding these difficulties, the market has been active with volumes traded soaring during the latter half of 1986 and during 1987.

The market was initiated primarily to give major investors in government bonds a means of hedging their exposure during the continuing large bond issuing programme, and also against interest rate volatility following the extension of deregulated interest rates.

The bond futures market started in Japan at a time when there was a growing opinion in financial circles that risk management and risk assessment needed to be improved at all levels of operation. To this end the start of the bond futures market is the first step in a development that is likely to bring about a substantial variety of new instruments.

Japan's institutional investors were given direct access to overseas financial futures markets during 1987 and corporate investors are expected to be able to follow suit during 1988.

Officials of MoF are broadly in favour of developing these markets further in Japan, although there are some severe regulatory obstacles. For instance, the Osaka 50 Stock Futures contract has no provision for cash settlement. Rather, physical delivery is demanded if the contract is not matched out prior to conclusion – the only such stipulation of a futures market in the world. This regulation is due to Japan's securities industry legislation.

Nevertheless, the establishment of the bond futures market in Tokyo has resulted in an extraordinary rise in volumes traded. Once the market overcame its initial difficulties, trading levels rose sharply, and during 1987 exceeded the volumes traded on the Chicago Board of Trade's US Treasury bond futures contract.

Trading volume in 1985 reached ¥45 trillion, which was overshadowed by the 1986 level of ¥939.15 trillion. Monthly turnover in the latter part of 1986 regularly exceeded the ¥100 trillion level, with all of the major financial institutions actively involved. In 1986, securities houses accounted for over 55 per cent of all trading, with the banks making up an additional third. Most other investors, apart from the corporate sector, are minor participants at best. Individual investors in particular may be deterred by the large denomination of each unit traded.

During 1987 trading volumes have continued to rise, with a record ¥229 trillion traded in March. Trading volumes in the first half of 1987 exceeded those of the whole of 1986, indicating the extraordinary level of demand for hedging instruments on the part of Japan's investors.

The success of the bond futures market is likely to lead to a diversification of the instruments traded; a contract for 20-year bonds is expected to be the next instrument.

Development of the yen bond market

The opening of the yen bond market to foreign issuers was one of the seminal events in the internationalisation of the yen. Progress after the first public issue, in December 1970, by the Asian Development Bank was slow, but there has been exceptionally strong growth, especially in the Euroyen bond market, after further liberalisation measures were adopted in 1984.

The principal forms of yen-denominated bonds are Samurai, Shibosai (private placements) and Euroyen bonds. Other variants include Daimyo and Shogun bonds.

Since the Samurai market was opened in 1970, there has been substantial growth of all yen-denominated issues, with Euroyen issues temporarily surpassing Eurodollar issues in the first quarter of 1987.

Growth since 1985 has been rapid, in sharp contrast to the 1970s, when the authorities kept the Samurai market under close controls, severely limiting its growth. Initial caution was due to the fact that the authorities were keen to limit the impact of yen-denominated bond issues on the external account. More recently, the aim has been to isolate developments in the Euroyen market from affecting the domestic deregulatory process, an aim that has proved impossible to achieve.

Samurai bonds

The Asian Development Bank (ADB) issue of yen bonds in December 1970 followed two private placements, one by the World Bank and the other by the Inter-American Development Bank. The decision by MoF to approve the issue by the ADB represented as much Japan's traditional control over the ADB as its responsibility for the expansion of the bank's capital base.

The authorities were cautious in allowing the market to expand, initially restricting borrowers to sovereign entities with strong links with Japan. Interest by some borrowers, for example Brazil and some African countries, was rebuffed.

In addition, as Japan's balance of payments came under pressure, the number of new issues approved was limited, and the market closed down entirely for a time during the 1970s.

The market was not opened up to corporate borrowers until 1979, when Sears Roebuck made an issue, taking advantage of the authorities' embarrassment over the fact that Japanese corporates were able to tap North American capital markets but American groups could not access Japan. Issues by foreign corporate borrowers were sparse, and up to 1982 there were only three issues: by

Sears Roebuck, Dow Chemical and NCR.

By the mid-1980s, the level of new issue activity had flagged severely, causing the authorities further embarrassment. In 1985, for example, there were only 35 issues, raising ¥1.11 trillion, which fell to just 21 issues in 1986, raising ¥590 billion – well below the level of activity in the late 1970s. The test of the market's viability came with the explosion of activity on the Euroyen market, where issuing conditions and, more importantly, timing are much more flexible. As a result, borrowers have switched from the Samurai bond market, where it can take three months from the time an initial application is made to when the issue is completed.

Moves to allow shelf registration, expected in the first half of 1988, as well as easing the registration system will help, but the market needs a complete overhaul if it is to compete with the much freer conditions applying to the Euroyen market.

The other recent challenge to the market stemmed from the desire of some borrowers to retire issues early as interest rates fell. Some came back to the Samurai market, raising funds at cheaper rates, others opted for the Euromarkets.

In particular, for many borrowers the fall in interest rates meant that they were carrying Samurai issues with a coupon of over 9 per cent at a time when new issues were being offered at 6.5 per cent. The borrowers' difficulties were compounded by the currency shift, which added to the cost of these fund raisings.

It took time for the issue to be resolved, but ultimately MoF stepped in and forced the securities houses to back down. The first early redemption was a sovereign issue by Singapore in the mid-1980s. It signalled that it did not intend returning to the market so that, while there was opposition to the move, the ramifications were more limited. The first early redemption of note was by Sweden, which was followed by Australia – a frequent borrower which signalled that it intended returning to the market in the future. These redemptions were followed by several other sovereign borrowers. Official approval for early redemption was signalled in January 1987, when the ADB decided it would pre-pay its sixth Samurai issue, an important milestone given the close links between the ADB and the Japanese government.

Even though early redemptions have occurred, the securities houses can circumvent it by reaching an unofficial agreement with new borrowers prior to the launch of an issue that, while there is provision in the underwriting agreement for early redemption, this option will not be exercised by the borrower. Some houses have taken to removing the early redemption clause altogether.

Since it is less competitive than the Euroyen market, the Samurai market is likely to remain the domain of supranational organisations such as the World Bank, and sovereign borrowers, especially Asian borrowers.

Part of the difficulty with the Samurai bond market is the lack of liquidity, which adds to the cost of tapping the market. To help circumvent this problem, MoF put pressure on the four big Japanese securities houses to maintain a secondary market, which they undertook to do in 1986.

In a bid to give the market additional depth, it was decided from February 1987 that along with the four big securities houses, 10 medium-sized houses would also endeavour to create a secondary market to improve liquidity and hence cut borrowing costs. This move, similar to the initial steps undertaken by the big Japanese houses, has had only marginal impact on new issuing trends.

With the medium-term future of the Samurai bond market in some doubt, in the light of the extraordinary success of the Euroyen market, the World Bank was allowed to issue Daimyo bonds. This bond, a hybrid between the Samurai and Euroyen bond, may point to the way the authorities intend to allow the market to develop in the future. These bonds, of which by mid-1987 there had been two issues, both by the World Bank, are issued in Tokyo and listed on the Luxembourg Stock Exchange. Issues by the World Bank are not subject to withholding tax, and the bonds can also be cleared through either Cedel or Euroclear.

The bonds are not subject to the 90-day lock-up period demanded for Euroyen bonds, and commission costs are low, as is the case with Euroyen bonds. The first Daimyo bond issue for ¥40 billion carried a coupon of 4.625 per cent for 10-year paper, at a time when Samurai bond issues were carrying a 4.9 per cent coupon. The second issue, in June 1987, also for ¥40 billion, carried a coupon of 4.25 per cent, when other Samurai issues were pitched at 4.8 per cent.

The permission for the World Bank, the pre-eminent supranational borrower, to issue on such favourable terms may eventually be extended to other supranational organisations such as the ADB, although the authorities have yet to signal their views.

Shibosai

The market for privately placed yen bonds, or Shibosai, has typically been much smaller than the Samurai bond market, and as such has usually attracted much less prestigious issuers and has been subjected to tighter controls by the authorities. The market has been open to both banks and securities houses to act as lead arrangers, and from mid-1987 regional banks with overseas offices were also allowed to participate. Because of the slightly lower quality of paper, and the fact that the paper by its nature cannot be publicly traded, coupons are usually pitched around 0.7 per cent to 1 per cent higher than straight Samurai issues, depending on the quality of the borrower. In mid-1987, for example, when Samurai issues were attracting coupons of around 4.8 per cent, Shibosai were concluded at around 5.5 per cent. Even with the slightly higher coupon, the downward trend of interest rates in Japan has meant that some borrowers have achieved sub-Libor rates. For example, the City of Bergen raised ¥5 billion at a coupon of 5.2 per cent, the first time a Shibosai issue had attracted such low rates.

With the slightly higher coupon, some of these issues became more popular with domestic institutions as interest rates declined during 1987. In a further measure aimed at stimulating this market, MoF allowed a change to the pricing method in early 1987: issuers who had previously made a public offering were permitted to make a private placement at a yield of just 0.1 per cent over their public offering price.

Under this new scheme, qualified borrowers are limited to six issues annually, with a maximum limit of ¥10 billion per issue.

Euroyen bonds

The first Euroyen bonds were issued in 1977 and, as with the Samurai market, MoF was extremely cautious in allowing the market to develop, largely because it was concerned that a too fast growth could have severe repercussions on Japan's balance of payments. Therefore, usually only one issue a quarter was allowed and tight limits were set on the amount of any one issue.

The Euroyen market appeared doomed to remain a backwater of Japan's capital markets but direct pressure from the US government changed that scenario completely. As part of its moves to force Japan to liberalise its capital markets, the US government brought considerable pressure to bear as part of the yen/dollar committee proceedings. Debate over liberalising the Euroyen market became a notable feature of the argument between the two countries. The decision, effective from 1 December 1984, to allow non-Japanese corporations rated A or better and others to issue yen-denominated bonds in the Euromarket proved to be the catalyst not only for much of the subsequent financial deregulation in Japan, but also for unleashing Japan's securities houses onto the international market.

The growth of the Euroyen market has been spectacular although doubts linger about the genuine level of underlying activity. Demand among international borrowers for yen is limited, with only an estimated 5 per cent of Japan's imports and 35 per cent of exports denominated in yen. Because of the low underlying demand for yen, much of the new issue activity in the Euroyen market has been swap driven, with Japanese banks eager to get access to long-term yen funds to even out their mis-matched portfolios.

Market activity has also been driven by the needs of Japan's institutional investors, which have fuelled an extraordinary variety of novel issues, such as heaven-and-hell bonds and survival bonds. During much of the early development period of the Euroyen market, there were vociferous complaints from rival banks and securities houses based in Europe that many of the issues were clearly unprofitable, with a large number of 'hara-kiri' deals. Much of this reflected the fact that the market had only just started, with fierce competition between rival banks and securities houses to establish their ranking and pecking order.

MoF tried to mitigate the impact of the Euroyen market on domestic financial markets by forcing its domestic institutions to delay buying Euroyen paper for 180 days after the initial issue, a ruling that was easily circumvented by simply holding the paper offshore for the requisite period. MoF subsequently reduced this 'seasoning period' to 90 days.

Even though the level of activity on the Euroyen market has been, and will probably continue to be, swap driven, MoF appears pleased with the market's rapid expansion, despite the impact on domestic market developments.

One of the most notable features of the development of the Euroyen market was the extraordinary array of sophisticated structures that were quickly invented, an important spur in attracting investor interest for much of this paper.

Many of these structures carried with them sizeable risk, and MoF was fearful of the implications for some of the large domestic institutional investors if they needed, for whatever reason, to try and liquidate some of these holdings. As a result, from late 1986, MoF began putting pressure on all institutions to back off from these issues. This accounted for the sudden drying up in the volume of new activity in the more complex structures from the early part of 1987 and a revival in issues of straight Euroyen bonds.

Although most of the activity in the market is swap driven, some sovereign borrowers have been attracted to the market because it offers a cheaper borrowing alternative to the Samurai market.

Another notable feature of the market is that no Japanese government or semi-government bodies have tapped the market for funds.

The advantages of the market

The first Euroyen issue was floated in 1977, with a ¥10 billion offering by the European Investment Bank, lead managed by Daiwa. Up to 1983, there were only ¥420 billion of issues made. Domestic groups were unable to access the market but the supermarket chain Ito-Yokado made a ¥5 billion private placement with the government of Kuwait, taking advantage of a loophole in the regulations. This was followed by a limited number of similar issues. With the liberalisation agreed to in early 1984, from December of that year foreign corporations with an A rating or better were allowed access to this market. Minimum maturities of five years were demanded, and a 180-day 'seasoning period' was instituted.

Euroyen issues by non-Japanese corporations are tax-exempt, although a withholding tax is applicable to the interest paid on Euroyen issues by Japanese corporations. This acted as a slight restriction on the development of this market for domestic borrowers.

The real growth of the market occurred in April 1985, when MoF approved dual currency bonds, zero coupon bonds, deep discount bonds and floating rate notes.

With most of these novel structures driven by swap deals, the arbitrage opportunity between Euroyen bond rates and Japan's long-term prime rate underpinned much of the activity.

The ballooning of borrowing through the Euroyen market by foreign corporations attracted by the ability to obtain cheap finance through swapping the yen proceeds into US dollars, and by Japanese corporations looking for access to cheap long-term funding free of domestic restraints, has given birth to conditions which will force further wholesale deregulation of Japan's domestic capital markets.

The flexibility of the Euroyen market for issuers contrasts sharply with the severe restraints on domestic bond issues. When the domestic market will be liberalised depends heavily on the trade-offs that the long-term credit banks in particular can obtain from MoF.

In a similar vein, the attraction of the Euroyen market has cast a pall over the future of the Samurai and Shibosai markets. If these markets are to survive, further steps will need to be taken to liberalise issuing terms and conditions. Much of this will hinge on the attitude of the securities houses.

Even though limited moves have been made to develop a secondary market for Samurai issues, Japan's securities houses have been driven by the need to expand their presence in the Euroyen market, which promises much greater returns in the future. The Samurai market thus is likely to become much more of a regional market, with some limited attraction for Asian borrowers who may find it difficult to access other markets.

Some steps have been taken to liberalise the Shibosai market by allowing smaller broking houses a greater role. Regional banks with overseas offices have, for example, been given approval by MoF to arrange private placement. Indicative of this was a ¥10 billion placement for the World Bank in July 1987, which was lead arranged by the Bank of Yokohama and co-lead arranged by the Hokuriku Bank and the Shizuoka Bank. The underwriting included only regional banks, 40 in all.

Steps such as this may be helpful in enabling the Shibosai market to expand, although given the more limited capabilities of the regional banks, they will not be able to bring a large number of new issuers to the market.

As well as allowing the steady expansion of the variety of instruments, MoF agreed in mid-1987 to allow foreign banks with Tokyo branches to tap the Euroyen market. This development caused concern to Japanese banks and securities houses alike since it promised foreign banks for the first time access to cheap funds which would allow them to develop their operations in Japan.

But the power of Japan's financial institutions is evident in that they have dominated activity in the Euroyen market, with foreign firms getting only a minor share.

Innovation

One of the most popular instruments in the Euroyen market has been the dual currency bond, which is issued in yen and carries a yen coupon, although the redemption is usually in US dollars. For the borrower, it obtains low-cost financing without any forex risk, with the principal and the coupon converted to a non-yen currency. The investor assumes the currency risk, although this is partly compensated for since these issues offer yen income at a higher rate than straight yen bonds, with redemption usually at a slight premium above the spot rate prevailing at the time of the issue.

Other innovations included the reverse dual currency bond, the first of which came to the market in 1986. This variety is purchased and redeemed in yen, with interest paid in US dollars.

Deferred interest bonds are typical of the variety of bonds brought to market to satisfy the needs of Japanese investors, especially the trust banks, which, due to the sharp rise in their earnings during 1985 and 1986, needed instruments to spread their income gain across an extended period for tax purposes. No interest is paid on these bonds for, usually, the first three years of the bond's five-year life. After the first three years, the bond can be sold at a premium, to unlock the profit and also to take advantage of the higher yield paid in the last two years of the bond, which is attractive to most investors. By selling, the institution earns a handy capital gain, avoiding taxable income gain on these instruments.

The split dual currency bond gave investors a low yield in the initial years but a much higher yield in the final years of the bond, with a part of the principal repayment in yen and the balance in a foreign currency, typically US dollars. There were a number of variations on this theme.

Others, such as the heaven-and-hell bond, were linked to stockmarket movements, with the investor taking a position on either a rise or a decline in equity markets. The rise in equity markets for much of 1986 made these instruments particularly attractive.

The only limit to the level of innovation is the attitude of MoF. Concerned about the rising risk that many of the institutional investors were locking themselves into by aggressively pursuing these investment options, it intervened in late 1986 to halt the flow.

Innovation has not been limited just to Euroyen instruments. The Sushi bond aimed to take advantage of a specific loophole in the regulations for offshore investments by Japan's institutional investors. Under existing guidelines, the foreign investments of the life companies and the trust banks are limited to 30 per cent of their total assets. But foreign currency bonds issued by domestic borrowers are not classified as foreign bonds. As a result, these Sushi bonds can be held by domestic institutions without impacting on the overall level of their foreign currency holdings.

The other principal variations are the Shogun bond, a foreign currency-denominated bond issued in Japan, and the Geisha bond, a foreign currency issue placed privately with Japanese investors.

The Shogun bond market was opened in 1985 by the World Bank and has largely been limited to foreign agencies, with little corporate interest. However, tax changes in the US in late 1986 to some extent stimulated interest in issuing these securities. The US Treasury Department allowed US corporations to issue bearer bonds abroad without fear that these issues would violate US tax laws. In addition, rules for Shogun issues were eased, waiving for companies with an AA rating or better the requirement that the capital to assets ratio be higher than 30 per cent, and also for companies with an A rating and assets of over US$1.5 billion.

The first Shogun issue by a private corporation was made in October 1985 by Southern California Edison Company. Issues have been sparse, totalling less than US$1 billion annually.

The major disincentive is that, like Samurai issues, the registration period for Shogun issues is comparatively long and the documentation requirements are onerous. Both of these difficulties will be partly overcome during the first half of 1988, once MoF obtains Diet approval for streamlining, which will give these issues greater flexibility, although still not enough if they are to compete successfully with the Euroyen markets.

東京相互銀行

CHAPTER EIGHTEEN

Short-term money markets

Central to much of the effort to deregulate interest rates have been the steps taken to boost the volume of trading on Japan's short-term money markets, which had been dull and sleepy during the 1960s and 1970s. The progressive introduction of new instruments and the active support of the Bank of Japan have resulted in the volume of activity expanding dramatically.

In broad terms, the volume of trading on the short-term markets more than doubled from ¥21.4 trillion in 1980 to ¥52.3 trillion in 1985.

During the 1960s, the outstanding balance of the short-term money markets equalled just 4.5 per cent of Japan's GNP. By 1980 this had expanded to 5.8 per cent, rising to 12.9 per cent by 1985 and 14.4 per cent of GNP by the end of 1986. Japan's short-term money markets are now proportionally slightly larger than West Germany's short-term capital markets, which stand at around 12 per cent of GNP, but still markedly smaller than those in the US, which total over 30 per cent of GNP.

The historical dominance of the interbank market, which accounted for three-quarters of all activity, has been slightly reduced with the moderate expansion of the open market, especially during the 1980s. Nevertheless, the interbank market still accounts for around 60 per cent of total outstandings.

The introduction of new instruments, as well as shortening the maturity and reducing the denomination of other instruments, has fuelled much of the growth in the open short-term money market. Expansion of the short-term markets has been a deliberate policy of the Bank of Japan, which has also been keen to deepen the market in short-term government debt, a development consistently opposed by the Ministry of Finance (MoF).

The biggest influence on the money markets is the window guidance of the Bank of Japan. The bank may soak up liquidity by selling short-term paper, or boost liquidity by buying paper. In addition, it gives unofficial guidance to the main players in the interbank and the open market, and directly influences market developments through its direct and indirect controls over the money market brokers.

The traditional role of the market in filling the capital needs of the banks has also changed. The dominant users of the interbank market have historically been the city banks. Over-lent for much of the post-war period,their funding needs dominated activity in the call market: in the 1960s and 1970s, they accounted for over 80 per cent of all borrowing from the call market. During the 1980s, this has declined as their over-lent position has been reduced. At the end of 1985 the city banks accounted for only 51.8 per cent of borrowings through this market, which further declined to 45 per cent at the end of 1986, although these figures hide some seasonal variation. The decline in the city banks' funding needs has been offset by increased funding through the uncollateralised call market by foreign banks. The market has changed on the lending side as well; the trust banks are now the dominant lenders to the market and the role of other institutions is declining.

Increasing sophistication

In the initial post-war period, the short-term market simply consisted of overnight money, unconditional borrowings and over-the-month money.

Opposite: Sunrise over Tokyo: the short-term money markets have also seen the dawning of a period of high activity.

In the call market, there is now half-day money, either morning or afternoon, seven-day money, fixed maturity funds (for up to three weeks), unconditional money (payment is deferred for two days but payment after that is due within one day's notice from either borrower or lender) and over-the-month money, where a certain day of the next month is designated as the settling day. Historically, most call loans were over-the-month money, but with the more recent changes to the market, they are now usually unconditional loans.

Even though trading through the short-term money markets has increased considerably, Bank of Japan officials admit the need for significant change in several areas, pointing out that many of the bank's moves are only short-term measures to limit some of the excesses. The biggest distinction between Japan's short-term capital markets and those of most other major financial centres is the role of unofficial guidance provided by the central bank, which often enables it to achieve its objectives without overt actions. For example, the central bank has played an important role in trying to increase arbitrage opportunities between the official and unofficial markets, so as to achieve much greater control over and stability of interest rates.

Interbank market

Japan's short-term money markets were historically centred on the interbank market which comprised the call and bill markets. The open market consisted solely of the 'gensaki' market. Gensaki are securities with repurchase or resale agreements. This market, which had existed in a basic form in the late 1940s, did not begin to expand until the early 1970s.

By the mid-1970s, the total size of the short-term money market – both the interbank and open market – was ¥6 trillion, or around 4 per cent of GNP at that time. The limited size of the short-term capital markets was due to the relative unimportance of the secondary bond market, since until the mid-1960s there had been no issues of government bonds as MoF pursued a balanced budget. In addition, the corporate sector had only limited amounts of surplus cash, which were usually deposited with the institutions that lent the funds in the first place. There was therefore little demand for other investment instruments. Given the rudimentary nature of the short-term capital markets, monetary control exerted by the Bank of Japan was elementary, consisting of the sale and purchase of securities, purchases of private bills and lendings to the short-term money market dealers and security finance corporations.

There has also been direct lending to financial institutions at the official discount rate with funds effectively rationed to borrowers. The repayment of lendings could be forced at any time, giving the Bank of Japan strong control over short-term liquidity.

In addition to its direct controls on market rates in the interbank market, the Bank of Japan holds significant powers through moral suasion and through the quarterly lending limits it imposes on the banks, which can be revised if market conditions change. These are what are termed 'window guidance'. The Bank of Japan has relied on a mixture of both techniques, since lending rates of the banks are often difficult to adjust quickly so that significant changes in short-term interest rate movements can take some time.

More recently, the Bank of Japan has begun to rely more heavily on interest rate movements to effect control over the short-term money markets, largely because of the expansion in the overall size of the short-term money markets.

Liberalisation

The general increase in the level of liquidity of the corporate sector brought about a steady expansion of the gensaki market during the latter part of the 1970s. As a result, the open market finally surpassed the size of the interbank market in 1980. Subsequently, the introduction of a larger variety of instruments in the open money market fostered its growth.

In 1979, for example, after a lengthy series of negotiations between the Bank of Japan and MoF, banks were allowed to issue a limited volume of CDs for the first time. In 1978 and 1979 there was also some liberalisation of the quotas on the sales of securities in the gensaki market by the city banks, followed by the authorisation of short-term untied loans (impact loans) by authorised foreign exchange banks.

Also, a series of steps were taken to smooth transactions in the interbank market. These changes were made in several distinct phases, underscoring both the caution of Japan's authorities when taking deregulatory measures and the fact that there was an element of uncertainty about the impact of many of these steps. As part of the measures aimed at increasing the degree of flexibility in quoting the call rate, the Bank of Japan established call money with a seven-day term and also a one-month term at a free rate, and liberalised interest rates on bills maturing three months forward.

This was followed, in early 1979, by the decision to abolish the quoting of call rates, establishing call money with a two- to six-day term, and other similar moves. These moves were designed to introduce more market flexibility, so that the daily shortage or surplus of funds would be readily reflected in rates in the interbank market.

The second phase, which began in 1980, was to facilitate arbitrage between the interbank and the open markets. To this end, gensaki transactions were liberalised, the ceilings on currency swaps into yen were eased and securities companies were given access to the call market. The driving force here was the expansion of the open market, particularly after the introduction of CDs and the liberalisation of foreign currency deposits.

The overall growth of the open market was due to the need to develop a secondary market in government bonds following the rapid expansion of the primary issue market after the heavy government spending during the 1970s.

In 1984, the Bank of Japan removed completely the ceiling on swap limits, and approved the introduction of bills with a five- to six-month term, call money with a two- to three-week term and unsecured call transactions.

And in 1985, the maturities on negotiable CDs were shortened, while the minimum denomination was reduced and the manner of selling treasury bills was altered.

Outstanding balances in the short-term money market, 1979-86

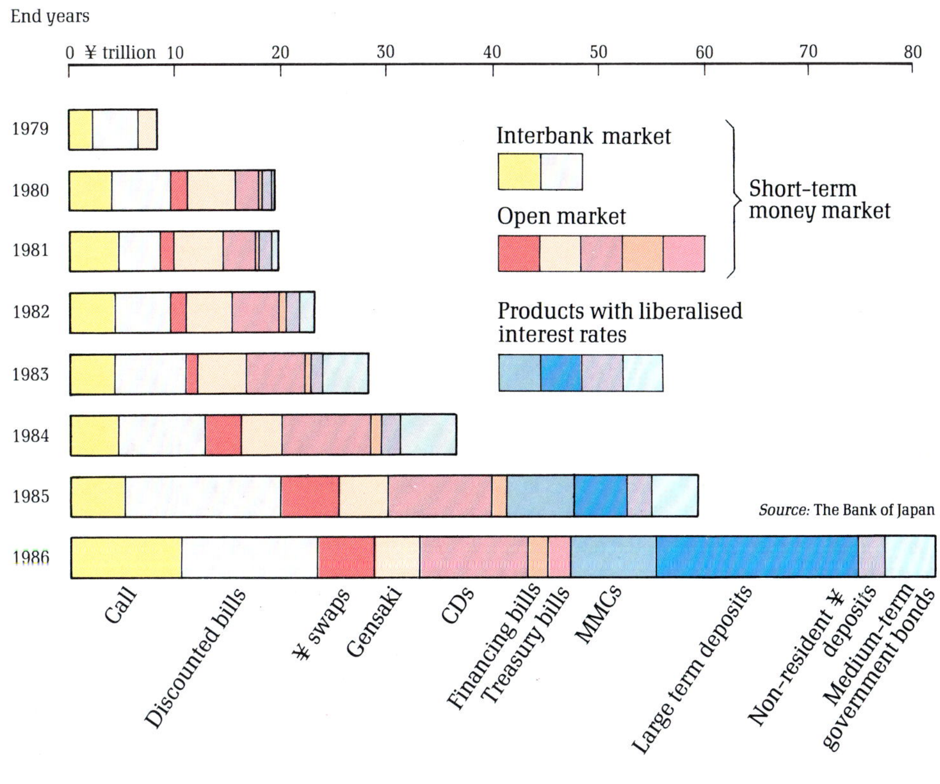

Source: The Bank of Japan

The Bank of Japan also began making loans to the tanshi brokers to buy CDs in an attempt to give this market additional depth, a move which attracted considerable attention at the time. In fiscal 1986, it did this on 11 occasions, advancing a total of ¥1.4 trillion. This was not the first time that the central bank had done this; in the early 1960s, it advanced loans to the tanshi brokers as part of its preparations for the launching of national bonds.

Along with deepening the short-term money markets, the Bank of Japan has changed its qualitative controls over the markets. The abolition of the quotation system, whereby the tanshi brokers set formal quotes, has enabled a much more accurate movement of call and bill rates reflecting the underlying liquidity of the official markets. Simultaneously, the Bank of Japan has changed its controls to place more emphasis on interest rate controls, instead of relying on providing credit to meet a shortage of funds or absorbing surplus funds in the interbank market. This greater reliance on interest rate controls is evidenced by the much larger changes in unconditional call rates during the 1980s compared with the 1970s.

One of the main aims of the Bank of Japan is to develop the markets by liberalising a number of minor controls in order to ensure much greater interest rate arbitrage between the interbank and the open markets. The bank's pressure on rates in the interbank market would then be reflected quickly in the open market. To this end, the central bank has carried out extensive studies into the correlation between movements in interbank and open market rates as a means of determining market efficiency.

And to maintain its control and influence, the Bank of Japan has sought to expand the short-term treasury bill market, which it anticipates will consolidate its control over the open market. During 1986, for example, the Bank of Japan engaged in the sale of short-term government bills 45 times, involving a total of ¥19.4 billion.

At the same time as the Bank of Japan seeks to develop this market, there has been an increase in the issuance of shorter-term government bonds, again with the overall aim of expanding the market for shorter-term paper in Japan. The smooth expansion of this market will also be important for handling the amortisation of government debt that will increase dramatically during the late 1980s.

But, while moving to allow much greater interplay of market forces in setting interest rates, the central bank still relies heavily on window guidance to restrict the volume of activity in the market and the volume of bank lending.

The call and uncollateralised call market

With the development of the CD market, the earlier heavy reliance of the city banks on the call market has steadily declined, with only a slight increase in their borrowings through this market.

Outstanding balances in the short-term money market as percentage of GNP, 1979-86

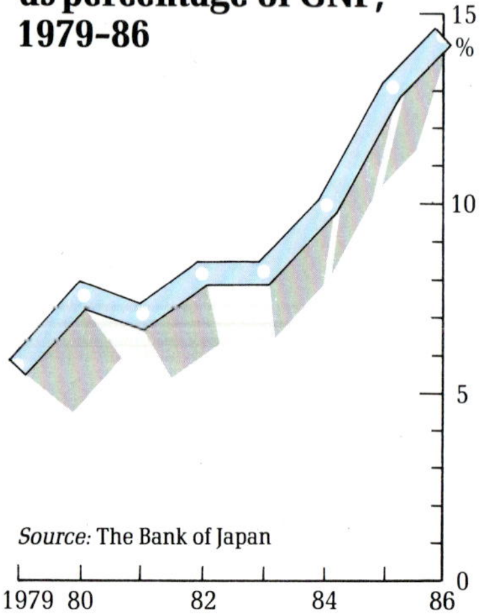

Source: The Bank of Japan

Even with the steady increase in the variety of call market instruments available, the growth of this market has been overshadowed by the expansion of the uncollateralised call market.

In the mid-1970s, the city banks traditionally accounted for around 90 per cent of all funds borrowed through this market. By the mid-1980s, this had fallen to less than 50 per cent, with a sizeable increase in funding by foreign banks.

Indeed, the shift away from the over-lent position of the city banks has seen them gradually emerge as lenders to the call market for the first time. The amount was small until 1986, when the city banks advanced ¥243 billion to the market. By June 1987, their net outstandings had risen to ¥298.9 billion, after reaching a seasonal peak of ¥545 billion in March of that year.

The bulk of the funds are supplied by the trust banks and the Norinchukin and Zenshinren Bank. Between them, these institutions supply over 50 per cent of the funds for the call market.

The decision to introduce an uncollateralised call market in August 1985 has underpinned much of the call market's growth since then, which has given

Average call market balance by lender, 1976–June 1987 (¥100m)

End	Total	City banks	Regional banks	Trust banks	Long-term credit banks	Foreign banks	Sogo banks	Specialised banks*	Insurance companies	Others
1976	24,172	—	4,636	5,213	1,895	636	2,520	5,661	2,011	1,597
1977	26,255	—	4,755	6,953	2,676	454	2,424	5,377	2,254	1,357
1978	28,085	—	4,760	8,204	2,903	350	2,554	5,529	2,554	1,226
1979	36,177	—	4,773	9,412	3,104	1,361	3,285	9,217	3,289	1,732
1980	32,575	—	4,087	8,713	1,591	1,428	2,895	9,215	3,246	1,395
1981	44,594	55	6,464	11,102	3,170	2,101	4,106	11,869	3,866	1,858
1982	45,281	108	4,445	12,274	1,722	3,414	3,530	13,666	4,138	1,979
1983	38,355	18	4,512	14,274	1,795	794	3,279	8,554	3,421	1,702
1984	45,442	223	4,498	18,169	2,405	1,717	3,396	10,035	3,457	1,538
1985	50,455	892	3,311	24,105	1,061	1,641	3,178	10,884	3,652	1,725
1986	79,571	2,431	3,674	50,655	540	823	3,849	11,023	4,392	2,179
June 1987	142,587	2,989	4,378	110,764	7	539	6,193	11,525	4,549	1,643

*Includes Zenshinren Bank and community banks, agricultural financial institutions, and securities and securities financing companies. *Source:* Bank of Japan.

Average call market balance by borrower, 1976–June 1987 (¥100m)

End	Total	City banks	Regional banks	Trust banks	Long-term credit banks	Foreign banks	Others
1976	24,843	21,994	644	239	3	253	1,712
1977	26,991	23,297	700	169	—	746	2,077
1978	28,948	23,624	993	173	—	1,384	2,771
1979	37,091	28,803	1,577	150	4	991	5,563
1980	34,086	24,745	2,544	227	17	1,111	5,440
1981	45,301	31,292	1,570	146	27	2,126	10,138
1982	46,391	33,334	2,955	126	172	2,115	7,686
1983	39,199	22,017	3,615	104	198	5,223	8,040
1984	46,374	28,371	3,946	238	194	4,795	8,828
1985	51,400	27,852	6,591	1,004	1,558	5,563	8,829
1986	80,158	36,845	6,895	3,870	3,077	19,435	10,033
June 1987	139,518	60,683	9,675	7,983	8,299	43,409	9,469

Source: Bank of Japan.

foreign banks easier access to funding. The uncollateralised portion of the call market now accounts for 15 per cent of the total outstandings in this market.

In addition, there has been a gradual extension of the instruments available through the uncollateralised call market, and these instruments are now the same as those available through the collateralised call market. This was finally achieved in 1987, with the decision to allow uncollateralised call loans of between two and six days.

Much of the achievement in establishing the uncollateralised market followed pressure from the US in the follow-up discussions after the yen/dollar committee accord of April 1984. Foreign banks have complained repeatedly that they have to meet collateral requirements in accessing the call market, which puts them at a disadvantage to Japanese banks in raising funds competitively.

With the uncollateralised call market in operation, the differential between funds raised through it and funds raised through the collateralised call market has steadily narrowed to the point where by 1987 it stood at between two and three basis points, although brokerage in the uncollateralised call market is paid solely by the borrower. This has been a great advantage for the foreign banks. By June 1987, for instance, the total outstandings of the uncollateralised call market were ¥2.2 trillion; foreign banks were the borrowers of ¥2.17 trillion of this, accounting for 98.2 per cent of all borrowings. For the foreign banks, funding through the uncollateralised call market account for 60 per cent of all their call market financings.

The expansion of the uncollateralised call market has also helped the overall expansion of the interbank market which has expanded strongly since the end of 1984, with total outstandings almost doubling.

Discount market

The city banks, while reducing the volume of funds sourced through the call market, have been much more active in sourcing funds through the discount market, accounting for around 90 per cent of all borrowing through this market. The bulk of the funds come from the cash-rich agricultural institutions such as the Norinchukin and the Zenshinren Bank.

Both the call and the discount markets undergo regular seasonal fund shifts, with a rundown in liquidity particularly in the March–April period because of tax payments, and in June and December because of bonus payments to employees. The Bank of Japan moves to smooth out such seasonal variations through direct market intervention by either buying or selling bills to control overall liquidity.

Average discount market balance by lender, 1979–June 1987 (¥100m)

End	*Total*	*City banks*	*Regional banks*	*Trust banks*	*Long-term credit banks*	*Foreign banks*	*Sogo banks*	*Specialised banks**	*Insurance companies*	*Others*
1979	56,844	—	1,749	7,535	1,601	345	876	25,072	959	18,705
1980	61,204	—	1,654	8,236	766	2,619	1,111	10,680	1,705	34,429
1981	39,894	—	3,422	5,759	923	730	1,306	14,429	1,198	12,123
1982	38,670	—	1,891	5,360	865	1,992	685	20,588	784	6,500
1983	56,823	—	2,987	6,379	2,302	3,710	594	27,125	1,071	12,651
1984	66,667	—	1,203	4,999	2,655	1,865	616	32,044	548	22,735
1985	94,402	206	2,668	8,660	1,821	4,021	1,342	43,960	939	30,781
1986	132,548	738	4,297	16,116	1,107	10,073	2,211	47,494	963	49,545
June 1987	155,941	—	6,940	28,798	—	10,233	6,397	55,113	478	47,982

*Includes Zenshinren Bank and community banks, agricultural financial institutions, and securities and securities financing companies. *Source:* Bank of Japan.

Average discount market balance by borrower, 1979–June 1987 (¥100m)

End	*Total*	*City banks*	*Foreign banks*	*Others*
1979	56,844	51,220	5,464	159
1980	61,204	55,364	5,653	186
1981	39,894	32,270	5,976	1,647
1982	38,672	30,623	3,774	4,275
1983	56,827	52,292	3,183	1,350
1984	66,669	58,735	5,889	2,044
1985	94,404	84,833	2,906	6,663
1986	132,550	115,547	2,353	14,650
June 1987	155,941	135,174	2,406	18,361

Source: Bank of Japan.

The interest rate on funds available through the bills discount market varies in line with the seasonal flow of funds, although it usually moves within a band of between 1.0 and 1.3 per cent above the discount rate, with the call market moving in a band between 0.8 and 1.1 per cent of the discount rate.

Dollar call market

Established to give domestic banks access to trading in short-term unsecured foreign currency loans, the US dollar call market has experienced dramatic growth since it opened in 1972. The balance by 1981 exceeded the size of the call market, and by 1985 was double the size of the call market and exceeded the discount bills market.

The US dollar call market is of considerable importance to regional banks and other smaller financial institutions which have no overseas offices or only limited access to US dollar funds. They constitute the most active borrowers through this market, and the city banks with their much greater volume of dollar funds are the most active lenders.

This market underwent a boom in trading conditions prior to the start up of the Japan offshore market in late 1986. Trading levels, which expanded rapidly in the early 1980s with annual growth rates of more than 50 per cent, slowed markedly in 1985, although they picked up again in 1986 before the start of Tokyo's offshore market. Most of the smaller institutions decided to increase their expertise in trading in the US dollar call market, so that they could take advantage of trading in the offshore market once it started.

The expansion of the US dollar call market has moved in line with the increase in foreign liabilities of Japan's banks and, because of this, is expected to continue to expand in the future, albeit at a more conservative pace. Typically a market for only short-term transactions, historically overnight, it has gradually changed, and now dealings of more than one month can often account for up to 20 per cent of total outstandings in the market.

Open market

Along with the expansion of the interbank market there has been an equally significant increase in the size of the open market. The introduction of new instruments and the liberalisation of terms and conditions on existing instruments has underpinned much of the growth. The change has been startling. In the mid-1960s, the inter-bank market accounted for 75 per cent of all money market transactions and there was only one open market instrument, the gensaki. By 1987, the open market made up 40 per cent of the total market, and had a range of instruments from gensaki to CDs, Treasury bills and bankers' acceptances.

The outstanding balance of all instruments available through the open market was just ¥600 billion in 1965. It rose to ¥20.6 trillion by the end of 1985 and reached ¥25 trillion by mid-1987. It will become much larger over the coming decade, and Bank of Japan officials think that it will eventually overshadow the interbank market in size and importance.

Much of the growth of the interbank market since 1985 has stemmed from the introduction of the uncollateralised call market, which has been dominated by the foreign banks, and also the US dollar call market. The open market has grown more slowly, held back by the poor start of trading in the bankers acceptance market and MoF's caution in developing the Treasury bill market.

The introduction of new instruments, such as commercial paper from late 1987, will give the open market additional growth in the future. Also, the progressive lifting of restrictions on the CD market is likely to result in more banks tapping this market.

Gensaki

In the past, the sole open market instrument was the gensaki, a term bond with a repurchase agreement which allows it to be treated as a short-term instrument. In recent years, the outstanding balance of gensaki has been steady as it lost out to newer instruments, although this temporarily changed in 1986 with a rising volume of funds seeking a safe return.

For much of the 1980s, the outstanding balance of gensaki was around ¥4 trillion, although during 1986 the balance topped ¥10 trillion at one stage before drifting back to around ¥7 trillion by the end of calendar 1986. By mid-1987, the level had expanded again, exceeding ¥10 trillion.

It is the least restricted of all instruments, and the bulk of the funds are supplied to the market by cash-rich corporations seeking a safe return on their investment funds. There is no limit on the denomination of the gensaki on offer but maturity is limited to less than one year.

Negotiable CDs

Since the inception of the CD market, city banks have dominated its activity, on average accounting for 50 per cent of all funds raised through this instrument. As deregulation has progressed, the city banks have increased their funding through this source, and recently they have accounted for over 60 per cent of all funds raised through CD issues. Most other banks, especially regional and foreign banks, have moved away from relying so heavily on CDs.

The authorities moved quickly to expand the CD market once the long-delayed decision to establish the market was taken. Within the first year of its start up in 1979, there were several steps, initially allowing banks to raise 25 per cent of their capital through CD issues, then 50 per cent. In the third quarter of 1983 this limit was gradually raised to 70 per cent. In 1984, the limit was raised to 90 per cent of capital, and the minimum issue size was reduced to ¥300 billion, down from ¥500 billion. The following year, the minimum issue size was lowered to ¥100 billion and the minimum maturity shortened from three months to one month. The maximum that could be issued by the banks was raised to 100 per cent and then 150 per cent of capital.

CDs outstanding by issuer, 1983–June 1987 (¥100m)

End	*Total*	*City banks*	*Regional banks*	*Trust banks*	*Long-term credit banks*	*Sogo banks*	*Shinkin banks*	*Foreign banks*	*Others*
1983	56,645	27,502	11,458	3,801	3,361	4,313	1,228	4,293	685
1984	84,611	45,956	17,605	5,233	3,312	5,310	2,910	4,049	233
1985	96,572	48,905	17,630	7,476	5,784	6,755	2,032	7,540	447
1986	99,263	61,044	11,914	4,080	7,418	6,511	6,203	1,563	528
June 1987	117,721	69,789	14,291	5,973	10,011	9,180	5,992	1,832	648

Source: Bank of Japan.

In 1986, the maximum maturity of CDs was raised from three months to one year, and during 1987, banks were given approval to expand the total of CDs outstanding to three times shareholders' funds and reserves.

The gradual easing of the restrictions on the issuing of CDs is symptomatic of the usual approach of the Japanese authorities to market development: first to establish a basic market, and then step-by-step extend maturities and free the size of issues that can be made.

Money market certificates

Closely linked with the expansion of the CD market are the money market certificates (MMCs), with interest rates pegged at a slight discount to CDs. The gradual reduction on interest rates of large bank deposits has increased the volume of funds seeking higher returns.

After a dispute between the city, regional and sogo banks, the first MMCs were brought to market in 1985 by the sogo banks and the trust banks. They were followed a short time later by the city banks and regional banks.

MMCs initially had a minimum unit size of ¥50 million and an interest rate ceiling of 0.75 per cent less than the CD rate. The maturity of these certificates has been extended from the original period of six months to one year and, during 1987, to two years.

Further substantial deregulation of this market is expected and this will boost interest in these certificates, especially once the decision is taken to free interest rates and to make terms and maturities more flexible.

Fiscal bills

One of the more unusual instruments available is the so-called fiscal bill, issued by MoF to even out its financing, and which is almost solely taken up by the Bank of Japan.

There has been a steady increase in the number of these issues, with 47 issues in 1986, raising ¥19.9 trillion; in the first half of 1987, there were 28 issues for ¥13.1 trillion. Issues are limited to 60 days.

Fiscal bills are issued at a premium of one or two points above the official discount rate and, while included as part of the short-term money market, are a captive financing for MoF from the Bank of Japan. However, it is thought likely that they will be offered more widely for distribution in due course.

Treasury bills

Treasury bills (TBs) are issued for terms of less than six months, and it is this market which has been the principal test of wills between MoF and the Bank of Japan. The Ministry has consistently been opposed to any rapid development of the market for short-term government paper, while the Bank of Japan is keen on this.

The narrowness of this market in Japan is in sharp contrast to the US, where the TB market is one of the largest of the short-term money markets. In Japan by December 1986, TBs on issue totalled ¥2.07 trillion. By mid-1987, this had fallen to ¥1.95 trillion, or less than 2 per cent of the size of the total short-term money market. Dealing in TBs is restricted solely to banks and corporations and the minimum denomination is ¥100 million.

Tendering for TBs is through a large number of institutions, with 89 securities companies, all of the city banks, long-term credit banks, trust banks, regional banks, mutual banks, a number of life and general insurance companies and a limited number of foreign banks allowed to participate.

There is sufficient demand for short-term government bills, but MoF's determination to limit the impact of short-term interest rate trends on the government's long-term borrowing programme has stifled the development of this market.

Even so, given the strong push for the expansion of this market, some ground is likely to be given in the future, and MoF will eventually yield.

Bankers' acceptances

Established in 1985 as part of the government's measures to deregulate domestic markets, the bankers' acceptance (BA) market has been an abject failure. Total outstandings by mid-1987 had declined to just ¥13.7 billion. The reason is that most large borrowers, such as the big manufacturers and trading houses, can obtain cheaper funds through other markets. The authorities argue that the deregulation of interest rates will spur the development of the BA market. More to the point, however, would be the reduction of the onerous stamp duty, which has limited the usefulness of the market for most likely borrowers.

Tanshi brokers

At the heart of much of the market's developments, and the Bank of Japan's controls, are the activities of the six long-established tanshi broking companies. Some trace their origins back to pre-war money broking. The oldest, Tokyo Tanshi, was founded in 1909 and was merged with Fujimoto Bill Broker, formerly part of, and a forerunner to, Daiwa Securities, and one of the most important pre-war bill brokers. Daiwa Securities retains strong links with the company. Nippon Securities Finance has a large stake in Nippon Discount and Call Money, and Osaka Securities Finance holds a large interest in Yagi Tanshi, headquartered in Osaka.

The board members of the tanshi broking companies are usually former Bank of Japan officials, which ensures continued close links between the bank policy and the tanshi brokers. As the primary instrument of the Bank of Japan in influencing trading in the interbank market, they form an extension of the central bank's activity.

In line with the rapid expansion of the interbank market over the past decade, the earnings of the tanshi brokers have risen significantly. During calendar 1986, for example, the average daily balance of interbank call loans and bill discounts rose by 27.6 per cent, or ¥4.4 trillion, to ¥15.9 trillion.

In addition to their money market broking activities, the six tanshi brokers have also long-established foreign exchange broking arms and have stepped up their links with overseas groups.

The largest, Tokyo Tanshi, established Tokyo Forex, in which Tullet and Tokyo Forex International now hold a 20 per cent stake. Ueda Tanshi transferred its foreign exchange division in 1985 to a subsidiary, Ueda Harlow Ltd, in which the Mills and Allen International group has taken up equity. Yagi Tanshi moved into international money broking in 1986, with a trading agreement signed with the Kirkland-Whittaker Group of London and Caridon of Hong Kong. Yamane Tanshi has established links with Charles Fulton (Asia) for the same purpose.

The tanshi brokers have had little choice but to begin diversifying their activities if they are not to be locked into declining opportunities in the long term. Even though the interbank market has been the area of primary growth of Japan's short-term money markets during the 1980s, the focus of activity is likely to shift to the open instruments in the future.

In addition, pressure will mount for a deregulation of the tanshi brokers' commissions, and it is inevitable that negotiated commissions will be introduced eventually.

All the tanshi brokers have stepped up their moves to diversify and internationalise operations. As Japan's financial markets become more sophisticated, they are expected to offer a broader range of services, from simple money broking to foreign exchange dealing, as well as becoming increasingly active in futures and other domestic financial markets.

Opposite: Even in street demonstrations, the Japanese do not lose their sense of discipline.

岡大
中曽根たおせ
反安保・中曽根たおせ!
安保をつぶせ
軍拡を許すな
青年行動委員会

CHAPTER NINETEEN

Foreign exchange markets

The growth of foreign exchange trading in Tokyo has been dramatic. Two rounds of liberalisation of foreign exchange controls, initially in 1980 and again in 1984, laid the ground for the growth in foreign exchange dealing, which now rivals New York in terms of daily volumes traded. The growth has acted as a magnet to foreign banks, eager to expand their foreign exchange trading capabilities in Tokyo so that they can round out their international currency trading services.

Foreign exchange brokers have a large presence in the market, although they are faced with a more limited role in the market as trading continues to expand. Direct interbank dealing now accounts for almost 50 per cent of trading – a dramatic shift in a short period of time. And with strong implications for future developments, an offshore market has been established which has grown to the point where the new market in Tokyo is larger than either Hong Kong or Singapore (see Chapter 20).

Tokyo has emerged as the key foreign currency trading market in the Asian region. It is commonly expected in Tokyo that it is only a matter of time before it convincingly eclipses New York, and emerges as the largest market after London.

Increased currency volatility, combined with heavy intervention by the Bank of Japan and other central banks, has added to the volume of foreign currency trading worldwide, with particular focus for much of the time on the yen in the light of Japan's large external surplus, especially in its trade with the US.

Foreign currency dealing in Tokyo is denominated by yen/US dollar trading. Trading in other currencies has continued to expand – both in value and absolute terms – and now accounts for almost 20 per cent of daily volumes traded.

Unlike in both New York and London, comparatively little speculative trading is carried out in Tokyo, with most foreign currency dealing still linked to real demand. In part, this is due to the powers of 'moral suasion' held by the Japanese authorities, which have from time to time, successfully moved to limit undue currency speculation by Japanese investors, and are cautious about speculative dealing of any kind.

Volume of business

A survey carried out by the financial authorities in New York, London and Tokyo in 1986 estimated that at that time daily foreign exchange trading in Tokyo averaged US$48 billion, compared with US$60 billion in New York and US$90 billion in London. Since then, trading volumes have continued to expand in Tokyo, and there is widespread feeling among market participants that it now rivals, and often exceeds, New York.

Much of the growth in foreign currency trading has been fuelled by the exchange rate volatility during the 1970s and 1980s, combined with the removal of many restrictions. In the mid-1970s, for example, when domestic controls were much stricter, the yen/US dollar exchange rate moved by an average of 9 per cent annually.

Since 1980, when Japan began relaxing its foreign currency controls, the annual fluctuation between the two currencies has risen to 20 per cent, with few

The Japanese occasionally prefer the more speculative forms of investment.

signs of any immediate stability. The dramatic overvaluation of the US dollar against most other leading currencies in the first half of the 1980s has been replaced, in the Japanese view, by a period of overvaluation of the yen against the US dollar.

Until recently, there was a marked reluctance by many of Japan's trading partners to accept payment in yen, preferring to receive US dollars, which have been much easier to convert into third currencies. That is changing, particularly now that the yen is no longer undervalued.

For much of the 1970s, for example, a negligible share of Japan's imports and only about 17 per cent of its exports were denominated in yen. But by the mid-1980s, about 40 per cent of exports and a growing share of imports, estimated at over 5 per cent, were denominated in yen.

The very low figure for imports is due to the fact that most of Japan's imports, until 1987 at least, were basic commodities, such as oil, which have a world market price denominated in US dollars. Few Japanese importers have been willing to switch to yen-based contracts.

The big currency shift, however, has resulted in a sizeable, although as yet largely unquantifiable, boost in the volume of intermediate manufactured goods imported by Japan. Again, the import contracts for most of these goods are based on US dollars, which gives Japanese importers a natural hedge against the expensive yen. But the volume of imports written in yen is expected to rise further in the future.

The other factor influencing present developments is the attractiveness of the yen as a reserve currency. Most countries seek to diversify their official reserve holdings to give them a natural hedge against future currency movements. The reasons vary, although it often follows the overall changing pattern of a country's trade flows – countries with a large trade 'exposure' to Japan may seek to hold a portion of their currency exposure in yen, even though the bulk may be denominated in US dollars.

The strength of the Japanese economy during the 1980s and the rise of the yen have resulted in many governments seeking to denominate a portion of their international borrowings in yen. The interest of sovereign borrowers in the yen to obtain a balance of currencies underwrote the initial expansion of the Samurai bond market during the 1970s, even though for much of this time expansion was either proscribed or controlled by the Japanese government.

The large shift in the value of the yen that has occurred since 1985 changed the perceptions of a number of governments towards raising yen funds for a time, although once the yen began to stabilise against the US dollar, many sovereign borrowers effectively sought to roll over their Samurai borrowings, to capitalise on lower interest rates or to remove much of their currency losses.

As part of this, the use of the yen as a reserve currency has doubled from 2 per cent to more than 4 per cent, and will continue to grow in the medium term.

Legislative reform

Controls surrounding Japan's foreign currency trading have undergone two decisive reforms during the past decade. The first occurred late in 1980 when the government made a sweeping reform of foreign currency regulations. Foreign exchange dealings were declared 'free in principle' compared to the previous 'proscribed in principle'. However, even with this decisive change, unofficial controls remained.

The next step forward came in 1984, as part of the deregulation agreements reached with the US government. The restriction that foreign exchange dealings of non-banking institutions must be backed by underlying commercial transactions was removed with effect from 1 April 1984. Following this, the volume of foreign exchange dealing in Tokyo, stagnant in 1983, surged in 1984 and 1985.

Other reforms have also been instituted, largely following consideration of the issues by the Market Practices Committee, which is chaired by the Bank of

Tokyo. The most important move by this committee was in mid-1984, when it was agreed to lift the requirement that all foreign exchange dealing be conducted through the authorised foreign exchange brokers, although at first this was limited to dealing in currencies other than the US dollar, which at that time accounted for only a negligible proportion of foreign currency dealing. In response, trading in third currencies, such as Deutschmark, Swiss franc and sterling, surged. From accounting for less than 10 per cent of all trading volumes, their share rose steadily and now approaches 20 per cent of all foreign exchange trading in the Tokyo market.

To offset the impact of this shift on the foreign exchange brokers, they were given some access to international broking for the first time. At the same time, brokerage rates for larger transactions were reduced. Brokerage fees were subsequently reduced further.

The settlement procedure was also changed in 1984 with the decision to shift settlement for direct dealing from the day following to the second business day after the transaction is carried out. Then, in early 1985, direct dealing was extended to include yen/US dollar deals, the most important part of market dealing.

International comparison

Compared with most of the larger foreign exchange markets, Tokyo has several points of distinction, not the least of which is the continued operation of the foreign exchange brokers. Even though direct bank-to-bank dealing can now be undertaken, trading through the brokers is still the preferred method of dealing for many participants, especially newcomers to the market. Secondly, Tokyo has a comparatively low level of third currency dealing, with trading dominated by yen/US dollar transactions.

In addition, in Tokyo the volume of spot trading is overshadowed by the volume of swap dealing, contrary to both New York and London.

When the financial authorities in London, New York and Tokyo carried out their last international comparison in 1986, spot dealing accounted for 39.5 per cent of transactions in Tokyo, 63.2 per cent in New York and 73 per cent in London. Swap deals in Tokyo accounted for 49.9 per cent of all turnover, in London for 26 per cent and in New York for 29.8 per cent.

Foreign exchange dealers in Tokyo argue that this is due to the ill-formed and underdeveloped nature of foreign exchange dealing in Tokyo. Even though the most important restraints on active trading have been lifted, there is still administrative guidance, which is one reason why the volume of swap trading is larger in Tokyo than in other centres. It is also argued that the high level of swap dealing indicates the continued market inefficiencies in Tokyo, since theoretically there should be only limited distortions between a free market and the cost of the yen/US dollar swap. Because these distortions do exist in Tokyo, they create an environment that encourages a great deal of swap-driven foreign exchange transactions.

Ironically, as the authorities in Japan have freed foreign exchange trading, the volume of swap trading has risen sharply.

Speculation is still minor by comparison with other centres. This is indicated by the fact that interbank dealing accounts for two-thirds of the volumes traded in Tokyo, compared with well over 80 per cent in both New York and London. By way of contrast, non-financial counterparties account for one third of dealing in Tokyo, whereas in both New York and London their participation is negligible.

The Japanese economy relies much more on trade than the US economy, and this is usually interpreted by bullish forex dealers in Tokyo to mean that the potential for future growth in Tokyo is much greater, so that trading volumes will comfortably exceed those in New York in the medium term.

Despite the optimism, problem areas remain. Securities companies, for example, are hampered in their foreign exchange transactions, since they are forced to clear all of their dealings through the foreign exchange banks. So, too, are the trading companies.

Despite the fact that most of Japan's big exporters have begun trading aggressively in foreign currencies in order to limit their exposure, their access to the market is still directed through those banks which have foreign exchange licences.

Future deregulation

The decision to give Japan's financial institutions direct access to foreign capital markets so that they can hedge their currency exposure from the latter part of 1987 points to future deregulatory steps.

After the sizeable foreign currency losses incurred by the life insurance companies in 1985 and 1986, the Ministry of Finance (MoF) decided to give them direct access to foreign markets. Previously, access was only possible through foreign affiliates of these institutions. Given the cost of hedging foreign exchange risk, however, few were willing to cover their exposure, since it would cut substantially into their returns on foreign investments.

With the freedom given to the financial sector, MoF officials concede that it is only a matter of time before similar freedom is given to the larger industrial groups, especially the trading companies, most of which already have large currency trading divisions operating as a separate profit centre.

But even if some of the overt controls are lifted, the trading companies will remain hampered. During the second quarter of 1987, for example, when there was very heavy selling of the US dollar by both Japanese banks and the industrial sector which moved the yen sharply higher against the US dollar, the authorities stepped in.

Both sectors were instructed to limit their selling of US dollars, and all trading was closely scrutinised by either MoF (for financial institutions) or MITI (for industrial groups). As a result, sales of US dollars were sharply reduced, for a time at least. So, although Japan's foreign exchange controls are 'free in principle' the reality is a little different.

Foreign exchange brokers

One of the anomalies of the foreign exchange market is the continuing large role of the foreign exchange brokers. Originally divisions of the 'tanshi' brokers, the exclusive short-term money market dealers, most of the foreign exchange brokers were spun off from their parent companies in the early 1980s. Following this, a number have established links with some of the international money brokers.

The start of direct dealing between the banks, first in third currency transactions in 1984, and subsequently in yen/US dollar trading, would appear to indicate that the forex brokers have a declining future in the Tokyo market, especially as many of the medium-sized banks gain more experience in foreign exchange trading.

As with stockbroking commissions, the rates applying to foreign exchange dealing in Tokyo are higher than in most international centres. To obviate the criticism, the Market Practice Committee has moved to cut commission rates, especially through the application of volume discounts, which has been achieved by the implementation of negotiated commission rates for larger deals.

The last cut in commission rates was implemented on 1 April 1987, following a previous cut imposed in August 1986. Even with the reduction, many banks still complain that rates are much higher than those in other foreign exchange markets. For many foreign banks, for example, which do not have a strong domestic client base in Japan, brokerage commissions on forex dealing operations are one of their largest overhead expenses.

Even those banks with an established client base often still have little choice but to conclude their deals through the forex brokers since they will often quote a slightly better rate than that available in dealing directly with some of the larger banks active in the market. For the brokers, one of the most important changes was the move in 1984 to allow direct interbank dealing, by-passing the brokers. To offset the impact of this, they were given access to international broking for the first time.

The forex brokers in Tokyo have found that international broking commission rates are roughly half of those they can obtain in the domestic market. Nonetheless, the absolute increase in foreign exchange trading in Tokyo has underwritten a continued increase in their profitability during the 1980s.

With the squeeze in domestic commission rates, the brokers have moved to strengthen their international links. Tokyo Forex teamed up with Tullett and Riley International. Ueda Tanshi linked up with Mills and Allen International and renamed its Tokyo affiliate Ueda Harlow. In turn, the two companies have moved into the Asian region, with a jointly-owned affiliate established in Singapore. Others have also moved into Hong Kong.

Much of the reason for the continued role of the brokers in the Tokyo market stems from tradition – banks that have in the past dealt mostly through the forex brokers prefer to continue to do so. Although the larger banks, with their more extensive experience, are willing to move independently, the increase in the number of medium-sized and small banks that have established foreign exchange trading operations assures a continued role for the forex brokers.

Growth of business

In the wake of the liberalisation of foreign exchange controls in 1984, foreign exchange trading in Tokyo has soared, thanks to both the deregulation that was effected and subsequent market developments – specifically the revaluation of the yen against the US dollar.

The tumultuous developments in foreign exchange markets during 1986 can be divided into two periods. First, the extended period from January to August, when the yen moved ever higher against the US dollar. During this period, the Bank of Japan reversed its earlier policy of selling US dollars to force the dollar down against the yen, emerging as a buyer of US dollars during March in a vain attempt to stop the rise of the yen.

In the process, activity in Tokyo's foreign exchange market rocketed, with the total volume traded almost doubling from US$1.75 trillion in 1985 to US$3.19 trillion in 1986. A record volume of US$322.5 billion was traded during July 1986 alone.

The second stage of foreign exchange developments was from August to mid-October 1986. For much of this time, the yen was stable against the US dollar, trading in a band between ¥160 and ¥150 to the US dollar, as the view broadened that the yen had peaked.

At the Group of Five and Group of Seven meetings in late February 1987, broad agreement was reached to intensify the coordination of economic policies in order to stabilise exchange rates. During 1987, trading in the yen remained extremely sensitive to both the continued disappointing US trade performance and the strength of Japan's export performance.

Currency markets remained volatile for much of 1987, which underpinned large trading volumes in the Tokyo foreign exchange market. The yen continued to edge higher against the US dollar, reaching a peak of ¥137.25 in late April. Fearing a continued slide of the US dollar against the yen, the Japanese government became extremely concerned, since it realised that intervention could not contain the market's bearishness over the outlook for the US dollar. As a result, MoF used stiff moral suasion on both the financial and industrial sectors to restrain the heavy selling of the US dollar which took place at that time. Subsequently, all foreign exchange dealing was closely scrutinised, and only small-lot selling was approved. The impact was immediate, and the yen eased against the US dollar for a time.

One consequence of the firming of the yen against the US dollar was that it sparked a change in the use of the yen as a currency of settlement for Japan's trading transactions. The peak in the usage of the yen as the currency of settlement for Japan's exports was reached in the third quarter of 1985, when it reached 42 per cent, before declining slightly again. There has, however, been an increase in the settlement of imports in yen, which has reached around 10 per cent of the total volume.

Louvre accord

The most important step taken to stabilise foreign exchange markets during 1987 was the 'Louvre Accord', reached in late February. In broad terms, the agreement was to hold exchange rates close to levels ruling at that time.

The agreement, reached following a meeting of the Group of Seven countries (although Italy did not participate), was arrived at along with a commitment by Japan to boost Government spending in a bid to boost economic growth and to take some of the pressure off the US economy's role of underpinning world economic growth.

Whether there would be co-ordinated intervention in foreign currency markets to achieve the goal of stabilising exchange rates and exactly what the limits of currency movements were was a matter for conjecture throughout much of 1987.

The issue of policy co-ordination between the US, Japan and West Germany was also promoted, as it had been since the 1986 World Bank and IMF meetings in Seoul, although it remained an elusive goal.

The future

Further liberalisation is likely in the medium term, with securities houses commonly expected to obtain direct access to the forex market. In return, banks are likely to get full access to dealing in the domestic government bond market. At present they are limited to trading only in their own account.

At the same time, overall growth in foreign exchange trading in Tokyo can only continue, as second-ranked traders become more adept at assessing market trends. At present, much of the dealing is still closely related to underlying transactions, with the authorities very cautious in allowing an undue amount of speculation. Both the Bank of Japan and MoF closely monitor trading, and on occasion directly intervene to try and limit the amount of speculative selling.

Some accommodation to currency speculation will come about, although for the Japanese authorities to adopt a fully hands-off approach will take a long time, if it ever occurs. Among the most handicapped of Japan's institutions in the foreign exchange market are the big trading houses, which do not have direct access to the market, and as yet cannot directly access overseas hedging markets.

Most already have sizeable equity and currency dealing operations but, since the trading houses are regulated by the Ministry of International Trade and Industry, which has no influence whatsoever over MoF, their ambitions will largely remain unfulfilled. Even so, given their large forex exposure, smoother access to the market appears overdue.

CHAPTER TWENTY

Japan's offshore market

One of the principal developments in Japan since the deregulatory process began has been the formation of the Japan offshore market (JOM), which has been operational since 1 December 1986.

Heavily criticised prior to its establishment as being too tightly controlled, the market has been at least a partial success. The Ministry of Finance (MoF) estimated that within its first week the market had assets of US$50 billion. By mid-1987, assets had reached US$179 billion. The start of the offshore market in Tokyo was a tangible sign of MoF's commitment to deregulation and the internationalisation of the yen. An offshore financial centre in Tokyo would confirm its position as the financial centre of Asia, as well as putting it on an equal footing with both London and New York, ministry officials argued.

But, as with the entire process of financial liberalisation in Japan, the authorities were keen to limit the impact of the offshore market on the domestic markets, which was underscored by the tight controls instituted.

Given the sheer size of Japanese financial institutions in international capital markets, both the Hong Kong and Singapore governments were extremely concerned at the possible negative impact the start of the offshore market in Tokyo could have on their own markets.

Accurate figures are difficult to obtain, but the Hong Kong and Singapore markets are estimated to have assets of around US$150 billion each. Tokyo surpassed the size of both of these markets by mid-1987.

Japanese officials confidently expected that before 1990 the size of the offshore market in Tokyo will approximate that of the New York market, which has assets of around US$280 billion. Both trail far behind London, which has assets estimated at more than US$750 billion.

The Tokyo market was modelled on that of New York, and this is a major handicap for the market to grow to anything like the size of the London market. The most trenchant criticism of the Tokyo market is that local taxes and duties are still levied on transactions.

History

The belated decision to establish an offshore market in New York in 1981, which was aimed at reviving its role as the leading international finance centre, provoked the Japanese government to look more closely at the issue, especially following the liberalisation of Japan's foreign exchange controls in 1980.

In early 1983, the then head of the Overseas Economic Cooperation Fund, Takahashi Hosomi, made a proposal for the setting up of a similar offshore market in Tokyo, after leading an official mission to study the New York market. In the light of the underdeveloped nature of Japan's domestic capital markets, which were still tightly controlled, he recommended a market along the lines of the New York offshore market.

There was no immediate response to his proposal and, apart from occasional discussion of the prospect of establishing such a market in Tokyo, little progress was made. With the mounting pressure by the US government on Japan to start a full-scale process of financial deregulation, the original proposal was eventually re-evaluated.

The Kashiwagi Committee

Immediately after the publication of the recommendations of the committee on the yen/US dollar exchange rate in April 1984, MoF released a separate report, which also noted the need to consider the establishment of an offshore market.

Following support at this level, the matter was considered at great length by the Committee on Foreign Exchange and Other Transactions, which gradually evolved a consensus on the possibility of establishing an offshore market in Tokyo.

A special sub-committee headed by the chairman of the Bank of Tokyo, Yusuke Kashiwagi, assessed the specific issues to be resolved if an offshore market was established. Again, this committee opted for an offshore market along the lines of that of New York, although the final shape of the market was more limited than the one envisaged by the committee.

A key feature of the recommendations, which ran through the entire discussion on the establishment of an offshore market, was that if the proposal was pursued, any such market should be insulated as far as possible from domestic capital markets. One of the prime concerns was that if an offshore market was set up, it could hamper domestic monetary policy controls, which was to be avoided at all cost.

The market in detail

Access to accounts in Tokyo's offshore market is limited to banks authorised to undertake foreign exchange transactions in Japan and to those groups which receive specific approval from MoF.

Participation in the dealings transacted through the offshore market are limited to non-residents: banks domiciled overseas (including the offshore branches of Japanese banks and securities companies), foreign corporations (which includes offshore subsidiaries of domestic groups), and foreign governments and agencies. Excluded from accessing the market directly are non-residents and overseas branches of domestic companies.

A basic feature of the operation of the offshore market is that it is limited to 'out–out' transactions – that is those dealings which would be exempt from withholding taxes. To comply with these controls, foreign exchange banks with offshore accounts have to ensure that the counterparties to any transactions are non-residents, and that any funds transacted through the market are used outside Japan. In addition to this, the daily net flow of funds between a bank's domestic and overseas account is limited to 5 per cent of the average balance of the bank's offshore assets held for non-residents during the previous month.

This latter control was a particular issue of contention which, it was argued at the time, would severely hamper both the growth and the future role of the market. As a result, some banks, including the Bank of Tokyo, argued strongly that this control be replaced by reserve requirements.

Another onerous restraint on the market's expansion is that transactions processed through this market are still subject to local taxes and stamp duties, a clear disincentive to channel deals through the Tokyo market rather than through other markets such as Hong Kong, for example, which offers a more favourable tax regime.

Even with the controls presently in place, the offshore market in Tokyo has grown steadily since its launch on 1 December 1986. By July 1987, total outstanding assets of the market stood at US$178.8 billion. Of this, US$107.1 billion was denominated in US dollars, with yen-denominated assets making up the balance. The bulk of the funds in the offshore market are funds deposited in offshore accounts primarily by domestic banks for management by their overseas branches.

Soon after the launch of the market, Japanese banks began to provide syndicated loans through their accounts held in the market, although the level of activity has been subdued in line with the low demand for syndicated loans in recent years.

The main interest in accessing the market came from the larger Japanese banks engaging in arbitrage transactions by monitoring interest rate movements in the Euroyen, call and bill discount markets, together with the cost of raising yen funds by selling US dollars on the foreign exchange market. As a result, interbank transactions accounted for most of the activity in the market.

The growth of the offshore market has been achieved by domestic banks transferring funds to their offshore accounts, but the very low level of lending channelled through the market is seen as an indication that the market still lacks depth, and cannot realistically be justified. Indicative of the lack of attraction of the market is the fact that there has been virtually no participation by foreign banks since the market commenced.

Apart from tax liability and limits on the net inflow into the offshore accounts, a major stumbling block to the development of the Tokyo market is that securities issued by non-residents cannot be held in offshore accounts.

The restrictions on either transacting securities business or completing issues through the market reflects the clash of interests between banks and securities houses. Banks are keen to ensure that securities houses cannot participate as underwriters through the Tokyo offshore market. For their part, the securities houses are anxious lest an issuing market begin through the offshore market, which would give banks a means of circumventing domestic controls which prevent them from participating as underwriters or dealers in domestic securities markets.

For once, the conflict between banks and securities houses in seeking to protect their respective areas of interest domestically has resulted in a joint interest to limit the offshore market from developing as a market for issuing securities along the lines of the Euromarket in London.

This agreement between the banks and securities houses has restricted the expansion of the Tokyo offshore market as a potential competitor to the Euromarket. At the same time, it has ensured that the Tokyo offshore market remains little more than an extension of the interbank market, except that it operates between the various offshore branches of Japanese banks. If the controls which presently restrict the development of the Tokyo offshore market were brought into line with those operating in London, for example, then Tokyo would clearly develop as the dominant capital market of the Asian region.

MoF is under pressure to remove some of the constraints surrounding the Tokyo offshore market, especially in terms of tax treatment, but the power of the Taxation Bureau of MoF is such that little ground will be given unless there is a complete revision of Japan's taxation system.

Just how committed the Japanese authorities are to establishing a large offshore market in Japan is a moot point. Some argue that the present organisation of the offshore market in Tokyo is purely transitional, and that further steps will be taken in the future to liberalise activities in the market.

CHAPTER TWENTY-ONE

Funds management

The most dramatic change in Japan's financial system, which will also have a large impact on its future developments, is the move to institutionalise the funds management industry. The large annual increase in the size of pension funds under management, the sharp increase in the use of various investment trusts such as tokkin and kingai by the corporate and financial sectors, and the large flow of individual savings into investment trusts have fuelled the boom in Japan's equity markets, and also led to a reweighting within Japan's financial sector. The change in the flow of funds has pushed the trust banks, insurance companies and securities houses to the fore.

Excluding pension funds under management, total investment funds passed the ¥80 trillion level during 1987, and further rapid growth is expected. Japan's biggest institutional investors are the insurance companies, followed by the trust banks. Both groups have the sole management right over pension funds. The insurance companies also have funds from their own policyholders under management, and the trust banks have control over the investment funds entrusted to their care.

The securities houses have substantial investment trusts under their management, as well as sizeable funds handled separately by their investment management company affiliates.

Fuelled by tax changes and the rising level of corporate sector affluence, active funds management is the area that has shown the most dramatic growth in Japan's financial system over the past five years. Funds management, outside these areas, had been a largely unregulated cottage industry in Japan until late in 1986, when the Investment Advisory Act was introduced. This legislation was sparked by the *Toshi* journal incident of 1984.

This monthly publication was primarily a tip sheet for investors. Its bankruptcy resulted in over 10,000 investors losing an estimated ¥350 billion, resulting in a public outcry which forced the government to introduce controls over the investment advisory industry.

The new investment advisory legislation incorporates a registration and licensing system. Under the new legislation licensed investment advisers are allowed for the first time full discretion over investments. (See Chapter 25 for further discussion.)

A large number of both Japanese and foreign investment advisory companies will eventually be licensed and given discretion over funds management.

There have been many tie-ups, including, for example, Yamaichi Securities and the Murray Johnstone group of the UK, Sumitomo Bank and Bankers Trust, and Diamond Asset Management (an affiliate of Mitsubishi Bank) and the US Fidelity Group.

Yamaichi Securities' moves are indicative of the rush by the Japanese securities houses to build up their expertise in this area. Along with its tie-up with the Murray Johnstone group, it has forged links with the Batterymarch Investment group of the US, bought equity in Daishin Securities (a South Korean securities firm) and Bangkok Tokyo Finance and Securities of Thailand, and took a stake in China Securities Investment Trust, the advisory company to the Taiwan Fund. All the other big Japanese houses are involved in similar moves to prepare for the increasing pressure on funds management performance.

A large number of Japan's smaller security firms have moved to increase their capital and some, such as Kokusai Securities and Tokyo Securities, have made share offerings. A number of investment management firms affiliated with the big city banks and general insurance companies have also been established, as well as foreign firms, in the hope of obtaining licences.

Investment trusts

After the dramatic shake-out of the investment trust industry in the early 1960s when prices on Japan's stock exchanges tumbled, investment trusts have experienced a slow, but steady, return to popularity. During 1986 and 1987, they emerged as the fastest growing area of Japan's savings sector with rates of growth outstripping all other major competitors for savings.

The sharp fall in domestic interest rates, combined with the continued climb in stock prices since 1984, and the lack of promising investment alternatives resulted in a surge of funds into both equity and bond trusts.

Most of the recent growth has been recorded by equity investment trusts. At the end of 1985, the net assets of all equity investment trusts stood at ¥10.38 trillion. Within one year they had climbed to ¥19.12 trillion, and by the end of June 1987 they had expanded to ¥27.22 trillion. Bond investment trusts have been left behind in the rush. After falling to ¥9.59 trillion in 1985, total net assets expanded to ¥12.95 trillion by the end of 1986 and to ¥13.81 trillion by the end of June 1987. The downturn in interest rates has limited the popularity of these trusts and most investors channel their surplus funds into stock trusts, which typically combine both stocks and bonds. The lure of high rates of return has proved to be a powerful incentive. By June 1987, net assets of unit trusts had risen to ¥41.03 trillion, up from ¥32.07 trillion at the end of December 1986.

The attraction of investment trusts is the indicated rates of return of more than 6 per cent at a time when bank deposits are typically offering only around 2 per cent.

There are two basic varieties of investment trusts – the unit (closed) type and the open-ended type. Most funds are raised through unit type funds, which operate for a fixed term – three, four, five, seven or 10 years. Returns are paid out yearly and at the time of redemption all trust assets are liquidated. Unit type trusts have achieved much higher returns than the open-ended trusts, which accounts for their continued popularity.

The first bond trusts were launched in the early 1960s as a natural extension to the existing equity trusts. Their growth was also encouraged by MoF during the mid-1970s, as the level of construction bonds issued by the government exploded and there were fears that new bond issues could not readily be absorbed by the market.

Specialist funds

In line with the growing sophistication of Japanese investors' needs, there has been a gradual diversification of the variety of funds on offer. Various jumbo funds, and other offerings such as international equities funds, have been launched. There has also been a variety of funds in both the fixed income and the equities areas, offering solely capital gain, or dividend income, or a mixture of both, reflecting the diversity of investor needs.

More recently, funds specialising in second section and OTC stocks have been launched, giving potential investors a broader range of investment options. Approval has also been given in some circumstances for funds to be invested in warrants and, increasingly, foreign bonds and securities.

The steady growth of these investment trusts is in line with the decline in direct individual holdings of stocks, which is a reflection of the increasing maturity of the Japanese economy, combined with the fact that unless an investor is well connected with his broker, the gains on direct investments will be minimal.

Chuki-Kokusai funds

In 1979 the securities houses received approval to start trusts devoted to medium-term government bonds (the so-called 'chuki-kokusai' funds) which witnessed an explosion of investor interest in the first half of the 1980s. In 1980, shortly after their establishment, investment in chuki-kokusai funds was a modest ¥231 billion. By the end of 1985, had expanded to ¥4,012 billion.

The establishment of these funds has taken the securities houses one step closer to the banks, since they are very similar to cash management funds in the US. MoF has, however, refused repeated pressure to give the securities houses the potential for same-day withdrawal from these funds. Even so, most of the big securities houses have teamed up with regional banks to offer clearance facilities for investors.

The steady popularity of these trusts, which account for 20 per cent of total outstandings, has also boosted the weighting of bond holdings in all funds. With most equity funds balanced, with a mixture of bonds, equities and funds invested in the call market, this meant that at the end of 1985 70.4 per cent of total funds raised were invested in bonds.

Corporate investment – tokkin and kingai

As investment trusts have shown the strongest growth of any section of the personal savings industry, similarly corporate investments through trusts have been a significant factor in corporate investment patterns during the 1980s.

Principally the corporate sector, but also the finance sector itself, have through tokkin and kingai devoted an increasing portion of assets to indirect investment, as opposed to direct investment. Corporate sector investments in funds trusts more than doubled in 1986, with those deposited in trust bank accounts rising by 43 per cent. Of the two, tokkin funds are the more significant as a result of changes in tax law interpretation which made it possible for the corporate sector to take advantage of the boom in equity markets.

The sudden rise to prominence of both tokkin and kingai reflects the zaiteku financial techniques carried out by an increasing proportion of the industrial sector, as they seek profits from financial markets at a time of low earnings from traditional operations.

Tokkin

Tokkin accounts consist of funds entrusted by financial institutions and corporations seeking to separate securities trading from their existing securities investments.

If an investor buys new securities directly, they are added to the existing portfolio, considerably boosting the average purchase cost since all holdings are in the books at cost. As most of the shareholdings by the corporate and finance sector are long-term, the book price bears no relation to present market prices. Tokkin accounts, which are held through the trust banks, enable a separation of securities accounts for tax purposes, making securities trading much more attractive.

The key tax change enabled corporations to separate out shares bought for trading purposes, with a different tax treatment. Typically, the investor in tokkin funds gives broad details of the preferred investment mix to the trust bank, which in turn then instructs the securities house.

Kingai

With kingai, the fund manager holds much greater discretionary investment powers and can hence take full advantage of the manager's perceptions of future market trends. Usually, kingai funds are managed in a co-mingled manner, which makes them similar to mutual funds.

Both tokkin and kingai have broadly similar investment approaches, with an estimated 30 per cent in government bonds, 15 per cent in foreign securities, 30 per cent in domestic equities and the balance in a range of other sectors.

Growth of tokkin and kingai

Because of declining interest rates and the necessity for some clarification of the revision of the tax law in 1980 it was not until 1982 that there was scope for a significant growth in the management of corporate funds through either tokkin or kingai.

Even so, limits still apply. Life insurance companies, for example, have been able to invest only 3 per cent of assets in tokkin, although they have lobbied for some time for this to be increased to 5 per cent.

All other sectors of the finance industry – credit banks, mutual banks, regional banks and city banks – are active investors in tokkin funds, as are pension associations related to the Ministry of Home Affairs.

From slow initial growth, total investments in tokkin have risen to high levels and show no sign of slowing down. Since their establishment, the increase in the volume of funds invested has been dramatic. For tokkin, it rose from ¥3.6 trillion in March 1985 to ¥10.6 trillion by September 1986 – an expansion of 2.9 times in less than two years. By April 1987, investments in tokkin had reached ¥16.3 trillion.

Funds invested in kingai rose from ¥1.75 trillion in March 1985 to ¥4.69 trillion the following year, reaching ¥11.9 trillion by April 1987.

The total for the two stood at ¥28.2 trillion by April 1987, up ¥3.19 trillion over the previous month. Growth continued steadily during 1987, and investments exceeded ¥30 trillion by the end of August 1987.

The rapid expansion of tokkin and kingai have been a boon for the foreign trust banks that entered the Japanese market in 1986. Formed primarily to gain a share of pension fund management, the extreme popularity of tokkin and kingai accounts gave them some quick business. By the end of March 1987, the nine foreign trust banks had garnered ¥850 billion in these trust accounts, accounting for 3.4 per cent of the total outstanding.

Over the same period of time, investments in mutual funds rose from ¥8.5 trillion to ¥32.1 trillion. With the mutual funds, around half of the funds is earmarked for investment in equities, although in fact a large portion of this is placed in the call markets, with further funds invested in public bonds.

Similarly with tokkin and kingai funds, which by the middle of 1987 showed a sizeable increase in their overall liquidity as fund managers became increasingly wary of the short-term outlook for equity markets.

The investors

Apart from the tax advantage for the corporate sector, another factor which has encouraged the usage of tokkin and kingai funds is that they promise anonymity for the corporate investor, so that the beneficial ownership of the funds is not disclosed.

Along with the banks, particularly large users of tokkin and kingai funds are trading companies as they take full advantage of active securities markets to boost overall rates of return. The four biggest trading companies – Sumitomo, Mitsubishi, C. Itoh and Marubeni – were estimated to have had ¥9.7 trillion invested in tokkin and kingai by the end of March 1987.

In broad terms, financial corporations have a much greater exposure to tokkin funds, with industrial groups investing more heavily in kingai. By March 1987, 65 per cent of all funds invested in tokkin came from financial institutions, while for kingai, 80 per cent of the funds invested in kingai came from the corporate sector.

The particular difficulty for many of these trust accounts is that the fund managers have indicated rates of return that may not be achievable. Notwithstanding this, a number of fund managers have usually indicated annualised returns of around 8 per cent to corporate investors, which they feel is low enough to be achievable.

In addition, for many corporate managers, avoiding risk is paramount, so they are usually content with the indicated rate of return which is roughly in line with that earned from long-term government bonds over the past decade.

Eigyo tokkin

Since their introduction, there have been numerous allegations of excesses, and loss controls, leading to regular investigations by MoF.

Much of the interest of the authorities has been aroused by so-called 'eigyo tokkin' which, devised by the securities houses, usually offer corporate clients specified rates of return, usually pitched at around 8 per cent, or in line with the coupon of maturing long-term government bonds.

These funds are illegal, since the institutional investment desks of the securities houses are not empowered to raise funds for discretionary investments.

Notwithstanding this legal limitation, these funds are believed to have flourished during 1986. Disturbed at their proliferation, the authorities have attempted to stop these excesses, although with little apparent success. However, it is hoped that with the introduction of the new Investment Advisory Law, the worst of these excesses will be stamped out.

Valuation of funds invested in tokkin and kingai accounts has also caused some headaches for the regulatory authorities at first, in trying to enforce uniform accounting practices.

Typically, many of the investors first began to value their investments at cost, although MoF applied strong pressure for this to be changed to the lower of cost or market value in an attempt to improve the accuracy of the valuations.

Along with the prospect of higher returns, many of the life insurance companies have been keen to participate since they could generate capital profits through tokkin or kingai investments which went some way towards offsetting the impact of their sizeable capital losses on foreign investments during fiscal 1985 and 1986.

Investment fund management

The introduction of the new Investment Advisory Act and the move of more foreign fund managers into Japan will result in a general shake-up of this sector.

Most of the investment management companies of the bigger securities houses were small, if they existed at all, prior to the oil price rises of the 1970s. The resulting flow of funds to the Middle East saw a steady stream of investment advisers trying to garner a share of fund management.

The four big securities houses subsequently made some inroads into North American funds. Usually, US fund managers devoted only 2 or 3 per cent of their funds to foreign markets so that, given the small size, they were prepared to hand the management of funds earmarked for the Japanese market to investment management companies affiliated with the big Japanese houses. Given their expertise on markets in the Asian region, there has been a progressive shift towards giving Japanese securities houses discretion over funds not only for Japan but also for the Asian region.

Middle East money still forms an important part of the overall funds under management, often accounting for as much as 50 per cent, although it has dwindled significantly as a proportion of the total over the past five years.

Thanks to their power within the Japanese market, the four big securities houses have ¥4.3 trillion in funds managed by their affiliated investment management companies. The growth of total funds under management by the four big houses has been impressive but the competition that will arise with the new Investment Advisory Act is likely to threaten their dominance in time.

Propelled by clients' requests, some of the Japanese houses have also established units in Europe for fund management, adding to their power in international capital markets.

Deregulation

Pressure is mounting for a deregulation of the management of Japan's pension funds, which is at present limited to trust banks and life insurance companies. Pressure is also increasing for the government to boost the returns of the public pension funds it controls. The investment management companies anticipate obtaining access to pension funds over the next few years, which will result in a substantial expansion of their funds under management.

The introduction of new legislation has also resulted in a large increase in the number of foreign groups seeking to establish a presence in this market in Japan.

By mid-1987, MoF had licensed nearly 300 investment advisory firms, a significant number of which were foreign groups. The main initial attraction was to obtain access to the tokkin and kingai investment trusts, with the added lure of gaining access to pension funds management in the medium term.

Many of these new investment advisory companies are directly affiliated with existing insurance companies and banks and with securities houses.

Mortgage securities

One of the fastest growing lesser markets in Japan is the mortgage securities market, where the level of activity has expanded rapidly over the past three years, particularly following the involvement of the bigger securities houses.

But like most new markets in Japan, it soon suffered from excesses. A number of cases in the latter part of 1986 and 1987 where investors were defrauded of their investments eventually led MoF, in conjunction with the main industry participants, to establish new guidelines, primarily through new legislation.

Originally, the mortgage securities sector had been dominated by companies affiliated with the major banks. With the industry's growth since 1984, it has become a battle field between the banks and mortgage securities companies affiliated with the bigger securities houses.

The industry's rankings have changed dramatically over the past three years, and Nippon Godo Securities, linked with Nomura Securities, has emerged as the largest issuer of mortgage backed securities in fiscal 1986. Its quick emergence at the top of the industry is evidence of the fact that both banks and securities houses regard the development of a mortgage securities market as having some significance.

CHAPTER TWENTY-TWO

General insurance

Insulated from the rate cutting wars that have regularly ravaged general insurers in most world markets, Japan's industry has prospered and some of its groups have emerged as the strongest and most profitable in the world. Thanks to the protection of the Ministry of Finance (MoF) their prosperity is assured. And, with the introduction of various savings-linked policies, the general insurers are now one of the fastest growing sectors of the financial system.

Strict controls over rates and the type of policies that can be introduced have ensured their financial strength. Equally, the industry is strongly opposed to MoF making any change from the present cosy cartel which would diminish the insurers' position of strength. The general insurance groups point to the experience of the general insurance industry in Australia, where controlled rates were abolished overnight, as an example of the dire effects of free competition.

However, even with the lack of competition, the nature of the industry is changing, and traditional insurance policies now account for only about half of all premiums written. Savings-linked policies, now accounting for almost half of all direct premiums, have fuelled the overall growth of the general insurance sector which, with total assets expanding by 23.9 per cent in fiscal 1986, is one of the fastest growing sectors of the insurance industry.

The general insurance companies, while powerful, will never be in a position to challenge the financial strength of the life insurance groups. In particular, the life companies have access to pension funds management, which has provided much of their growth over the past decade. Nonetheless, the general insurers are poised to introduce products remarkably similar to annuities, which they hope will underwrite much of their future expansion.

Given the very strict controls over rates for most of the big insurers, innovation is marginal, so that one of their prime tasks to improve underlying profitability is simply controlling costs.

History

The first Japanese general insurer to be established was Tokio Marine and Fire, which began business in 1887. Prior to that some marine insurance syndicates had been established to provide this form of cover and foreign insurance companies had also established operations in Japan from 1859. A large number of domestic companies were subsequently established, and in 1900, the Insurance Business Law was introduced, which attempted to bring the industry under control and introduced the demarcation between general and life insurance.

As in most other sections of the finance sector and industry in general, all the zaibatsu, or business groups, established their own general insurance companies, which handled most of the general insurance cover needed by each group. As a result, new firms starting up, or foreign firms, have found it difficult to generate much business in Japan, due to the closed nature of the industry.

Of the biggest general insurers, Tokio Marine belongs to the Mitsubishi group, Yasuda Fire to the Fuyo group, Taisho Marine to the Mitsui group and Sumitomo Marine to the Sumitomo group. These four together control an estimated 46 per cent of the net premiums written, with Tokio Marine controlling an estimated

17.3 per cent, Yasuda Fire 13.2 per cent, Taisho Marine 8.4 per cent and Sumitomo Marine 7.1 per cent.

In total, there are 21 general insurance companies in Japan and two re-insurers. Only two of the general insurance companies are mutually owned; the rest are joint-stock companies.

Even though the general insurance sector has enjoyed strong growth over the past two decades, there is a sharp distinction between the level of public support for life insurance and general insurance. Per capita life insurance coverage in Japan is the highest in the world; general insurance is among the lowest ranking with premiums of US$181.9 per head, or just 1.74 per cent of GNP, lower than, for example, Holland, France or Austria. In the US, the largest market, per capita premiums are US$672.9, or 4.35 per cent of GNP.

Ratings associations

In the post-war period, there was a fundamental reorganisation of the industry, with the decision to establish industry-wide ratings. At the initiative of the occupation authorities, the industry was reorganised using the Connecticut Insurance Law as the base. Ratings associations were established, which were specifically excluded from the provisions of the anti-monopoly legislation.

The first ratings association, the Fire and Marine Ratings Association of Japan, was established in 1948. Subsequently, in 1964, the Automobile Insurance Rating Association of Japan was established, taking over motor insurance from the Fire and Marine Ratings Association.

The Fire and Marine Ratings Association moved slowly in establishing ratings for most major classes of cover. Fire tariffs for housing were established in 1952, but it took until 1955 for fire cover for warehouses to be introduced, and until 1966 for some types of earthquake cover. Ratings for personal accident cover were not established until the 1970s.

For much of the post-war period, the industry has grown steadily, if at a comparatively unexciting pace. The introduction of compulsory motor insurance in 1955 set the industry on a path of assured prosperity during the 1960s and 1970s, as car ownership increased.

The various ratings associations closely monitor loss ratios and rates for all major classes of insurance. As a result, premiums for most major classes of cover have been progressively reduced, although each proposed reduction is usually strongly opposed by the insurers. A recommendation is made by the relevant ratings association to MoF, which then decides independently what the appropriate size of the rate reduction should be.

Premium income by type of cover, 1986 (¥m)

	Amount (¥m)	*Growth (%)*	*Share (%)*
Fire	1,320,155	6.1	17.7
(Maturity refund type)	(672,399)	(10.4)	(9.0)
Voluntary motor	1,689,021	6.9	22.6
Personal accident	2,842,106	99.1	38.1
(Maturity refund type)	(2,499,198)	(114.6)	(33.5)
Miscellaneous casualty	322,127	3.4	4.3
(Maturity refund type)	(9,735)	(−36.7)	(0.1)
Marine hull	103,979	−12.8	1.4
Marine cargo	114,860	−22.2	1.5
Inland transit	43,061	1.0	0.6
Sub-total	6,435,309	32.1	86.2
Compulsory motor liability	1,030,236	12.6	13.8
Total	7,465,545	29.0	100.0
(Maturity refund type)	(3,181,332)	(77.9)	(42.6)

Premium income

For much of the 1950s and 1960s, fire and marine premiums formed the mainstay of the general insurance companies' premium income. The introduction of compulsory cover and the increase in car ownership progressively changed that. By the mid-1980s, the share of direct premium income from fire cover had dropped to 17.7 per cent, compared with almost 80 per cent in the 1950s. Voluntary motor cover peaked with a share of direct premiums of 31.6 per cent in fiscal 1978. Similarly, all other forms of cover have declined, and personal accident cover is now the dominant form of insurance. In the mid-1960s, this accounted for just 0.7 per cent of direct premium income; by the end of fiscal 1986, it had expanded to 38.1 per cent of direct premiums.

In broad terms, direct premium income, which expanded by an average of 15 per cent annually during much of the 1970s, expanded by an average of 18 per cent between fiscal 1984 and fiscal 1986.

The growth of both voluntary and compulsory motor cover provided much of the growth during the 1960s and 1970s but it was a mixed blessing. Overall, the underwriting results from voluntary motor cover have been satisfactory, with a loss ratio during the 1980s of between 57 and 65 per cent.

In compulsory motor cover, however, heavy underwriting losses were accumulated in the latter part of the 1960s, when the loss ratio reached a peak of 160 per cent. Losses continued for seven years before they were brought back into balance. Difficulties arose again in the first half of the 1980s, when underwriting losses were incurred between 1982 and 1984. Agreement was finally reached for a rise in premiums, implemented recently, which should put this back onto an even base.

In addition to the straight cover provided for most personal and commercial forms of insurance, there are a number of insurance pools in operation which help spread the overall risks. The principal pools are the Japanese Aviation Insurance Pool, the Japan Atomic Energy Insurance Pool and the Japanese Hull Insurers Pool. Normally, all the domestic general insurance groups, and on occasion one or two of the larger non-Japanese companies, will participate in these pools.

Earnings growth

Even with the highly regulated nature of the industry, the general insurance industry as a whole has managed to continue expanding its earnings, with the growth in net premiums written exceeding net losses paid. In fiscal 1986, net premium income rose by 4.7 per cent and net losses declined by 3.0 per cent, enabling a continued improvement in underlying profitability.

Profit performance between the major firms varies significally since the larger companies are able to spread their higher costs across a broader mix of business.

The leader, Tokio Marine, has the best operating margins in the industry, with a ratio of net income to net premiums written of 3.64 per cent. The nearest to this is the ratio of 2.84 per cent achieved by Sumitomo Marine.

Also, companies that placed greater emphasis on savings-linked policies showed better performance than those that were slower to introduce these policies. Taisho Marine, for example, achieved an annual growth rate of 43 per cent of net savings premiums written during the 1980s, with savings-linked policies accounting for 27.4 per cent of all policies written in fiscal 1985 – second only to Sumitomo Marine with 28.4 per cent of all policies written in the same year being savings-linked policies.

Traditional marine hull and cargo policies have declined, with cover affected by the rise of the yen.

Policy developments

Savings-linked policies were first introduced in the mid-1960s but it was not until the early 1970s that the insurance companies began offering a range of these policies. Growth was steady, if unspectacular, until the early 1980s.

Investor interest was fuelled by the gradual increase in the savings component of these policies, which now stands at 92 per cent of the total amount of 'premiums' paid to the insurance companies. Interest was also generated by the steady relaxation of the 'loss' portion of the cover. Initially, the savings portion could be jeopardised if there was a sizeable claim against the underlying policy. This provision has gradually been relaxed, so that the savings element is now usually kept intact even if a maximum claim is made.

However, with interest rates declining, some of the general insurance companies found it increasingly difficult to honour their 'indicated' 5 per cent interest rate on the savings element of these policies. As a result MoF, after stiff lobbying by the industry, agreed in early 1987 to reduce the indicated rate to 4 per cent. When a return is generated, over and above the indicated rate, much of this is paid as a bonus to the policyholder.

Investments

The investments options of the general insurance groups have been tightly controlled by MoF. But substantial progress has been made since 1985 in lifting many of these controls, in particular for offshore investments. This has helped the major companies to achieve a slight, but steady, improvement in net investment yields in recent years. Most companies posted yields of around 6.36 per cent in fiscal 1986, up from less than 6 per cent the previous year. The largest, Tokio Marine, posted a net yield of 6.1 per cent in fiscal 1986, up from 6.01 per cent the previous year, and Yasuda Fire, the second largest, showed an average yield of 6.15 per cent, up from 5.83 per cent.

For the industry as a whole, 44.9 per cent of assets are invested in securities, 20 per cent in loans to industry, a further 17 per cent is held on deposit and property investment amounts to about 5 per cent. Over the past five years there has been a steady decline in cash on deposit and a gradual expansion of funds lent. Securities loans and deposits are favoured by the fund managers of the general insurance companies since they promise both a higher rate of return and security.

As with the life insurance companies, MoF subjects the general insurance companies to direct and indirect controls over investment options. Until quite recently, for example, foreign investments could only comprise up to 10 per cent of total assets. In March 1986, that ceiling was raised to 25 per cent. At that time, the total foreign holdings of the general insurers amounted to 8.3 per cent of total assets – a doubling over the previous three years. The upper limit was raised to 30 per cent from August 1986. By November 1986, the overseas investments of the general insurers stood at 9.6 per cent of the total assets.

Key figure for the non-life insurance industry, 1985–86

	1985 Amount (¥bn)	*1986 Amount (¥bn)*	*Growth (%)*
Net premiums written	3,990	4,178	4.7
Net losses paid	2,105	2,041	−3.0
Net operation expenses	1,553	1,662	7.0
Provisions (net) for liability reserves and outstanding claims	1,179	2,646	124.4
Underwriting balance	93	170	82.8
Profit for the current year	121	131	8.3
Earnings from investment of the savings portion of long-term premiums, etc. and interest revenues and dividends	646	725	12.2
Total assets	12,173	15,080	23.9
Liability reserves and reserves for outstanding claims	9,609	12,254	27.5

Offshore activities

Japan's general insurers moved offshore particularly in the early 1980s but the subsequent rate wars diminished their enthusiasm significantly. As a result, they have generally reduced their overall level of international activity since. In fiscal 1985, for example, there was a 1.9 per cent decline in direct premiums written abroad by Japanese companies. Policies written in all the main areas, such as fire, automobile, marine hull and marine cargo, have consistently declined although there has been growth in other areas.

There has also been a general reduction in re-insurance activity. In line with the difficulties experienced by the re-insurance industry worldwide, Japan's insurers have incurred a net deficit on their re-insurance activities in recent years. In fiscal 1985, for example, their net deficit was ¥79.9 billion.

Foreign insurers

The introverted nature of much of the insurance industry in Japan, with most conglomerates placing their business with their in-house general insurer, means that the role of the foreign insurance groups is peripheral at best.

Foreign companies' share of the market has steadily declined, so that they had just 2.5 per cent of total direct premium revenue in fiscal 1985. The disadvantage of not having longstanding links with the large industrial combines makes it hard to make any inroads with general industrial cover.

They have also performed less well with savings-linked policies, as few have achieved sufficient size and income to be able to afford the costly computerisation that is necessary for operating these policies. However, if savings-linked policies are excluded, then the foreign insurers have steadily expanded to reach a 3.4 per cent share of the market.

The largest foreign insurer is AIU Insurance Co, followed by the Cigna Group and BIG (British Insurance Group). AIU initially succeeded in Japan with motor policies and has gradually expanded from this base. It is estimated to hold 70 per cent of the entire share held by the foreign general insurers, with Cigna holding an estimated 20 per cent and BIG around 5 per cent.

In total there are 36 foreign insurers reasonably active in Japan, although eight of them are joined in the BIG consortium. A number have little more than a representative function in Japan, largely for re-insurance purposes, although many are confident that there will be sufficient liberalisation in the market to give them a role. There are also a small number of international insurance brokers increasingly active in Japan. They have carved out a useful niche working with those of Japan's big manufacturers which are moving production facilities offshore. This may in turn give them access to some further business in the domestic market as and when there is any liberalisation.

Direct premiums written abroad by Japanese non-life insurance companies, 1985 (¥m)

Class of Business	*Premiums (¥m)*	*Growth (%)*
Fire	17,443	−8.1
Motor	10,593	−6.7
Marine Hull	1,824	−13.9
Marine Cargo	9,134	−10.0
Others	16,397	18.3
Total	55,391	−1.9

Assets of non-life insurance companies, 1984–86 (¥bn)

	1984		*1985*		*1986*	
	Amount (¥bn)	*Share (%)*	*Amount (¥bn)*	*Share (%)*	*Amount (¥bn)*	*Share (%)*
Cash and deposits	1,586.4	14.6	1,896.2	15.6	2,487.9	16.5
Call loans	159.4	1.5	172.2	1.4	330.7	2.2
Securities	4,854.4	44.9	5,471.1	44.9	7,084.8	47.0
Loans	2,159.9	20.0	2,466.6	20.3	2,922.6	19.4
Real estate and movables	661.1	6.1	709.0	5.8	826.2	5.5
Other assets	1,392.8	12.9	1,458.3	12.0	1,428.1	9.4
Total assets	10,813.9	100.0	12,173.4	100.0	15,080.3	100.0
(Growth ratio)	(9.9)		(12.6)		(23.9)	

Source: Daiwa Bank

The Nihon Bashi bridge: Can the performance gap be bridged between Japanese and foreign insurance companies?

The future

While most of the world's attention on the financial power of Japan's general insurers was focused on the ¥5.3 billion purchase of van Gogh's 'Sunflowers' in April 1987, the industry itself was looking further afield. For at about the same time, the Non-Life Insurance Committee of the Insurance Council made a detailed assessment of the future directions of the general insurance industry.

The committee's report, submitted to the government in May 1987, suggested a variety of new forms of cover, including cover for computer software, care for the elderly and for invisible assets, such as technological and corporate expertise. Most of the broad features of the report's suggestions will be adopted by the government over time, in line with the consensus view formed by the industry.

CHAPTER TWENTY-THREE

Life insurance

Capitalising on the urge to save has underwritten the emergence of Japan's life insurance companies as large-scale institutional investors. Insurance is one of the few sectors of the Japanese industry that has shown consistent growth over the past five years, with life insurance companies now accounting for 6.4 per cent of all savings, up from 4.9 per cent in the mid-1970s. In addition, the life insurers, together with the trust banks, are the only groups allowed to handle pension fund investments, giving them an extraordinary franchise over one of the key growth areas of the financial sector.

At the heart of their success has been the introduction of an increasing diversity of policies, taking advantage both of the strong urge to save on the part of Japanese consumers and of openings provided by reductions of government spending in, for example, the medical insurance area.

Overseas life insurance groups, while active in Japan for some time, have not built up a large position. Some have achieved strong growth during the 1980s on the back of specialised policies in areas not considered worthwhile by domestic life companies. Equally, Japanese life companies have not been adventurous in moving offshore, with modest operations in only Hawaii and Brazil.

Traditionally, investments of the life insurance companies have been under strict controls by the Ministry of Finance (MoF), but there has been a significant liberalisation since early 1986 as the authorities have moved to boost Japan's capital outflow. This has given the insurance companies much greater freedom to invest internationally than previously.

So, after being one of the sleepiest sectors of the financial system, the life insurers, along with the trust banks, have moved into one of the more dynamic areas. One indication of this is that a job with a life insurance company has become one of the most sought-after positions for graduate job seekers. And the life companies have become more adventurous in their strategies. For example, they had become increasingly active in some of the more sophisticated areas of Euroyen swaps, until a ban by MoF stifled much of this activity from late 1986. Direct access to overseas futures markets from mid-1987, together with their interest in tapping domestic futures markets as they develop, will keep the life companies at the cutting edge of much of the development in financial markets in Japan.

Indicative of the way they intend expanding their influence in the future was the decision by Nippon Life to take up a direct stake in the American Express securities subsidiary Shearson Lehman Brothers and the move by Sumitomo Life to buy a small stake in Paribas after its privatisation.

Keen to tap the investment expertise of others, the life companies have steadily moved to expand their international investment strategy. From initial cautious investments in Canadian and Australian government securities in the early 1980s, they have broadened their approach to include most international markets, both bonds and equities, and, most notably since 1986, international property. They have also progressively expanded their presence in the domestic finance sector. Most of the larger life companies have established leasing company affiliates, as well as building up a presence in mortgage securities and establishing investment management companies, either singly or in joint ventures.

Most of the major companies have also expanded their consumer finance activities, both in direct loans to policy holders and consumer credit card financing activities.

History

Japan's first life insurance company, Meiji Life, was established in 1881. Prior to this, various forms of mutual insurance existed, especially in the general insurance sector covering, for example, marine risk.

After the establishment of the first life insurance company, a number of others followed suit and, to reduce abuses in the industry, the Insurance Business Law was enacted in 1900. This required that all participants be either joint-stock companies or mutual companies. It also introduced the formal division between general and life insurance, requiring that an institution could not participate in both markets. Gradually, as with most other sectors of finance and industry in Japan in the pre-war years, the life industry fell under the control of the large zaibatsu, or industrial combines. And the life companies learned how to act in a cooperative manner, with the formation of the Life Insurance Securities Company in 1933 to prop up prices on the stockmarket as it went through a major crisis.

As part of the general wartime policy, the number of life companies was reduced from the former level of 28. The policies on offer were simple, and it was not until the 1960s that there was any significant diversification.

After the war, there was a slight increase in the number, with 20 life companies established by the mid-1960s, of which 16 were mutually-owned, and the balance organised as joint-stock companies.

The subsequent expansion has been due to the rise in the number of foreign participants, either entering the market through joint ventures, for example Sony-Prudential, or independently, such as American Life. In mid-1987, Sony-Prudential indicated that it would reorganise this venture, with Prudential's participation being reduced, following Prudential's decision to establish its own fully-owned venture.

The industry, led by Nippon Life, has several large groups such as Sumitomo Life, Asahi Life, Dai-Ichi Life, Yasuda Life, Mitsui Life and Meiji Life which dominate the industry, accounting for over 75 per cent of annual sales of policies.

Policy developments

At the heart of the traditional life insurance marketing effort is an army of over 400,000 direct salesmen and women. The largest company, Nippon Life, has over 60,000 sales representatives alone. The direct sales forces capitalise on the compulsion to save, which is driven in turn by the fears of inadequate social security cover, in particular concerns that the government will not be able to maintain social benefits in the future due to the rapid ageing of the population.

Competition on policies offered, while closely controlled by MoF and largely static for much of Japan's post-war period, has witnessed a dramatic growth since the start of the 1980s.

After growing moderately, at around 10 per cent annually during the late 1970s, the general assets of the life companies have expanded at a quickening pace during the 1980s, with assets doubling every six years. By the end of fiscal 1985 they had reached ¥53.87 trillion, up from ¥45.7 trillion the previous year. In fiscal 1986, assets expanded by a further 21.2 per cent to ¥65.3 trillion – the third consecutive year that the rate of increase in assets had exceeded the increase of the previous year.

Much of the life companies' growth is due to their steady expansion in pension funds management. On average, growth here has exceeded 20 per cent annually during the 1980s, with total funds under management reaching ¥8.6 trillion by the end of fiscal 1986, up from ¥4.03 trillion in fiscal 1982. Expansion in this field is now showing signs of slowing to a steadier pace.

Life insurance policies by value (percentage of total), FY1976 and FY1986

	FY1976 (%)	*FY1986* (%)
Term insurance	15.9	18.1
Whole-life insurance	7.6	43.4
Ordinary endowment policies	7.0	12.5
Term age insurance	58.1	11.4
Child insurance	0.8	2.4
Savings-linked insurance	0.7	0.6
Other	9.9	11.6
	100.0	100

Source: Life Insurance Association.

In broad terms, the income of the life companies has steadily expanded, with premium income rising 19.1 per cent in fiscal 1985 and a further 21.1 per cent in fiscal 1986. Investment income increased 16 per cent in fiscal 1986, with overall income increasing by 24.5 per cent to ¥27.7 trillion.

Investment

For much of the post-war period, the investment options of Japan's life insurance companies were limited by a number of dictates set by MoF. Investment in securities was limited to domestic and foreign government bonds, local bonds, government guaranteed debentures, industrial debentures, shares and money in trust. Share holdings were restricted to less than 30 per cent of total assets.

Loans to any one company were limited to less than 10 per cent of the capital of the company, and had to be secured. Deposits could not be placed with financial institutions other than banks, credit associations or the Post Office. Deposits with a bank could not exceed 10 per cent of assets, and money in trust and insurance policies in trust with the same bank were also limited to less than 10 per cent of total assets. In addition, property investments were limited to less than 20 per cent of total assets. Any other investments had to have the express approval of MoF.

For much of the post-war period, the main outlet for funds was lending to industry which, with demand strong and outrunning supply, generated a sufficient rate of return to satisfy policyholders. The corporate sector's excess of funds since the mid-1970s has changed that, leaving the life companies with a substantial surplus of funds seeking alternative outlets. During the 1970s, loans made up over 60 per cent of the life companies' total investments. Since then, this has gradually fallen to less than 40 per cent of total investments, and further decline is anticipated. Most of the new investments have been made in securities, especially corporate and government bonds. The total securities holdings of the life companies now make up over 40 per cent of investments, a figure that will continue to rise.

The life companies have also emerged as active investors in 'tokkin' funds, which are classified in their investments as cash. The life companies are limited to holding only 3 per cent of their funds in tokkin, but have been seeking to boost this to 5 per cent. However, MoF is keenly aware of the impact that this would have on domestic equity markets and is reluctant to change the limit.

The preference for lending new funds remains, however, and while loans as a percentage of total investments have declined, the absolute volume of loans has continued to expand, although at a slowing rate, reaching ¥25.6 trillion by the end of fiscal 1986.

The life companies are looking to international investments and new domestic markets, such as financial futures, to absorb extra funds in the future. Since 1985, they have emerged as significant investors in US government securities as the amount of new debt issued in that market has spiralled. But currency losses on this have been large as almost all of this exposure was unhedged. The liberalisation of access to foreign futures and options markets will progressively limit that exposure in the future, although the life companies argue that if they fully hedge their exposure, it will reduce their returns substantially.

Central to the investment strategies of the life companies, both domestically and internationally, is the ruling by MoF that they must maintain separate accounts for capital gains and income gains from investments. Whereas income gains can be accessed in determining returns to policy holders, capital gains cannot. Life companies therefore prefer income gains, such as from investments in bonds, to capital gains from investments in equities. However, this ruling is likely to be relaxed in the future, which will have a fundamental impact on their investment alternatives and on most of the larger international capital markets.

The other principal ruling that restricted investments by the life companies was that less than 10 per cent of their total assets could be invested in overseas securities. In the first half of the 1980s, the life companies gradually raised their

Growth of pension funds management by life insurance companies, FY1982–FY1986

Fiscal year	*Total (¥100m)*	*Growth (%)*
1982	40,315	126.4
1983	49,779	123.5
1984	60,644	121.8
1985	72,982	120.3
1986	85,967	117.8

Source: Life Insurance Association.

offshore exposure and most of them were close to this ceiling by late 1985. Towards the end of fiscal 1985, the overseas security holdings of the life insurers totalled ¥4.67 trillion, or 8.67 per cent. As a result, pressure was mounting for a relaxation of the ruling.

Anxious to rein in the soaring yen, MoF raised the ceiling on the life companies' foreign investments in successive stages in a bid to boost Japan's capital outflow. In the first quarter of 1986, it raised the limit from 10 to 25 per cent but this higher limit included foreign currency-denominated bonds issued by Japanese companies, previously excluded. And in August 1986, MoF allowed the life companies to join syndicates for long-term loans of more than 20 years' maturity without limit on the level of their participation, which previously had been limited to no more than 50 per cent of the amount being raised.

In addition, MoF raised the maximum size of individual loans from ¥2.5 billion to ¥5 billion, giving the life companies much greater flexibility. Up to 10 per cent of the assets of a life company can be advanced in yen loans. Life companies are allowed to lead manage an issue although typically, 50 per cent of the funds are advanced by life companies with the balance coming from Japanese banks.

In late 1986, MoF relaxed its regulations still further with the decision to allow up to 30 per cent of assets to be invested in foreign securities. The definition of

Investments by life insurance companies, FY1985–FY1986 (¥100m)

	FY1985			*FY1986*		
	Amount (¥100m)	*Proportion (%)*	*Change over previous year (%)*	*Amount (¥100m)*	*Proportion (%)*	*Change over previous year (%)*
Cash and deposits	62,485	11.6	205.2	75,705	11.6	121.2
Call loans	1,466	0.3	128.6	1,301	0.2	88.7
Securities	189,813	35.2	118.3	267,918	41.0	141.1
(Shares)	(81,138)	(15.1)	(117.2)	(111,005)	(17.0)	(136.8)
(Other)	(108,675)	(20.2)	(119.0)	(156,913)	(24.0)	(144.4)
Loans	243,722	45.3	105.7	256,366	39.2	105.2
(General loans)	(223,986)	(41.6)	(105.3)	(234,623)	(35.9)	(104.7)
(To policy holders)	(19,735)	(3.7)	(109.5)	(21,742)	(3.3)	(110.2)
Property and real estate	31,962	5.9	116.6	37,770	5.8	118.2
Others	9,254	1.7	127.5	14,109	2.2	152.5
Total	538,705	100.0	117.8	653,171	100.0	121.2

Source: Life Insurance Association

foreign securities was broadened to include Samurai bonds and private placements, but Sushi bonds were excluded as they were counted as domestic securities.

There is a separate regulation, however, which limits the exposure of the life companies to foreign currencies to 30 per cent of assets. In addition to this MoF limit, the life companies agreed between themselves to limit the increase in foreign assets of each company to the same rate as the overall rate of increase of assets of the company.

With all these changes, the foreign securities holdings of the life companies stood at 11.52 per cent by the end of fiscal 1986. Including foreign lending, total overseas assets amounted to ¥10.02 trillion, 15.34 per cent of assets, up 30 per cent over fiscal 1985.

One notable change has been the life companies' decision to move much more aggressively into equity markets worldwide, especially in North America. Although equity holdings are still minimal, they are rising quickly. By the end of fiscal 1985, for example, they stood at just 0.86 per cent of total assets but by the end of fiscal 1986 they had almost doubled to 1.29 per cent of total assets.

Growth of total assets of life insurance companies, FY1980–FY1986 (¥100m)

Fiscal year	*End-FY assets (¥100m)*	*Asset growth (¥100m)*	*Yield (%)*	
1980	262,577	35,135		(7.56)
1981	300,987	38,409		(7.69)
1982	346,137	45,150		(7.74)
1903	395,200	49,130		(7.72)
1984	457,401	62,132		(7.77)
1985	538,705	81,304	7.50	(7.72)
1986	653,171	114,465	7.13	(7.39)

Note: Yield figures in parentheses calculated according to the Hardy system.
Source: Life Insurance Association.

Foreign exchange losses

With the rapid expansion of their foreign holdings the foreign exchange losses of the life companies have risen substantially. In fiscal 1985, the seven largest life companies lost an estimated ¥600 billion on the currency shift, and in fiscal 1986 they lost a further ¥1.70 trillion. Almost all of the foreign exchange exposure of the life companies was unhedged, in contrast to the trust banks, whose offshore exposure, at the behest of MoF, was much more fully covered.

Initially, the life offices wrote off their losses on investments in Canadian and Australian government securities since those currencies had fallen against the yen and the US dollar and in both cases their exposure was comparatively large. Write-offs were made against their accumulated capital profits. With the larger losses on the currency shifts against the US dollar, the life companies have moved more slowly. Initially, some were confident that the US dollar would recover and restore a portion of their losses, so they were more reluctant to bring their losses to account. However, most life companies have made provisions against at least a portion of their losses, although there is still a considerable amount outstanding.

Future developments

The most revolutionary change that has occurred in the life insurance industry was the introduction of variable policy insurance. The industry in Japan had been slow to follow the lead provided by Equitable Life in the US, which began marketing variable policies in the mid-1970s.

The introduction of these policies in Japan followed lengthy deliberations by the Insurance Council. In 1985, it proposed to MoF that variable policies be introduced. It also sought the introduction of a range of new policies, including policies to make up for the reduction of medical cover by the government.

The first variable policies were launched in October 1986. Significantly, MoF allowed the life companies to establish separate accounts for managing the funds raised for such policies, and these accounts were free from the restrictions that only up to 30 per cent of assets can be invested in equities and 10 per cent of assets in the bonds of any single company.

Of greater interest in pointing the way to the future is that MoF allowed both capital return and dividend return to be aggregated for policyholders. The major feature of this development is that it has focused attention on aggressive funds management for the first time.

The introduction of variable policies has been highly successful. All the major insurance companies achieved rates of return of over 30 per cent in the first year of operation as fund managers took advantage of record movements in domestic bond and equity markets. Maintaining such high rates of return will prove difficult in the light of the increasing volatility of markets in Japan.

All the major insurance companies reported sharp rises in the returns generated for these policies in the initial six months, although in the June quarter of 1987, due to increased volatility of both bond and equity markets in Japan, returns fell. Mitsui Mutual Life, for example, which generated the highest return of 54 per cent in the period to end March 1987, reported that its average return on variable-sum insurance fell to 38 per cent in the June quarter. Nippon Life registered a decline from 37 to 25 per cent.

In line with the overall blurring of the lines of distinction between insurance policies such as variable-sum policies and the investment trust savings industry, the life companies began pushing in mid-1987 for the introduction of more specific variable policies, for example, policies with up to 80 per cent of the funds invested in stocks, others with the bulk of the funds invested in government securities, and a further variety with funds predominantly invested in mortgage-backed securities, savings and deposits. MoF was not expressly opposed to the introduction of such policies, and there is some expectation that these policies will be introduced in late 1987.

Indicative of the volume of funds that can quickly be mobilised for the new investment instruments, ¥1.76 trillion (US$11.73 billion) was invested in these flexible policies by 30 March 1987, only five months after their introduction.

Prudential Life, which held a half interest in Sony-Prudential, considered the prospects for variable insurance policies so promising that it decided in mid-1987 to reduce its holding in the joint venture in favour of establishing its own wholly-owned affiliate to specialise in this form of insurance.

MoF has also allowed banks to begin marketing products in association with foreign life companies. For example, Mitsubishi Bank and United of Omaha Life Insurance began offering time deposits, with the interest used to pay for insurance premiums. The marketing of insurance-related products by banks will give the foreign life insurance companies a broader distribution network in Japan, which will help them boost their share of the market. As part of the continuing diversification, some of the joint ventures with foreign firms have taken distinctly individual approaches in seeking to increase their market share in Japan. Sony-Prudential, for example, has eschewed the traditional approach of a huge sales force in favour of a group of 'life planners' who advise clients, and potential clients, on the best method of investing their financial assets, rather than simply marketing insurance policies. With this, the company is well-positioned to advance with the progressive deregulation of Japan's capital markets. The company has also targeted high net-worth individuals who, it argues, are not well serviced by the Japanese financial system. While there is considerable conjecture within the industry whether the company's approach is justifiable in the Japanese market, Sony-Prudential has achieved a far lower cancellation rate than the mainstream Japanese groups.

Foreign insurance companies

As in general insurance, foreign insurance companies hold only a negligible market share in the life sector of the industry. There are, however, far fewer foreign operators in life insurance than in non-life insurance, with only five majority-owned foreign insurers active – Combined Insurance Company of America, American Life Insurance, United of Omaha, National Life (a subsidiary of Nationale Nederlanden) and American Family. In addition, Prudential is expected to establish a wholly-owned operation from late 1987, and Allstate Insurance has a joint venture with the Seibu retailing group.

Even though the foreign companies' share of the market is very small, their income has risen much faster than the industry average in recent years, rising 31.3 per cent in fiscal 1984, 28.6 per cent in fiscal 1985 and 33.6 per cent in fiscal 1986.

They are poised for even faster growth in the future following MoF's approval of the introduction of variable policies. The rising affluence of society, and concern for adequate provision for retirement, are creating among savers a much greater awareness of return, and a greater willingness to take risks, which gives the foreign groups the potential to write a larger, even if still modest, amount of business.

While the foreign life insurance groups were much slower to move into Japan than the non-life companies, the environment is much freer and is likely to become more so over the coming decade. The introduction of variable life policies, and the likelihood of policies being introduced which are much closer to investment trusts, demonstrate MoF's willingness to permit policies carrying higher risks, which may also generate for policyholders higher returns than achievable through traditional, tightly regulated policies.

CHAPTER TWENTY-FOUR

Pension funds

The rapid ageing of Japan's population, together with the continued pressures on national government finances and the projected ballooning in the cost of providing national pensions, has focused increasing attention on Japan's pension funds. More particularly, the debate has focused on whether there will be sufficient funds available to ensure that retirees will be adequately catered for in the medium term.

The fears are more than academic, since the impact of a rising tax burden on a dwindling taxation base threatens the bankruptcy of the existing social welfare system. The result has been a startling growth in private pension funds. Life insurance policies and pension policies have become increasingly popular. Total assets increased by more than 16 per cent annually during the 1980s, and double digit growth is expected to continue.

It is estimated that corporate pension funds alone will more than treble to ¥70 trillion by 1995, compared with a total of ¥22.75 trillion accumulated as of March 1987. In 1970, the total stood at less than¥500 billion.

Corporate pension funds are exceeded by the funds accumulated under national pension plans which totalled almost ¥60 trillion by the end of 1986, but the rate of increase here is a more modest 5 per cent a year.

The need to ensure an adequate rate of return on the funds invested, as well as the security of the funds for pensioners, is placing enormous pressure on the authorities.

The increasing burden

In early 1986, the ratio of those aged over 65 years to the total population was approximately 10 per cent. This ratio is expected to reach 15 per cent by the turn of the century, and according to Ministry of Finance (MoF) forecasts it will reach 21.8 per cent by the year 2020 – the highest of any of the major advanced countries.

In the mid-1980s, one person aged over 65 was supported by 6.9 people between 15 and 64 years of age. By early next century, this ratio will be cut to 4.6, and it will be reduced further to a forecast 3.3 by the year 2020.

A report released by the Council of Economic Affairs in 1982 estimated that social security transfers measured as a ratio to national income will rise from

Proportion of population aged over 65 years, 1965–2035

Year	*Total population (10,000)*	*Aged over 65 years (10,000)*	*Aged over 65 years % of total population*	Year	*Total population (10,000)*	*Aged over 65 years (10,000)*	*Aged over 65 years % of total population*
1965	9,920	628	6.3	2000	12,812	1,994	15.6
1970	10,466	739	7.1	2005	13,001	2,223	17.1
1975	11,194	886	7.9	2010	13,028	2,418	18.8
1980	11,706	1,064	9.1	2015	12,933	2,731	21.1
1985	12,102	1,239	10.2	2020	12,812	2,795	21.8
1990	12,283	1,429	11.6	2025	12,718	2,708	21.3
1995	12,538	1,708	13.6	2030	12,079	2,551	21.1
				2035	11,840	2,325	19.6

Source: Ministry of Health and Welfare.

Ratio of the number of people aged 65 years or more to total population, 1950–2020

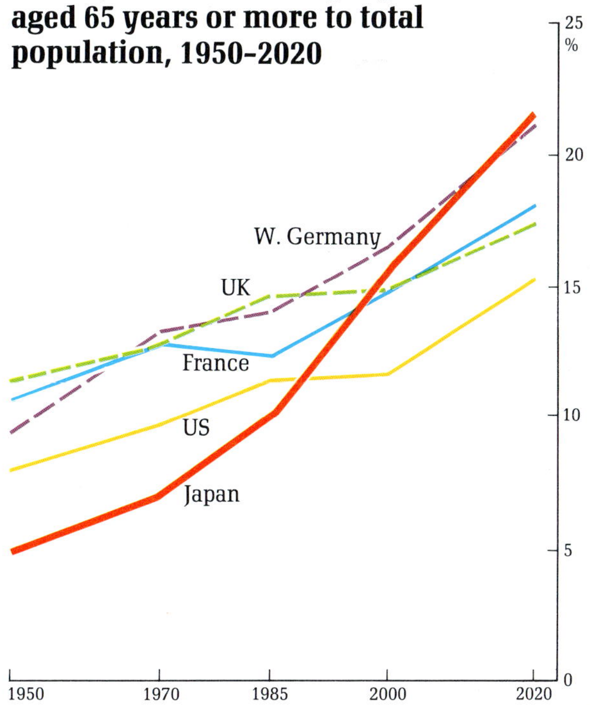

12.8 per cent in 1980 to 24.7 per cent by the year 2000 and 34.7 per cent by the year 2020. The reason for the sharp rise is the burden of the national pension system, whose ratio to national income will reach 19.4 per cent by the year 2025, up from just 4.3 per cent in fiscal 1980.

In 1986, the Economic Planning Agency said that the proportion of payments to the national pension plans would rise from 5.6 per cent of national income in 1985 to 13 per cent in the year 2025. Similarly, there will be a doubling of the payments by the government into the national pension systems, which will add significantly to the taxation burden.

History

Japan's pension system originated in the Meiji era (1868–1912) with the provision of a form of pension for retired army and navy servicemen. Gradually, the system was extended with the provision of various mutual aid associations, principally for government employees. Private sector employees only had the retirement allowance, paid by their employer.

The first provision of private sector pensions followed the enactment of the Seamen's Insurance law in 1939, which provided a pension programme and health insurance cover. In 1941, the Employees' Pension Law was passed, and this was the forerunner of the present Employees' Pension Insurance. This plan was orginally intended to discourage employees from leaving their jobs, to stimulate employment stability and to help control wartime inflation.

In 1959, the National Pension Law was passed, which gave some cover, initially through a non-contributory programme, and from 1961 through a contributory programme, to self-employed workers such as farmers and others excluded from the main Employees' Pension scheme.

Along with the extension of cover by the government, there has been a gradual increase of pension plans provided by the corporate sector. All public companies now provide some sort of scheme to employees but only an estimated 30 per cent of unlisted companies provide employees with cover.

As a result, the attention of the savings industry is firmly focused on both life companies and pension funds. And the pressure on MoF to relax some of its controls to enable fund managers to boost returns will contine to grow, as will the pressure for an expansion of the number of pension fund managers. At present, the trust banks and the life insurance companes have sole access to pension fund management. Investment advisory companies are increasingly pressuring the authorities to allow them access to this lucrative sector – pressure that is being equally strongly opposed by the trust banks and life companies.

The industry

The largest pension fund manager in Japan is Daiwa Bank which, even though it is a city bank, refused to hive off its trust banking division in the post-war period. It is followed by Mitsubishi Trust Bank, Sumitomo Trust Bank and Nippon Life Insurance. The pension system is divided into two broad streams – government programmes which are organised through the Ministry of Health and Welfare, and private programmes.

The two principal government programmes are the Employees' Pension programme and the National Pension Programme. Total assets of the Employees' Pension programme stood at ¥50.78 trillion at the end of 1985, and the National Pension had assets of ¥2.59 trillion. The Employees' Pension scheme is for employees of businesses. It has approximately 25 million subscribers, with 40 per cent of the contributions paid by employees, 40 per cent by employers and the remaining 20 per cent by the government. The National Pension programme, which is for self-employed workers, has an estimated 27 million subscribers with the government paying one-third of the contributions.

All but a small fraction of the pension funds of the government programmes (¥1 trillion) are channelled through the Fiscal Investment Loans Programme (FILP), administered by the Trust Fund Bureau of MoF. These funds generated a moderate rate of return of 6.2 per cent in fiscal 1986.

Starting from fiscal 1986, a portion of these funds, ¥1 trillion, was set aside for investing in alternative areas, with ¥500 billion managed by the trust banks. In fiscal 1986, the portion of pension funds managed by the trust banks generated a net yield of 7.65 per cent, 1.4 per cent higher than the return on funds lodged with the Trust Fund Bureau. This initial amount of ¥1 trillion is likely to be expanded gradually over the next decade.

The low rate of return on the funds invested through FILP amounts to an implicit subsidy paid by tax payers to the semi-government organisations, allowing them to raise funds cheaply. Pressure for a further increase in the rate of return is mounting.

The main focus of attention, however, is on the corporate and individual pension plans, which are managed by the trust banks and life companies. Corporate pension funds management is organised through a syndicate, with a principal manager, almost always a trust bank, commanding a higher fee. Participation in the syndicate is primarily based on performance, although for newcomers it is difficult to establish a track record, so it normally takes time to expand the size of funds under management.

The two principal corporate pension programmes managed by the trust banks and life companies are the employee pension plans, or adjusted pensions (chosei nenkin), and the tax-qualified plans (tekikaku nenkin).

The tax-qualified pension plans were introduced in 1962, and were aimed at encouraging the development of pension plans. The fear then was that corporate liabilities to employees at the time of retirement could be insufficient, so various tax concessions were given to encourage companies to form pension trusts out of the company retirement allowance programmes.

A tax-qualified pension plan needs to comply with a variety of specific conditions, including providing a scheduled annual interest rate of 5 per cent or more. In addition, the company's contributions are treated as non-taxable income for employees, although benefits are subject to tax at the time of dispersal.

Corporate pension plans commenced in 1966, and now include 1,174 pension funds with assets totalling ¥14.4 trillion at the end of fiscal 1986. At the same time, total assets of the tax-qualified pension plans stood at ¥8.26 trillion. In the management of tax-qualified pension plans, the trust banks are limited to plans for companies with over 100 employees, whereas for the life companies the minimum company size, over 15 employees, is very much smaller. This distinction, due to administrative guidance by the authorities, has given the life companies a significant advantage over the trust banks in winning new business since the early 1970s.

Under MoF controls, the trust banks and life companies are limited to investing less than 30 per cent of pension funds in foreign bonds and stocks, less than 30 per cent in domestic equities and less than 20 per cent in property. In addition, 50 per cent of all pension funds must be invested in guaranteed instruments.

Breakdown of corporate pension funds, March 1987 (¥100m)

	¥100m	*%*
Daiwa Bank	27,803	12.2
Mitsubishi Trust Bank	22,771	10.0
Sumitomo Trust Bank	22,196	9.8
Nippon Life	21,235	9.4
Mitsui Trust Bank	19,740	8.7
Toyo Trust Bank	19,110	8.4
Yasuda Trust Bank	18,914	8.3
Dai-Ichi Life	15,516	6.8
Sumitomo Life	11,295	5.0
Meiji Life	9,307	4.1
Chuo Trust Bank	7,795	3.4
Asahi Life	5,707	2.5
Yasuda Life	4,946	2.2
Chiyoda Life	3,706	1.6
Mitsui Life	3,679	1.6
Nippon Trust Bank	2,615	1.1
Daido Life	1,497	0.7
Fukoku Life	1,487	0.7
Nippon Dantai Life	1,466	0.6
Toho Life	1,326	0.6
Others	5,371	2.3
Total	227,482	100.0

Source: Daiwa Bank.

Controls over the investment options of the pension fund managers move in tandem with the limits on foreign investments by the life companies. When MoF relaxed some of these controls during 1986, for example, when the low limits on offshore investments were raised, the changes applied equally to the pension funds and the insurance funds managed by life and non-life insurance groups. As with insurance funds, capital gains on investment funds cannot be passed on to policyholders, which severely limits the potential yield to fund managers. Some easing of this restraint is expected.

In broad terms, the investment patterns of insurance and pension funds are the same. Looking at the investments undertaken by the trust banks, declining demand for new funds by the industrial sector has resulted in a drop of loans to industry from 42.3 per cent in 1975 to 25.1 per cent in 1985. At the same time, the total funds invested in bonds have risen to 55 per cent, with shares reaching 16.5 per cent, up from 9.5 per cent.

This trend continued into 1986, with over 80 per cent of new funds being invested in equities. But the bulk of investments remain in public bonds, which stood at 55 per cent of all investments at the end of fiscal 1985.

Competition for funds management

The battle between the trust banks and the life companies is intense, and will continue. For much of the latter part of the 1970s, the life companies generated a higher return than the trust banks, which aided their overall expansion of funds under management. But since 1982, the trust banks' rate of return has been about 0.5 per cent higher than that of the life companies.

However, a full comparison of the relative investment performance of the two groups is difficult. For instance, the trust banks claim that if there was full disclosure by the life companies of the returns on the pension funds under their management, a much more accurate assessment could be made of the returns generated by the two groups.

To this end, an association of corporate pension fund managers was formed in 1985, and has strongly argued, among other things, for an increase in the level of disclosure by the life companies. The fundamental difference is that the life offices handle all of their investments in a comingled manner – there is no distinction between investment of their pension fund assets and their insurance assets. The trust banks, on the other hand, handle all of their pension funds separately. Much of the trust banks' loss of market share stems, however, from the ruling that the trust banks can only manage tax-qualified corporate pension schemes for companies with over 100 employees, substantially higher than the minimum size (15 employees) allowed for the life offices. Consequently, the life companies now command a majority of the tax-qualified pension plans, moving above the 50 per cent level in the mid-1980s, and by the end of fiscal 1986, they commanded a 51.6 per cent share of these funds.

But the trust banks control 70 per cent of the employee pension funds, a much larger share of the market. So, overall the trust banks manage 62 per cent of all corporate pension funds.

Ranking of trust banks in pension funds management, end June 1987 (¥bn)

	Employee pension plan		*Tax-qualified pensions*		*Total*	
	Amount (¥bn)	*%*	*Amount (¥bn)*	*%*	*Amount (¥bn)*	*%*
Daiwa Bank	2,097,359	20.2	761,571	19.0	2,858,930	19.8
Mitsubishi Trust Bank	1,596,355	15.4	720,360	18.0	2,316,715	16.1
Sumitomo Trust Bank	1,558,122	15.0	698,078	17.4	2,256,200	15.7
Mitsui Trust Bank	1,425,358	13.7	584,288	14.5	2,009,646	13.9
Toyo Trust Bank	1,519,734	14.6	443,004	11.0	1,962,738	13.6
Yasuda Trust Bank	1,437,903	13.8	501,359	12.5	1,939,262	13.5
Chuo Trust bank	586,570	5.6	210,893	5.2	797,463	5.5
Nippon Trust Bank	176,786	1.7	94,772	2.4	271,558	1.9
Total	10,398,187	100.0	4,014,325	100.0	14,412,512	100.0

Source: Daiwa Bank.

The life companies' successful push into pension funds management has changed the nature of their funds under management. In 1960, for example, corporate pension funds accounted for just 2.9 per cent of total funds under management. By the end of fiscal 1986, this proportion had risen to 13.2 per cent. The threats to the entrenched position of the trust banks and the life offices stem from the probablility that their franchise over pension fund management will be eroded over the next decade. First, a limited number of foreign trust banks have been allowed into the market in 1986, although it will take them several years to make major inroads. While the foreign trust banks have been quick to accumulate a number of 'tokkin' accounts, accumulating pension funds will prove more difficult. Of the foreign trust banks, the fastest to move has been Japan Bankers Trust, which secured from Sumitomo Bank the management of the pension fund of employees of the former Heiwa Sogo Bank, which made up the bulk of the ¥8.7 billion under its management by the end of fiscal 1986.

However, the biggest threat will come from the growing number of investment management companies who are applying steady pressure to be allowed access to a part of the expanding pension funds market.

Of some importance is the decision by the Ministry of Health and Welfare

1986 that the return on funds invested through FILP, just 6.2 per cent, was too low. Accordingly, FILP sought approval to place a portion of its funds under independent management. Out of the ¥53 trillion under its control, an initial amount of just ¥1 trillion was allocated for independent management. It is widely expected that at least one-third of the government pension fund will be managed privately in the future in a bid to generate higher returns. So this will tend to offset the new competitive pressure the life companies and the trust banks may experience as a result of any decision to give the investment management companies some access to the market.

With private pension funds totalling over ¥22 trillion, handled by only around 30 companies, the pressure to ease some of the severe controls will continue, especially if the government expands its plans to hand more of the public pension funds over to private funds management.

Representatives of both the life companies and the trust banks privately admit that change will come, although they are preparing to fight a tough rear-guard action to protect their lucrative position.

CHAPTER TWENTY-FIVE

Law and regulation in Japan and its financial markets

by Kate Perry
Clifford Chance, London

Legal restrictions have greatly influenced the development and structure of the Japanese financial system. Until recently, financial markets were rigidly compartmentalised with a strict delineation (on the Glass-Steagall model) between banking and securities activities.

However, in recent years the Japanese authorities have implemented significant deregulation with the Diet enacting important legislation including extensive amendments in 1979 to the Foreign Exchange and Foreign Trade Control Law of 1949 (FEFTCL) and a New Banking Law (NBL), which was promulgated in 1981 and which also required amendments to the Securities and Exchange Law (Law No.25 of 1948) (SEL). In addition, MoF and the Bank of Japan have generally adopted a more permissive attitude towards both domestic and overseas transactions, across the whole spectrum of Japanese financial institutions.

The purpose of this chapter is twofold: first, to provide an overview of the Japanese legal and regulatory framework within which various Japanese financial markets and institutions operate, and secondly to give some guidance to those foreign institutions, or individuals, who are looking to Tokyo as the third international financial market in which to do business.

Legal and regulatory framework

Sources of Japanese banking law

Japan's modern legal structure reflects, to a large extent, the civil law tradition of continental Europe with much of its law being codified in the 1880s and 1890s. In addition to the present Japanese constitution (promulgated in 1945), there are five codes: (1) the Civil Code, (2) the Code of Civil Procedure, (3) the Criminal Code, (4) the Code of Criminal Procedure and (5) the Commercial Code. The codes have since their enactment undergone several revisions but they remain the source of regulation for legal relationships and transactions in Japan. The Civil and Commercial Codes have the greatest relevance for banking transactions. Both these codes reflected the German system although in places there are clearly influences of French, English and early Japanese law. These codes and complementary and supplementary legislation such as the Bills Act and the Cheques Act regulate primarily banking transactions, while other statutes such as the NBL, the SEL and the FEFTCL regulate banking activities of commercial banks. The Bank of Japan Act (which established the Bank of Japan), the Trust Business Law of 1922, the Trust Law of 1923, the Law on Trust Business of Ordinary Banks of 1943 and the Loan Trust Law of 1952, along with the NBL, are the principal pieces of legislation which regulate the trust banks. The Long-Term Credit Bank Law of 1952 regulates the three long-term credit banks and their branches. Securities companies are regulated under several laws, but primarily under the SEL. As well as the major statutes and Cabinet orders and regulations relating thereto, notices, notifications and releases provided by the central administrative agencies, such as MoF, inform their departments of the appropriate administrative interpretation of the various legislation and assist in the implementation of administrative regulation.

There is a further powerful tool in the regulation of banking transactions which takes the form of unofficial guidance known as 'gyosei-shido', or administrative guidance. This term eludes precise definition but can perhaps be best described as embracing all the various means whereby ministries and agencies of the Japanese government exert formal and informal regulating authority over business in Japan.

Administrative guidance is strictly unofficial and may or may not have any statutory basis of action in guiding, suggesting and advising. Compliance is voluntary and no penalties are imposed for non-compliance (although sanctions statutorily available in other areas are often imposed), nevertheless, it is obeyed almost without exception. It has been described by some legal observers as 'officially voluntary and unofficially binding'.

The effect of the administrative guidance is that MoF may influence Japanese banks and other financial institutions to undertake or avoid certain activities through directives (shiji), requests (yobo), warnings (keikoku), suggestions (kankoku) and encouragements (kansho). Such administrative guidance will usually take the form of a number of notifications or official liaison letters issued to appropriate representatives of the banks and financial institutions at which it is aimed.

The advantages of administrative guidance are flexibility and speed. Action can occur without the need for statute, issues can be resolved quickly and unofficially, and administrative guidance can be altered at short notice. The disadvantages, on the other hand, are that there are no legal checks to control the power of the bodies employing the administrative guidance and no formal legal recourses for its abuse.

The final two sources of Japanese banking law are custom and case law. Custom and customary law may often determine the outcome of a banking transaction and will sometimes prevail despite provisions in the codes to the contrary. Also, Japan, like any other country in the civil law tradition, looks to its courts to interpret the codes: theoretically, judges are not bound by judicial precedent but in practice a judge is unlikely to refuse to adhere to a well-established court decision, particularly one of the Supreme Court.

The role of lawyers and litigation

Tokyo law firms differ markedly from their counterparts in other major financial centres. The law offices are small; only a few employ more than 20 attorneys and most have fewer than 10. However, a large number of major corporations have their own in-house legal departments staffed not by lawyers but by employees (usually with law degrees) who handle almost all domestic and some international matters, particularly contract negotiations.

From April 1987, it became possible for foreign lawyers who satisfied the prescribed qualifications to practise in Japan as foreign law consultants (gaikoku-ho jimo bengashi). As a consequence, a number of the larger London and US law firms have established offices in Tokyo.

The single most striking aspect of the legal system in Japan is perhaps the Japanese attitude towards litigation. It is difficult to say whether the dearth of lawyers is a result of the Japanese dislike of litigation or whether the lack of litigation is a result of the small number of lawyers available.

Several factors contribute to this. First, the system of legal education does not lend itself to the development of a tradition of adversarial relationships and the ability to debate or defend a point of view; learning by rote without being encouraged to evaluate or criticise the material is common to all types of education in Japan.

Secondly, all future lawyers, prosecutors or judges must be admitted to, and graduate from, the Legal Research and Training Institute which effectively has a monopoly on the training of lawyers. In order to be admitted to the Institute the applicant must pass an extremely competitive exam, and less than 2 per cent of those taking the examination are accepted. Uncertainty of admission inevitably leads many aspiring lawyers to choose a career elsewhere, such as with the government or a company.

Thirdly, the cost of bringing an action is very high and the ability of the successful party to obtain a costs award from the loser is very limited. The result is that lawyers in Japan occupy the rather anomalous position of being highly trained specialists to whom the average man in the street would not turn for advice.

Submitting a dispute to the courts is considered very much a last resort. The Japanese will instead look for compromise (wakai) or conciliation (chotei). If the parties do resort to settling their dispute in the court, the exercise will usually be lengthy and costly. There is no distinction between barristers and solicitors as, for instance, in England. A Japanese bengoshi (lawyer) may appear before any court on behalf of his client. Usually, claims over ¥900,000 will be brought in the District Court (there is a separate small claims procedure). Appeal against a judgment may be made to the High Court. Further appeal may be made to the Supreme Court on a point of law. It is not unusual for more complicated cases to take several years before final judgment is given.

A non-Japanese faced with the prospects of litigation in Japan should note that, as Japanese is the official language of the Japanese courts, all documents not in Japanese must have official Japanese translations. In addition, where a foreign plaintiff is not domiciled in Japan (in the case of an individual) or does not have an office or a place of business in Japan (in the case of a company), the court may order such plaintiff to offer security for costs.

Legal documentation and negotiations

Generally, contracted documentation will be in English where transactions involve one or more non-Japanese parties, and sometimes even where both parties are Japanese if the transaction has an international flavour. The choice of law will depend largely on the type of transaction involved, but it should not be assumed automatically that Japanese law will be the appropriate choice. The following examples illustrate this.

Yen-denominated loan by a Japanese lender to a foreign borrower

From a legal standpoint, the first issue for consideration will be that of the governing law. MoF has expressed a preference for domestic yen-denominated loans to be governed by Japanese law, whereas in the case of a Euroyen loan, any law other than Japanese law is to be used (typically, English law will be chosen).

However, this is not a hard and fast rule and often a case can be made to MoF for a document which should, on the face of it, be governed by Japanese law to be governed by a foreign law. For example, if the transaction is secured and the nature of the security demands that its construction be governed by the laws of another country (as is often the case, for instance, in real estate deals), MoF may be persuaded that all the transaction documents should be governed by the same law in order to avoid the use of several jurisdictions which could give rise to conflicting constructions.

Another instance in which the choice of law may vary is where reciprocal enforcement of judgments is available between the borrower's jurisdiction and a neutral but well-known jurisdiction such as New York or England. In such a case, if the borrower is unlikely to have assets in Japan and the neutral courts will accept a submission to their jurisdiction, it may be preferable to choose as the governing law the law of the country in which judgment would be sought.

There are circumstances in which a Euroyen loan, despite MoF's general wish to the contrary, may be governed by Japanese law. The legal systems of some borrowers will not recognise an insulated choice of law (such as New York or English law) unless there is a connection between those laws and the transaction. In such circumstances, if the syndicate of institutions is wholly

Japanese, then the choice is between the laws of the borrower's country (which is likely to be unacceptable) or the laws of Japan.

An unsecured domestic yen loan without extenuating circumstances to suggest the use of a law other than Japanese law may look very similar to a loan agreement governed by English or New York law and in many instances there will be little difference in terms of the effect of the various clauses. However, there are some pertinent differences such as, for instance, the effect of regulations regarding maximum limits on interest.

Domestic yen loans extending beyond one year generally apply interest at the long-term prime rate (LTPR), which is a rate fixed by the long-term credit banks and generally adopted by the other Japanese banks. LTPR is either fixed at drawdown for the life of the loan, fixed on a drawdown-by-drawdown basis or will be subject to renewal and variation periodically by reference to the then prevailing LTPR. Other rates are based on the certificate of deposit rate and the bills discount rate, especially in relation to short-term rollover loans.

In the context of a loan with a lengthy availability period or of a loan with a variable rate of interest, it is essential to adopt a definition of LTPR or some other benchmark rate and, in view of the changes that have taken place in the Tokyo financial markets and the likelihood that at some stage the structure of interest rates in Japan will undergo a dramatic overhaul, it is also advisable to make some provision for the possibility that LTPR will cease to exist altogether.

The enforceability of a submission to the jurisdiction of Japanese courts by a sovereign or state agency borrower is not certain under Japanese law. The 1928 case of *Re Matsuyama* seems to provide that a Japanese court will have jurisdiction only if the subject matter of the claim is real estate in Japan or if there has been a voluntary submission to the jurisdiction either by international treaty or an agreement between sovereign governments. A submission in a loan agreement (or, indeed, most other documents) does not comply with these tests.

In addition, it is doubtful whether any appointment by a foreign borrower of an agent for service of process out of one of Japan's District Courts (usually Tokyo) will be effective (although, in practice, an agent and usually an address for service is nearly always appointed), as there is no precedent in Japan's procedural rules. If the borrower has a branch or other presence in the relevant jurisdiction, however, service may freely be made on that branch.

It is not uncommon in the context of project-related loans for a borrower to request that interest be capitalised during the construction or development phase of the project. Japanese banks are required to report 'non-performing loans' to the Bank of Japan and make certain reserves for them; a loan on which interest is not being paid would constitute a non-performing loan, whatever the reason interest was not being paid. One solution to this problem is, instead of capitalising interest, to achieve the same aim by having the banks make advances on each interest payment date in an amount equal to the accrued interest and for the borrower to apply those advances in payment of the interest, thereby increasing the overall principal amount of the loan.

Loans by foreign banks to, or offshore issues by, Japanese corporate borrowers

In the context of a Japanese entity undertaking a loan, bond or guarantee obligation, a foreign lender will be looking in particular for confirmation of due organisation and corporate status, power and authority to enter into the transaction. Searches at the local Company Registration Office of the Legal Affairs Bureau, a division of the Ministry of Justice, will provide evidence of due organisation. The constituent and internal documents of the borrower, principally the Articles of Incorporation (which will include an objects clause) will set out the powers of the borrower to enter into the transaction. There is a limited doctrine of *ultra vires* (i.e. matters which are beyond the legal power of the company) under Japanese law, but basically a wide interpretation of a company's powers is applied. The requirements for corporate action and for stockholder and/or board approval of a transaction will be found in the Commercial Code or sometimes in the Articles of Incorporation. Stockholder approval for incurring a debt or issuing a guarantee is unlikely to be necessary, but the position as to board approval can be less certain and it is always advisable for the lender to obtain board resolutions in connection with a transaction.

Another important consideration is whether or not a foreign judgment will be enforceable against a Japanese entity in the courts of Japan. Various conditions must be satisfied before a foreign judgment may be enforced in Japan without further enquiry into its merits, the most important of which is that there should be mutual reciprocity in respect of enforcement or execution of judgments between Japan and the relevant foreign state.

Basically, this means that a Japanese court will not recognise a foreign judgment unless a Japanese court's judgment would be recognised by the courts of the relevant foreign country under the same or similar conditions as those in Japan. In practice, this is a difficult condition to fulfil, as many foreign courts will review the merits of a judgment of another country in the absence of a specific treaty and Japan is not a party to any reciprocal enforcement treaty. The foreign party will, therefore, have to rely on precedents, if any. To date, there has been no case concerning the enforcement of an English judgment in Japan but a glimmer of hope has been provided by a recent Supreme Court decision involving a German judgment. In this instance, the strict adherence to reciprocity was overriden on the basis that the principles involved in the case were dealt with so similarly by both legal systems that the judgment could be upheld without retrying the merits of the case. For the moment, however, the outcome of any attempt to enforce a foreign judgment is still likely to be uncertain, involving substantial investments in terms of both time and costs.

In addition to the authorisation formalities and the question of enforcement of foreign judgments other points are worth noting. First, a Japanese company is lawfully entitled to submit to the non-exclusive jurisdiction of non-Japanese courts without qualification. If a submission to the exclusive jurisdiction is required, it must be not unreasonable, contrary to public policy or relating to a subject matter over which a Japanese court should have jurisdiction (such as Japanese real estate).

Secondly, the appointment by a Japanese entity of an agent in a foreign jurisdiction for service of process is valid (subject to any local requirements). This is important, since to serve a foreign-sourced process on a Japanese defendant in Japan, it would be necessary to effect such service through diplomatic channels which can be costly and time-consuming.

Thirdly, in certain circumstances a lender may wish to consider arbitration as a means of settling disputes. Agreements to arbitrate are enforceable and exclusive under Japanese law, and the additional advantage in the case of Japan is that a procedure exists for the enforcement of foreign arbitral awards.

Transferable loans

As in the Euromarkets, there has been some desire in Japan to render participations in syndicated loans more easily transferable and to create a secondary market in such participations. In London, the answer was to introduce devices such as the transferable loan instrument and the transferable loan certificate, both of which have proved to be inappropriate in Japan. When MoF was approached with the suggestion that such devices be introduced in Tokyo, it classified them as quasi-securities. And since banks would, therefore, be encroaching on the territory of the securities companies, MoF would not agree to Japanese banks dealing in such instruments. As a result, an alternative had to be found.

The Euromarket concept was successfully adapted under Japanese law by providing in the loan agreement for the relevant transferor and transferee and the agent to sign a brief assignment and assumption agreement whereunder the transferee assumed the transferor's remaining rights and obligations under the loan and notice of this was given to the borrower who, in the terms of the loan agreement, had already expressly agreed in advance to be bound by any such assignment and assumption. Under Japanese law, if a party to a contract desires to transfer its obligations, the other party's consent is required, but a general consent in advance will suffice provided the eligible class of transferees is pre-agreed. Thus, the desired objective of transferability was achieved albeit in a modified form necessary to accommodate the particular requirements of the Japanese legal system.

Swaps

The form of documentation used by Japanese banks need not vary from that governed by English or New York law save in two major respects. First, whilst banks do frequently wish to stipulate a formula which will apply on termination (as opposed to a general indemnity) in order to be confident of the extent of their exposure from time to time, the legal concerns that arise in England or in the US in connection with a general indemnity do not apply in Japan. Under English and New York law, apart from any commercial considerations, compensation provisions expressed by way of a general indemnity pose concerns about the enforceability of such provisions in the English or New York courts, and whether or not any particular provision might be held to be a penalty. Except in extreme cases penalties are, however, not repugnant in the eyes of Japanese law.

Secondly, Japanese banks, even those authorised to conduct foreign exchange business, should not agree to net payments provisions in the context of fixed and floating interest rate swaps denominated in the same currency. This is because the FEFTCL imposes restrictions upon what are described as 'special methods of settlement' between residents and non-residents and one such method is the settlement of outstanding balances on the basis of netting off. The only exception to this is where the Japanese bank is licensed as a specialised foreign exchange bank.

There is no specific tax or accounting treatment of swaps and it is generally thought that Japanese withholding tax is not applicable to payments made under a swap representing the other party's interest obligation.

Negotiations

The differences in attitudes towards the law are obviously reflected in the expectations of what a contract should contain and how it is negotiated. It is not an exaggeration to say that generally in the minds of the Japanese the contract is the end result of having established a relationship of mutual trust and understanding. In the West, a contract is seen as a legal document containing the rights and obligations of each party, enforceable by law. Whereas there is a tendency in the West – although this is perhaps as much due to the over-zealousness of lawyers as any social tradition – to ensure that contracts contain the greatest possible detail, the Japanese prefer more open-ended agreements that can be modified as circumstances change. The principle is that if a good working relationship with the other party has been developed, the contract is merely an affirmation of the joint understanding.

It is not unusual, for example, to have a provision in a Japanese contract that in the event of a dispute the parties will 'confer in good faith' or 'settle the dispute harmoniously by consultation'. The concept of trying to reach a settlement in good faith is not unknown to the West but such a provision is perhaps treated in the West with a great deal more cynicism, and there is a preference to know in advance that there is a definite procedure by which disputes may be resolved. In the context of international financial transactions, those Japanese financial institutions more frequently involved in such transactions and more acquainted with the expectations of foreign corporations have come to accept far lengthier and more involved documentation than their domestic counterparts.

Foreign institutions

Prior to liberalisation and deregulation in its financial markets, Japan maintained a highly rigid, segmented set of financial institutions and closed markets, from which foreign financial institutions were to a large extent excluded. Liberalisation has given such institutions opportunities for wider access to the Tokyo markets. This section examines the options and legal and regulatory framework within which foreign institutions may operate in the Japanese market.

Trust banking

In December 1984, MoF established the criteria for foreign bank participation in the Japanese trust business, and by June 1985 nine foreign banks had gained entry. Prospects for an increase in this number in the near future, however, are bleak: it appears that entry of additional foreign trust banks is conditional upon MoF approval of Japanese city banks entering the sector, which is unlikely in light of MoF's concern to keep commercial and trust banking separate.

The Tokyo Stock Exchange

In 1984 MoF requested the Tokyo Stock Exchange (TSE), which lies outside the control of MoF, to investigate possibilities of providing additional opportunities for non-Japanese securities houses to become members. In late 1985, the TSE increased the number of seats from 83 to 93, with six seats going to foreign brokers. On 1 February 1986, Merrill Lynch became the first foreign member to start trading on the TSE. In November 1987, the TSE selected further qualified applicants amongst foreign as well as domestic securities firms and will allow them to operate from May 1988, when once more the number of TSE seats will be increased.

Nevertheless, the Japanese securities market remains one of the most heavily regulated in the world. Complex procedures must be followed in the listing of stock, with large amounts of paperwork to be produced in both English and Japanese and gestation periods within the TSE and MoF resulting in a process that can last several months or even longer. A TSE listing is governed by a combination of the provisions of the SEL and the detailed listing regulations of the TSE. The main parties will be, on the issuer's side, the securities company sponsoring the issuer, which must be a TSE member, and the issuer's lawyers, and on the authorities' side, the Securities Bureau and the International Finance Bureau of MoF and the TSE.

Basically, there are two separate but often simultaneous procedures. First, there is the procedure to obtain a listing on the TSE (largely governed by the TSE regulations and negotiated with the TSE) and secondly there is the procedure for a public offering of foreign stock under the SEL and negotiated with MoF. A listing can only be obtained without the necessity for a simultaneous public offering if there are already 1,000 shareholders of the foreign company resident in Japan or if there is a good probability that the number of such shareholders resident in Japan will rise to 1,000 or more at a time of listing.

The main criteria which need to be satisfied before the TSE will consider a listing are as follows:

1. The applicant must already have been listed for two years on a stock exchange recognised by the TSE, and if that exchange is not in the country of domicile of the applicant then its shares must also be traded continuously on an organised over-the-counter market in such country.

2. There must be a minimum number of shares listed and the number of shareholders in Japan must be reasonably expected to be 1,000 or more. A simultaneous public offering will achieve this or, alternatively, the sponsoring Japanese securities company can arrange the necessary distribution of existing shares.

3. The TSE must consider that the shares have a good level of liquidity on its home exchange (or over-the-counter market).

4. The applicant must have been established as a stock corporation at least five years prior to the application and must have been continuously carrying on business activities during such five-year period (although this requirement can be waived for recently privatised companies).

5. The amount of shareholders' equity (net assets) must have amounted to over ¥10 billion in total and over ¥100 per share at the end of the business year immediately preceding listing application. The pre-tax profit of the applicant in each of the last three years must have been at least ¥2 billion.

6. Dividends from earnings must have been paid in the last business year and there must be a good prospect that, after listing, the applicant will continue to be able to pay a dividend at least equal to ¥5,000 divided by the number of shares making up a unit of stock.

7. The form of the applicant's share certificates must conform to the requirements of the TSE and if they do not, there must be a resolution of the board of directors resolving that they will, in future issues, so conform. There must also, in principle, be no restrictions on the transferability of shares. Exceptions may be made if restrictions are imposed by law and such restrictions are not deemed detrimental to transactions in the shares.

8. The applicant must have designated a local shareholder service agent and a dividend payment handling bank, both approved by the TSE, to ensure local service to its Japanese shareholders.

9. Purchased securities of TSE listed foreign companies are not physically brought into Japan. A book-entry clearing system will be operated by the Japan Securities Clearing Corporation (a wholly-owned subsidiary of the TSE) which will in turn, in consultation with the applicant, appoint a custodian in the country of incorporation of the applicant.

If the applicant complies with the TSE criteria, it will submit various documents in Japanese, on the basis of which the TSE will primarily make its assessment. Briefly, the applicant will submit formal Application for Listing of Securities (including details of its equity structure, its current business, terms of any public offerings, names of shareholders and distribution of ownership of shares), a Securities Report for Application for Listing, the contents of which are governed by regulations made under by the TSE regulations (including details of the applicant's corporate regulation, a history of the applicant, an outline of its business, its assets and copies of the audited financial statements of the company for the last five years) and a Stock Listing Agreement in the form of a letter to the President of the TSE agreeing to accept the regulations, directions and rulings of the TSE.

The applicant will also submit an opinion of legal counsel on the accuracy and truthfulness of descriptions on matters pertaining to laws and regulations contained in the Application for Listing of Securities.

Finally, the applicant will submit various corporate documents and copies of agreements for shareholder services, copies of all reports filed with registration authorities in the country of the applicant and copies of all statements and publicity materials distributed to shareholders during the last two years.

The documentation to be filed with MoF is broadly similar to the documentation required by the TSE to obtain a listing. The central documents are a Securities Report (giving details of the shares and the offer terms and of the corporate regulation and administration system in the issuer's home country, along with details of the issuer's business and equity structure) and the Prospectus which will set out the same information as required by the Securities Report with certain additional statements that must be prominent, such as a disclaimer by MoF as to the quality of the shares and that the shares are denominated in foreign currency and that their value would, therefore, be affected by exchange rate fluctuations.

A listed company must disclose periodically certain matters both to MoF under regulations made under the SEL and to the TSE according to the TSE Regulations for Supervision of Listed Securities to which the listed company is bound by its Stock Listing Agreement. An Annual Securities Report must be filed with MoF within six months of the end of the accounting year of the company. The effect of the Report is basically to give MoF a yearly update of the information provided in the Securities Report. Interim reports must also be submitted and special reports will be filed from time to time upon the occurrence of such events as a change in a shareholder owning over 10 per cent of the issued equity or a change in the consolidated structure of the company group.

Securities operations

In addition to the provision for greater access by foreign financial institutions to the Japanese markets, by increased foreign membership of the TSE, Japan now permits foreign securities companies owned by commercial banks to enter the securities field on condition that the parent's equity holding in the subsidiary is not more than 50 per cent and the remaining share is held by a non-banking institution.

The basic law relating to securities companies and securities dealing is the SEL. Foreign companies are outside the scope of the SEL, although the SEL established the ground rules which were then followed in a parallel body of law enacted specifically to deal with foreign companies, which comprise in particular the Law on Foreign Securities Firms (Law No. 5 of 1971 as amended) (LFSF), the Enforcement Order of the Law on Foreign Securities Firms (Cabinet Order No. 267 of 1971 as amended) and the Ministerial Ordinance on Foreign Securities Firms (MoF Ordinance No. 61 of 1971 as amended). The law gives a great deal of discretion to MoF's Security Bureau in deciding whether or not to issue a licence.

Foreign securities companies that wish to be represented or to operate in the Japanese market place may choose from three vehicles through which to conduct business: a representative or liaison office, a branch or a limited company. Each type of organisation has strictly defined areas of activity and the company will therefore need to determine the nature of its operations in order to choose the most appropriate vehicle.

Representative office

The Law on Foreign Securities Firms (LFSF, a statute which is dealt with in more detail in relation to branches) provides for advance notification by MoF of the intention to establish a representative office. Establishment does not require approval or permission as a matter of law, although in practice the Securities Bureau will send a letter of welcome when it receives the advance notification.

A representative office has a very limited sphere of activities and is not subject to the same detailed laws and regulations which apply in the case of a branch. Where there is only a representative office, all dealing must be done outside Japan. The basic activities of the office will be limited to marketing information collected for its head office and promotion and advertising on behalf of the head office. One of the few laws with which the representative office may have to comply will be the Labour Standards Law: if the office employs more than 10 staff, 'working rules' will have to be filed with the Labour Standards Inspection Office.

A representative office is not treated as a permanent establishment for tax purposes and will not be liable in respect of Japanese corporate income taxes. The office may, however, be subject to depreciable assets tax depending on the value of its fixed assets.

Branch

The LFSF authorises the licensing of foreign securities dealers. Its provisions govern the establishment, day-to-day running and dissolution of licensed branches.

Licences are available in the following four categories:

- buying or selling securities as a dealer;
- acting as an intermediary, a broker or an agent in respect of buying or selling securities for third parties either directly or through Japanese securities exchanges;
- underwriting distributions of new securities or secondary offerings; and
- handling public offerings of new or outstanding securities.

A licence must be obtained in respect of each branch established in Japan and there is a minimum capital requirement for the securities company ranging from ¥30 million to ¥3 billion, depending on the type of licence being requested by the branch.

In order to facilitate the application procedure, it is important, as with all dealings with the Japanese authorities, to establish good relations with the Securities Bureau from the outset. Initially, the Securities Bureau should be notified of the desire of the company to submit an application for a licence. This will be followed by several meetings with officials of the Securities Bureau in order that they may explain the procedure and also assess the applicant. Only then may the application procedure properly begin.

The first stage is to obtain prior approval and the applicant must comply with the following criteria:

1. The applicant must be a limited liability company incorporated outside Japan. It should be noted that partnership is not sufficient and this may mean, therefore, that a subsidiary will first need to be established, and the subsidiary will then make the application.

2. The applicant must have been carrying on the business for which it is seeking a licence for at least three years, but in the case of a newly formed subsidiary, it may rely on the business experience of the partnership.

3. The applicant is ineligible if it engages in 'Incompatible Business' (basically banking business and any other business which may not be carried out by securities dealers in Japan, which includes virtually all businesses other than securities business and business incidental thereto). There are also restrictions on the affiliation which the applicant may have with any company engaged in Incompatible Business (an 'Incompatible Company').

Essentially (although the rules are complicated), an Incompatible Company will be an affiliated corporation of the applicant where:

(i) the management of the applicant is controlled by the Incompatible Company by means of more than 50 per cent of the shares of the applicant being beneficially owned (*a*) by the Incompatible Company (and/or its officers or 'major shareholders' (any person owning more than 10 per cent of the total issued shares of the Incompatible Company)) or (*b*) by a company or 'non-juridical association' more than 75 per cent owned by the Incompatible Company (and/or its officers or major shareholders); or

(ii) the applicant controls the management of any such Incompatible Company by means of the applicant (and/or its officers or major shareholders) owning (*a*) more than 50 per cent of the issued shares of the Incompatible Company or (*b*) more than 75 per cent of the shares of a company or non-juridical association which itself owns more than 50 per cent of the Incompatible Company.

The prohibition does not apply, however, in three cases. First, where the Incompatible Company does not engage in Incompatible Business in Japan. Secondly, it does not apply if the Incompatible Business is either not that of a financial institution or is otherwise not regarded as contrary to the public interest or conflicting with the proposed securities business. Thirdly, it does not apply if it is the applicant itself that conducts an Incompatible Business which complies with the first or second exception, and the securities business is or will be accounted for separately in the books of the applicant.

After a period of some uncertainty, a formula was decided upon by the Securities Bureau to cut through the complicated provisions in practice: securities companies with 50 per cent bank ownership and 50 per cent ownership by sleeping partners will be treated as being eligible. In one case 100 per cent bank ownership has been permitted: the Securities Bureau allowed Vickers da Costa to continue after its acquisition by Citicorp, but this is considered an exception by the Securities Bureau.

The second stage in the application process is a detailed review by the Securities Bureau using guidelines for assessment set out in the LFSF which are based on the following:

1. The company must have sufficient capital and income to ensure that it is a going concern and that it has sufficient reserves to survive a prolonged downturn in the market.

2. The company's personnel must have the necessary expertise and experience to enable them to conduct the intended business efficiently.

3. The Securities Bureau has to evaluate the competitive and economic conditions of the area in which the applicant intends to operate.

For this review the Securities Bureau will call for detailed information regarding the company and its group such as shareholder and director details, financial statements, details of the volume of business transacted with Japanese securities dealers, the history of the group's involvement with the securities market in Japan, financial projections, and procedures on business operation. The company will have to submit a formal document with the licence application detailing how the business is to be operated and controlled and this document will effectively become its manual for operations.

Provided that the Securities Bureau considers that there are no grounds to justify refusal and the criteria above have been complied with, the company will be instructed to make a formal application. This stage involves the submission of an application form and various accompanying documents relating to the company, some of which will already have been informally presented at the second stage.

Once satisfied with the documentation, the Securities Bureau will issue a licence that will specify the categories of business which the branch may undertake and will stipulate compliance with the relevant legislation (including the Rules of the Stock Exchanges), membership of the Securities Firms Association of Japan (a self-regulatory body formed by the securities companies under the SEL which has only voluntary membership for Japanese securities dealers, unlike the foreign branches) and observation of the procedures for business operation.

The process of obtaining a licence is lengthy and commentators are of the view that reciprocity of treatment of Japanese securities companies abroad plays an important role in final success.

A branch of a foreign securities firm is regarded as a permanent establishment in Japan and is, consequently, subject to Japanese taxes. The branch is required to submit a tax return each year and corporate income taxes are payable in two instalments, in the case of securities branches on 31 May and 30 November each year. The other tax of specific relevance is the Securities Transfer Tax which is levied on the seller of securities when the transfer takes place; a securities branch benefits from a lower transactions tax than a public investor.

Finally, the Securities Bureau is empowered to order securities inspectors to examine the business, books and records on a surprise basis. The inspection could involve an unscheduled visit by eight or more officials for a fortnight, and an examination of all records down to the telex files.

Company

Until the enactment of the Investment Advisory Act, a Japanese subsidiary of a foreign company could carry on only limited activities, in the form of trust banking or liaison activities, similar to those of a representative office. The Act has offered new opportunities for securities companies in Japan.

Although there are four different types of company that exist in Japan, in practice the only one of relevance to a foreign company is the Kabushiki Kaisha, or joint stock company. The procedure for the creation of such a company is set down in the Commercial Code and permission is usually not required. If, however, the intended business of the company requires a licence or permission, the application for setting up a company must be accompanied by such licence or permission.

There are two particular pieces of legislation which are of importance. First, under the anti-monopoly legislation the establishment and operation of a holding company is prohibited and no company (including a foreign company) can operate as a holding company in Japan. Secondly, the FEFTCL requires that all direct investment into Japan be reported to MoF through the Bank of Japan. The report will provide information on the business activities, the date of establishment of the company, the capital investment and forecasts and details of shareholders and company officers.

Investment advisory services

The Investment Advisory Act, which was passed on 27 May 1986, to take effect in November of the same year, came in the wake of such incidents as the *Toshi* journal scandal in 1984, when the Japanese speculative stock-consulting group company, which had published monthly tips on investment and had offered to invest the money of its readers, went into liquidation leaving some 10,000 of its readers ¥350 billion out of pocket.

The aim of the Act was to create a legal framework for the responsible management of surplus funds through a system of registration and approval of investment advisers. Much of the detailed implementation of the Act has been left to cabinet and ministerial orders and in some cases only the *Nikkei* newspaper has published details as yet. The first licences were granted in May 1987, including discretionary investment management licences to 17 subsidiaries of foreign entities.

Two types of activity are permitted by the Act: investment advice and discretionary investment management, that is managing funds for investors as opposed to giving advice for a fee. The former requires registration whilst the latter requires a licence.

Investment advice

An investment adviser must be registered with MoF. An application has to be made to MoF which will include details such as share capital, names and addresses of directors, auditors in the case of a joint stock company and in the case of an individual, the names and addresses of certain employees. In addition, details must be given of business location and operation and the nature of any other business carried on by the applicant. The applicant will also have to declare that he is eligible under the Act (those who are ineligible include the mentally disordered, minors, bankrupts and persons who have been refused registration or have had their registration revoked within the last three years, or companies or individuals whose employees include a person in one of these categories).

Once an application is accepted, details of the company or individual will be entered into a Register of Investment Advisers. This is a public register. Once registered, the investment adviser must inform MoF of any change in the application details within two weeks of such change.

Before commencing any investment advisory activities, the investment adviser is required to lodge a business security deposit, in the form of a non-interest bearing cash deposit, against non-performance of investment advice with the legal affairs bureau nearest to its place of business. The amount of cash deposit is ¥5 million, plus ¥2.5 million for each additional branch established. The Act provides that certain prescribed government securities may be deposited as an alternative to cash, or a bank guarantee may be given. Registration costs in the form of stamp duty are ¥90,000 for each registration. Applications may be filed for more than one branch at the same time.

Discretionary investment management

Where an investment adviser (which under the Act can only be a Japanese joint stock company, or its foreign equivalent, but not an individual) is given discretion by a client over all or part of that client's investment decisions together with the necessary authority to make investments on his or her behalf, it must obtain a licence from MoF in order to carry out such discretionary investment management. The Act specifically prohibits discretionary investment management except under a discretionary investment contract, or where otherwise given specific authority, such as the trust banks which are authorised under the Securities Investment Trust Law.

The licence application will contain details of the company similar to those in the application for registration, but the application must be accompanied by the copy of the constitutive documents of the company (in the case of a Japanese joint stock company the Articles of Incorporation and an extract from the Commercial Register) and documents describing the nature and the method of business.

There are certain criteria and rules under which a licence will be granted, of which the basic ones are:

1. The company should be incorporated in Japan, or be the parent of a foreign-owned branch which should be duly incorporated in its own country. The minimum capital requirement of the subsidiary or branch is ¥100 million.

2. The net assets of the company should be maintained at a minimum of ¥100 million over three years. Fees from funds management should be sufficient to cover costs within three years.

3. The company must aim for assets under management to total at least ¥20 billion within a fairly short time after obtaining a licence. In the case of foreign companies, where the branch or subsidiary does not qualify under the criteria for assets under management, a licence may be granted if the parent company has ¥100 billion under management and the branch or subsidiary meets all the other requirements. Again, the assets under management criteria might be disregarded if the company has special expertise and means of protecting investors' interests.

4. The minimum value of an account must be set at ¥100 million for a customer, which must be described in the company's literature, and MoF will require information about the work experience of the fund managers.

5. The company must have a sufficient number of fund managers to cope with the accounts but in any event not less than two. However, MoF may permit a Japanese branch of a foreign company to have only one fund manager if the parent company operates a centralised management system outside Japan.

6. The company must be able to provide nearly real-time information to customers with an appropriate computer system.

7. The company must operate without subsidies or financial aid from its parent company or shareholders.

Once MoF is satisfied that the criteria have been met, a licence will be granted and the fact of issuance of the licence will be recorded on the register. MoF must be approached for approval of any changes to the nature or method of the company's activities.

Before commencing its discretionary investment management activities, the company must, as with the registered investment advisers, lodge a business security deposit of ¥5 million against non-performance. However in this case the company must also deposit ¥20 million, plus ¥10 million for each branch.

The Act provides that a licensed discretionary investment management company must not engage in any other activities. However, there is a possibility of MoF approval being given for the discretionary investment management company to carry on activities *related* to investment advice and discretionary investment management, provided that the company can demonstrate that this would not be to the detriment of the investor. Similarly, directors of the discretionary investment management company, or in the case of foreign companies operating in Japan, its representatives and directors, must not engage in any other business without specific MoF prior approval. The cost of obtaining a licence is ¥150,000 for each approval.

Regulation of business

The Act also regulates the conduct of the business of the investment adviser, in particular with respect to advertising, details of the type of documentation which must be provided to the client (basically, an initial proposal followed by a formal contract and six-monthly progress reports containing information about whether amongst the investments which the investment adviser may have bought or sold for his own account there have been investments which are also the subject of advice given to the client) and the procedure for cancellation of the contract by the client within 10 days of receipt of the contract. The Act lists those activities which are not to be carried out by an investment adviser (i.e. those registered but without a licence):

1. Dealing in securities either with or on behalf of a client.
2. Accepting deposits or negotiable securities from clients.
3. Making loans or lending negotiable securities to clients, acting as an intermediary, agent or proxy in such lending by a third party to the client.
4. Employment of deception, violence or threats in relation to the signing, cancellation or termination of a contract.
5. Offering unsubstantiated advice only with a view to taking advantage, for his own benefit or the benefit of a third party, of price fluctuations arising from transactions by the client.
6. Soliciting clients with a promise to bear all or part of their losses.
7. Any other acts from time to time set out in Ministerial Ordinance as being contrary to the protection of the investor.

The regulations apply equally to the discretionary investment management companies but with some differences. The company is permitted to deal in securities on behalf of a client and is also able to act as intermediary, agent or proxy in lending monies or negotiable securities to clients by securities companies arising out of the use of margin transactions. The other significant difference is that in addition to a three-monthly progress report with the same information as provided by investment advisors, the company must also submit a three-monthly report on assets under management.

Leasing

The growth of leasing in Japan is a fairly recent event. Leasing has to a significant degree developed as a result of city bank initiatives to expand into new areas of business.

The leasing companies are not, nor are they treated like, banking institutions. This has three important consequences. First, many of the restrictions of the FEFTCL apply to the leasing companies, whereas entities authorised to carry on foreign exchange business are free from such restrictions. For instance, leasing companies cannot make loans without MoF consent. Secondly, they are generally free from laws specifically applicable to lenders. Thirdly, as MoF does not regard leasing companies as banks, its administrative guidance is neither aimed at nor is it intended that it should be obeyed by them. As a result, the leasing companies are seen as having certain advantages over the commercial banks. For instance, the leasing companies have been able to offer longer-term financing than the commercial banks and are not subject to any guidance with respect to the choice of governing law.

Japanese leasing companies acquired considerable experience in cross-border transactions during the shipping boom and later turned their attention to aircraft with the introduction of the Samurai lease programme by the Japanese government in 1978.

The activities of the leasing companies have created a role for foreign banks, as well as Japanese banks, in developing and arranging financing 'packages' which both maximise the potential role of leasing companies in cross-border transactions and tailor schemes to fit a borrower's requirements in situations where the traditional simpler schemes do not suffice.

Although each transaction will have its own particular features, the majority of transactions will derive from one of a fairly small number of basic structures.

It should be noted that neither the relevant ministry nor the tax authorities will usually issue written rulings, binding or otherwise, on specimen structures and their implications. Approaches are often made on a no-names basis to sound out the position and, with the correct approach, a fairly strong feel for the official view of a proposed structure can be obtained.

Conclusion

This chapter presents a collage of sign-posts, concerns and hurdles for the foreign financial institution doing business in Japan. As it develops as a full-service centre, Tokyo will need greater depth in the professional assistance it can provide to the financial services industry. Guidance through the maze of legal, accounting and administrative regulations is one thing, the ability to implement a complicated transaction and document it to the satisfaction of institutions from all points of the globe is another.

CHAPTER TWENTY-SIX

Taxation and accounting requirements for the foreign investor

by Kazuhide Kondo and Shigeru Fujita
Partners, Showa Ota International Department

As the Japanese economy has progressed, restrictions on the inflow of foreign capital have been gradually removed. Restrictions on foreign investment were reduced by the government through its capital liberalisation programme in line with the Capital Liberalisation Code of the Organisation for Economic Cooperation and Development (OECD).

In 1980, the restrictive Foreign Investment Law was revised and incorporated into the new Foreign Exchange and Foreign Trade Control Law. The basic concept of the law provides for freedom of investment unless expressly prohibited. Government policy is to allow the inflow of foreign capital as freely as possible and to limit government intervention to exceptional situations only. Direct investment is allowed without restriction in most industries except in those specific industries where, according to the OECD Capital Liberalisation Code, national interest and security are at stake.

In July 1985, the Japanese government announced a series of measures to open markets which will help foreign investors gain greater and easier access to the Japanese market. Local governments are also promoting campaigns to attract foreign manufacturing investment in their regions.

Foreign direct investment in Japan has continued at high levels in recent years: US$749 million in 1983 (1,052 firms), US$812 million in 1984 (2,363 firms) and US$780 million in 1985 (690 firms). This brings the cumulative foreign direct investment to US$6,653 million (6,286 firms) at the end of fiscal 1985.

Foreign investment regulations

In order to meet the requirements of the Foreign Exchange and Foreign Trade Control Law, foreign investors planning direct capital investment in Japan must give prior notification to the Japanese government regarding their investment proposals. They are required to file, through the Bank of Japan, a report with MoF and the ministry in charge of the industry in which they propose to invest, within three months prior to the projected time of investment. Under the Law, the following forms of investment are considered direct foreign investment in Japan:

1. Acquisition of shares in a Japanese company listed on the stock exchange which amounts to 10% or more of the total issued shares.
2. Acquisition of shares or equity in a non-listed Japanese company, whether an existing or newly established company, either a wholly-owned subsidiary or a joint venture with a Japanese partner.
3. Establishment of a branch office.
4. Long-term loans to a Japanese company.
5. Acquisition of long-term private bonds.
6. Conclusion of a technical licensing agreement with a Japanese company.

The foreign investor is not allowed to proceed with his investment for 30 days after filing the report, during which time the report will be reviewed by the appropriate government ministries to decide whether the proposed investment is acceptable. This waiting period may be shortened to 15 days if the investment is considered to pose no particular problem. In most cases, investors can proceed with their investments two weeks after filing their reports.

If the proposed investment is considered undesirable for reasons of national interest or security, or possible adverse effect on the domestic industry in which the investment is proposed, the investment may be delayed for up to five months after filing, to allow time for further review by the government. The authorities may then advise the investor to consider an alteration in, or suspension of, the investment.

Under the OECD Liberalisation Code, the following industries remain restricted: agriculture, forestry and fisheries; mining; petroleum; leather and leather products manufacturing. Also, in view of their direct impact on national interest and security, direct foreign investment in the areas of public utilities, arms or explosives manufacture, atomic power, aircraft, and space development is subject to review.

For the purpose of the Law, "foreign investors" applies not only to non-resident individuals and foreign corporations, including branches of foreign corporations operating in Japan, but also to any Japanese company which is owned 50% or more by a foreign corporation and to any Japanese company of which more than half the directors are non-residents.

Foreign exchange transactions are free in principle, although restrictions may be imposed by the government as deemed necessary in special circumstances.

Operating funds for a branch can be brought in without restriction. The borrowing of funds by a subsidiary or a branch in Japan from its parent or home office in any amount for a loan period not exceeding one year can be made freely if such transactions are reported in advance to MoF through the Bank of Japan. Borrowings of less than ¥10 million are permitted without prior reporting.

The remittance of dividends, royalties, or service fees can be performed without restriction. Branch profits are also freely remittable, as is repatriation of equity capital and debt capital.

Anti-monopoly regulations

Anti-monopoly regulations are administered by the Fair Trade Commission (FTC) which is an independent government organisation. International contracts and agreements extending over one year, concluded between a resident and a non-resident, must, under the provisions of the Anti-Monopoly Law, be reported to the Commission within 30 days after the contract or agreement has been signed.

International contracts or agreements include joint venture agreements, licensing agreements, sales agreements, and trade mark, patent and copyright agreements.

The Law provides for restrictions on stock holdings and directorships in competitive companies. It requires foreign corporations with shares in a Japanese company to file an annual report with the FTC within three months after the end of each fiscal year. The report can be filed by the Japanese companies if they are granted power of attorney.

The Anti-Monopoly Law prohibits a company from establishing or becoming a holding company. A foreign corporation is prohibited from establishing a company in Japan which will perform the function of a holding company.

The Law also prohibits foreign financial institutions from acquiring 5% or more of the stock of other financial institutions or companies in Japan.

Setting up business in Japan

Form of business

There are four alternative forms of business which a foreign investor can choose for doing business in Japan. They are: a representative office, a branch, a subsidiary, or a joint venture.

Representative office

A foreign investor can open a representative office without filing any report with the government ministries. A representative office of a foreign bank, foreign securities or foreign insurance company, however, requires notification to MoF. Since a representative office is not a legal entity, it need not be registered legally. However, it is not allowed to engage in any commercial transactions. Its activities are limited solely to information gathering, market research, and general liaison with the head office of a foreign corporation. A representative office is not subject to Japanese corporate tax for its liaison activities on behalf of a foreign corporation.

Due to restrictions on the activities of the representative office, that status is generally suitable only for temporary operations, such as market research before developing into a legally recognised branch or subsidiary operation. Changing from a representative office to a branch or subsidiary is common and can be accomplished with little difficulty.

Branch of a foreign corporation

A foreign investor can set up a branch of a foreign corporation to engage in any commercial activity in Japan by filing a report with the appropriate government ministry under the Foreign Exchange and Foreign Trade Control Law. The establishment of the branch must also be registered under the Commercial Registration Law.

Although a branch operation is acceptable in any business category, it is considered most suitable for liaison, purchase, sales and service operations. A branch normally does not engage in manufacturing.

Under government regulations, foreign investors are allowed to conduct business activities only through branch operations in the following business categories: banking, long-term credit banking, foreign securities, gas and electric utilities.

For tax purposes, a branch operation is treated the same as a Japanese company. It is taxed on its Japanese source income at the same rate as Japanese companies. Branch operations have certain tax benefits. Losses incurred by the branch are generally deductible against the income of the home office and, subject to recapture, losses may be carried forward to offset future taxable income.

Fund transfers between the branch and the home office can be made without difficulty. Branch profits are also freely remittable and there is no withholding tax on such remittance.

Restructuring a branch to a subsidiary is legally possible but requires careful considerations. It is a rather time-consuming and costly process. The foreign corporation must set up a subsidiary and then transfer the branch assets to the subsidiary. If the branch had incurred losses, the carryforward benefit cannot be transferred to the subsidiary. On the other hand, if the branch was profitable, taxable goodwill may arise. If a foreign investor plans to conduct business in Japan over a long period, it would be more desirable to consider setting up a subsidiary at the outset.

Subsidiary or joint venture

A subsidiary or a joint venture can take one of the following four corporate forms recognised under Japanese law: partnership company (gomei kaisha), limited partnership company (goshi kaisha), joint stock company (kabushiki kaisha), limited liability company (yugen kaisha). The major difference between the four corporate forms is how and to what extent a shareholder is liable for the company's debts and obligations.

A joint stock company is the form of business most widely used by foreign investors to set up a subsidiary or a joint venture with Japanese partners. Shareholders' liability is limited to the capital invested. Incorporation procedures, management, and accounting and auditing requirements of a joint stock company are all provided in detail in the Commercial Code. Since the provisions of the law governing a joint stock company are designed for a company with a great number of shareholders, applying this form to a subsidiary or a joint venture entails some technical difficulties. Nevertheless, a joint stock company generally has greater advantages in the conduct of business than other forms of business. For example, a joint stock company enjoys financial and business credibility and a better public image.

Procedures of establishment

Branch of a foreign corporation

A foreign investor who intends to set up a branch in Japan is required to file a "Report Concerning the Establishment of Branch, etc." with MoF and the ministry in charge of the industry involved, through the Bank of Japan, three months prior to establishing the branch. The report must be in Japanese and must be filed by proxy by a resident in Japan. Under normal circumstances, the report will be accepted within a few days and the investor will be allowed to establish the branch. If the government ministries need a longer period to review the proposed establishment (for reasons of national interest or security), this period may be extended to a maximum of five months.

The Commercial Code provides that a foreign corporation continually engaging in commercial transactions in Japan must appoint a representative in Japan (branch manager), set up a place of business, and register with the commercial registry office.

Japanese joint stock company (Kabushiki Kaisha)

The same incorporation procedures apply to the establishment of both a wholly-owned subsidiary and a joint venture with a Japanese partner, when it takes a form of a joint stock company or a Kabushiki Kaisha under the Commercial Code.

A foreign investor must, through the Bank of Japan, file a Report Concerning Acquisition of Stocks with MoF and the ministry in charge of the applicable industry within three months prior to acquiring the stock. The report must be in Japanese and must be filed by proxy by a resident in Japan.

Within 30 days after acquiring the stock, the foreign investor must, through the Bank of Japan, report the acquisition of the stock to MoF and the ministry in charge of the industry involved.

Accounting and audit requirements

The Commercial Code requires all businesses to maintain double-entry books of account, including a general ledger and supporting ledger. Books are required to be kept for a 10-year period.

A joint stock company is required to prepare financial statements which include a balance sheet, income statement, business report, proposal for appropriation of retained earnings (declaration of dividends, etc.) and supporting schedules as of the end of each fiscal year.

Although auditing standards as published by the Business Accounting Deliberation Council (an advisory organ to MoF made up of members of the Japanese Institute of CPAs, users of financial statements and academics) are similar to US standards, there are variations in practice, generally related to documentation, degree of reliance on internal control, etc.

Accounting principles generally accepted in Japan are also similar to those in the United States. However, Japanese accounting practices are strongly influenced by the income tax law and, as a result, certain practices allowed under Japanese tax law would not be considered appropriate for a fair presentation under US generally accepted accounting principles.

Statutory audit requirements vary depending on the size of the company. A joint stock company is classified as follows:

1. A large corporation whose capital stock is ¥500 million or more or whose total liabilities are ¥20 billion or more.

2. A medium-sized corporation whose capital stock is more than ¥100 million but less than ¥500 million.

3. A small corporation whose capital stock is ¥100 million or less.

The financial statements and supporting schedules of small and medium-sized corporations are subject to audit only by statutory auditors (a member of the company organisation), whereas those of a large corporation must be audited not only by statutory auditors but also by an independent Certified Public Accountant (CPA) or an audit corporation.

Under the Commercial Code, the audit opinions of both the statutory auditor and the independent CPA must be submitted to the annual general shareholders' meeting.

Under the Securities and Exchange Law, corporations which have offered securities and filed registration statements in the past or corporations whose shares are listed on stock exchanges or traded in the over-the-counter market are required to file securities reports which contain non-consolidated financial statements on an annual and a semi-annual basis with MoF. The financial statements included in such reports must be audited by an independent CPA. All companies whose stock is listed on the stock exchange are required to prepare consolidated financial statements as an attachment to the securities report and these consolidated financial statements also must be audited.

Taxation

Corporate tax return

National and local corporation tax is assessed on the worldwide income of a domestic corporation and on income from sources within Japan of a foreign corporation having a permanent establishment in Japan. A branch in Japan of a foreign corporation is considered the permanent establishment of a foreign corporation and is subject to corporation tax on its Japan sourced income. In addition, an agent of a foreign corporation who has authority to conclude contracts or performs habitually important activities in Japan exclusively for or on behalf of a foreign corporation, may be deemed a permanent establishment of the foreign corporation and be subject to Japanese corporation tax on income attributable to the permanent establishment.

Blue form tax return

The blue form tax return system, which is used by most corporations, entitles a taxpayer to various tax benefits. Under the return system, a taxpayer is required to keep a set of books that reflect clearly all transactions affecting assets, liabilities, and capital in accordance with the principle of double-entry book-keeping, and to settle accounts on the basis of those books.

Benefits accruing to blue return taxpayers include a five-year carry-over of operating losses following the taxable year of such loss. A net operating loss may be carried back one year provided a blue return was filed for the earlier year as well as the loss year. However, as an interim measure, this provision has been suspended for the two fiscal years ending between 1 April 1986 and 31 March 1988. Other benefits relate to reassessments made based on the results of an actual tax examination, if a mistake was made in computing taxable income, deductible reserves and depreciation expense.

Computation of taxable income

Japanese national income tax is based on a determination of a taxpayer's taxable income. Net income, however, as reported under GAAP does not necessarily constitute taxable income for corporation tax purposes. The definition of taxable income is quite broad and the way income is generated is irrelevant. Thus, gross income is an expansive concept under the Japanese tax system. On the other hand, expenditures incurred in the conduct of the business – except as otherwise provided by the law, i.e. directors' bonuses, specified amounts of entertainment expenses, and contribution expenses – are allowed as deductions from gross income.

Tax rate

The effective tax rates are calculated as follows:

National tax	43.30%
Enterprise tax	13.20%
Inhabitant tax (43.3% × 20.7%)	8.96%
	65.46%

Considering that enterprise tax is deductible for national and inhabitant taxes in the following fiscal period, the effective tax rate (excluding the per capita levy) is calculated as follows:

$$\frac{65.46\%}{(1 + 0.132)} = 57.82\%$$

Tax return filing and due date of payment of corporate tax

Corporations must file a tax return within two months of the end of their fiscal period and pay the tax at the same time. Corporations whose fiscal year is longer than six months, except a newly established corporation, should file an interim return and pay an interim tax as of the end of the first six months of a fiscal year. Corporations are not allowed to file consolidated tax returns.

Going public in Japan: accounting and other listing requirements for the foreign corporation

Introduction

Multinational companies requiring access to funds on a worldwide basis will find their access to the Japanese financial centre enhanced if their stock is listed on a Japanese stock exchange. Like all credit grantors, Japanese financial institutions are most comfortable dealing with those they know. The Japanese registration process, designed to disclose all relevant facts about the corporation's capital structure, financial condition, management and operations, is said to be more stringent than that of the US. Once registered the corporation is obligated continually to up-date its disclosures in annual and semi-annual securities reports.

The listed company is able to issue new capital stock at a known market value. It will find it can issue bonds and other financial instruments at more favourable rates; and there are other benefits as well. The listed company doing business in Japan finds enhanced prestige which is attractive to Japanese employees and executives and facilitates business transactions. The free publicity which comes from the disclosure and reporting process and the attention of the financial press also enhances the corporation's public image.

The underlying objective of the Commercial Code is to provide information to protect credit grantors and current investors. Therefore, financial disclosures concentrate on the availability of earnings for dividends, creditworthiness and earning power. The Securities and Exchange Law is orientated to general investors. Its requirements therefore embrace the Commercial Code requirements and include management and operating information, cash flow and operating projections and consolidated financial information.

Historically, Japanase financial disclosures have concentrated on non-consolidated financial statements. This reflected the nature of Japanese business which tended to concentrate on Japanese activities with few overseas operations. The exceptions were the trading companies; but their overseas subsidiaries were looked on as investments rather than operating entities, hence the longstanding accounting rule, only recently amended, that foreign subsidiaries should be accounted for at cost. Now that Japanese companies are major overseas investors in operating entities, the accounting rules have been changed to require equity accounting and consolidated financial statements, as well as the traditional non-consolidated, cost-basis statements. Foreign corporations seeking registration in Japan will long since have adopted the consolidated form of reporting, and so will have no problem in meeting this portion of the requirements. Except in very special circumstances, non-consolidated financial statements are not required of foreign registrants.

There was a time when auditors' reports on the financial statements of foreign corporations listed on the Japanese exchanges had to be signed by a Japanese CPA. This was accomplished by allowing the Japanese CPA to review the work of the foreign auditors and obtain satisfaction to the same extent as if he had performed the audit. Now the report of the foreign auditor is acceptable by itself so long as the report and the accompanying financial statements have been filed with and accepted by the regulatory authorities of the corporation's home country. This liberalisation has also been extended to the financial statements. Financial statements which have been filed by the corporation with the US Securities and Exchange Commission, for example, are acceptable for filing in their entirety without amendment in Japan. That is not to say, however, that additional information might not be required in the form of schedules and supplementary disclosures.

The registration procedure

While the Securities and Exchange Law is the responsibility of MoF, in actual practice the examination of the foreign corporation applying for listing is delegated to the relevant exchange. After reviewing all the required filings the exchange passes its recommendation to MoF which, after due deliberation, makes the final approval decision.

The first step in the registration process is the appointment of an underwriter from among the member companies of the exchange. The underwriter coordinates all steps of the registration process with the exchange and MoF. The underwriter is essential to the corporation, as all documents filed must be in Japanese. The underwriter handles translation of all parts of the registration statement and supplemental filings except the financial statements which are customarily translated by the Japanese office of the corporation's CPAs. In practice some parts of the translation (except the financials) are delegated to the corporation's Japanese attorneys.

The following criteria must be met for the listing application to be accepted by the Tokyo Stock Exchange:

1. The applicant must be listed in its home country on a stock exchange recognised by the Exchange.
2. The minimum number of shares to be listed is 20 million if the shares are to be traded in normal units of 1,000 shares. Fewer shares may be listed if shares are traded in units of less than 1,000 shares; but this is not usual.
3. The applicant must have been incorporated and continuously in business for at least five years.
4. The applicant's stock must have good liquidity in its home market.
5. There must be a good prospect that the number of shareholders in Japan will be 1,000 or more at the listing date.
6. Shareholders' equity (net assets) as at the end of the fiscal year immediately preceding the listing application date must have been at least ¥10 billion.
7. Income before income tax in each of the last three years must have been ¥2 billion or more.
8. The applicant must have paid dividends in each of the last three years and, in addition, there must be a good prospect that the applicant will be able to pay dividends continuously after listing.
9. There must have been no false statement made in the financial statements or other documents relating to the applicant's financial position in the last three years and the auditors' report of the applicant's certified public accountants in the latest year must have been, in principle, without qualification.

10. The applicant must place no restriction on the transferability of shares of stock. (The Exchange may recognise circumstances warranting exemption from this requirement.)

11. The share certificates must be in conformity with the requirements of the Exchange.

12. The applicant must have appointed a shareholder service agent in Japan and a bank to disburse dividends, or have obtained informal acceptance of such appointments.

The following documents in the Japanese language are required, in principle, to be submitted to the Exchange.

1. Application for listing of securities.
2. The minutes of the Board of Directors' resolution authorising listing.
3. A set of specimen share certificates.
4. Articles of Incorporation.
5. A Securities Report for the application for listing, Sections I and II.
6. Opinion of legal counsel as to the truthfulness and accuracy of statements pertaining to laws and regulations contained in the documents submitted to the Exchange.
7. A document certifying that the stock is listed on a stock exchange in the country of origin.
8. A document certifying that the person acting as representative of the applicant in applying for listing is duly authorised.
9. A Stock Listing Agreement.
10. Copies of the agreement with informal or written acceptance of appointment from the shareholder service agent and the bank responsible for disbursing dividends.
11. Copies of documents filed with regulatory authorities, stock exchange and similar bodies in the country of origin and of documents sent to shareholders, all within the past year. These documents need not be translated into Japanese.
12. Prospectus for listing.

The Application for Listing of Securities is a set of documents to be submitted by the applicant in making formal application for listing to the President of the Exchange. It must carry the name and seal (or signature) of the authorised representative of the company applying for listing. The major items of information to be furnished in the Application are:

1. Description of the stock for which application is being made, i.e. name of the issue; registered or bearer form; class; par value or non-par value; amount of par value, if applicable; and the amount of stock outstanding.

If the number of shares for which application is being made includes unissued shares, approval of which has been made by vote of the shareholder, or if any additional shares beyond the number for which application is being made are expected to be issued as a result of the exercise of a conversion privilege or "equity elements" of the company's other securities, the number of such shares is to be furnished.

2. Other securities issued by the company.
3. Detailed information regarding the number of shares outstanding and the amount of capital.
4. Purposes of the company.
5. Outline of business.
6. Terms and conditions of any public offering or secondary distribution conducted during the three-year period preceding the listing application date.
7. Number of shares held by directors and statutory auditors.
8. Number of shares held by principal shareholders.
9. Distribution of ownership of shares by type of holder, size of holding, and geographical distribution in Japan.

The form and contents of the Securities Report (registration statement) are prescribed by regulations of MoF pursuant to Form 7, the form applicable to foreign registrants.

To support the acceptance of the foreign corporation's financial statements in the form and content required by regulatory authorities in the country of origin without change, and the acceptance of the audit report of the corporation's regular auditors, it is necessary to submit a summary of differences in accounting principles reflected in financial statements generally accepted in the country of origin which differ from those in Japan and a summary of differences in qualification standards for CPAs in the country of origin and in Japan. The summary of qualifications of CPAs follows a prescribed form which is technical and need not be reproduced here.

Investing in the Japanese Stock Market

Introduction

Liberalisation rules adopted in Japan have made the Tokyo stock market accessible to foreign investors and the zooming Nikkei index made it attractive. But what kind of reliable financial information is available to the prudent investor anxious to follow the history and prospects of his investment?

Disclosure requirements for Japanese companies

All Japanese companies in which the foreign investor might own shares are subject to the Commercial Code. The underlying objective of financial statements prepared in accordance with Commercial Code requirements is to protect creditors and current investors. Accordingly, disclosures relating to availability of funds for dividends, creditworthiness and earning power are emphasised. The statements and supporting schedules, prepared only in Japanese, include a single year parent-company-only balance sheet, income statement and proposal for appropriation of retained earnings. A business report, similar to the financial review found in the annual reports of US companies, is also included. The financial statements and business report are available to stockholders, but is not distributed to them automatically, prior to the annual general meeting, which must be held within three months after the close of the fiscal year (most commonly 31 March in Japan.) After approval by the AGM, the financial statements are filed with MoF and a condensed balance sheet and income statement must be published in a newspaper.

In contrast with the Commercial Code requirements, companies subject to the Securities and Exchange Law are required to supply financial reports and other pertinent operating disclosures which are orientated more toward general investors. These companies include all those listed on Japanese stock exchanges and, as a result, probably include all those companies in which foreigners are likely to invest. As the accounting principles are the same for Commercial Code reports and SEL reports, net income and earnings per share as reported will be the same but considerably more information will be available in the SEL report, including consolidated financial statements which must be filed as an attachment. All financial statements in the Securities Reports, which the SEL reports are called, including the consolidated financial statements, must be accompanied by an auditors' report issued by an independent CPA or an audit corporation.

Further, in accordance with SEL rules, a semi-annual Securities Report is required to be submitted to the exchange and MoF within three months of the end of the first half of the fiscal year. This report is fairly condensed in comparison with the Securities Report. The semi-annual report is subject to limited audit by an independent CPA, in accordance with procedures specified by the Business Accounting Deliberation Council, an advisory body to MoF.

In addition, in certain circumstances, a supplementary Securities Report is required to be submitted to MoF under the following circumstances:

1. When the company issues new stock, bonds or warrants outside Japan with a value of more than ¥100 million.
2. When a principal shareholder or a significant subsidiary changes.
3. When the company is seriously damaged by a disaster.

The above reports are not sent to shareholders but made available at MoF, company headquarters or the exchange.

Information available in the English language

Unfortunately for the foreign investor, all of the above Securities Reports are prepared only in Japanese. However, some Japanese companies prepare English language annual reports which contain the consolidated financial statements foreign investors are accustomed to seeing – the balance sheet, statements of income and changes in shareholders' equity, and the statement of changes in financial position or cash flows (which is not included in Japanese financial statements), all in comparative form – as well as enhanced footnotes. If the companies have previously issued ADRs in the English language, financial statements will be prepared in accordance with the US GAAP in order to fulfil requirements of the US SEC. Companies which have issued bonds in the Euromarket prepare their English language financial statements in the US style, but in accordance with Japanese GAAP. Approximately 1,800 companies, about 30% of listed Japanese companies, prepare an English language version of their financial statements and annual reports.

Furthermore, it is common for Japanese companies to prepare a supplementary brochure in English which gives the company's history, describes its main products, gives a directors' profile, and contains a brief explanation about operations of subsidiary companies. The financial statements are rarely included in such a brochure; but some financial data like trend of sales for the last five years and trend of capital stocks are usually included.

Information available from Japanese securities companies

Leading Japanese securities companies provide several publications in English to fund managers abroad in order to invite equity investment in Japanese companies.

Those publications include the following:

Investment Report

This report is prepared periodically in the English language by securities companies in order to explain economic trends in Japan, business trends, foreign exchange rates, monetary conditions, etc. This report generally also includes information about market activity and market statistical data.

Investment brief

Written in English, this publication provides general information about a recommended company. It includes a short profile of the company and business trends of its industry group. Comments on future prospects of the company are also included. Statistical data such as sales breakdown, business trends, operating profit, net profit, and dividends for the last three or four years, are included.

Follow-up report

This report provides further information about the recommended company. The report addresses the business background or trend of the particular industry group of the company, the business trends of this company for the last seven years, explanation of its business plan or future projections, financial statements for the last two years, and price trends of the company's stock for the last two and half years.

Foreign exchange controls

Non-residents who purchase securities in Japan are required to inform MoF in advance that their purchases are for personal investment portfolios, unless the investing is carried out through authorised securities companies or other specific exemptions are obtained.

CHAPTER TWENTY-SEVEN

Tokyo's potential as a financial centre

by C. Tait Ratcliffe
President, International Business Information

Once described as a 'fragile blossom', following the first oil crisis, Japan has shown a strong ability to adapt to severe shocks and to continue to build its position as an industrial and financial power. Since the early 1980s, Japan has moved from having a deficit in its current account to becoming the world's largest exporter of capital. Barring stoppages of raw material supplies, Japan's position as supplier of capital and Tokyo's standing as a financial centre will continue to rise.

Only four or five years ago, talk of the possibility of Tokyo becoming a leading financial centre would have met with some scepticism, and any suggestion of Tokyo being the world's *leading* financial centre would have been regarded as quite optimistic. After all, as recently as 1980, Japan was running a deficit in its current account as it struggled to pay for oil costing more than US$30 a barrel.

Since the early 1980s, Japan has shown a strong ability not only to adapt, but also to move out in front in many areas. Looking at the current account balance alone, Japan has moved from a deficit of US$10.7 billion in calendar 1980 to a surplus of US$86 billion in calendar 1986. Over the same period, the long-term capital balance moved from a net inflow of US$2.3 billion to a net outflow of US$131.8 billion – more money than any country has ever placed overseas in a single year.

Assisted by a strong dollar and a weak yen during the first half of the 1980s, many Japanese industries moved to consolidate their international positions in strategic industrial sectors, particularly in electrical and electronic equipment. Drawing on the strengths of a business system that encourages long-term planning and acquisition of a leading market share internationally, and on the advantages of cooperative business and government relationships, many Japanese industries have taken internationally dominant shares in strategic markets. And, until the sharp appreciation of the yen beginning in 1985, many Japanese companies remained virtually unchallenged by foreign competition in the home market.

By 1984, it had become clear that the Japanese industrial establishment had developed a money-generator likely to be more powerful and long-lasting than Opec. Japan's trade balance exceeded US$44 billion in 1984, and net capital outflows rose close to US$50 billion.

An equally important development, of far-reaching significance, was the emergence of signs that Japan's invisible trade balance deficit was beginning to decline. During the post-war period, Japan had usually run a deficit in its invisibles account as Japanese companies paid more to foreigners for insurance and shipping services than was received in income from overseas investments and other sources. But the rise in overseas investments, both in plant and equipment and in securities, began to bring a higher inflow of earnings to offset payments for insurance and freight. The invisibles deficit dropped from US$13.6 billion in calendar 1981 to US$7.7 billion in 1984, and then to US$4.6 billion in calendar 1986.

As forecasts of the OECD and international banking institutions suggest, even with a strong yen Japan's current account surplus in US dollar terms will decline more slowly than hoped for. At the same time, the outflow of long-term capital will continue, leading to a further reduction in the invisibles deficit.

In contrast, the United States is on a course to become a debtor nation of unheard of proportions. Even strong measures in the US to reduce fiscal and current account deficits are likely to take four to five years to succeed. Japan will be the principal foreign financier of this external debt of the US.

Forecasts of where these trends will lead differ in detail, but the magnitudes and implications are similar. By the early 1990s, Japan may have net external assets of US$500 billion. The United States may well have net external liabilities of between US$700 billion and US$1 trillion. The attitudes and apparent strategies of Japanese securities companies and institutional investors are already having a significant effect on the placement of US Treasury bonds and on dollar interest rates. This influence could increase by a significant order of magnitude by the early 1990s.

In addition, a very rough calculation suggests the United States may be paying over US$60 billion a year in interest charges to foreigners holding its debt by the late 1980s. Thus, if Japanese investors hold only half the external debt of the US, Japan's current account may still be in surplus, even if Japanese industry loses some of its ability to compete and if the trade surplus is eliminated.

The potential

A comparison of the world's three major financial centres suggests Tokyo has some important strengths that may enable it to move into a leading position. These include a large and growing base of domestic savings, a basically strong domestic economy that is likely to adapt to the effects of a stronger yen, and important social underpinnings that will support the development of a sophisticated financial centre.

One of Tokyo's principal strengths is the large volume of monetary assets in the economy. Recent estimates put total monetary assets at ¥600 trillion, growing at about 8 per cent annually. One of the principal factors leading to this large volume of liquidity has been the consistently high rate of personal savings in Japan. Despite a decline from more than 20 per cent in the 1970s, the savings rate from household incomes remains well above 15 per cent.

Other indicators of the size of Tokyo's financial muscle include the total outstandings in financial markets. According to estimates made in late 1986, Tokyo's financial market size stood at the equivalent of US$1.5 trillion, compared with US$2 trillion in the US. The figure for Japan was about three times that of West Germany. The Japan offshore market, which began in late 1986, has expanded to US$130 billion as of the end of March 1987, already rivalling Hong Kong and Singapore in size.

The large volume of liquidity in Tokyo is in part responsible for some of the remarkable statistics. For example:

- the average price/earnings ratio on the Tokyo Stock Exchange in late 1986 was 60 times, far above those of other markets;
- the total market valuation of Tokyo Electric exceeds that of the exchanges of Hong Kong, Singapore and Sydney combined; and
- the total market value of Nippon Telegraph & Telephone exceeds that of IBM, AT&T, Exxon, General Electric and General Motors combined.

There are no changes in the offing which appear likely to reduce the savings rate in Japan or to lower significantly the volume of monetary resources available in Japan. If the yen continues to strengthen in the medium term, the overseas purchasing power of Japan's monetary assets will rise, contributing to Japan's potential as a capital exporter.

Some discussions of the future of Tokyo as a financial centre link its eventual position to Japan's current account surplus. The argument goes that the current account surplus enables Japan to export its liquidity. If Japan became less competitive, this would place a limit on Japan's role in providing financial resources to the rest of the world. In fact, this linkage appears to be weaker than many suppose. From 1984 to 1986, Japan reported growing trade and current account surpluses, but exports of net long-term capital have far exceeded these surpluses. In 1986, Japan's overall balance, after net long-term and short-term outflows, was US$44.8 billion in deficit.

This means that foreigners have a willingness to accept yen assets. Until the early 1990s, the United States will be occupied with the task of regaining its international competitiveness and its ability to pay its way internationally. The yen may very well remain attractive to international investors and even become more so as the US moves further into debt. At least in the medium term, yen assets seem likely to be in demand, and Japan can continue to run an overall balance of payments deficit, providing the world with liquidity.

Tokyo compared with London and New York

Besides a large base of domestic savings, what other features characterise Tokyo? A brief comparison with London and New York highlights these factors.

London, as the centre of the Euromarket, handles a massive volume of international transactions. The focus of operations of large UK institutions and foreign institutions in London is providing international services. The domestic market for financial services in the UK is much smaller than in the US and Japan, but London has a secure position because of the drawing power of international banks and securities houses either based there or with substantial operations there. The institutions, the personnel, the communications infrastructure, and the location of London in the highly industrialised European time zones all attract business to London and make it, by most indications at present, the largest international financial centre.

What would happen if another major city in Europe offered similar advantages? Ignoring the costs of relocation, there is really no reason why most of the transactions now carried out in London might not be carried out in another equally well-equipped centre elsewhere in the European region. Although this is not likely to happen, the point is that the economy of the United Kingdom and sterling alone are not sufficient reasons for locating the world's largest international financial centre in London.

New York is in some ways the reverse of London. The domestic market in the United States is very large, and the US dollar is still the principal international currency. Providing financial services to corporations operating in the United States and financing the US government fully justify the existence of New York as a financial centre. An important difference compared with London is that the international component of business is a smaller percentage of the total. New York is the leading domestic financial centre for the world's largest economy. International activities take place on a large scale, but are secondary to domestic activities.

Tokyo at present is rather more similar to New York than to London. Japan has a large domestic market for financial services. The largest part of operations of leading Japanese financial institutions is still domestic, even though they have built up substantial international banking and securities businesses. If anything, the emergence of large volumes of liquidity in Tokyo has shifted the attention of Japanese financial institutions back to their domestic market and promoted the links between their domestic and overseas offices.

Another important difference between New York and London on the one hand and Tokyo on the other is the extent and pace of deregulation. New York, and the US market in general, is highly deregulated compared with Tokyo. The US has already experienced and made adjustments to the deregulation of interest rates, equity commissions and other measures that Japan has yet to adopt to the same extent.

In part, as a result of deregulation, the role of foreign financial institutions in the US economy is substantially larger than in Tokyo. In the United States, foreign banks and securities companies, some of them Japanese, own major US institutions. Leading Japanese commercial banks, for example, have operations in California that rank within the top 20 institutions in that state. Two Japanese institutions are already primary dealers in US government securities, one directly and the other through the acquisition of a US primary dealer.

potential of the Tokyo market, training of the personnel needed and larger investments in the infrastructure to curb runaway real estate costs.

Continued deregulation appears to be one of the central requirements for further development of the market. Some of the main areas for consideration are:

1. Expansion of the types and volume of short-term financial instruments available to domestic and foreign investors.

2. Expansion in the availability of futures and options instruments. The bond futures market, which began operations in late 1985, has shown explosive growth because it plays an important role in helping investors to hedge the risks of their large portfolios of government bonds.

3. Futher deregulation of interest rates is another requirement. As Paul Hofer, Chairman of the Institute of Foreign Bankers in Tokyo, stated in a speech in February 1987: 'I have watched the process of deregulation in Tokyo now for more than five years. I think the monetary authorities have taken major strides toward deregulation. But one difference I detect in the process of deregulation is greater emphasis on survival and soundness of even smaller institutions in Japan. The two Samurai principles, "Work for long-term survival" and "Cooperate with the authorities", seem to come into play here. The process of liberalisation in Japan has been, in my view, a brilliant job of defending and protecting the interests of Japanese financial institutions. Every change has been made carefully and orchestrated to prevent disruption and to nurture Japanese institutions into strong domestic and international players.'

This is another clear example of the private and government sectors working together in Japan. If we refrain from making any value judgements, we can at least say the approach to deregulation in Japan is different from the emphasis in Europe and the United States. There, the thrust of deregulation has been to use competitive forces to increase market efficiency and stimulate market growth. In Japan, domestic interests are very carefully weighed and the final decision need not represent a victory for efficiency in the short to medium term. The fact that Japanese corporations have issued more bonds in international capital markets in recent years than in the domestic market is eloquent testimony to the rigidity of rules in Japan. Also reflecting the priority placed on domestic interests is the fact that Euroyen financial instruments have been deregulated far more rapidly than domestic yen instruments.

At present, many foreign banks are reducing their loans outstanding to Japanese corporations and are emphasising marketing of fee-based services. This is in strong contrast to the strategies of Japanese banks in the United States as they continue to build strong relationships, including credit exposure. Foreign banks in Japan would be in a stronger position to expand their loan portfolios if they had access to yen funding at rates competitive with Japanese banks.

In addition to further deregulation, another requirement appears to be generating a stronger consensus on the potential of the market. Numerous instances can be cited where decisions on deregulation could probably have been speeded up significantly if development of Tokyo as an international financial centre had received higher priority over purely domestic concerns.

Recruitment and training of personnel

The third major requirement appears to be increased emphasis on training of personnel. In rough terms, about 800,000 people are employed in the financial industry in New York, 500,000 in London, and only 170,000 in Tokyo. Given the current size and potential of the market, personnel will have to be trained very quickly to keep pace with the growth of the market. Looking at the foreign securities companies alone, 36 have branch licences, and by the end of 1987 or early 1988, another 30 will apply for licences. These newcomers all have plans for expansion, in some cases for raising the number of staff in Tokyo by multiples of three or four. As these figures suggest, the issue of personnel has already become important, as the sharp rise in salaries suggests, and is likely to become even more prevalent in the years ahead.

Cost of real estate
Another very practical problem is to provide for sufficient office space in the Tokyo area to curb rapidly rising land costs. In mid-1987, the rental costs of prime office space had risen sharply compared to only a few years earlier and were substantially higher than rents in London and New York. The rate of office vacancies in Tokyo stood at only 0.2 per cent, essentially zero for all intents and purposes. Estimates by leading banks and real estate companies suggest that by the year 2000, an additional 10 million square metres of office space will be needed, but even if all the ambitious development projects now in progress or planned are carried out, only 7 million to 8 million square metres in new space can be made available.

The pitfalls

The rise of Tokyo to the position of the world's premier financial centre in the coming years will also not be without pitfalls for Japan. Two of the most significant of these will be the accompanying rise in Japan's international political position and overseas reactions to Japan's success, not only in strategic industrial sectors, but now also in financial services.

With Tokyo as the leading financial centre by the early 1990s and the leading creditor of the United States – which has become the world's largest debtor – the potential for friction appears likely to rise rather than diminish. As C. Fred Bergsten pointed out in *Economic Imbalances and World Politics* (*Foreign Affairs*, Spring 1987), '... with America as massive debtor and Japan as massive creditor, [this] will pose major challenges to global management in both the economic and political spheres. In both areas a newly pluralistic world power structure must be arranged, with a revised leadership role for America – perhaps using its security position to pursue economic goals – and an increasing leadership role for Japan. The only precedent dates from the 1920s, when Anglo-American cooperation attempted but ultimately failed to reconcile the decline of Britain and the rise of the United States, due to the unwillingness of both countries to understand and adapt to their new positions. The new Administration in 1989 will have to address these matters with highest urgency.'

It is to be hoped, however, that Japan can direct its capabilities for adaptation to assume its new responsibilities in the world economy.

Another pitfall may be a phenomenon observed in recent years, but which with each incidence seems to become more intense. The emergence of Tokyo as the leading financial centre is bound to create resentment. This resentment will be all the sharper because of the basic difference between government and business interaction in Japan and elsewhere. In Japan, business and government generally cooperate to attain economic objectives and, particularly in the financial sector, the government has taken special pains to look after the interests of private financial institutions. In the US and Europe, considerations of competition and efficiency have often taken precedence over careful supervision and nurturing of individual financial institutions. As Japan and Japanese financial institutions have risen to pre-eminence internationally, the feeling has grown that these two systems may be incompatible. Other countries may therefore adopt a more protective role to assure that competition is conducted on a more or less level playing field. From the Japanese point of view, this may imply the need to examine and reconsider the ambitions of Japan as a country and the ambitions of Japanese corporations, to permit smoother adjustment to Japan's growing role.

When the newness of Japan as number one in finance begins to wear off, a sobering realisation will emerge, hopefully, that Japan now has massive responsibilities for revitalising not only its own economy but also the economies of Europe and the United States and to promote the continued development of the industrialising nations. The challenge for Tokyo will be enormous. The cooperation and assistance of financial institutions, governments and other interests around the world will be essential for Tokyo's continued success.

Sponsors

CIBC

CIBC structures itself for global competition

CIBC is the 10th largest bank in North America with assets in excess of C$85 billion, employing some 33,900 people in more than 1,600 branches, offices, agencies and subsidiaries in 23 countries. CIBC has a particularly strong presence in North America. In Canada, it has the largest market share of corporate business. In the United States, independent market research shows that CIBC is one of the most effective foreign banks in market penetration of the corporate sector. It is from this base that our strategic thrust has been made.

Adapting to meet global needs

With the rapid advance in deregulation of the banking and securities industry in Canada, CIBC has structured itself to be a vigorous global competitor in both fields.

Commercial banking has to adapt to an environment of securitisation. Many commercial banks have sought ways of enhancing their capability in this field. CIBC addressed this challenge directly in 1986, when it reorganised itself into three distinctly focused and managed business units.

Individual Bank, CIBC is responsible for servicing CIBC's four million retail customers. Corporate Bank, CIBC is responsible for maintaining CIBC's corporate relationships and for performing the credit function for the bank. Investment Bank, CIBC is responsible for providing the necessary transactional capability in the capital markets that will enable CIBC to meet the investment banking needs of all its clients.

The separate structure of each business unit, each with its own management team and allocated capital, enables it to concentrate directly on the specific requirements of its mandate. As a result, Investment Bank, CIBC was able to create an organisational and cultural environment suited to investment banking.

Because of these initiatives taken in 1986, Investment Bank, CIBC now has a substantial global investment banking operation with a total complement of around 1,000 people. It has offices throughout Canada and in major centres around the world and has established a merchant banking joint venture, Gordon Investment Corporation, with Gordon Capital Corporation.

Major dealing rooms around the world

State-of-the-art major dealing rooms have been installed in London, Tokyo and Toronto. A new dealing room in New York will be completed shortly. These are supported by satellite dealing rooms strategically located throughout the world, which have all been completed within the last two years.

CIBC's headquarters building in Toronto.

Paul Cantor, President of Investment Bank, CIBC.

Product specialisation

Investment Bank, CIBC has a focused approach to investment banking where it specialises in a number of fields. Wherever we have created strengths in a local market, we have also built a network allowing the bank to deliver these products or services globally.

In the Americas, Investment Bank, CIBC has specialised in the following areas:

- public and private debt of governments and corporates;
- domestic money market investments;
- foreign exchange;
- bullion;
- swaps and other risk management products;
- mergers and acquisitions; and
- corporate finance.

These products and services are also delivered internationally through Investment Bank, CIBC's global network which extends across Europe, Asia and Australasia.

In 1988, discount brokerage and mutual funds will be offered in Canada.

In addition, the following products and services sourced from Europe, Asia and Australasia are offered through this global network:
- fixed-rate government debt;
- fixed-rate Eurobonds with a bias towards Canadian and Australian dollar securities;
- floating-rate securities and money market instruments;
- loans and credit facilities;
- investment management; and
- stockbroking and equity underwriting.

While we have altered our organisational structure radically to meet current and future changes, we remain true to our heritage. Our basic strategy is to provide access for our Canadian clients to major markets in the world. Conversely, Investment Bank, CIBC seeks to provide our areas of speciality to our international clients. The mechanism for achieving this aim is the effective interplay between the three separate business units that make up CIBC. Separately the three business units are focused on their specific roles, together they provide the most professional answer to our clients' needs.

Working with Japan

The emergence of Japan as the largest net exporter of capital has had profound implications for participants in the global financial community. Canada has been a significant beneficiary of Japanese capital export in plant and production facilities, and in investment in Canadian dollar-denominated securities. The realignment of CIBC into three separate business units has enhanced the bank's ability to satisfy these requirements.

In Tokyo, CIBC is represented by both Corporate Bank, CIBC and Investment Bank, CIBC which, while having separate functions, nevertheless work as an integrated force. In Japan, Corporate Bank, CIBC's activities focus on

Government finance team in Toronto. Right to left: Leon Lambert, VP; Barry Bruce, SVP; Geoff Browne, SVP; Hank Cunningham, VP.

Tokyo senior management: John Welch, VP Japan (left) and Lowery Christie, VP Asia (right).

the bank's North American strengths in order to capitalise on the ever increasing business activity between Japan, Canada, and the United States. Concomitant with this objective is the creation of a strong presence in the local domestic wholesale lending markets of Japan.

In Japan our investment banking activities are primarily focused on delivering Canadian dollar-based products and services to Japanese clients. Our secondary objective is the development of capabilities in yen-based products.

Working closely with its counterparts in Toronto and London, the Tokyo office makes two-way prices in a comprehensive list of public domestic Canadian and Euro securities. Complementing this business is CIBC's promotion of private placements with the major Japanese life and trust companies.

In conjunction with these capital market activities, CIBC in Tokyo is at the forefront of Canadian dollar-related interest rate and currency swaps. This Tokyo-based capability enables CIBC to play an active role in swaps transactions in conjunction with new international issues for Japanese borrowers. CIBC has also developed a significant foreign exchange capability in Tokyo. In line with the overall strategy of CIBC, the bias of this foreign exchange activity is toward the Canadian dollar.

With regard to yen securities, CIBC was recently admitted as a foreign bank underwriter in the Government of Japan bond underwriting syndicate. As a consequence of this, CIBC was also invited to join the select group of banks which receive tender invitations in the regular auction of medium-term bonds.

Working throughout Asia and Australasia

CIBC's position in Japan has to be seen in the broader context of Asia and Australasia.

In Hong Kong, where CIBC has had a presence for 15 years, CIBC and the prestigious Cheung Kong Group have established a joint venture, CEF Capital Limited. CEF Capital Limited's activities include the underwriting of securities for local and international borrowers, mergers and acquisitions and portfolio management for high net worth individuals. Aware of the importance of Japan's capital flows to Asia, CIBC is intimately involved both directly and through CEF Capital Limited with many major Japanese projects in the region.

Completing CIBC's Asian link is CIBC Asia Limited, a merchant bank based in Singapore which is well positioned to service clients in this region's financial markets.

Australasia, like Canada, is expanding its trading and investment links with Japan and the rest of Asia. CIBC has a substantial presence in Australia where it operates through CIBC Australia Limited, a wholly-owned investment banking subsidiary, and in partnership with the Melbourne-based stockbroker D & D – Tolhurst. In New Zealand the bank operates through a wholly-owned investment banking subsidiary, CIBC New Zealand Limited. In Australasia, CIBC provides a broad range of investment banking products and services. Internationally the bank markets Australian dollar-denominated products.

The strategic initiatives taken in 1986 have allowed CIBC to build on its strong Canadian and international foundations so that today it functions as a strong competitor in the world's financial markets.

CIBC's new dealing room in London.

Chase Manhattan Bank: A new strategy for a new age

Under the leadership of Chairman Bill Butcher, Chase has broadened its activities from being a major lending institution to embracing all facets of financial engineering worldwide. And the development of Chase's activities in Japan epitomises the success of that global strategy.

'We've proved our ability to harness technology and an international banking network to add value to our traditional services and in so doing re-energised our ability to compete very effectively in this market', says Robert Binney, Country Manager responsible for all of Chase's activities in Japan. 'We've chosen our clients carefully, focused our resources and as a result, we're expanding our market share.'

Central to Chase's renewed thrust are four core businesses that have successfully been put in place. These are:

- **Investment banking;**
- **Securities trading and distribution;**
- **Trust banking and funds management; and**
- **Commercial banking.**

1987 marks Chase's 40th year in Japan and a year that represents the completion of the shift in strategy which began to take shape four years ago.

With these four pillars of its operation in Japan, Chase is uniquely placed to help overseas businesses – especially US and European – access Japan's capital markets, as well as helping cash-rich Japanese corporations and institutions to invest overseas.

Chase's extensive global banking network and strong client relationships puts it in a very strong position to compete head on with Japanese banks which, although powerful, lack Chase's international network and strong client base.

Management integrates strategy to meet the competition head-on.

Chairman Bill Butcher embraces all facets of financial engineering worldwide.

INVESTMENT BANKING

A full range of services

The first core is an investment banking capability, through which Chase provides a full range of investment banking services, both to clients in Japan and to the increasing number of overseas clients seeking to tap Tokyo's capital markets. Through Chase's long-standing institutional relationships in Japan, Chase is able to seek out investors for paper of all kinds.

The Chase investment banking arm has established itself as a leader in a number of fields, particularly in leasing, private placements, swaps, and Eurocommercial paper. In addition, Chase has boosted its trading and distribution capability through the securities trading licence recently awarded to Chase Securities.

'We are amongst the most active players in Japan in several products – swaps and Eurocommercial paper are prime examples. In addition, we pioneered the Japanese leverage lease and also were the first to introduce commodity swaps into this market', says Senior Managing Director, Hasan Askari, who heads up Chase's investment banking operations in Japan.

In Japan, the investment bank has focused its resources on meeting the emerging investment banking needs of Chase's traditional wholesale banking client base. This focus is underscored by Chase's international organisation, with both product specialists in the Investment Bank and the wholesale bank's client executives (who manage all relationships) reporting directly to Askari.

'Over the years', says Michael Zavelle, Chase Investment Bank's Managing Director for Corporate Finance, 'we have built up strong relationships with many of Japan's leading corporations and financial institutions. There is a great respect for the Chase name in this market. We think relationships are important, and we manage our business on a relationship basis.'

'Traditionally', says Zavelle, 'investment banks have tended to be deal oriented and wholesale banks relationship oriented. We have structured our business to offer our clients the benefits of both.'

Two of the key products in which Chase takes a leading role are Eurocommercial paper and Eurobond underwriting.

Chase's strong position in the Eurocommercial paper market has powered it into an unrivalled position with its Japanese clients. Of the 18 Japanese corporations to launch EuroCP programmes in 1986, six chose Chase as a dealer and two as a lead dealer.

In Eurobond underwriting during 1986, Chase was in the management group or an underwriter for 100 Japanese issues in the public and private markets, including five lead management positions. One-third of all Eurobond issues made by Japanese borrowers found Chase in the management group. In turn, one-third of Chase's fund raisings in this area were equity related, either as equity warrant bonds or as convertibles.

'The equity area is one in which we have been placing increasing emphasis', says Zavelle. 'Due to our purchase of Laurie Milbank and Simon & Coates in London and their merger into Chase Manhattan Securities, our equity capabilities worldwide have expanded rapidly.'

The appetite for sophisticated financial products in Japan has also led to exceptional growth for Chase in the less publicly visible product areas of swaps, private placements, leasing, and mergers and acquisitions.

Chase's strong position in swaps comes from the funding book of the entire bank. 'That is why we can efficiently do some of the more exotic swap transactions, such as amortising internal rate of return swaps, that other financial institutions cannot', says Director Mary Ginsberg, who heads up this activity. 'Positions taken in Tokyo are put in the global book, which is passed around the world as each market opens.'

A global book enables Chase to take wider gaps and absorb much wider mismatches than competitors, who operate only local books. Using a global book also enables Chase to quote firm prices in Tokyo on currencies such as the Canadian dollar, for example, even though the Canadian market may be closed. Chase's ability to quote firm prices in Tokyo applies, also, to all other major currencies.

'Private placement activity at Chase is growing rapidly', says Director Tag Murphy. 'Last year we placed over US$1 billion in this market. This year we expect to double last year's figure. We have a good knowledge of the market, particularly the leasing industry, where we have been a leading player since the industry began to look offshore for investment opportunities. Of transactions placed by foreign institutions within the leasing industry, for example, our market share is 40 to 45 per cent. In addition, we have rapidly developed our placing power with the major Japanese life insurance companies.'

The emerging mergers and acquisitions business evident in Japan is perfectly suited to an investment bank like Chase, which has a superior global network and long-standing expertise.

As buy-side mandates are rare in Japan, Chase tends to look for likely acquisitions first, and then match them up with Japanese buyers. The businesses Japanese corporations are most interested in buying into are electronics companies, hi-technology businesses such as factory automation industries and, increasingly, pharmaceutical companies.

'This is where Chase's practice of building up industry by industry expertise gives us an advantage', says Managing Director Kazuo Hayakawa, who is responsible for Chase's mergers and acquisitions business. 'When the field of search is industry specific and in more than one location, as in the pharmaceuticals industry, you could be looking as easily in Europe as the US. In a search of this kind, we are able to draw on our global network and our industry expertise to identify possible candidates. We also benefit from our having a large client base in middle market companies.'

Left: Chet Brauch provides a crucial third link to global securities trading. Right: Robert Binney heads the integrated effort to compete effectively in the Japanese market.

SECURITIES TRADING AND DISTRIBUTION

Key link in 24-hour trading

Chase's second core business is securities trading and distribution, where, now that a securities licence is held by its securities subsidiary in Tokyo, a global network is in place.

Along with Chase's operations in New York and London, the Tokyo office adds the crucial third link to the chain, enabling the group to trade securities globally on a 24-hour basis.

'We can now act as principals, broaden our client base and deepen our product range', says the head of the Tokyo securities operation, Senior Vice President Chet Brauch. 'We expect to be very active in yen securities, US government securities, Eurosecurities, equities and gilts, and we also expect to bring to the Japanese marketplace Chase's worldwide capabilities.'

Left: Ed Cooper maintains the successful position in commercial banking. Right: Hasan Askari offers the benefits of both wholesale and investment banking.

At present, Chase operates in 18 different securities markets around the world, and the bank's objective is to bring all of these securities into place for Japanese portfolio managers.

'In the old environment we were limited to doing business with Japan's largest institutions', says Brauch. 'With the licence we will be able to approach anyone.'

Chase Manhattan Securities Japan also expects to benefit from, and in turn further expand, Chase's custodian business, the largest of any foreign institution in Japan.

As one of the first three foreign institutions licensed to deal in yen government bonds, gaining a securities licence will also broaden the range of business Chase can carry out, with a variety of yen-based products such as municipals, bank debentures and convertibles targeted.

Chase Manhattan Securities Japan will also emerge as a force in underwriting as well, rounding out the present activities of Chase Investment Bank in London and Chase Manhattan Asia Limited in Hong Kong, which are already active as underwriters of Japanese bond issues.

TRUST BANKING AND FUND MANAGEMENT

Leveraging for market differentiation

The third core business in place is investment mediation in the form of a licensed trust bank and the fund management capabilities of Chase Investors Management Corporation in New York.

Established in 1985, Chase Manhattan Trust and Banking Co (Japan) Ltd is already outperforming its own ambitious financial targets. According to Senior Managing Director Kohji Hijikata, being a subsidiary of a commercial bank gives Chase Trust an advantage shared by only one of its established Japanese rivals, and it is already leveraging that association, to gain market differentiation.

One such leveraging of its commercial banking franchise was the pioneering of the securitisation of loans booked by Chase's commercial bank, packaging them, and passing them on as investments to Trust Bank clients. So, at a stroke, the commercial bank improves its balance sheet, and the Trust Bank books new business.

'We were the first to do this', says Hijikata. 'Last year we did more than US$100 million of business in these securitisations.'

Chase is looking for similar synergy to drive the trust bank's investment management business. 'Chase already has within its worldwide operations the elements we need for a very good investment management business. I want to incorporate these capabilities in Japan.'

COMMERCIAL BANKING

Key to success

The fourth component of Chase's strategy is in the traditional commercial banking arena, in the form of international payments, trade finance, foreign exchange and global custody. In each of these, Chase can justifiably claim a top-line reputation.

Traditionally, Chase in Japan has been a major participant in the foreign exchange markets and a major provider of trade finance services, especially US dollar letters of credit. Today, Chase is the largest foreign bank in the yen/US dollar foreign exchange market in Tokyo. The market has grown very rapidly since the 1984 liberalisation of the Tokyo foreign exchange market by the Ministry of Finance.

In the fields of international payments and global custody, Chase Japan is in a unique position. Chase is, by far, the largest provider of US dollar funds transfer services to the Japanese banking industry. Recently Chase Japan was named as the only foreign bank to participate in a pilot of the Bank of Japan's next round of automation for yen payments processing. Dominance in the US dollar payments field was achieved, as least in part, due to Chase's development of a micro-based funds transfer system which operates entirely in the Japanese language. 'We have achieved levels of processing accuracy and efficiency unmatched in the industry', says Ed Cooper, Deputy General Manager for Service Products. 'Successful implementation of the enhanced yen processing system will give Chase Japan a multicurrency processing capability unrivalled by any competitor in any market.'

Global custody entails the provision of custodial services in Tokyo, covering both debt securities and equity instruments. The ultimate owners of these securities are principally North American and European investors, particularly pension funds and insurance companies, who use Chase Tokyo to safekeep their yen-denominated securities. Chase is the largest foreign bank in this business in Tokyo.

Maintaining Chase's successful position in commercial banking will form a key part of Chase's long-term success.

Conclusion

'In the face of severe Japanese competition, many of our foreign competitors have taken the view that they want to get out of the commercial banking business and concentrate entirely on investment banking', says Robert Binney, Chase Japan's Country Manager. 'Our view is that there are very real advantages for our clients in our ability to provide a wider range of financial solutions. Our experience over the past three years has proved that there is a synergy between investment banking and commercial banking, and that you can make money in both.'

The advanced Tokyo trading room adds value to traditional services through technology.

Left to right:
Peter Castenfelt,
Deputy Chairman,
Cresvale Partners;
Pierre Moussa,
Chairman,
Cresvale Partners;
Ephraim Margulies,
Co-Chairman,
Cresvale Partners;
Steven Burnham,
President,
Cresvale Partners.

James Foster,
Director, Cresvale Partners.

Malcolm Stevenson,
Director, Cresvale Partners.

Paul Taylor,
Director, Cresvale Partners.

Harry Wiltshire,
Director, Cresvale Partners.

London trading room.

Cresvale today

The Cresvale companies are leading specialists in the international equity and equity-linked securities market. The basic business is market making, which is complemented by a strong sales capacity.

The operating companies which make the Cresvale group are Cresvale Limited in London, which has also opened a representative office in Tokyo, Cresvale International Inc in New York and Cresvale (Far East) Limited in Hong Kong. The group has approximately 170 employees.

In July 1987, Pallas Group SA, a Luxembourg-based holding company, joined with S. & W. Berisford PLC and the senior management and employees of the Cresvale companies to form Cresvale Partners SA. Cresvale Partners is the new Luxembourg-based holding company of the Cresvale group which is now fully geared to take advantage of the growing opportunities in an expanding market for equity and equity-related products. Pierre Moussa and Peter Castenfelt of Pallas have joined the Cresvale Partners Board of Directors as Chairman and Deputy-Chairman respectively.

The group is committed and well placed to continue its expansion. Its future plans fall into two main categories: the continued growth of the group's core business and, from this base, entry into other areas of the international securities business.

As the market in convertible bonds and equity warrants has developed, Cresvale has expanded its operations. Over the last five years, growth in the international equity-linked securities market has been exceptionally strong. The nominal value of Japanese and American Eurodollar equity-linked securities issued in 1982 was just over US$1bn. By 1986 the nominal value of new issues had reached US$14bn. Not only is the market growing, it is also diversifying in terms of the products available. During the first half of 1987, there were 19 new Eurosterling convertible bonds issued by UK companies. There was also an increasing awareness among investors of the attractiveness of European equity warrants.

Cresvale is committed to making markets in equity-related securities and believes that, as the market develops, profitable opportunities will increase. Cresvale has made sure that it is able to keep in touch with developments in this market, and is now looking to diversify into new markets and new products, where its management skills can generate further profitability. At the same time Cresvale will remain cautious in its approach to risk management.

STRENGTH OF CRESVALE INVESTMENT BANKING

SALES AND TRADING

With its offices well located in time zones, Cresvale is well positioned to operate in international financial markets.

Cresvale has developed a highly sophisticated and successful international trading and sales network. Market making in over 800 equity-linked securities is complemented by a large salesforce which services a broad range of international clients.

Cresvale has a global book philosophy in its trading. Positions and customer orders are transferred from office to office in a well coordinated operation, allowing Cresvale to offer its entire client base a 24-hour service in all its products.

The international sales and trading activity of the group is coordinated by Paul Taylor, Managing Director of Cresvale Limited and a Director of Cresvale Partners.

OPERATIONS

Since its foundation, Cresvale has recognised the importance of its operations, finance and administration departments. It has always considered the relationship between trading and operations as a vital key in the successful running of the business. Cresvale has built up a strong internationally based team which provides the controls and management reporting procedures that are essential for the successful day-to-day running of the company. The team also ensures that current and planned expansion programmes develop in a well regulated manner and meet management's stringently imposed financial controls and objectives.

A further strengthening of Cresvale's operations department took place in May 1987, when a Group Treasurer was appointed.

Cresvale companies are members of Euroclear, Cedel and the Depository Trust Corporation.

James Foster is the Group Chief Financial Officer and is on the board of Cresvale Partners.

RESEARCH

Cresvale prides itself on producing professional research publications, geared to meet the needs of its large institutional client base, from its technical research departments located in London, New York, and Hong Kong. Cresvale clients have at their disposal a number of publications, ranging from weekly newsletters and a month-end pricing service to information booklets and quarterly chart books.

The research teams work in close cooperation with the salesforce. Salesmen are provided with regular investment ideas and strategies, supported by the latest charts and information. These views are quickly made available to clients of all the offices.

All the offices are linked by a computer network so that communications within the group can occur in the fastest and most efficient way possible.

Sarah Allen is Manager of International Research.

RESEARCH PUBLICATIONS

International Equity-Linked Securities – A Technical Perspective.
Tokyo Market Weekly; Convertibles/Warrants.
Guide to International Convertible Bonds and Warrants.
Japanese Euroconvertible Bond Chart Book.
American Euroconvertible Bond Chart Book.
European Euroconvertible Bond Chart Book.
Japanese Eurowarrant Chart Book.
A Guide to Japanese Eurowarrants.

CRESVALE LIMITED

Cresvale Limited is the largest operating company in the group. Over the years it has developed as the fastest-growing subsidiary, employing over 80 people, including a 40-strong trading and sales unit, servicing a large number of UK and European-based institutional clients. Cresvale Limited has an average monthly turnover in excess of £1 billion.

Cresvale Limited, well positioned in a time zone between New York and Tokyo, serves as the coordination centre for the management of market risk exposure. Trading and investment strategies are decided by Paul Taylor and his fellow directors, Peter Garrott and Andy Herbert.

CRESVALE INTERNATIONAL INC

Cresvale International Inc, the group's first venture overseas, opened in New York in 1981 as a natural extension of the successful London trading operation. The office is under the direction of Cliff Siegel, President.

Cresvale International joined the National Association of Security Dealers (NASD) in 1982. Now, in 1987, the company has achieved NASDAQ-listed market maker status, is a member of the New York and American Stock Exchanges and has become self-clearing in all transactions.

From its early strength as a broker/dealer in US and European convertibles, Cresvale International has recently expanded its activities in Far Eastern markets, in order to take advantage of the group expertise in those areas. Staff at its headquarters in New York now exceeds 35, with expansion occurring in the trading, sales and research departments, ensuring that Cresvale can fully benefit from the increasing internationalisation of the US securities market.

Peter Garrot, Director, Cresvale Limited.

Andy Herbert, Director, Cresvale Limited.

John Horsham, Specialist, Far East equity market, Associate Director, Cresvale Partners.

Hays Galleria, an exciting new building on the river Thames. Cresvale Limited moved here in late 1987.

CRESVALE FAR EAST LIMITED

Cresvale opened its Hong Kong office in May 1985, and since then has made considerable progress in the Far East. Cresvale Far East Limited now employs over 50 people and has obtained membership of the Unified Stock Exchange in Hong Kong through its wholly owned subsidiary, Cresvale Hong Kong Limited.

Cresvale Far East Limited acts as a market maker in Japanese and South East Asian Euroconvertible bonds and Japanese Eurowarrants. Additionally, capital is committed to running books in Hong Kong, Australian and Singapore shares. Recent expansion in both the trading and sales departments has been complemented by the addition of a research team and the introduction of a regular weekly market letter, which is distributed to Far Eastern clients.

Cresvale Far East Limited is well located to follow the Japanese market during local trading hours. Additionally it will serve as the base from which Cresvale is expanding its business in other South East Asian areas, namely Singapore, Malaysia, Australia and other South East Asian markets.

CRESVALE LIMITED TOKYO REPRESENTATIVE OFFICE

Cresvale Limited obtained permission from the Japanese Ministry of Finance to open a representative office in Tokyo in October 1986. The Tokyo office is working towards obtaining branch status and to employing a full complement of senior staff. The office plays a valuable role in disseminating information regarding Japanese companies and the Japanese economy to the other offices in the group. Should branch status be obtained, Cresvale plans to trade equity-related securities in Japan.

Len Kruse, Managing Director, Cresvale Far East Limited.

Cliff Siegel, President, Cresvale International Inc.

The Lloyds Bank Group in Japan

The Lloyds Bank Group has been present in Japan since 1970 when the first representative office of the Bank of London and South America Limited was opened.

A full banking and foreign exchange licence was obtained in 1973 in the name of Lloyds Bank International Limited, Tokyo Branch, and a second branch was opened in Osaka in 1981. The name of these branches was changed to Lloyds Bank Plc following the merger of Lloyds Bank International with its parent on 1 January 1986. The National Bank of New Zealand Limited, also now a member of the Lloyds Bank Group, has been in Japan since 1969, when its representative office was established.

Today, the Lloyds Bank Group in Japan is well positioned to offer a selected range of financial services to major Japanese financial institutions and industrial corporations, as well as to multinational corporations and other entities seeking access to the Japanese market. The services offered by Lloyds Bank in Japan are characterised by their quality and selectivity, with a high value-added content.

The evolution of the Tokyo market

During this long period of operating in Japan, personnel of the Lloyds Bank Group have been able to follow closely the many changes which the Tokyo financial markets have undergone over the last 10 years. More recently, the pace of change has accelerated to the point where revolution is perhaps a better word than evolution to describe this phenomenon. Changes in financial markets are always driven by changes in the economic environment which they service, and the financial services industry responds to its clients' changing needs. In turn, regulators are usually pulled along by these changes and even in Japan regulatory change can be characterised as only a recognition of the market's new realities based on the profound changes the Japanese enconomy is undergoing.

The single biggest fundamental changes in Japan's economic situation over the last 10 years has been the unprecedentedly rapid swing from being a major capital importer to becoming the single largest exporter of capital in the world today. The pace of this change has been accelerating, and most of it has occurred in the last three years. It is not a coincidence that the same period has also seen the most rapid liberalisation and expansion of the financial markets in Tokyo to the stage where it is poised to become one of the three major financial centres in the so-called global market place.

The most important liberalisation measures adopted by the Japanese authorities during this time have been the liberalisation of the foreign exchange market, the lifting of a variety of restrictions on overseas investment by Japanese residents – both individuals and corporate – and the opening of the Euroyen market. Yet with hindsight we can see that these measures were essentially dictated by the over-riding necessity for Japan to be able to recycle its trade surpluses and huge internal accumulation of savings.

There is one further major change we may anticipate in the economic environment in the very near future, and that will be the final emergence of the Japanese yen as a major international trading and reserve currency. This is foreshadowed by the recent rapid growth of the Euroyen bond market, but we are yet to see wide use of the Japanese yen in trading and international balance of payments lending or accumulation in other countries' foreign exchange reserves. This inevitable development is being accelerated by the recent renewed weakness and instability of the US dollar on the foreign exchange markets resulting from the continuing American fiscal and trade deficits. The so far stillborn proposal that the Federal Reserve should issue yen-denominated 'Reagan Bonds', in order to stabilise the foreign exchange position of the US, is perhaps a sign of the kind of developments to be expected in the coming years. Similarly we have seen the Japanese government offering additional support to the Latin American debtor countries in the form of further balance of payments loans, but this time denominated in yen.

Thus, just as the Eurodollar market was created by the need to recycle the Opec countries' surplus dollars from oil exports, so the Euroyen market is being created to help recycle Japan's trade surplus.

Treasury services

Lloyds Bank Treasury in Japan started with a very small operation in Tokyo, in common with many other institutions who in allocating resources gave priority to the 'glamorous' offshore centres of Bahrain, Hong Kong and Singapore.

However, in 1983 we began to make serious efforts to address the obvious potential of the Japanese marketplace, in anticipation of the expected liberalisation of the market which materialised in a timely fashion in April 1984 with the abolition of the 'real demand rule'.

Since that time we have remodelled our dealing room twice and now have capacity for seven-times the number of traders we had in 1984. Tokyo has now become one of the major foreign exchange trading centres on a par with New York after London, and this is reflected at Lloyds by the enormous growth we have seen in trading volumes in the Tokyo Branch.

Our current objective is to maintain an active presence in the 'plain vanilla' foreign exchange and treasury products area whilst offering a judicious selection of the more useful innovative products available to the informed customer. Thus we have taken a leading role in yen interest rate swaps and have further protected our clients' interest rate exposures by offering forward rate agreements (FRAs). Indeed, Lloyds concluded the first publicly acknowledged FRA in the Tokyo brokers' market.

It is in the area of 'old-fashioned' foreign exchange, however, where Lloyds has developed its strongest presence using our own expertise and the strength of both our London Head Office and our worldwide network. Our pre-eminent position in the New Zealand market, both through our wholly-owned National Bank of New Zealand and our associated merchant bank, South Pacific Merchant Finance, give us a crucial edge in the hiatus after New York closes and before Tokyo opens.

Concentrating on its customers' greatest needs, Lloyds offers a full market-making service in US dollar/yen and sterling spot and forward exchange dealing and a first class execution service in other major currencies such as Deutschmark, Swiss franc, Australian and New Zealand dollar, and Ecu. Indeed, on a number of days Lloyds has accounted for around 5 per cent of total US dollar/yen exchange volume transacted in the Tokyo market. Thus, in the newly liberalised environment we are able to compete on equal terms with major Japanese and foreign banks alike.

The foreign exchange dealing room in the Ote Centre Building.

Lloyds Bank Plc is also participating actively in the yen bond markets, which are of growing importance to our international client base. In this regard, Lloyds Bank is a fully licensed dealer in Japanese government bonds and is one of the more active foreign banks in this sector.

It is our firm intention to continue to develop our services in relation to the demands of our customers however this occurs. In particular, we foresee great potential for the development of a major market in options and futures of all kinds in Japan.

Corporate and trade finance services

Lloyds Bank has forged close relationships with many of Japan's leading corporations since establishing a presence in Tokyo, and many of these ties are international in scope because of the wide coverage which the Lloyds Bank network is able to give to Japan's multinationals.

Whilst foreign banks, including Lloyds, looked to medium-term foreign currency lending as the basis for developing corporate relationships during the 1970s, lending has assumed diminishing importance since borrowers have been able to turn increasingly to the capital market to satisfy their financing requirements. Pressure on margins has accompanied the decrease in lending opportunities, and asset rankings have long since ceased to constitute a valid measure of success for foreign banks operating in Japan.

De-emphasis of lending has gone hand-in-hand with the need to deliver innovative products to Japanese companies as their needs have changed, and market liberalisation has paved the way for foreign banks and securities companies to meet these needs. Whilst continuing to offer a wide range of traditional commercial banking products when required by our customers, Lloyds Bank's business development efforts in Japan are focused increasingly on delivery of specialised banking and treasury-related products to develop new sources of income and provide the comprehensive range of banking services demanded by major corporations.

In the area of interest rate swaps, for instance, Lloyds Bank has been able to assist its customers to realise appreciable cost savings on the servicing of their debt, particularly through the use of yen and US dollar interest rate swaps and Swiss franc swaps, an instrument in which Lloyds is a market leader and which is seeing increasingly active use.

With an international network of offices covering 47 countries, the Lloyds Bank Group has also been well-positioned to participate in the trade flows to and from Japan, and to support the overseas investment activities of Japanese corporations as their operations have become increasingly internationalised. Issuance of contract guarantees in support of Japanese companies' tenders for overseas projects and the financing on a non-recourse basis of Japanese companies' export documents are examples of trade-related activities where benefits are delivered to customers as a result of the Lloyds Group's strong international representation. A leading bank in the field of international barter and countertrade, with a specialist unit based in London, Lloyds is also able to assist its customers in structuring and administering the most complex trade transactions.

Lloyds Bank's corporate and trade finance services are delivered to its customer base through a small team of Corporate Banking account managers who, through their access to Treasury and specialised trade finance and banking products, are able to bring a high level of technical expertise to their relationships, whilst at the same time providing the personal attention necessary to evince Lloyds' commitment to those relationships over the longer term. By allocating resources in a focused manner and delivering those products which offer the greatest value-added to its customers, Lloyds has built a successful corporate and trade finance based business which is well-placed to develop further as the continued proliferation of opportunities in the market-place is matched by financial liberalisation.

Jack Wadsworth, President Morgan Stanley Japan, with Hidekichi Tanaka, Executive Director and Head IBD–Japan.

Morgan Stanley International Ltd

At the cutting edge of developments in Japan's rapidly expanding capital markets is Morgan Stanley International Ltd, using its diversified services and highly regarded expertise to guide clients' investment strategies. As one of the largest foreign securities firms in Tokyo's capital markets, Morgan Stanley International offers a full service approach – from sales and trading of all types of domestic securities in Tokyo to advising on the numerous investment opportunities in the major capital markets in the world.

Morgan Stanley has been a member of Japan's financial community for over 17 years. In 1970, the firm opened a representative office in Tokyo, and in 1984 the office was upgraded to full branch status, licensed to conduct a full securities business in Japan. In early 1986, Morgan Stanley was among the first foreign firms to be admitted to the Tokyo Stock Exchange (TSE), which has added a new dimension to our worldwide equity capability.

In line with the firm's overall expansion in Japan's financial markets, Morgan Stanley began futures trading on the Osaka Stock Exchange in June 1986, helping further to round off the services it offers clients.

Morgan Stanley has developed a name for itself not only in the areas of fixed-income securities and equity sales and trading, but also with its investment banking activities. The firm is particularly well-known in Japan for its extensive mergers and acquisitions activities, for its swap capabilities, and also in the increasingly active field of convertible bond and debt with equity warrants distribution.

Since it established a full branch in Tokyo in 1984, the office has grown from a staff of 35 to over 400, ranking it with its operations in both New York and London as one of the three world centres from which Morgan Stanley coordinates its securities brokerage, sales and trading, capital markets and investment banking activities.

The strategy driving Morgan Stanley's expansion in the Tokyo market is to develop a creative array of products to meet the needs of Japanese institutional and corporate clients.

Fixed-income securities

A cornerstone of the firm's activities in Japan is the sales and trading of a wide variety of debt products. The firm currently has nine traders and 50 salesmen in Tokyo offering Japanese domestic, Euro and US fixed-income securities. The high level of investment by Japanese institutions in US Treasuries has been important to Morgan Stanley's growth in Tokyo.

In addition to the expanding public debt business there is a special focus on privately sourced transactions, some of which are packaged with swaps.

Equity

Since joining the TSE, Morgan Stanley has continued to expand its Japanese stock business, establishing a leadership position in terms of daily volume among foreign members. Taking full advantage of its London and New York offices, the firm has developed a strong global sales and trading capability in convertibles, warrants and Japanese stocks in overseas markets.

Other equity products offered in Tokyo include the sales and trading of US stocks. Morgan Stanley is one of the few US firms which make active markets in Tokyo for a group of NYSE stocks which are not listed on the TSE. One of the keys to continued penetration of the Japanese stock business is high-quality research. The expansion of this area is a major initiative for 1987.

Investment banking

Morgan Stanley was the first US firm to have a special team covering M&A in Tokyo. This has resulted in a high market share on behalf of Japanese clients making overseas acquisitions. The total market value of transactions completed over the past five years exceeds US$2.5 billion.

Although Japan's major securities houses or Japanese banks lead manage most international offerings for Japanese companies, Morgan Stanley's underwriting record is one of the best among foreign firms. In 1986, for example, Morgan Stanley International lead or co-lead managed US$23.2 billion in the international capital markets, including US$4.4 billion for Japanese and other Asia-based clients. As a result, in 1986 the firm was ranked fifth in terms of overall international activity for Japanese clients, and first among foreign firms.

Its expertise in all facets of capital market activities enables Morgan Stanley to tailor products to suit the specific needs of institutional investors. By working closely with clients, it has become a leader in private placements, including many with interest rate and currency swaps.

Forex

Morgan Stanley has a forex operation which complements its other securities activities in Tokyo. This business is also targeted for expansion in 1987.

There follows an interview with David S. Phillips, Managing Director and General Manager, Morgan Stanley International Ltd, Tokyo:

A view of the Investment Banking Division.

Fixed-income traders.

Q. Morgan Stanley has achieved significant growth in Tokyo over the past three years. What is your optimal size in the Tokyo market?

A. It is difficult to be specific about optimum size since this depends, in part, on the continued rate of liberalisation of the Japanese capital markets. However, we are targeting our size to be 550-600 by the end of 1988. We will continue to add people in sales and trading of Japanese and US stocks, expand our research team, and further increase the fixed-income sales force.

Q. What are your objectives on the equity side?

A. With regard to Japanese equities, we would like to be among the top 15 firms on the TSE in terms of volume. At the present we have been holding at 30th position, and by the end of this year we hope to lift our position to the 20th largest in Tokyo. One of the keys to our objective will be broadening our research coverage of Japanese stocks. This may take a little longer than we originally anticipated since there is strong competition for good people from the many foreign firms who have entered the market over the past few years.

Q. What about your fixed-income activities?

A. We want to be a major intermediary in the US$50 billion investment Japanese institutions are making in the fixed-income markets annually. This will require broadening our sales staff to cover more institutions in Japan and adding specialised traders to expand our real-time market making during Tokyo's business day.

We are also aiming to be a major factor in the market for Japanese government bonds. In a recent tender for four-year government bonds we were awarded the fifth

Gene Dattel, Managing Director – Equities, discussing the markets with the trading desk.

largest amount and outbid one of the big four Japanese houses. Our future growth in this sector depends on the speed with which the Japanese government moves to a full auction system for its bond issuing programme, and also on getting better access to information.

Q. What is Morgan Stanley's main client base in Japan?

A. When Morgan Stanley set up its representative office in Tokyo in 1970, we had a small group of high-quality clients including Mitsubishi Bank, Mitsubishi Corporation, Mitsubishi Heavy Industries and several other members of the Mitsubishi Group, Hitachi, Nippon Steel and IBJ. Our investment banking group has gradually expanded and now covers the top 200 financial institutions and corporations in Japan.

In the mid-1970s, we began relationships with many of the major institutions for fixed-income investment, and more recently have done the same for our equity business. Today we probably cover the 150 largest investing institutions.

Q. For your Japanese clients, what is the particular advantage of coming to Morgan Stanley over other foreign or Japanese groups?

A. We really have different clients or at least different departments at our clients for each of our three major businesses – fixed-income, equity and investment banking.

Our fixed-income clients in Japan choose us because we have the right products at the best price and because we are innovative – bringing modern portfolio theory to Japanese institutions.

On the equity side it is a matter of good research, established client relationships and also good execution.

For our investment banking clients we have some products, like mergers and acquisitions, where we are clearly the market leaders, and others like our underwriting capabilities where we have had a long history of service and maintain good coverage. Another factor, which is difficult to measure, is our ability to communicate market opportunities between London and Tokyo.

Q. What new markets do you intend targeting?

A. We have a very successful foreign exchange business here but we are constrained by law from expanding it further. We hope to overcome this barrier in the near future.

What is often overlooked in Japan is the growing population of high net worth individuals. We successfully service this important market segment in the US and in Europe, and we intend to make inroads in Japan as well.

Q. On the institutional side?

A. We wish to add to our successful base of innovative private placement and high-yield products: for example, we have sold a leveraged buyout fund to selected Japanese institutions, two venture capital funds and a special fund based on stock index futures.

One area in which we are looking for dramatic growth is asset management. We have a good start dealing with trust banks and life insurance companies, but we wish to obtain a licence to handle discretionary accounts from corporations and smaller institutions.

The Tokyo Stock Exchange.

Nikko's professional staff are constantly engaged in looking ahead and developing new financial services and products that anticipate customer needs.

Nikko Securities at the forefront of international finance

The Nikko Securities Co Ltd is recognised as one of the leading investment banks and capital market traders worldwide. Founded in Japan 70 years ago, Nikko has consistently led the industry in offering responsive and innovative services to clients. With an established presence in the major financial centres, Nikko provides clients with a comprehensive range of financial services, including a highly-regarded array of research and investment advisory services, underwriting and market making in all major capital markets, and assistance for non-Japanese corporations listing and raising funds in the Tokyo capital market. With the advent of global financial deregulation and securitisation over the past few years, Nikko has positioned itself strategically to enable clients to capitalise on the most timely and cost-effective market opportunities.

As the advantages of the Tokyo market will increasingly enter the international financial equation, Nikko has taken steps to enhance its domestic and international capabilities with the infusion of new capital and experienced financial professionals. Nikko has also invested heavily in information technology and product development to stay at the forefront of the financial revolution. These, along with a market-minded approach to serving the needs of clients, will allow Nikko to sustain its growth and continue to stay ahead of the pack in a highly competitive environment.

The Nikko perspective on globalisation

From an international perspective, Nikko Securities is a firmly established investment bank with a major presence in both principal and emerging markets. It has significantly expanded its global network with the opening of representative offices in Milan and Madrid, and the upgrading of its office in Paris to subsidiary status. The proposed establishment of a merchant bank in London will further strengthen Nikko's international operations and will heighten its ability to offer clients critical advantages at the most opportune moments.

Nikko Securities was one of the first financial firms in Japan to recognise that the distinction between domestic and international finance was beginning to blur because of the increasing globalisation of corporate activity. Furthermore, Nikko saw that deregulation and shifts in the flow of international capital – with Japan emerging as the largest provider of capital – would open up new options and opportunities for investors worldwide. In order to take advantage of these developments and to continue meeting the increasingly diverse needs of clients in Japan and overseas, Nikko reorganised itself to a more product-oriented, market-minded footing. Nikko also endeavoured to familiarise Japanese staff with international operations, and overseas staff with Japanese finance. The synergies created by these efforts have brought Nikko to the forefront of international finance, as investment banker and investment manager.

An established competence in investment banking

Nikko Securities is highly regarded for its tremendous placing power in Japanese capital markets and for its abilities as an organiser of innovative financing packages. Nikko was quick to recognise the attractiveness of equity-linked debt issues to Japanese borrowers, and took strategic measures to leverage the opportunities thus presented.

Nikko, already a leading contender for the top position in bond league tables, is becoming a major force in the underwriting and placing of international equities. These strengths are becoming crucial advantages to Nikko in its drive to become a top international investment bank, as corporations and governments, large and small, increasingly securitise their debt.

In response to the increased segmentation of global capital markets, Nikko has adopted a market-minded approach to investment banking – bringing markets and clients together under the most favourable terms. Nikko's expertise in cutting across currencies and traditional product lines has enabled it to create new financing vehicles that are tailored exactly to the diverse needs of international borrowers.

First and foremost in investment management

Nikko Securities is a leading provider of global investment advisory and capital management services. Against a background of growing personal and corporate assets in Japan, more relaxed regulations governing capital investment by Japanese institutional investors, a surging yen and declining global interest rates, Nikko has implemented capital management strategies designed to meet the requirements of a demanding clientele worldwide.

The services provided by Nikko International Capital Management Co Ltd (NICAM), Nikko's asset management subsidiary, have won favourable recognition from clients – including Japanese institutional investors, sovereign governments, US, UK and European pension funds, and several international accounts – due to its excellent overall performance. This performance has been supported by highly regarded research and analysis operations and a state-of-the-art information network which together provide Nikko clients in Japan and overseas with up-to-the-minute information and advice on investment opportunities worldwide. Furthermore, Nikko is one of the most innovative investment managers, working to advance in-depth qualitative and quantitative research and application of the most up-to-date portfolio decision models.

The BARRA/Nikko Japanese Equity Risk Model, developed jointly with BARRA of California, is but one example of the sophisticated capital management methodologies Nikko is incorporating into its investment operations to maintain its position at the leading edge of investment technology.

A leader in investment trust management

With more than 25 years of experience as a separate company in the Nikko Securities group, Nikko Securities Investment Trust & Management Co Ltd has compiled an impressive record in the management of investment funds. As of February 1987, Nikko Investment Trust has about ¥6 trillion, or approximately US$40 billion, in assets under management. This figure represents about 18 per cent of the total net assets of all Japanese investment trusts. Investment trusts provide one of the most convenient and efficient ways for Nikko's clients, including both individuals and corporations, to secure the benefits of diversified portfolio management.

Investment trusts managed by Nikko Investment Trust are structured in a number of ways and include the following types of funds: equity, balanced, government bond, convertible bond, medium-term government securities, and international. The success of these funds in meeting investment needs is reflected in the rapid expansion and high level of funds under the company's management. In its management activities, Nikko Investment Trust draws on the full resources and experience of the Nikko Securities group.

Role of Nikko Research Center

One of the major supports of Nikko's activities is the Nikko Research Center Ltd (NRC), a subsidiary of Nikko Securities Co Ltd. NRC provides Nikko's clients in Japan and overseas with up-to-date information and advice on investment opportunities worldwide. As one of Japan's largest research and investment analysis organisations, NRC is distinguished by an international orientation. With operations based in Tokyo, NRC has a branch in Osaka, and offices in New York, London and Hong Kong. These offices have the dual functions of gathering information on overseas economies and financial markets, and providing investment information on Japanese securities to Nikko's clients overseas.

To facilitate timely investment decisions, NRC is constantly engaged in analysing economic trends and forecasting movements in interest rates and foreign exchange markets. NRC also has one of the most extensive programmes of research on industries and individual corporations.

NRC publications cover a wide range of industries and companies, and the annual publication *Analysis of Japanese Industries for Investors*, which covers more than 100 industrial sectors, has been acknowledged as one of the most comprehensive sources of information on Japanese industry.

Nikko's market-minded approach to trading services

Nikko Securities has an exceptionally strong and responsive trading capability in Japan and in other principal capital markets. Nikko has earned its place among the top brokers and securities dealers, against especially strong competition, by taking a market-minded approach – the capacity to offer clients in any market access to any security on any market at any time. In order to accomplish this, Nikko has upgraded its global communications and on-line market information network systems. It has also shored up the capital positions of its main subsidiaries – thus allowing Nikko to hold greater inventories of securities to meet client demand – and enhanced its back-office operations.

Nikko is a top broker in equities, with seats on all eight Japanese stock exchanges and on the New York, London, and other major stock exchanges around the world. By being one of the most active participants in the Japanese equity markets, Nikko can offer overseas investors competitive, timely quotes on all Japanese issues around the clock.

In fixed-income securities, Nikko has traditionally been one of the largest traders of Japanese government bonds. It has also become a recognised dealer in Eurobonds and equity-linked issues. Today, against the backdrop of huge capital surpluses in the hands of Japanese investors financing the US budget deficit, Nikko, along with other Japanese securities houses, is becoming one of the most active dealers of US Treasury securities in Japan as well as in the United States. If Nikko's hope to become a primary dealer of US Treasury issues is realised, Nikko will, together with its established role as a market maker in Eurobonds, solidify its position as a world-class bond dealer. Further contributing to Nikko's position will be its strategy of incorporating financial engineering techniques, such as interest rate and currency futures and options, in leveraging risk.

Nikko and the Tokyo capital market

The emergence of Japan as the largest provider of capital in the world, supported by cash flows generated by its massive current account surpluses, the sharp appreciation of the yen, and historically low interest rates have caused a rapid shift in the flow of international capital. Coupled with the ongoing deregulation of Japanese financial markets and the liberalisation of yen-related financial transactions, Tokyo has gained acceptance as an international money centre equalling New York and London. The number of non-Japanese financial firms opening new offices in Tokyo, or upgrading existing ones, has grown rapidly over the last two years, reflecting Tokyo's increased stature as an international financial centre.

Nikko anticipated these trends early on, and was able to make strides in gearing itself strategically to meet the challenges and opportunities presented by the growing importance of Tokyo in global finance.

Especially important to the growth of the Tokyo market has been the increase in Tokyo Stock Exchange (TSE) listings of foreign corporations. Nikko acted as sponsor and lead manager of the TSE listing of the Spanish telecommunications monopoly, Telefonica, in 1985. The success of this issue touched off the subsequent rush to list equities on the Foreign Section of the TSE, and eventually established Tokyo as a viable option for international corporations raising new equity capital. Attractions of a TSE listing also include expansion of the shareholder base among Japan's large and highly liquid institutional investors and the establishment of around-the-clock trading in an issuer's shares. Since the Telefonica listing, Nikko has continued to foster the development of the Foreign Section of the TSE by bringing successive issues to the market.

While the issuing of debt securities on the Tokyo market by overseas borrowers during the past year has been somewhat circumscribed by the appreciating yen, further easing of regulations governing issues by foreign entities and the wide use of swaps and other risk-hedging

Investment professionals at Nikko keep on top of emerging market trends.

tools has created opportunities as well. Nikko has been a top-performing managing underwriter and arranger for numerous public offerings and private placements in Japan by overseas borrowers; recent offerings have included an innovative continuously issuable bond for the World Bank. Nikko was also one of the first investment banks in Japan to manage an offering through the bought-deal method. Nikko's placement capabilities in the Tokyo market benefit issuers with better terms.

The incorporation of Japanese securities into their portfolios by overseas pension funds and other institutional investors has grown in importance with the ascent of the Tokyo market. Nikko has continued to play an important and expanding role in assisting overseas investors with their equity, bond and convertible bond investments in Tokyo. Nikko offers highly competitive investment opportunities, drawing on its position as one of the largest brokers and dealers in Japan.

Nikko: Looking to the future

As opportunities have expanded in Tokyo, so has competition from domestic and foreign securities firms and banks. Nikko welcomes this competition, as it can only serve to nurture the growth of the Tokyo market, thereby benefitting international borrowers and investors. Nikko's strategy in trying to maintain its lead as a top-rated financial firm is to further build and broaden the base of its operations, devote resources to the training and recruitment of highly qualified personnel, strengthen its financial position, introduce innovative new services and products to satisfy the needs of specific clients and markets, and work to improve its information development, analysis and delivery capabilities.

Traditional segmentation of the financial services industry in Japan and elsewhere is breaking down as deregulation takes hold and as the world of finance moves into an era of global markets that operate around the clock. In this challenging environment, Nikko has adopted the goal of being a market-minded, full-service supplier of financial services that is capable of responding to the financial needs of clients worldwide. Nikko's commitment to providing clients with quality services at the leading edge of financial technology will allow Nikko to continue to shape the global markets of tomorrow.

日本生命
第一勧業
地下鉄
京阪電車

Nippon Life Insurance Company: An ambitious global investor

Ever since its foundation in 1889, Nippon Life Insurance Company has continued to strive steadily for a healthier, more prosperous society. Nippon Life, the largest life insurance company in Japan, has through its financial activities been able to support the rapid expansion of the Japanese economy.

Nippon Life ranks first worldwide in terms of life insurance in force at US$1.4 trillion (¥204.4 trillion), while its total assets at US$104 billion (¥15.1 trillion) rank second, preceded only by Prudential Insurance Co. This exceptional scale of operations is supported by 121 branches nationwide, with 1,991 sub-branches under Head Offices in Osaka and Tokyo, assisted by some 72,000 sales representatives who carry out various customer-related activities.

Nippon Life in Tokyo's financial markets

With total assets at over US$100 billion, Nippon Life is an important participant in Tokyo's financial markets. As the largest institutional investor in Japan, its investments range from equities, bonds, corporate loans and real estate to other related financial activities. No other company in Japan encompasses such a wide range of investments on a scale as large as Nippon Life, nor has its reputation for expertise.

Since assets of life insurance companies are derived from insurance premium income, they are of a long-term nature, extending to 20–30 years, and the continued increase in funds can be anticipated. This aspect of the company's funds makes it possible to make long-term investment decisions on a grand scale, an advantage denied to other financial institutions. In fact, total assets have been growing at an annual rate of 20 per cent, an amount equivalent to US$17.6 billion in fiscal year 1986. This rate of increase, unequalled by other domestic financial institutions, gives the company a very favourable position in the rapidly expanding global financial markets.

In equity investments, Nippon Life is literally a giant, with over 10 billion shares, accounting for 3.2 per cent of all shares listed on Japanese stock exchanges, making it a major shareholder in 753 companies, or 40 per cent of those listed. Although the company's equity portfolio consists mainly of stakes in major long-established firms, purchase of stocks from new companies with an encouraging future is also on the increase, a strategy which is likely to be fully justified in the years to come.

Presently the company's equity portfolio at US$17.1 billion constitutes 16.8 per cent of assets. But since the book value of Japanese companies is based on the lower of cost or market (LCM) procedure, the current value should be something in the region of US$50 billion. Since leading Japanese banks are estimated to have hidden equity assets of US$12 billion on average, the implicit strength of Nippon Life's equity portfolio can be discerned.

Through the years the company has acted as a stable shareholder, supplying capital to industry, while backing efficient management and unobtrusively supporting Japan's economic expansion. In the past Nippon Life, like most institutional investors, took a passive position on its shareholders' rights. However, recent changes in the financial community, which have put more and more emphasis on corporate earnings and competitiveness, have induced changes in the company's stance on equity holdings. Although the company has no direct interest in exercising its rights as a shareholder in management decisions, it is beginning to assert its position as an investor where it affects the return on investment.

Nippon Life's presence in Japan's financial markets is not only limited to the equity market. The company continues to be highly active in the bond market, especially that for government bonds, in which it plays a significant role in such areas as the underwriting of ultra long-term government bonds for private placements, as well as being a major holder of long-term government bonds in the 10-year range. Moreover, it actively invests in bonds issued by Japanese firms in both domestic and oversea markets, thereby keeping abreast of changes in their fund procurement policies. The domestic bond portfolio at US$13 billion is also a close match to that of equities.

The company also plays a substantial role in providing long-term funds to corporate borrowers, with total loans outstanding amounting to about US$35 billion. Furthermore, the company is one of Japan's foremost owners of buildings for lease and a leading developer on a national scale, with holdings reaching US$6.5 billion.

Nippon Life in the global market

Nippon Life's scope of investment is not limited to the domestic market. With the growth of the company's assets, the domestic market could no longer offer enough attractive investment opportunities, and with the internationalisation of the financial community the company sought to explore investment opportunities abroad as a means of diversifying its portfolio and maximising returns.

The company's overseas investment began in 1971, when it first entered the US stock market. Since then overseas investment has been growing by leaps and bounds, extending into real estate investment as well. Foreign assets are now 18.1 per cent of the company's portfolio at US$18.7 billion, and the organisation of Nippon Life's overseas investment was restructured into several specialist departments at the company's Tokyo Headquar-

Nippon Life's Head Office in Osaka.

ters, assisted by seven overseas representative offices in New York, London, Sydney, Frankfurt, Singapore, Toronto and Beijing.

Yen syndicated loans

Nippon Life has been an active participant in the area of yen syndicated loans since 1978. By March 1987, loans had been extended to the World Bank and nine other international organisations, as well as to sovereign, municipal and private borrowers in 38 countries. Together they totalled US$3.6 billion, a staggering 38.7 per cent increase over the previous year.

In March 1983, Nippon Life became the first life insurance company to lead manage a syndicated loan by acquiring a sole mandate from the Province of Manitoba, and since then the company has acted as a major coordinator in the Japanese life insurance industry's participation in large-scale overseas lending programmes, as well as being a leading firm in the syndication of loans in the Tokyo capital market. This is illustrated by the fact that Nippon Life has been the principal coordinator for the life insurance industry in arranging loans to the World Bank on each of the 15 occasions it has raised funds from the Tokyo capital market. Furthermore, on the last occasion, in December 1986, the company succeeded in the syndication of a loan with two remarkable features that marked a new departure in Tokyo's capital market: this loan to the World Bank was advanced by a syndicate consisting solely of life insurance companies, and was for an ultra long term extending to 30 years.

In a way, 1986 was a year of remarkable achievement for Nippon Life's international lending operations. The company lead managed 31 loans, totally US$4 billion, and at the same time made two breakthroughs with promising implications for the future. First of these was the introduction of ultra long-term loans (those extending over 20 years), which are likely to be provided mainly by life insurance companies due to the long-term nature of life insurance funds. In this area, Nippon Life lead managed not only the aforementioned loan to the World Bank, but also loans to the Province of Quebec and the government of New Zealand. The second breakthrough was the loan to Girobank, which marked the first occasion in which a UK government agency had raised capital in yen, as well as being the first time the bank raised funds from abroad. This lead management confirmed the company's high repute within the international financial community.

Yen syndicated loans to foreign borrowers have been subject to several restrictions which have somewhat limited the extent of active participation by life insurance companies. Nippon Life has always been among the first to take advantage of new deregulatory measures, and with the recent deregulation of financial activities in Japan, Nippon Life's presence in this field has become progressively greater. Current international trends such as low interest rates and drastic currency fluctuations, along with the variety of instruments afforded to potential borrowers, have produced an increasingly specific and individual demand for loans. Realising these requirements, Nippon Life in the past has adopted flexible lending policies to fulfill the borrower's needs, and as financial regulation in Japan becomes further liberalised, more flexibility in the company's lending policies can be expected.

Investment in foreign securities

Nippon Life is not only the largest institutional investor in the Japanese securities market, but also has a substantial amount invested in foreign securities. The company's foreign securities portfolio has been rapidly expanding and currently stands at nearly US$10 billion.

A major part of its foreign securities portfolio is composed of foreign bonds, with an emphasis on high quality, liquidity and profitability. Since the basic investment strategy of life insurance companies is to obtain high income gains in the long term, the company's bond portfolio tends to be made up of high-yielding bonds with

The signing ceremony for a yen syndicated loan to Société Nationale des Chemins de fer Belges.

long-term maturities. In terms of currency diversification, investments cover 11 currencies including the US dollar, Canadian dollar, sterling, Ecu, Deutschmark, French franc, Dutch guilder and Australian dollar.

Although smaller in volume compared to the foreign bond portfolio, overseas equity investment also has been steadily increasing. US corporate stocks currently are a major portion of the company's foreign equity portfolio, but the portfolio is being diversified into blue-chip stocks in Europe, Asia and Oceania that show promising increase in value. In addition, a substantial amount is being placed in foreign currency-denominated term deposits related to various international capital market transactions.

Moreover, recent trends to emphasise maximum return on investment have had noticeable effect on the company's management of its securities portfolio. One aspect of this is seen in the increasing amount of resources diverted to research and management of investment risks, in order to protect the portfolio from unexpected fluctuations in today's volatile markets. Another is to pursue a more flexible approach to various investment opportunities offered in various markets, including use of more sophisticated techniques and financial instruments.

One result of this move to implement a more active and efficient securities investment was the establishment of investment subsidiaries in the world's largest capital markets. The first of these subsidiaries, Nissei International Investment Luxembourg SA, was established in April 1981 to exercise effective investment in the Eurobond market. Another subsidiary, the Nissei International Fund Panama Corporation established in March 1984, specialises in investment in US and Canadian dollar-based bonds. Both have so far shown highly encouraging results, and recent capital increases should afford a substantial expansion in the scope of their operations. In 1987, three more investment funds were established in locations such as Jersey and the Cayman Islands. These and other subsidiaries, totalling 12 in all, as well as the seven overseas representative offices, form the core of this more flexible approach to foreign investments, and are the vehicles through which the company will be actively participating in the various investment opportunities offered in the world market.

Investment in real estate

Nippon Life's international investment portfolio has also expanded into foreign real estate investment. The company's overseas real estate operations are conducted through two subsidiaries, Nissei Reality Inc, based in New York, and Nissei Real Estate Canada Inc, based in Toronto. Through these subsidiaries Nippon Life has been investing in first-class properties located in the US and Canada, with an eye to initial cash return as well as potential capital appreciation in the long term. Nippon Life has accomplished 11 real estate projects as of end March 1987. These investments are represented by 645 Madison Avenue, a 22-storey office building located in the heart of Manhattan, acquired in partnership with a major US life insurance company, and the Crocker Center complex in downtown San Francisco, also a joint-venture project. The operation of the two subsidiaries is characterised by their sophisticated and professional style along with a hands-on management.

Further investments in office buildings, shopping centres and hotels in prime locations in the US and Canada are expected, and overseas real estate investment shows encouraging signs of becoming one of the cornerstones in the company's foreign investment portfolio.

Crocker Center, Nippon Life's real estate holding in San Francisco.

In search of new frontiers

Always prepared to break into new fields of investment, Nippon Life is now undertaking an ambitious expansion programme of its overseas network to deal with the rapidly expanding scope of investments in the global market. The establishment of various subsidiaries is one such measure.

Another step to enhance the company's global strategy was taken by Nippon Life's alliance with Shearson Lehman Brothers, a major investment bank of high repute. This new step opens a myriad of possibilities for the future. The move will further facilitate the company's participation in overseas markets as well as pave the way for Nippon Life's entry into new financial fields. This partnership symbolises a new era for Nippon Life in that it marks a step towards the goal of becoming a truely international financial institution.

Backed by its ample financial resources, Nippon Life is expected to expand further its operations as a multifaceted financial institution offering various related financial services. It is true that many of the company's strategic blueprints are still veiled, but as the company's past record suggests, Nippon Life can be expected to be in the forefront of the ever-changing financial community.

ARK Mori building.

Shearson Lehman Brothers in Tokyo

Shearson Lehman Brothers has the longest involvement with Japan of any major US investment banking firm.

In 1904, one of its predecessor firms, Kuhn, Loeb & Co, provided crucial financing for Japan during the Russo-Japanese War and, in the process, established credit resources for Japan in the United States, Germany and France, previously a heavy financial supporter of Russia. In 1962, still early in Japan's rise as an international economic power, Shearson Hammill, another predecessor firm, lead managed the intitial public offering of the US distributor of Nikon cameras.

Since May 1986, Shearson Lehman Brothers' Tokyo office has held full branch status. Under Japanese regulations similar to the US Glass Steagall Act, American Express Company, owner of American Express Bank and Shearson Lehman, could not engage in both commercial banking and securities trading. The parent company's decision to relinquish its banking licence enabled Shearson Lehman to extend its reach to Japan.

Shearson Lehman's presence in Tokyo is essential for the firm's global strategy. Tokyo, London and New York are the focal points for the firm's 24-hour worldwide investment banking and securities trading operations. Each city serves as the regional headquarters for the other offices in its area. Offices in Hong Kong, Singapore, Beijing, Sydney and Taiwan continue to be important Asian/Pacific links in the Shearson Lehman worldwide network.

Of the three focal points, Tokyo is the newest and fastest growing. The branch has demonstrated the same financial acuity, innovation and commitment apparent in the firm's historical Japanese dealings, and characteristic of Shearson Lehman around the world.

'The resources we've built throughout the firm have enabled us to move quickly in Japan,' says Kiyonobu Shimazu, Senior Managing Director of Shearson Lehman Brothers Asia, Inc. 'Capital strength, the willingness to risk our own capital in local market making and our strong presence in all the world's markets are important to Japanese institutional investors. All of these, plus the creativity to design new financing strategies and a powerful global securities distribution capability, are attracting Japanese investment banking clients to us.'

Increased capital resources

The link to American Express, one of the world's most respected financial organisations, has also been an asset for Shearson Lehman in the Far East. In order to expand Shearson Lehman's capital resources, yet retain a majority interest in the firm, American Express recently sold approximately 40 per cent of its Shearson Lehman holdings. In May 1987, 27 per cent of Shearson Lehman was sold to the public and to the firm's employees. Concurrently, Nippon Life purchased a 13 per cent equity interest in the firm for US$508.3 million. These transactions brought Shearson Lehman's total capital base to more than US$3 billion. In Tokyo, Shearson Lehman Brothers Asia, Inc has a capital base of over US$100 million.

Shearson Lehman should accrue considerable benefit from its partnership with this giant financial institution. However, the firm remains an important part of the American Express empire. With a 60 per cent ownership of Shearson Lehman, the international financial services company is continuing to expand cooperative ventures between the investment firm and other American Express operations. Nippon Life will also be involved with both American Express and Shearson Lehman in 'selected projects in key financial centres of Asia and other regions'.

A joint venture in London between Shearson Lehman and Nippon Life is being developed to focus on such areas as investment advice, asset management, research and consulting on financing. This venture will operate side-by-side with Shearson Lehman's existing London operations, which provide international investment banking and capital markets services as well as UK stock brokerage and investment services.

Nippon Life, with more life insurance in force than any other insurer in the world, is Japan's largest institutional investor. According to Gentaro Kawase, Nippon Life President, the insurance company expects the relationship with Shearson Lehman and American Express to 'contribute to more efficient management of Nippon Life's large assets'.

Kiyonobu Shimazu, Senior Managing Director of Shearson Lehman Brothers Asia, Inc.

Even before the recent capital additions, Shearson Lehman had the third-largest capital base in its industry and had long demonstrated a willingness to use the firm's money to facilitate client transactions.

'The strength of our capital position means we can execute client transactions of any size, even when market circumstances are difficult', says Craig Anderson, Deputy General Manager of the Tokyo Branch, who runs the capital markets area. 'The client has a high level of assurance that the transaction, no matter how complex, will be completed quickly and in the most efficient way.'

The firm offers a full range of trading in Japan, including equities, corporate and government bonds, collateralised mortgage obligations and money market instruments. It is a principal market maker in every security it offers in Japan, and provides 24-hour trading in most instruments.

Investment banking in Japan

Shearson Lehman has made impressive inroads into the Japanese investment banking market. In the past two years, the firm has lead or co-lead managed more than 40 external financings for Japanese issuers. In March 1987, Shearson Lehman lead managed a US$180 million fixed-rate Eurobond issue for Sumitomo Bank, one of the largest fixed-rate US dollar issues for a Japanese Bank.

Shearson Lehman's ability to develop innovative financing techniques has been a strong asset in attracting Japanese financial institutions to its client roster. The firm's highly successful introduction of capped floating rate notes to the market was followed by the development of variable money market certificates (VMMCs) for Japanese banks. The product is a certificate of deposit based on commercial paper rates rather than Libor. The instruments are repriced at periodic auctions.

'The product conforms to Japanese regulations which prohibit banks from issuing commercial paper, yet provides access to an entirely new investor base for the client', notes Vice President Gary Talarico. Since May 1987, Shearson Lehman sole-managed over US$1 billion in VMMCs for nine leading Japanese banks.

The VMMC product not only reflects Shearson's strengths in the money markets, but also in auction-linked instruments. In addition to the VMMC transactions, Shearson Lehman participates as dealer in all of the 10 uncommitted EuroCD programmes established by Japanese banks in the past year.

Craig Anderson, Managing Director.

Shearson Lehman's strength in commercial paper has been an important advantage in attracting non-bank corporate finance clients as well, according to Ken Shizunaga, who looks after corporate clients in Japan. 'Shearson Lehman's recognised money markets expertise has opened doors for us', he notes. The firm has quickly become a dealer in major commercial paper programmes for such prestigious clients as NEC, Toshiba, Honda Motor Company, Nippon Denso, Mitsui and Kumagai Gumi.

Mitsui Real Estates's US$99 million money market preferred (MMP) issue was lead managed by Shearson Lehman, the inventor of the product. This was one of the first issues of MMP, an auction-rate preferred stock, by a Japanese corporation.

Akio Aoki, Senior Vice President (sitting) and Gary M. Talarico, Vice President.

Investment banking clients from other parts of the world are taking advantage of Shearson's growing strength in the Japanese market. In the past year, the firm arranged more than US$600 million in private placements with Japanese insurance companies and banks for such clients as the Province of British Columbia, the Belgian bank ASLK-CGER and American Express Company.

Shearson Lehman has also been active in yen-related financings. Crédit Lyonnais chose Shearson Lehman to lead manage its recent highly successful ¥15 billion Euroyen bond issue – particularly notable because very few non-Japanese investment banks have lead managed a Euroyen issue. And in June 1987, Shearson Lehman lead managed a US$100 million Eurobond for All Nippon Airways which was swapped into Japanese yen.

'These transactions demonstrate not only our securities distribution ability, but also our strength in structuring swap-related transactions', Talarico points out. 'Each had a yen/US dollar swap attached to it that we were able to arrange quickly with leading Japanese banks.'

Placement power in Japan is an integral part of Shearson Lehman's global financing capabilities.

Trading floor.

'A strong local presence in each of the world's major capital markets enables us to offer full product service to all of our clients', states Anderson. 'US and European companies are increasingly turning to yen markets, while Japanese issuers are taking greater advantage of securities denominated in Eurodollars and other currencies.'

Shearson Lehman's traditional strength in US dollar products and more recent presence in yen-denominated instruments are complemented by aggressive growth in Europe. The firm acquired the UK stockbroking firm L. Messel & Co, and became a primary dealer in the UK gilt market in 1986. Investment banking operations have been established in France, Germany, Switzerland, and Italy.

Project finance

Shearson Lehman's ability to assemble specialists from various parts of the firm to accomplish a specific task is an important factor in its longstanding strength in major project finance. Experts in various disciplines from Japan, Hong Kong, New York and London worked together to make possible Hong Kong's Eastern Harbour Crossing, a rail and road tunnel under the world's busiest harbour.

Shearson Lehman put together the consortium of clients from Hong Kong, Japan, Britain and China that won the contract to build and operate the tunnel. The firm then designed and placed a HK$4.4 billion (US$564 million) financing package with institutions worldwide, many of them Japanese.

Debt restructuring

Another area in which Shearson Lehman demonstrates its ability to bring together a wide variety of skills in the international arena is in the financial restructuring of troubled companies. In the past five years, the firm has helped clients around the world restructure more than $30 billion in debt. The Shearson Lehman teams that carried out the restructurings comprised professionals with a wide range of skills who were drawn from all over the world.

Specialised expertise

The interrelationship among all parts of the firm is basic to Shearson Lehman's concept of full service.

'We have assembled a complete range of highly specialised expertise throughout the world', says Peter Cohen, Shearson Lehman Chief Executive Officer. 'We can configure our client service teams in almost infinite variations to meet a specific need, anytime and anywhere in the world.'

The firm also has a policy of using local people in all the markets it covers. 'We want our people to be part of the culture of the communities in which we operate', Cohen continues. 'We try to combine functional expertise which can be universally applied with the insights of nationals on the local scene.'

Shearson Lehman Brothers Asia reflects that philosophy. Of the branch's 160 staff, only 20 are non-Japanese. These are primarily experienced investment bankers and product and risk managers who bring the specialised resources of the firm to Japan.

The Tokyo office has more than doubled its size in the past year, but Shimazu says future growth cannot outpace the availability of talented, motivated and well-trained people. 'In a bull market, unchecked growth is a strong temptation, but we recognise the danger that we could exceed our ability to assure only the highest quality of service in everything we do. The superior capabilities of Shearson Lehman throughout the world must be delivered in Japan by people of equal talent and insight', he maintains.

In addition to bringing US and European professionals to Tokyo, Shearson Lehman rotates many Japanese employees through its other operations. The purpose of both is to develop a thorough understanding of the opportunities available in all the world's markets with sensitivity to the needs of the Japanese investment community.

'Japanese institutions are very visible in the world's markets today, but we must remember that they are still relatively new at the game', Shimazu notes. 'Deregulation is only beginning in the Japanese markets, and traditional Japanese conservatism will continue to be evident, even as our investors become more aggressive and worldly.'

'Japan's venture in world investment leadership is well underway, but it still requires us to be understanding, sensitive and very proficient guides.'

Peter A. Cohen, Chairman and Chief Executive Officer of Shearson Lehman Brothers Inc.

Left to right: M. Yano, Senior Manager, K. Kondo, Showa Ota Partner, and T. Kato, Show Ota Partner.

Left to right: R. C. Kingston, S. Fujita, Partners, and H. Miya, International Tax Coordinator.

T. Saito, Senior Manager, T. Inohana, Showa Ota Partner, and M. Muramatsu, Manager.

Left to right: M. Inoue, Director, H. Kato, Senior Manager, and H. Settle, Ernst & Whinney Partner.

Showa Ota & Co and Ernst & Whinney

Showa Ota, the Japanese member firm of Ernst & Whinney, can provide comprehensive services to its Japanese clients as well as to foreign corporations with operations in Japan. Showa Ota also has extensive expertise to assist Japanese corporations in seeking, planning and carrying out investment and financing opportunities overseas.

Our service capability is based on four complementary elements:

- our leading position as a Japanese audit corporation;
- the resources of our international department in Tokyo;
- the liaison provided by our Japanese Business Groups, operating in key business centres around the world; and
- the leadership of Ernst & Whinney in serving banks and financial institutions worldwide.

Leaders in Japanese Accounting Services

Certified public accounting and auditing were introduced in Japan through the enactment of the Securities and Exchange Law and Certified Public Accountants Law in 1948.

Dr Tetsuzo Ota, a founder of Showa Ota, was at that time a leading educator, teaching commercial science and accounting at Hitotsubashi University. An advocate of the need for a public accounting profession in Japan, he was one of the founders of the Japanese Accounting Research Academic Society, the forerunner of the present-day Japanese Institute of CPAs (JICPA), and the first chairman of its Accounting Principles Board. He was influential in drafting the legislation which established accountancy as a profession in Japan. He became first president of the JICPA, formed as a result of the legislation and can be said to have been the father of the CPA system in Japan.

Dr Ota established his office as a practising accountant as well as an academician in 1950 to serve the growing companies subject to the new Securities Exchange Law. Early clients included Nissan Motor, Ajinomoto, NEC, Fuji Film and Nippon Oil. The Japanese government appointed him auditor for the fledgling Japan Air Lines. Close ties to the Fuyo Group resulted in the appointment of his firm as auditors for Nippon Kokan, Oki Electric and Nihon Cement. Later, in 1976, when amendments to the Commercial Code and Securities Exchange Law required audits of banks, insurance companies and financial institutions, Dr Ota's firm was appointed to serve Fuji Bank, Yasuda Trust & Banking and Yasuda Fire & Marine Insurance.

In 1967, when the CPA law was amended, Dr Ota's firm became the first to incorporate as an audit corporation. Thus the present-day Showa Ota & Co, with 900 partners and staff and with offices in 11 Japanese cities, is the oldest audit corporation in Japan.

Today, our longstanding clients read like a *Who's Who* of Japanese business. Nissan Motor Co, a pioneer in the Japanese automobile industry, is now the second largest automobile manufacturer in Japan and the fourth largest in the world. Nippon Kokan is one of the five largest steel makers in the world. Ajinomoto is Japan's largest integrated food processor and ranks among the world's leaders in advanced amino acid application technology. Japan Air Lines, Japan's largest airline engaged in both domestic and international operations, ranks among the world's largest international carriers. Nomura Securities is the world's largest securities company. Fuji Bank ranks second among city banks in Japan and is expanding its overseas operations. Yasuda Trust & Banking is now the fourth-largest trust bank in Japan. Yasuda Fire & Marine Insurance is the second-largest non-life insurance company in Japan. The banks and insurers became audit clients following the enactment of the Commercial Code Special Measures Law Concerning Audit of Kabushiki Kaisha and the amendment of the Securities and Exchange Law requiring the audit of the financial statements of major banks and insurance companies.

Our history and professional service record are not only relevant as indications of the quality or our service

S. Fujita, Showa Ota Partner, International Department.

but, equally important, enable Showa Ota to develop an effective accounting and auditing approach for foreign corporations which must meet Japanese requirements which differ from those in countries where most investor companies are headquartered. Two key examples are:

- A major responsibility of independent auditors is to assist the full-time statutory auditor, which each corporation must have, meet his broad responsibility for overseeing operations and finances. Consequently, audit procedures must be designed to meet the statutory audit requirements, and the implications in terms of planning and timing can be considerable for firms preparing international consolidations.
- Japanese shareholders receive the audited non-consolidated financial statements of corporations which, after their approval, are filed with the Minister of Finance. By law, shareholders have important powers, including approval of dividend policy, directors' bonuses and retirement allowances, and issuance of debt and other important financial transactions. Management takes its responsibilities to shareholders very seriously and prepares extensively for shareholder presentations and responses to questions. Working with the statutory auditor, the independent auditor assists in this process.

One of the crucial services Showa Ota performs for foreign clients operating in Japan is interpreting Japanese requirements, both those arising from law and those based on business customs unique to Japan, and harmonising the Japanese approach to that of the corporation's home country.

The International Department in Tokyo

This is composed of Showa Ota's Japanese professionals with broad international experience and Ernst & Whinney personnel knowledgeable about doing business in Japan. Our professional staff in Japan includes resident expatriate executives, experienced in the US Security Exchange Commission (SEC) and other international accounting and financial reporting requirements and techniques. They are available to advise and assist in such matters as well as provide liaison with foreign securities, business and governmental institutions. We can provide comprehensive quality services in auditing, taxation and management consulting.

We believe we add value for our clients in those services by the breadth of our professionals' ability to work in English and the depth of our professional ability to interpret differences in requirements and in practice between the Japanese environment and other national environments.

Equally, we emphasise assisting our clients to achieve their desired results and we go far beyond the technical in providing service. We have been asked (and answered) many different questions by foreign executives investing and operating in Japan, such as: 'What can I do about the shortage of office space in Tokyo?; 'How can I recruit good Japanese personnel when I start up?'; 'Can I use the same type of financing techniques in Japan that I use at home?' and 'How can I use my "tax haven" corporations effectively in relation to my Japanese business operations?'

The Japanese Business Groups

To assist Japanese clients in planning overseas investment and financing we have formed Japanese Business Groups in key cities such as Sydney, London, New York, Toronto, Los Angeles, San Francisco and Vancouver. These groups consist of professionals who speak Japanese and understand the needs and concerns of Japanese management. They call upon Ernst & Whinney professionals to marshall the specialised resources of our worldwide firm.

T. Kato, Showa Ota Partner, International Department.

K. Kondo, Showa Ota Partner, International Department

Worldwide professional services

Ernst & Whinney is comprised of some 29,500 partners and staff in over 400 offices in more than 75 countries, and is one of the largest accountancy practices in the world. With headquarters in New York, Ernst & Whinney works constantly to develop, coordinate and monitor professional services throughout the world, and to assist offices in meeting their clients' needs.

Professional staff members are frequently exchanged between the offices; through them we are able to obtain current local information promptly. For example, to a Japanese corporation which intends to invest in a foreign country, we provide essential current information on that country and, after the establishment of a subsidiary or a branch, Ernst & Whinney professionals in that country provide necessary services through close co-ordination with the International Department of Showa Ota.

To most effectively deliver service to clients, Ernst & Whinney, and Showa Ota in particular, have from the beginning been committed to industry specialisation for partners and staff. The banking and financial services industry has always been a unique, complex business, relying heavily on timely recording and control of values for maintenance of confidence among customers, shareholders and regulatory authorities. Technical expertise is required of the auditor to understand foreign exchange dealings, for instance, or to apply judgment to credit evaluations. Accordingly, we have identified audit executives, both partners and managers, who have developed the necessary attributes to supervise services to banks and other financial institutions, and we have organised staff into groups with this specialisation.

This policy assures that staff receive training in banking and financial services early in their careers and develop experience to render quality service to their clients. And it assures experienced executives who keep informed of new business and technical developments and coordinate the firm's services to the industry.

Ernst & Whinney publications.

T. Inohana, Showa Ota Partner.

Serving banks and other financial institutions

Showa Ota is a leader in providing services to Japanese banks and other financial services institutions and their overseas operations, just as Ernst & Whinney is a leader in services to the banking and financial services industry worldwide.

Showa Ota audits 12 city and local banks, two of the largest trust banks, and one of Japan's three long-term credit banks. Showa Ota thus has more banking clients than any other audit corporation in Japan. In addition, Showa Ota audits seven securities dealers, including Nomura Securities, the world's largest, and several large property and casualty and life insurance companies.

Ernst & Whinney is a recognised leader in serving the needs of the financial services industry, providing a full range of accounting, auditing, tax and consulting services. The firm serves approximately one-fourth of the top banks, savings and loan associations, mortgage banking firms, and diversified financial companies in the United States.

Approximately 49 of the top 200 US banks are Ernst & Whinney clients. In the United Kingdom, Ernst & Whinney has been providing professional services to banks and other financial institutions since the late 1880s. The UK firm presently serves nearly 100 banking clients, including 30 'recognised' banks. In the Middle East the firm serves over 40 banks, including a number of government monetary agencies.

Services to banks and other financial institutions are co-ordinated by the Banking Committee of Ernst & Whinney International. This committee is responsible for ensuring that services provided are performed to the highest standard and that worldwide expertise is available to all practice areas. A Showa Ota partner is a permanent member of this committee.

Acknowledgements

Euromoney is very grateful to Professor Fumimasa Hamada, Professor of Economics at Keio University, Tokyo, to C. Tait Ratcliffe, President, International Business Information, to Kate Perry, Clifford Chance and to Showa Ota & Co for their contributions to the editorial matter of the book.

All photographs in the text portion of the book were taken by Lucy Birmingham. The sponsors provided their own photographs.
The charts were drawn by Richard Natkiel Associates.
The book was designed by John White.